THE UNIVERSITY OF
WINCHESTER

Martial Rose Library
Tel: 01962 827306

To be returned on or before the day marked above, subject to recall.

Crowd Actions in Britain and France from the
Middle Ages to the Modern World

Crowd Actions in Britain and France from the Middle Ages to the Modern World

Edited by

Michael T. Davis
Griffith University, Australia

First published 2015 by
PALGRAVE MACMILLAN

Palgrave Macmillan in the UK is an imprint of Macmillan Publishers Limited,
registered in England, company number 785998, of Houndmills, Basingstoke,
Hampshire RG21 6XS.

Palgrave Macmillan in the US is a division of St Martin's Press LLC,
175 Fifth Avenue, New York, NY 10010.

Palgrave Macmillan is the global academic imprint of the above companies
and has companies and representatives throughout the world.

Palgrave® and Macmillan® are registered trademarks in the United States,
the United Kingdom, Europe and other countries.

ISBN: 978–0–230–20398–3

This book is printed on paper suitable for recycling and made from fully
managed and sustained forest sources. Logging, pulping and manufacturing
processes are expected to conform to the environmental regulations of the
country of origin.

A catalogue record for this book is available from the British Library.

Library of Congress Cataloging-in-Publication Data

Crowd actions in Britain and France from the Middle Ages to the modern world /
Michael T. Davis.
     pages cm
    Includes bibliographical references.
    ISBN 978–0–230–20398–3
    1. Riots – Great Britain – History. 2. Riots – France – History.
  3. Crowds – Great Britain – History. 4. Crowds – France – History. I. Davis,
  Michael T., 1969– editor.
HV6485.G7.C78 2015
363.32′30941—dc23   2015015596

Contents

Acknowledgements

This volume has been a long time in the making. By exploring a topic that has deep historical roots and contemporary relevance, this book was originally conceived as something of a sequel to a volume co-edited with Brett Bowden entitled *Terror: From Tyrannicide to Terrorism* (2008). I would like to thank Brett for his initial involvement in conceptualizing this book. I would also like to thank all of the contributors for their enormous forbearance and continued support as this project faced unforeseeable challenges that hindered its progress. The first of these was the passing of Charles Tilly who agreed to contribute to the volume but most regrettably died in 2008 before being able to do so. More recently, another original contributor – Roger Wells – suffered a tragic fall that resulted in brain damage. Unfortunately, it has not been possible to include Roger's essay in the volume. At Palgrave Macmillan, this book was originally under the wing of Ruth Ireland, before passing to Holly Tyler and now Jade Moulds. I would like to extend my gratitude to each of these editorial staff at Palgrave Macmillan for their help and patience throughout the project.

Notes on Contributors

William Beik is Professor of Early Modern French Social and Institutional History at Emory University. He has written widely on French history, including *Absolutism and Society in Seventeenth-Century France: State Power and Provincial Aristocracy in Languedoc* (1985), which was awarded the Herbert Baxter Adams Prize by the American Historical Association; *Urban Protest in Seventeenth-Century France: The Culture of Retribution* (1997); *Louis XIV and Absolutism: A Brief Study with Documents* (2000). He is the co-editor of the *New Approaches to European History* series published by Cambridge University Press. He is especially interested in aspects of the social and institutional history of sixteenth- and seventeenth-centuries France, and one of his recent works is *A Social and Cultural History of Early Modern France* (2009).

John Bohstedt is Professor Emeritus of History at the University of Tennessee, Knoxville. His forthcoming work is an essay entitled 'The Politics of Food Riots in World History'. He is the author of two books: *The Politics of Provisions: Food Riots, Moral Economy, and Market Transition in England, c. 1550–1850* (2010) and *Riots and Community Politics in England and Wales, 1790–1810* (1983).

Cynthia A. Bouton is Professor of History at Texas A&M University. Her works include *The Flour War: Gender, Class and Community in Late Ancien Regime France* (1993) and *Interpreting Social Violence in French Culture: Buzançais, 1847–2008* (2012). Her current research focuses on the circulation of basic foodstuffs in the Atlantic during the Age of Revolution.

Brett Bowden is Professor of History and Political Thought at the University of Western Sydney. He also holds visiting appointments at the Australian National University and the University of New South Wales at the Australian Defence Force Academy. His recent major works include *Civilization and War* (2013); *The Empire of Civilization: The Evolution of an Imperial Idea* (2009), which was awarded the 2011 Norbert Elias Prize; and the four-volume edited collection, *Civilization: Critical Concepts* (2009).

Raphaël Canet is a professor in the School of International Development and Global Studies at the University of Ottawa, Canada. A sociologist and political scientist by training, he was educated in both France and Quebec. His research focuses primarily on forms of political action by crossing the study of collective representations, political institutions and social practices. Amongst his key works are *The Global Justice Movement: Social Forums, Resistance and New Political Culture* (2010); *Crisis of the State, Societies' Revenge* (2006); *The Neoliberal*

Regulation: Crisis or Adjustment? (2004); and *The Nation in Debate: Between Modernity and Postmodernity* (2003).

Michael T. Davis is a lecturer in the School of Humanities at Griffith University. His works include *Radicalism and Revolution in Britain, 1775–1848* (2000); *London Corresponding Society* (2002); *Newgate in Revolution: An Anthology of Radical Prison Literature in the Age of Revolution* (ed. with I. McCalman and C. Parolin, 2005); *Unrespectable Radicals? Popular Politics in the Age of Reform* (ed. with P. A. Pickering, 2008); *Terror: From Tyrannicide to Terrorism in Europe, 1605 to the Future* (ed. with B. Bowden, 2008); and *Liberty, Property and Politics* (ed. with G. Pentland, 2015).

Jack Fruchtman, Jr is Professor of Political Science and Director of the Program in Law and American Civilization at Maryland's Towson University, United States. He has written, edited or annotated ten books. His work includes studies of the political thought of Thomas Paine, Richard Price, Joseph Priestley, Thomas Reid, Helen Maria Williams and Thomas Hardy, as well as the Marquis de Condorcet and Jacques-Pierre Brissot. His most recent works include *The Political Philosophy of Thomas Paine* (2009) and the second edition of *The Supreme Court: Rulings on American Government and Society* (2014). He also serves as co-editor of the Pickering & Chatto series on The Enlightenment World.

Peter Hayes is Senior Lecturer in Politics at the University of Sunderland, UK. His research interests include political theory, ideology and social policy. His recent works include a co-edited book *Taiwan's Long Road to Democracy* (2009), and articles in journals such as *Pediatrics*; *The International Journal of Law*; *Policy and the Family*; and *Studies in History and Philosophy of Modern Physics*.

Jeff Horn is Professor of History at Manhattan College. He has written or edited four books on the era of the French and Industrial Revolutions. His next monograph entitled *Economic Development in Early Modern France: The Privilege of Liberty, 1650–1830* will be published in 2015.

Peter McPhee has published widely on the history of France 1780–1880, particularly on the social history of politics. His most recent book is *Robespierre: A Revolutionary Life* (2012). He was appointed to a personal chair in History in 1993 at the University of Melbourne, where he was also the University's inaugural Provost from 2007 to 2009.

Tadzio Mueller is a political scientist, climate justice activist and translator living in Berlin, where he works as a research fellow for the Rosa Luxemburg Foundation. He has co-edited *Contours of Climate Justice*, is a founding member of Turbulence: Ideas for Movement, and has published widely on green capitalism and the German 'Energiewende'. His current research focuses on strategies of social transformation in social movements working on questions of climate justice and energy democracy.

Mark O'Brien is a senior research fellow in the Centre for Lifelong Learning at the University of Liverpool. He served as Research Director at the Centre for the Study of the Child, the Family and the Law at the University of Liverpool during which time he carried out evaluation research for a government initiative called the Children's Fund. He has also carried out research into the experience of union activism for women activists. His works include *When Adam Delved and Eve Span: A History of the Peasants' Revolt of 1381* (2004).

Laurent Pech is Professor of European Law and Head of the Law Department at Middlesex University, London. Prior to his appointment at Middlesex University, Laurent worked at the National University of Ireland, Galway. A graduate of the Faculty of Law at the University of Aix-Marseille, Laurent specializes in EU public law and is the author of more than sixty scholarly publications on the subject.

Gordon Pentland is Reader in History in the School of History, Classics and Archaeology at the University of Edinburgh. He has degrees from Oxford and Edinburgh, and his works include *Radicalism, Reform and National Identity, 1820–1833* (2008); *Spirit of the Union: Popular Politics in Scotland, 1815–1820* (2011); and a large number of articles in journals including the *Historical Journal*; *Journal of British Studies*, *Past & Present*; and the *Scottish Historical Review*. He currently edits the *Journal of Scottish Historical Studies*.

Penny Roberts is Professor of Early Modern European History at the University of Warwick and co-editor of the Oxford University Press journal *French History*. Her most recent works include *Peace and Authority during the French Religious Wars, c. 1560–1600* (2013) and as co-editor with Graeme Murdock and Andrew Spicer, *Ritual and Violence: Natalie Zemon Davis and Early Modern France* (2012).

Nicholas Rogers is a distinguished research professor in the Department of History, York University, Toronto. He is the author of several books on British history, especially on different forms of popular contention. His most recent books are *The Press Gang: Naval Impressment and Its Opponents in Georgian Britain* (2007) and *Mayhem: Post-War Crime and Violence in Britain 1748–1753* (2012). He is currently completing a set of documents on naval impressment in Bristol, 1739–1815, for the Bristol Record Society.

Maura Stewart is Lecturer in French at the National University of Ireland, Galway. She has published on French presidential elections, France–EU relations, and political and media discourses. She has also provided analysis on related topics in her interviews with, and articles for, French and European media outlets. Her current book project examines how French presidential candidates have addressed the nation and Europe in their bids for the highest political office since 1988.

Sian Sullivan is Professor of Environment and Culture at Bath Spa University, and a co-investigator for the Leverhulme Centre for the Study of Value. Currently she is researching the production of 'nature' as 'natural capital' from an anthropological perspective that embraces different evaluative frameworks. She is the author of *Political Ecology: Science, Myth and Power* (2000), as well as articles in varied academic journals. Recently she has authored policy reports on approaches to biodiversity conservation for the Third World Network and the Green House Think Tank, UK. See http://siansullivan.net for more information.

John Walter is Professor Emeritus of History at the University of Essex. His research focuses on early modern British history, and his current project examines popular political culture during the English Revolution. His works include *Crowds and Popular Politics in Early Modern England* (2006) and *Remaking English Society: Social Relations and Social Change in Early Modern England* (ed. with S. Hindle and A. Shepard, 2013).

Chris Wrigley is Emeritus Professor of Modern British History at Nottingham University. His books include *David Lloyd George and the British Labour Movement* (1976); *Lloyd George and the Challenge of Labour, 1918–1922* (1990); *British Trade Unions since 1933* (2002); *A. J. P. Taylor: Radical Historian of Europe* (2006); an edited three-volume *History of British Industrial Relations* (1982–1996); and the edited *Challenges of Labour: Central and Western Europe 1917–1920* (1993). He was president of the British Historical Association 1996–1999, a vice president of the Royal Historical Society 1997–2001 and chair of the Society for the Study of Labour History, 1997–2001, and was awarded an honorary doctorate by the University of East Anglia, 1998.

Introduction: The Arc of Violence: Riots, Disturbances of the Peace, Public Protests and Crowd Actions in History

Jack Fruchtman, Jr

Disruptions of the peace and crowd action, public protests, mass demonstrations and mob violence have all attracted the attention of a variety of scholars from numerous disciplines: history, political science, sociology, psychology and even religion and philosophy. Riots and protests may have social or political or even financial goals, or they may not. Crowd actions may and perhaps often are peaceful affairs, but riots by nature cannot be so. Non-violent activities or passive resistance was a technique made most famous by Mohandas Gandhi, in striving to achieve an independent India, which came about in 1947. And of course in the United States, the Reverend Martin Luther King rejected the strategy during the following decade in an attempt to win desegregation in the American southland. But the essays in this volume look beyond non-violent crowd action and without exception drill-in on disturbing the peace through violent actions – in effect, on rioting.

Chalmers Johnson's observation about revolutions may easily pertain to riots: a non-violent revolution is a contradiction in terms, and so it is with riots. Defining the nature of this violence poses no easy task, as Johnson understood. For him, it has to be actions that are counter-intuitive at the moment, defying expectations of peace and stability, actions 'that deliberately or unintentionally disorients the behaviour of others'.[1] Historically, riots have entailed crowds of people intent on wreaking havoc, usually for some purpose: what George Rudé has famously called 'the crowd in history', trying to achieve its goals – political, social, economic or all three. Rudé focused on what he termed 'the "aggressive mob", or the "hostile outburst" – such activities as strikes, riots, rebellions, insurrections, and revolutions'.[2] But Rudé notwithstanding, there lies a crucial distinction. While the common denominator of 'crowd' and 'mob' is group movement, the radical difference is violence. A crowd can connote happy holiday shoppers; a mob will denote angry militants.[3]

Sometimes the rioters know one another, and sometimes they do not. When peasants are hungry or the crops have failed, riots may be in the form of food or bread riots. Or they may burn the manor house, kill the lord and perhaps his entire family and set fire to the crops. City and town dwellers, who are crushed by taxes, the denial of access to food or land or other heavy burdens like forced military conscription, may join together, often in organized ways, to attack town officials and wealthy merchants, even to the extent of burning their offices, official records and houses.[4] Alternatively, the strife may result from religious conflict, as the Catholic-Huguenot struggle demonstrates in the Wars of Religion and their aftermath during the sixteenth and seventeenth centuries or the Gordon Riots in 1780.[5] When political goals are at stake, like an overthrow of a government, the people's action will aim toward grand political, even social, transformation, with the downfall of an entire governmental regime to be replaced by a new one. The former examples constitute older forms of uprising, typically focused on attempts to improve daily life immediately. The latter are early-modern phenomena, dating from the seventeenth century, but more classically from the French Revolution in 1789, when the goal was to achieve social and political change on a monumental scale. It may involve the overthrow of monarchy and its replacement by a republic as occurred in France with the constitution of 1793 that Robespierre refused to allow to go into effect. Instead, the Reign of Terror began in earnest.[6] Or it may, in its twentieth-century form, entail the seizure of the economic means of production along with the end of the capitalist grip on social structure and its replacement with a communist dictatorship, as occurred in Russia in 1917 with the Bolshevik Revolution.

One thing is clear: these spectacles have been ubiquitous throughout history, displaying from ancient times to our own an arc of violence, resulting in riot, uprising and disruption of the peace. One single characteristic that encompasses all crowd action, public protest, whatever we call it, is that it poses a direct and immediate challenge to established authority. Law has no place; nor does peace. Monarchic or aristocratic decrees, parliamentary acts, judicial demands – none of these will have an impact on the crowd. Force must be used against force, even if it is only the threat of the use of force. Above all else, it signifies the collapse of the rule of law or the disregard of customary usage.

One incident from the American context clearly illustrates the power and disastrous consequences of crowd action. It also illustrates how and at what point the law fails completely. This was the galvanizing moment at Lexington, Massachusetts, on 19 April 1775, when shots were fired that left eight American militiamen dead and ten wounded. The British Crown and ministry demanded action in the colonies with the arrest and detention of the leaders of the rebellion. General Thomas Gage was the man in charge of British troops, a skilled and veteran officer who had cruelly put down uprisings in Scotland. He was certain the chances of the Americans achieving any of their goals were like a small hole allowing flour to run from its sack. When the colonists in the neighbouring town of Concord learned of his plans to subdue them by seizing their stocks of munitions and weapons, they quickly gathered in Lexington. There, Major John Pitcairn ordered his troops in six companies to fire on a crowd of some 70 American militiamen assembled on the village green in front of the meeting house. 'Lay down your arms, you damned rebels and disperse!' he is said to have shouted. 'Damn you! Why don't you lay down your arms?' Another British officer joined in the shouting, 'Damn them! We will have them.' And when the Americans refused, the shots rang out.[7] The law had expired in the sense that it died – lawlessness, violence and rebellion ensued.[8]

The activities at Lexington Green, and later in Concord where the British were routed by a crowd of American militiamen, leaving some 250 Redcoat casualties, was clearly crowd action. It was not a riot per se, but the term riot is fascinating because it carries so many meanings. Consider, for a moment, the meaning of the term riot. To determine that people are a 'riot' suggests a hilarious jokester or cut-up, who entertains others for their amusement. It also suggests a brilliant display of something, a bunch of flowers, for example, with their 'riot of colour'. The *Oxford English Dictionary* defines riot this way as 'unrestrained revelry, mirth, or noise' or 'an extravagant display *of* something'. In his 1768 unfinished memoir of his travels through France and Italy, Laurence Sterne expressed this meaning when he travelled in Bourbonnais, 'the sweetest part of France'. The sights were extraordinary, he wrote, such that 'there was nothing from which I had painted out for myself so joyous a riot of the affections, as in this journey in the vintage, through this part of France'.[9]

In Old English, the term had to do with wanton, loose or wasteful living; debauchery, dissipation, extravagance. Dr Johnson, in *The Rambler*, used it in this sense when he addressed 'the luxury of vein imagination'. To understand the context, hear the entire passage:

> There is nothing more fatal to a man whose business is to think, then to have learned the art of regaling his mind with those airy gratifications. Other vices or follies are restrained by fear, reformed by admonition, or rejected by the conviction which the comparison of our conduct with that of others, may in time produce. But this invisible riot of the mind, this secret prodigality of being, is secure from detection, and fearless from reproach. The dreamer returns to his apartments, shuts out the cares and interruptions of mankind, and abandons himself to his own fancy.[10]

Many years later, James Mill, in his 1817 history of British India, went further when addressing the early life of Hyder Ali, a Muslim ruler who 'proved the most formidable enemy whom [the English] had ever encountered in India'. His army won smashing victories over British forces in 1769 and 1780, but it was defeated in 1781 and Hyder died the following year. Mill reviewed his life and career and noted that Hyder, 'till the age of twenty-seven, could be confined to no serious pursuit, but spent his life between the labours of the chase, and the pleasures of voluptuous indulgence and riot'.[11]

The *Oxford English Dictionary* also tells us that the word riot initially had to do with disputation, 'debate, dispute, quarrel', which we definitely see when Wat Tyler behaved so dreadfully in front of the 14-year-old King Richard II at Smithfields. It was almost as if a difficult, disrespectful and naughty child was so recalcitrant and frustrating that his behaviour brings a mother nearly to tears and a father to an apoplectic state. Perez Zagorin describes the encounter this way: 'Tyler took Richard's hand and shook his arm, called him "brother", and rinsed his mouth before the king "in a rude and villainous manner". Then, after sending for a jug of ale and drinking down a great draught, he mounted his horse in the royal presence'. Speak of the demise of the rule of law, of the unbecoming behaviour of a commoner (and peasant, no less), and you have a picture of a riot in terms of disputatiousness and quarrel.[12] Tyler was 'rude' (unlearned and ignorant) and 'villainous' (churlish and ill-bred). So, originally a negative class distinction also attached itself to 'mob'. Indeed, the very word was a shortening of *mobile vulgus*, 'vulgar' or 'low' people in a destructive movement. Had Tyler lived at a later time, say in the eighteenth century, his insolence would have constituted treason, the penalty for which was death.[13]

Synonyms include violence, strife, disorder, tumult, especially on the part of the populace. Its earliest usage in these terms may be located in 1375 in the archdeacon of Aberdeen and Scottish poet John Barbour's commemoration of Scotland's independence from England. Barbour's epic poem, *The Bruce*, recounts the virtuous military deeds of Robert the Bruce, who became King Robert I. As part of his strategy, Robert invaded England while King Edward of England was fighting in Ireland. He chose two lords along with 15,000 men to ride with him:

> To England, there to burn and slay,
> And far and wide such riot play
> When they should hear the destruction done
> In England by their roving foe,
> Should be so fearful and so woe
> In case their children and their wives
> Should fear to lose their lives[14]

This meaning of 'riot' includes a second manifestation that draws us directly to the use of the term meaning a deliberate, often violent, uprising of several people, who intend to disturb the peace: more particularly, 'a violent disturbance of the peace by an assembly or body of persons; an outbreak of active lawlessness or disorder among the populace'. This is a more contemporary sense of the term, even though it dates from 1390. It carries with it the sense that we are seeking, namely upheaval and disruption of everyday life by a few or many, often destructive of property and threatening of life and limb, if not utterly dangerous.[15]

At common law, a violation of a breach of the peace occurred when three or more people gathered and three observers feared that violence may occur. In terms of statutory law, the British Parliament passed the Riot Act in 1715, which made it a crime for any 12 people to gather unlawfully to disturb the public peace. If the rioters refuse to obey a legitimate governmental authority's demand to disperse, they were subject to be tried as felons. The familiar term, 'to read them the riot act', takes its meaning from this statute. When an official formally commanded the rioters to cease and desist, he in effect 'read' them a portion of the act.[16]

The crowd in history, in Rudé's terms, requires more of an explanation because the crowd may be unruly, even destructive, while it may also be inchoate and amorphous in the sense that it may spontaneously develop. On the other hand, there may also be leaders who organize the mob and direct its activities in ways that the leadership believes will ameliorate the problems (political, social, economic or some combination of them) they all face. So, from Spartacus, Wat Tyler, Jack Cade and the Luddites, mobs and riots trace an arc to the twentieth century. One thinks of East Germany and Hungary in 1956, the Prague Spring in 1968, Kent State in 1970, Northern Ireland of 1972, Los Angeles in 1992, Tiananmen Square in 1989, Iran after the elections in 2009 and many meetings of the Group of 20, or G20: all actions as boiling points of recent history. And the arc continues. In the spring of 2010, after several years of ongoing corrupt rule and imminent economic collapse, the poor of Thailand erupted into street demonstrations and protests that led to several deaths and scores of injuries. At the same time in Greece, crowds of people stormed into the streets of Athens when it became likely that the government would have to undertake enormous budget cuts to save the country from economic disintegration. When the G20 met in June 2010 in Toronto, protestors were out in force, burning police cruisers and demanding an end to the iron financial grip that the nations making up the 20 economic elite allegedly has on the rest of the world.[17]

Most violent of all were the riots during the late spring and early summer of 2010 in the obscure country of Kyrgyzstan in Central Asia.[18] There, ethnic violence shuttered through the southern half of the country, leading to the destruction of the city of Osh and threatening to fragment the nation. Ethnic Kyrgyz and Uzbeks fought and murdered each other, culminating in the mass exodus of an estimated 400,000 Uzbeks, which number only about 15 percent of the population, into neighbouring Uzbekistan. Earlier, in April 2010, a coup had led to the establishment of a weak provisional government, which was unable to stop the rioting, pillaging, burning and killing. Some reports asserted that the rioting was stimulated by the former leaders of the over-thrown government in an effort to return to power. These reports claimed that hired thugs had committed atrocities against both the Kyrgyz and the Uzbek peoples to inflame ancient hatreds and suspicion. The provisional government asked the Russian government to send troops to restore order, but the request was refused. A referendum in late June 2010 on a new constitution overwhelm-ingly supported the provisional government in an attempt to bring peace and stability to the country when it passed by a large majority of votes.[19]

Public disorder, riots and mob violence occur only when there is 'crowd action'. Defining a crowd is subjective, but in 1715 an attempt was made when the Riot Act in England pinpointed the number of people at 12 as the minimum when the authorities could declare a gathering illegal. Often, however, that number has been as few as three individuals who join together in disorderly conduct. Often laws that prohibit 'disturbing the peace' indicate that a minimum of three people must be involved. Violations of these laws may occur when a law enforcement officer commands the three people to get off the street or if there is a legitimate threat that a firearm or other deadly weapon may be used (or even planned to be used). But then again, riots in history have always entailed far more than the Riot Act minimum of 12, much less three, individuals. The most familiar riots, mob violence or crowd actions are those involving the numerous social and political revolutions that have occurred throughout history, and they have all enjoyed thousands of people engaged in civil disorder. In the modern era, chief among these is the French Revolution, which culminated in the successful destruction of the entire social and political system of France 'from below': the action against the established order was undertaken by the people. Indeed, Martin Malia has outlined what he calls 'a convenient list of "grand revolutions"': England in 1540, America in 1776, France in 1789, Russia in 1917 and China in 1949.[20]

The most famous iconic moment in early modern history took place on 14 July 1789, and it involved, unsurprisingly, crowd action. This was the storming of the Bastille, an imposing military fortress and prison on the northern edge of Paris, which had strategic importance because its guns protected one of the northern gates of the city, especially from a possible English invasion.[21] Although it stood 73 feet high with eight round towers five feet thick, Robert turned it into a massive and frightening edifice.[22] A few days before the 14 juillet, throngs of people, who had grown disgusted with the French regime and who fell under the spell of the heated speeches of revolutionaries like Camille Desmoulins, considered the prison a symbol of absolutism. Simon Schama tells us of Desmoulins's mesmerizing rhetorical skills at the Palais Royal just two days before the Bastille was stormed by the mob. It is a moment often recounted in history textbooks when news of the dismissal of Louis

XVI's reform-minded counsellor, Jacques Necker, had reached Paris: in mid-afternoon, 'a crowd of six thousand or so milled about a young man, pale-faced and dark-eyed, his hair spilling freely onto his shoulders, shouting excitedly from one of the tables in front of a café'.[23] His fiery words embodied the frustrations and fears of the lower orders and middling sort.

With Necker out of office, soon all reformers, all partisans of liberty, were now threatened by an aristocratic plot to subdue them. Early on, he associated green, not red, with liberty and hope, and charged his huge audience, 'To arms! To arms!' overcoming the slight speech impediment that had inhibited his public speaking. 'Take all of your green cockades, the colour of hope. Citizens, there is not a moment to be lost....This evening all the German and Swiss battalions will come from the Champ-de-Mars to assassinate us!'[24] Call these words frenzied paranoia or unadulterated polemic, Desmoulins knew what he was doing. He knew how to move the crowd, and he also wanted to make a name for himself. He succeeded brilliantly on both fronts. Soon, the cockade was no longer green – it was red, and it, along with the *bonnet rouge*, became the symbolic colour of revolutionary liberation.[25] The prison governor, fearing for his life, attempted to engage the crowd in negotiations, but the crowd would have none of it. They attacked the prison, overwhelmed the guards, a mere 24 disabled veterans and 30 Swiss guardsmen, and killed the governor whose head was paraded through the streets on a pike.[26] Seven inmates, none of them political prisoners, were freed. Eighty-three of the rioters were killed, and 15 others later died of injuries.[27]

Just days after, Desmoulins's incendiary pamphlet, *La France libre*, appeared, urging more crowd action, more mob violence, more rioting, anything to bring down the *ancien régime*. 'Listen, listen, from one end of the country to the other, from Paris and Lyon, Rouen and Bordeaux, Calais and Marseille, the same universal cry is heard....The nation has everywhere expressed its will. Everyone wants to be free. Yes, my dear fellow citizens, we will be free, and who can prevent it?'[28] The great historian of the French Revolution, Georges Lefebvre, concludes that 'all classes of society were represented among' this massive crowd (masters, journeymen and merchants), though 'most were artisans from the [nearby] faubourg Saint-Antoine'.[29] The key element here is that this was mob action, a riot in effect, that precipitated the French Revolution and eventually led to the execution of hundreds of aristocrats, including the king himself on 21 January 1793, and ultimately the infamous Reign of Terror of 1793–94.

Familiarity, however, does not connote exclusiveness. Nearly 175 years later, an uprising involving mass crowd action took place in a far different venue, but in circumstances that possess salient parallels: among accusations of tyranny and corruption came the longing and a consequent call to arms in a fight for liberty. It was Camille Desmoulins written into a mid-twentieth century

American context. Berkeley, California, is the home of the flagship campus of the University of California, and in 1964, it was a hotbed of unrest, demanding free speech and soon shared student governance with the administration and end to military conscription, which was fuelling the Vietnam War.[30] Though chartered in 1868, the Berkeley campus did not develop its international reputation until after World War II when it began to attract highly respected and well-published scholars like Clark Kerr in Economics and Charles Muscatine in English, Gleb Struve in Slavic Languages and Literature, Sheldon Wolin in Political Science, John Schaar in Philosophy and Nicholas Riasanovsky, Carl Schorske and Robert O. Paxton in History.[31] The students followed. These included Mario Savio along with Bettina Aptheker, the best known spokesman for 1960s student radicalism, Jerry Rubin, and the irrepressible Abbie Hoffman, co-founders of the Youth International Party (the 'Yippies').[32]

The Free Speech Movement unexpectedly began in the fall of 1964.[33] It was the Berkeley equivalent of a group of like-minded young radicals in the Palais Royal when Desmoulins jumped up on his café table and exhorted his audience to fight for freedom. In the United States, it was the height of the Cold War and just after the misguided anti-communist attacks of Sen. Joseph R. McCarthy, who claimed he could detect the presence of Soviet influence throughout American life, including the United States Department of State and the White House. University officials, responding to the hysteria, decided to ban all advocacy political groups on campus with the exception of those directly related to the established political parties, the Democrats and Republicans. Some students were highly charged activists, having just returned from the American South where they had participated during 'Freedom Summer' to exercise their right to vote: they were known collectively as the Freedom Riders, having travelled to Mississippi and other states by motor coach. The university rule was clearly an effort to stifle speech at a time when the faculty at all institutions of higher education was required to take loyalty oaths to demonstrate their patriotism and to prove they were not tools of international communism. The policy seemed to be 'silence the students and get on with the business of the academy': senior faculty will do research and publish their work with the assistance of brigades of graduate students as their research assistants and primary teaching faculty.

Like the Bastille, resistance met with militancy. In October of 1964, a non-Berkeley student set up a table to educate passersby about the voter registration effort over the previous summer. He did so in front of Sproul Hall, which was the administration building named for a former president of the university. When the university police asked him to leave, he refused.[34] He was then placed in a police car where he remained for the next 32 hours as students paraded around it. Mario Savio, 'considerably barefoot', got up on the car bonnet and 'harangued the crowd' about free speech. Within a few months, hundreds of students, both liberal and conservative, still dissatisfied with the administration's recalcitrance to allow all political activity on campus, held numerous sit-ins in Sproul Hall. They demanded free speech for everyone on all issues, political or otherwise, or else: that is, or else they would see to it that no classes would be held. According to Sheldon Wolin and John Schaar, who were teaching there at the time, 'the students' major contention was that they should have the same political rights on campus that they enjoyed as citizens off the campus, and that determinations of the legality of off-campus actions should be reserved exclusively to the courts', not to the university adminis-tration. They sang folk songs, often led by Joan Baez, and heard fiery speeches delivered by many people, but it was clear that their leading spokesman was Savio. Not all of those involved in the student uprising held radical political beliefs. As Lefebvre noted about the mixed classes who stormed the Bastille, so Wolin and Schaar noted the united front the students posed, from Barry Goldwater supporters – the Arizona Republican senator who was a candidate for the American presidency in 1964 – to socialists.[35]

University officials seemed uncertain about how to respond. Roger Rapaport and Lawrence Kirschbaum, two journalists who were highly sympathetic to the 1960s student radical movement, having participated themselves in it at the University of Michigan, noted that the chancellor of the institution, Roger Heyns, was so inept that 'in the process of disciplining over 400 students,' he 'radicalized thousands'.[36] As at the Bastille, negotiations were attempted, and, as there, they failed. Unlike 1789, however, no one was killed in Berkeley. On 2 December 1964, during another seizure of Sproul, 600 students were arrested and sent to jail on the authority of the Alameda County district attorney, Edwin Meese, III, who later became the American Attorney General during the Reagan presidency. The university came to a complete halt when the graduate students went on strike. As Wolin and Schaar recalled, 'the students had ful-filled their vow; the machine was stopped'.[37]

The Free Speech Movement set off five years of student unrest at Berkeley, from 1964 until 1969. Some things were achieved. The ban on speech even-tually ended in mid-December of 1964, so students now openly advocated the causes that provoked them like their opposition to the Vietnam War. Protest demonstrations began the very next year with the creation of the Vietnam Day Committee, led by Rubin and Hoffman. Once the war ended in 1975, students returned to the classrooms and faculty to the library, archives or laboratories. Administrators were safe behind their closed-door offices. Some 14 years later, in 1980, in one late afternoon, I wandered through the campus while at a conference with Martin Malia, my former academic advisor in the History department. I saw some leaflets flying around in Sproul Plaza in the wind along with abandoned tables and chairs. I asked him what had occurred that day. He laconically answered, 'This is just some debris left from an earlier demonstration of some sort. No one showed up'. The student revolution, if that was what it was, had by then fizzled. The Free Speech Movement was rarely talked about, and the Vietnam War was no longer a divisive issue.[38]

The essays in this volume address the arc of violence in riot, public protest, crowd action and disturbances of the peace from the fourteenth century to the present. The role of the crowd that marks history throughout the world is examined through the lens of Britain and France during this broad chronological period. Some events recounted here are familiar, others more obscure. Each demonstrates the prevalence throughout human history of attempts by ordinary people to restore lost forms of social and political organization or, alternatively, to create the conditions for a new social and political order. While so many of these actions were unsuccessful in that permanent change did not result, the one uniting conclusion of these essays is that the people who were involved in them were never powerless. They successfully caused the unrest and turmoil that they set out to inspire. In some cases, many people died, and property destroyed. At other times, just the mere threat of violence was enough to motivate the authorities to begin to make changes. The universal interest, the very goal, of those engaged in these movements was to bring about improved living conditions and conditions of life – a goal so many people continue to seek well into the twenty-first century.

This volume also poses one major question for future scholarship: does a unifying principle join these episodes of crowd action together? The earliest examples of protest and rebellion examined here occurred when fourteenth-century England was primarily rural and the population was scattered throughout numerous villages and hamlets. The 1381 peasant uprising resulted from a variety of causes: the plague and theological contentions as well as fear, hunger and taxation policies. Only later did the insurgents reach London. In the next century, the Fronde in France, a series of uprisings led by the nobility against the king, ended with increased royal authority: here, much of the action took place in Paris. It was not, however, a modern insurrection equal to the events at the end of the eighteenth century. A definable transformation in the settings and roots of public protest and riot occurred during the 1780 Gordon Riots in London and the French Revolution just nine years later in Paris. Now, more than ever, cities predominated as centres of action. The most discernible change from 1381 to 1780 was that the city and its urban inhabitants became the fundamental elements of insurrection, even when insurgents moved to the countryside to extend the fighting to the rural areas. These remarkable essays display this change, but they also make clear that each incident possessed its own nuances and set of causes. The challenge they pose to future historians is for them to develop a general theory of riot, public protest and insurrection. In that way, our understanding of how, why, where and perhaps when these affairs occur and evolve will become heightened and enriched.

Notes

1. Chalmers Johnson, *Revolutionary Change* (Boston, 1966), pp. 7–8. For a theoretical consideration of riots, public protests and crowd actions, see John Stevenson, *Popular Disturbances in England, 1700–1832*, 2nd ed. (London, 1992), pp. 1–21. I would like to thank my Towson University colleague, H. George Hahn, for his keen and perceptive comments on a draft of this essay. Thanks also to Liana Colas, Hannah Johnston, Michael Johnston and Rob Primmer for reviewing an early draft.
2. George Rudé, *The Crowd in History, 1730–1848* (New York, 1964), p. 4. See also, George Rudé, *Ideology and Popular Protest* (Chapel Hill, 1995). John Walter points out, in this collection, that we are more apt today to speak of a 'variety' of crowds, rather than 'the' crowd, in history.
3. The term 'mob' derives from the Latin *mobile vulgus*, literally 'a readily movable crowd'. William Hogeland, *Declaration: The Nine Tumultuous Weeks When America Became Independent, May 1–July 4, 1776* (New York, 2010), p. 22.
4. As William Beik, in this volume, demonstrates, such uprisings in seventeenth-century France were often neither random nor uncontrolled.
5. Penny Roberts's essay in the collection explains in detail the confluence of riot, religion and social protest in the sixteenth century, and Nicholas Rogers's piece does the same for the Gordon Riots in 1780 in London.
6. See David Andress, *The Terror: The Merciless War for Freedom in Revolutionary France* (New York, 2005), pp. 191–94, 222–43.
7. Quoted in Robert Middlekauff, *The Glorious Cause: The American Revolution, 1763–1789* (New York, 1982), p. 270. See Jack Rakove, *Revolutionaries: A New History of the Invention of America* (New York, 2010), p. 67, and T.H. Breen, *American Insurgents, American Patriots: The Revolution of the People Before Independence* (New York, 2010).
8. For a collection of essays concerned with riot and upheaval in early America, see William Pencak, Matthew Dennis and Simon Newman (eds), *Riot and Revelry in Early America* (University Park, 2002).
9. Laurence Sterne, 'Bourbonnois', in *A Sentimental Journey Through France and Italy*, ed. Graham Petrie (Harmondsworth, 1967), pp. 136, 140.
10. Samuel Johnson, 'The Rambler, No. 89', in *The Works of Samuel Johnson, Vols. 3–5*, ed. W.J. Bate and Albrecht B. Strauss (New Haven, 1969), 4: p. 106.
11. James Mill, *History of British India*, 6 vols. (New York, 1968), 3: p. 319, 321.
12. Perez Zagorin, *Rebels and Rulers, 1500–1660, Society, States, and Early Modern Revolution*, 2 vols. (Cambridge, 1982), I: p. 18. Zagorin is quoting from the text by 'an indignant monastic chronicler', which may be found in a compilation of Wat Tyler sources: R.B. Dobson (ed.), *The Peasants' Revolt of 1381* (London, 1970), pp. 164–65, 170. For details, see the essay by Mark O'Brien in this collection.
13. John Barrell, *Imagining the King's Death: Figurative Treason, Fantasies of Patricide, 1793–1796* (Oxford, 2000). Gordon Pentland neatly shows, in his essay in this volume, how the mob was transformed in Britain after 1815 into militarised collective action when demobilised soldiers and those supporting them organised themselves into crowds with military-like units.
14. John Barbour, *The Brus*, preface by C. Innes (Aberdeen, 1856), p. 403.
15. See the various meanings of riot in the *Oxford English Dictionary* (Oxford, 1933), 8: pp. 699–700. John Walter, in his essay in this volume, demonstrates that riots may not only have a narrow focus, such as gaining access to land or food, but also a broader goal of seeking an engagement in dialogue with civil authority.

16. Michael Davis, in his essay in this collection, notes that radicals of the 1790s actively constructed an identity of reformers rather than rioters, who posed no threat to the public peace. The authorities, however, clearly believed otherwise, seeing radicals as conspiratorial, treasonous and revolutionary.

17. The Group of 20 Finance Ministers and Central Bank Governors, or G20, is an international organization comprising the 20 most economically advanced and developing nations of the world. The older, more elite group, initiated by France in 1975, is the so-called G8, consisting of the United Kingdom, the United States, France, Germany, Italy, Canada, and Russia. See the piece by Tadzio Mueller and Sian Sullivan in this collection.

18. Clifford J. Levy, 'In Kyrgyzstan, Failure to Act Adds to Crisis', *The New York Times*, 18 June 2010, p. A1, A10.

19. Andrew E. Kramer, 'Following Kyrgyz Vote, A Victory is Declared', *The New York Times*, 28 June 2010, p. A7.

20. Martin Malia, *History's Locomotives: Revolutions and the Making of the Modern World* (New Haven, 2006), p. 287. For whether the 1789 Revolution in France was or was not directly related to nineteenth-century revolts, see the essay by Peter McPhee in this collection. For the latest example of Parisian uprisings in the twenty-first century, see the essay by Raphaël Canet, Laurent Pech and Maura Stewart.

21. The sole remaining remnant of the Bastille is a pile of a few foundation stones on the right bank of the Seine in a small park. The best-known image of the structure is the Hubert Robert painting, now at the Musèe Carnavalet in Paris. Hubert Robert, 'La Bastille dans les premiers jours de sa démolition', 20 juillet 1789, Inv. CARP 1476. For a comprehensive study of art and riot, see Ronald Paulson, *The Art of Riot in England and America* (Baltimore, 2010).

22. For a full description of the fall of the Bastille, see Simon Schama, *Citizens: A Chronicle of the French Revolution* (New York, 1989), pp. 389–406, with an image of the Robert painting at 390. For a more realistic, though primitivist, version, see Claude Cholat's painting, at 401, with a colour plate available in François Furet and Mona Ozouf (eds), *A Critical Dictionary of the French Revolution* (Cambridge, MA, 1989), p. 106. This painting is owned by the Musée Carnavalet in Paris.

23. Schama, *Citizens*, p. 379. See also, Leigh Whaley, *Radicals: Politic and Republicanism in the French Revolution* (Phoenix Mill, 2000), pp. 11, 21–27.

24. Quoted in John Hartcup, 'Camille Desmoulins', *History Today*, 25 (1975), p. 240.

25. Patrice Higonnet, *Goodness Beyond Virtue: Jacobins During the French Revolution* (Cambridge, MA, 1998), pp. 226–27. The *bonnet rouge* may be directly linked to the *Bonnet Rouge* Movement in Brittany in 1675. See the essay, in this collection, by William Beik.

26. Denis Richet, 'Revolutionary *Journées*', in Furet and Ozouf, *Critical Dictionary*, p. 125. For machine-breaking activities, especially in Normandy, during the taking of the Bastille, see the essay by Jeff Horn in this volume.

27. Schama, *Citizens*, p. 404. There is no evidence Desmoulins participated in the fall of the Bastille.

28. Camille Desmoulins, *La France libre*, 4th ed. (Paris, 1789), pp. 4–5 (my translation).

29. Georges Lefebvre, *The French Revolution: From Its Origins to 1793*, 2 vols., trans. Elizabeth Moss Stanton (New York, 1962), 1: p. 124. Cynthia Bouton argues, in her essay in this collection, that the elites, especially among the bourgeois class, were at times involved in food and grain riots in eighteenth-century France until the 1760s and 1770s.

30. Brett Bowden's essay, in this collection, focuses on 1968, but it does not include the events in Berkeley in 1964. In the interest of full disclosure, I was a graduate student in History there, from 1965 to 1968.
31. The university also advertises its total 20 Nobel laureates, many having arrived in the 1950s and 1960s, including Donald Glaser in Physics who won in 1960 and Czeslaw Milosz in Literature in 1980.
32. Robert Cohen, *Freedom's Orator: Mario Savio and the Radical Legacy of the 1960s* (New York, 2009) and W.J. Rorabaugh, *Berkeley at War: The 1960s* (New York, 1989).
33. For the general context and history of the American student revolt in the 1960s, see Todd Gitlin, *The Sixties: Days of Hope, Days of Rage* (New York, 1987). Gitlin, a sociologist, has written a sociology of the student struggle as much as it is a memoir.
34. The non-student was Jack Weinberg, an alumnus of Berkeley and a former graduate student in Mathematics. Weinberg is said to have made the famous remark to a San Francisco *Chronicle* reporter in 1965, 'We have a saying in the movement that we don't trust anyone over thirty'.
35. Sheldon S. Wolin and John H. Schaar, 'Berkeley and the Fate of a Multiuniversity', in *The Berkeley Rebellion and Beyond: Essays on Politics & Education in the Technological Society* (New York, 1970), pp. 28, 24, 27. See Cohen, *Freedom's Orator*, pp. 98–120. Savior, along with Weinberg and Aptheker, was the true leader of the Free Speech Movement. He was an undergraduate Physics student there at the time.
36. Roger Rapaport and Lawrence J. Kirschbaum, *Is the Library Burning?* (New York, 1969), p. 82. The authors' reference in their title was meant to be self-evident: it was Hitler's alleged question to his commanders when Paris fell in June of 1940 when he demanded, 'Is Paris burning?' Wolin and Schaar also speak of Heyns's 'impotence' (Wolin and Schaar, *The Berkeley Rebellion*, p. 31). Savio viewed Clark Kerr, the nine-campus university system president, and not Heyns, as the true *bête noire* of the student protest movement. But the facts promote a more ambivalent role Kerr played. See Cohen, *Freedom's Orator*, pp. 79–82.
37. Wolin and Schaar, *The Berkeley Rebellion*, p. 30.
38. There were twentieth and thirtieth anniversary commemorations in Sproul Plaza. See Cohen, *Freedom's Orator*, pp. 279–81, 291–92.

Part I

Riots from the Middle Ages to the Age of Revolution

1

Heresy, Rebellion and Utopian Courage: The English Peasant Rising of 1381

Mark O'Brien

The social setting

By the mid to late fourteenth century, most of the population of England lived in small, scattered village communities. These people worked the *severalty* of small parcels of land divided between themselves. Increasingly, however, the villages clustered together, either near to, or certainly in the economic and social orbit of, one of the great manor houses of a region. Less often they would be located right alongside of a manor house and its land or *demesne*. The boundaries of the *vill* might even enclose the manor house if they were large enough.[1] The manor, around which the medieval village revolved, was a highly organized and hierarchical economic unit. This rule-bound and claustrophobic village society pressed heavily down upon the lowest in the social order. These were the peasants, whose lives were dominated by backbreaking, arduous and unremitting labour, and by the constant payment of tribute and tax. They were of two kinds – the free and the unfree, or *villeins*. The situation of the *villeins* was truly miserable. The essential primary producers of the feudal system, they were accorded a social status barely above that of the animal world. The Franciscan, Alvarus Pelagius, writing near the beginning of the fourteenth century, made his opinion of the lives of the peasants clear:

> For even as they plough and dig the earth all day long, so they become altogether earthy; they lick the earth, they eat the earth, they speak of earth; in the earth they have reposed all their hopes, nor do they care a jot for the heavenly substance that shall remain.[2]

The lord had legal control and possession of every aspect of the life of the *villein*. It was said of the *villeins* that they possessed 'nothing but their bellies'. In England, the *villeins* had no right of migration. This contrasted with their French counterparts who had the right to leave the estate on the condition that they relinquished all possessions. By contrast, English *villeins* were bonded with the land and were treated as being inseparable from it in law. There were no common rights in the sense that we understand today. Under feudalism, the peasant family and the individuals within it were regarded only in their economic aspect, in terms of their productive value.

In this medieval peasant world, the Christian Church reached deep and capillary like into the social body. Through tithes and rents, masses, blessings and sacraments, from the pulpit and through the confessional, it encompassed the life experience of the peasant. Its constant and pervasive presence was felt socially, economically and mentally. In many ways, this is where the peasant might feel their oppression the most. In the realm of religion, exploitation intersected with belief. In the popular imagination of the late middle ages, people understood society in terms of 'those who work, those who fight and those who pray'. There was a sense of reciprocity. Whereas the lord exploited his peasants, he was also expected to provide protection against thieves and brigands and to administer justice in the village. Similarly the Church was expected to provide a moral authority, a just fear of the Lord, reassurance of the afterlife and an example of Christ's teachings on earth. By the fourteenth century, the Church was woefully in deficit on its side of the social bargain. This was an age of ostentatious clerical wealth, and the Church of the thirteenth and fourteenth centuries was, in its own terms, decadent and corrupt.

The slow cumulative changes and improvements in farming technique and animal husbandry had by the thirteenth and fourteenth centuries created the conditions for a rapid growth of population. Population growth in turn stimulated productivity and had continued throughout the thirteenth century. In an age when human labour power was still a primary energy source, population growth was an engine of economic expansion. One result of this economic growth was a growth in trade and a resulting growth in town size. Within the towns themselves, social tensions were also apparent. By the fourteenth century, powerful guilds had emerged. These guilds had grown up from the increasing trade specializations within the general urban expansion of the time. The most powerful and wealthy of the masters within the trade guilds were now rivalling the old families which had dominated town and city life for centuries. They began to push increasingly for inclusion within the political structures, and in many cities, tensions between the established authorities and the guilds came to dominate public life. Within the guilds themselves, fragmentation was also evident. Guild members consisted of the masters, the apprentices and the journeymen. The journeymen were those who had finished their apprenticeships but had not yet become masters of the own workshops. Such journeymen were effectively wage labourers, and their interests were for the first time becoming openly antagonistic to those of the masters.[3]

English society by the fourteenth century was one in which immense forces of economic, social and ideological antagonism had become locked together. The wealth of the merchants as well as the corruption of the Church gave rise to social resentment and moral disgust. What the peasant saw gave the lie more and more to what the priest preached from the pulpit. The contradictions of fourteenth century society were setting the stage for revolution.

Background to the rising

The Bubonic Plague of 1348–49 struck on a scale that people could only explain as being the act of a vengeful God, angry at the sinfulness of the human world. In fact, the increasing trade between the Western regions of Europe and the Orient had provided a new vehicle for the transmission of disease that was carried in the blood of the black rat. The vector for the transmission to humans was the common rat flea, and their hosts had travelled on the boats of the grain trade. The symptoms of the disease itself added to the terror. Within two days of infection, the lymphatic areas of the neck, groin and armpits have swollen. These swellings, or buboes, begin to ooze vile smelling pus. Black carbuncles also appear. The victim dies within a week, tortured by intense points of pain over their body. The plague had immediate effects for those who survived both psychologically and socially. Some reported a mentality of abandon and dissoluteness. More commonly, though, the atmosphere in England seems to have been one of a strange malaise, with an outlook of pessimism and deep despair: 'In these days was death without sorrow, wedding without friendship, wilful penance, and dearth without scarcity, and fleeing without refuge or succour'.[4]

The longer term consequences of the plague, however, were social and economic. With the dearth of labour it created, harvests could not be brought in despite women and children being put into the fields. The *villeins* were now in a position to make demands. In particular, they insisted on payment for working the lord's land. In so doing, they were breaking centuries old customs, obligations and legal attachments to the land. The ruling class response came in 1351 in the form of the Statute of Labourers. The statute laid down the payment that could be asked for every type of work. In every town, *ceppes* or stocks were to be placed for the punishment of those who attempted to raise their wages beyond these levels or who refused to take an oath of obedience to the statute. The attempts to hold down wages proved ultimately unsuccessful. The repeated attempts to enforce it, however, meant that it became a pivotal focus for a class struggle of a new type. The class antagonisms, which had been unleashed by the plague now intensified into a more generalized unrest.

By the mid-1370s, the reign of Edward III was disintegrating. Edward himself was in his dotage and already senile. The real power behind the throne was a man who dominated the political life of England – John of Gaunt. With his own private armies, John of Gaunt was the most powerful subject in England in the period immediately before the outbreak of the Peasants' Revolt. He was third son to the king and the brother of the ageing heir to the throne, Edward of Wales – the so-called Black Prince. However, John of Gaunt also faced a challenge to his power in the form of an institution that was beginning to play a more independent and politically critical role. The 'Good Parliament', which lasted from April 1376 to July 1376, provided a platform for the growing opposition to Gaunt's power. The tensions of the time, however, were not only political but also religious. One name above all others stands out as being of key importance in this part of the story – that of John Wycliffe. John Wycliffe was one of a line of Oxford schoolmen who had been dissenters from church orthodoxy on theological matters. He preached against the wealth and ostentation of the official church. He denied the transubstantiation of the Eucharist, which struck directly against the power that the priest and friar held over their congregates. He denied the pope's authority over men's souls. In his doctrine of 'Dominion', he declared that God dispensed grace to men according to the state of their souls and not according to their preordained station. The overlapping crises represented by political schism and religious heresy reverberated downwards to meet the rising discontent emerging from the base of society. What hastened this rise was the issue of taxation. For most of the fourteenth century, England had been at war. The French expeditions had to be paid for, and by the eve of the revolt, three poll taxes had been imposed upon the population.

The scene was set for revolution when Richard of Bordeaux came to the throne in 1377 at the age of ten. But this historical moment might still have passed were it not for one essential ingredient – the patient work of revolutionaries. Throughout England, there were poor priests who articulated the social injustice of their times. A popular expression of their appeal for a human equality on Earth to match that in heaven drew on the radical image of the Garden of Eden. Often a sermon by a local or a travelling priest would include the couplet: 'When Adam delved and Eve span / Who was then a gentleman'. The meaning was that God had not created classes; instead, this was the work of humankind. And what had not been made by God could be unmade by human beings. The most important of these revolutionary priests was John Ball, who had begun his career 20 years previously. He was known to the authorities who repeatedly tried to silence him. He attacked Church and State alike with a militant rhetoric and won the predictable title of the 'Mad Priest of Kent' from his enemies. These radical, egalitarian ideas raised the imagination of the *villeins* beyond their most immediate concerns and fused their social anger with a new and utopian vision. That vision was creating a revolutionary consciousness, and the revolution which this had made possible was about to begin.

The stirrings of revolt

By 1380, the costs of the wars in France were crippling the English state, and the wars themselves had gone badly for the English armies. Meeting in Northampton for fear of the hostility of the London mob, the Parliamentary lords discussed ways by which they might raise more revenues for the further prosecution of the war. A tax was proposed and agreed. The tax was set at three groats – one shilling – for every person of the realm above the age of 15. This meant that even the very poorest peasants would have to pay the same three groats as the richest landowners. The first resistance to the poll tax of 1381 was massive evasion. Its scale suggested a level of organization and coordination that the rich and well-to-do could never have imagined of their serfs. England was seething with unrest. Mass desertions had occurred from many villages,[5] and peasants began to move from town to town in great convoys. By March, the king had been forced to appoint new tax commissioners with much greater powers of arrest and punishment.

Legend has it that the rising itself was started by a certain John Tyler of Dartford – not the Wat Tyler who is soon too play so prominent a part in the story. John Tyler, we are told, was at work when word came to him that his family and young daughter had been harassed by a tax collector, and so:

> being at work in the same town tyling of an house, when he heard therof [of the tax-collecting], caught his lathing staff in his hand and ran reaking [riotously] home; where, reasoning with the collector who made him so bold, the collector answered with stout words and strake at the tyler; whereupon the tyler avoiding the blow, smote the collector with the lathing staff that the brains flew out of his head. Whereupon great noise arose in the street, and the poor people, being glad, everyone prepared to support the said John Tyler.[6]

All over Essex and Kent, villages and towns were now assembling under quickly established leaders. At each village they visited, the peasants searched and destroyed the manorial rolls. These were the legal documents that recorded the status of the local *villeins* – whether they were free or unfree, their tithes to the lord and their tribute to the abbey and so on. On 5 June 1381, the peasants of Essex and Kent were at Dartford where more peasants of the locality joined the growing army. Now under the leadership of the baker Robert Cave, they set off to Rochester where the population was already in a state of excitement over the incarceration of a local man at Rochester Castle. As they combined with the Essex and Kent rebels, they became determined to take the castle. Robert Cave and his men laid siege to Rochester Castle and took it on the morning of 6 June. The fall of the castle became a clarion call to the peasants throughout England to rise.

As the rising spread, all forces were now making their way towards Maidstone. They were heading there to free John Ball, the spiritual leader of the rebellion. The town was already in the hands of local rebels when the armies of Kent and the surrounding districts converged there on 7 June. It now became the site of a conference at which the rebels discussed their aims. The peasants' loyalty was not to the rotten clique who surrounded the 14-year-old king but was rather to 'King Richard and the Commons of England'. John of Gaunt was named as a chief enemy of the people, and war was declared upon power and privilege. They would rid the king of his corrupt councillors and would put to death all who upheld the law of Gaunt. All manorial and court rolls were to be destroyed. Those responsible for administering the injustice of the Statute of Labourers and general feudal law would meet stern retribution at the hands of the revolutionaries.

It was also at the Maidstone conference that Wat Tyler steps out of obscurity onto the pages of history. We know little of Wat Tyler except that his followers were loyal to his call. He was of them and for them. He had their passionate fury at the injustice of lordly oppression but was also able to express it and harness it with brilliant tactical skill.

A group of the rebels under Tyler's command now set out to Canterbury where they hoped to find the Archbishop, Simon Sudbury, and settle accounts with him. They arrived in Canterbury on 10 June 1381. The city rose up to welcome him and to declare themselves for the commons. Tyler now turned back to rejoin the main peasant army still at Maidstone but not before swearing the mayor and bailiffs of the city to uphold the principles of a new society based upon freedom from bondage and equality and for the poorest. By this stage, all over Kent, the peasants had stamped their authority on the land. During the long summer days from 8 June to 10 June, the manorial rolls had been destroyed in their thousands, prisoners had been released and the great houses of the lords were ablaze. The peasants were now ready to take their message to the king himself and to seek out those they regarded as the traitors of England. The peasants returned to Rochester and began their march to London. The march to London was to take two days. With Canterbury, Dartford, Maidstone, Rochester and the other Kentish towns in peasant hands, they were now going to the capital to settle accounts with their enemies. On the night of 12 June, Wat Tyler's army arrived at Blackheath, south of the Thames, where 30,000 peasants made camp for the night there. On the other side of the river, the Essex army were encamped at Mile End under the leadership of Jack Straw. They knew that the following day they would enter London.

Occupying London

As the peasants camped outside London, the king and his advisors held a desperate conference in the Tower of London. They did not know how to act. Politically, they were isolated, and the loyalty of the London population was in question. Finally, they decided to send word to the peasants to enquire what might be their grievances. The reply was carried to the king. The peasants had risen 'to save the king and to destroy the traitors to him and the kingdom'.[7] Faced with little choice, the royal group agreed that the king would meet with the peasants the next day. The 13 June was the feast of Corpus Christi, and the peasants at Blackheath rose early to hear mass from John Ball. His sermon was more than merely a blessing before battle. With all of the peasant rebels from Kent and also from Surrey, Sussex, Hampshire and other counties of southeast England present, many of whom had only become involved in the rising in the last day or two, this was the moment to raise their sights to the highest level and to bring this army together in a single purpose. He began with his familiar theme of Adam and Eve. Lords and serfs had not been created by God. In the happy state represented by the Garden of Eden, Adam delved and Eve span. According to the Bible, in the beginning there were only workers. Classes had been created by Man and were a distortion of God's design.

This Christian communism tapped a deep sentiment amongst the commoners. Ball now began to bring the philosophical idealism of the revolt together with their practical objectives. He said that all were equal by nature and that their oppression was against the will of God. Now, he said, was the time of justice. He listed the so-called great men who were to be slain. With their oppressors dispatched, he explained, all would be alike in their nobility, authority and power. A new order was to prevail. But there was yet much work to be done. After Ball's sermon, a section of the peasant army moved off to the meeting place that had been agreed with the royal group, whilst the rest waited and prepared to take the city. The royal barge carrying the king with his earls and ministers had left the tower a little earlier. As they approached, they became unnerved. On the bank, they saw upwards of 10,000 peasants who had come to that place to meet with the king. The peasants were waving and shouting to Richard to come ashore. As the royal group observed this scene, they immediately were of the view that the king should not in any circumstances land. The king shouted to the bank: 'Sirs, tell me what you want'? The answer came back loud and clear: 'We wish thee to land where we will remonstrate with thee and tell thee more at our ease what our wants are'. There was a pause, and then the Earl of Salisbury rose and, replying for the king, bellowed: 'Gentlemen, you are not properly dressed, nor in a fit condition for the king to talk with you'.[8] The chronicler, Froissart, records that nothing further was said, and the royal barge was then rowed hastily back up the Thames to the tower. This rebuff infuriated the peasants, and now they determined to enter London.

Both of the peasant armies were soon poised to enter the city. Straw's army north of the river had moved from their Mile End encampment to the Ald Gate. On the south bank, Tyler's men had assembled at London Bridge. With the connivance of the London aldermen, the gates and bridges to the city were left open and unguarded.[9] And so, on 13 June 1381, the peasants entered London as a conquering army. They had already declared that there would be no wild rampage. The Londoners were not their enemies. Indeed, they had even promised to pay for all of the food and drink they were afforded by the London populace who welcomed them so warmly into the city. The peasants broke up into different sections that were dispatched to different parts of the city. Whilst the largest group set off to the Strand to find the Savoy, the palace of John of Gaunt, another group went further west. First, the Fleet Prison was besieged to free the prisoners there. The houses and shops of the wealthy were destroyed. The peasants then made for the Temple, the lawyers' quarter of the city. It was here that the feudal laws of England were devised and protected. Here were the people who created the legal edifice of bondage, of land ownership and of tribute. A bonfire was made of all parchments, documents and legal records. The laws of feudalism were burned to ash.

Next on the peasants' route were the houses of the religious order, the Hospital of St. John. The hated Robert Hales was head of the Knights of St. John, and so the buildings were burned. Now these rebels went on to join those who had gone ahead for the greatest prize of all – the Savoy. It was decorated in the very latest finery and was a treasure trove that rivalled the wealth of the king. Wat Tyler, however, had given strict instruction that there would be no looting for personal gain. Their aim was the destruction of feudalism. And so, they set about the systematic destruction of the palace of the most hated man in England with an almost detached and methodical calm. Everything was to be committed to the flames. By the complete destruction of the Savoy, the symbol of his prestige, the rebels had dealt Gaunt a humiliating blow. They moved on now, along the Strand, to Westminster. The Westminster Prison was attacked, and the prisoners released. They went then along Holborn to the Newgate prison and again freed those inside. All the way they attacked and burned down the properties of those they identified as enemies and traitors.

On the night of 13 June, the fires of London lit up the night sky. The rebels were in complete control of London, and the royal party was utterly defenceless. The king now sought the counsel of his advisors. As the Earls discussed their situation, two schools of opinion emerged. Walworth, Mayor of London, was for drowning the rebels in blood. The Earl of Salisbury, the most experienced of the nobles around the king and a military man, disagreed. They had no choice, he argued, but to make concessions and if necessary to concede everything in order to get the peasants to disperse. There was no question that the rebels hated every one of them, and that if they kept control of London, the royal group would lose their lives. There was one, however, in whom they had trust – the king himself. The nobles now began to push Richard into the foreground of their plan. Richard was sent with a statement for the commons. He stood at the east, facing St. Catherine's Tower, and passed down a statement, which was read out by a sergeant-at-arms standing on a chair to be heard. The statement promised immunity to all the rebels as long as they dispersed and returned to their villages. The shallowness of this gesture after such dramatic events offended the rebels, and they shouted back that such a response was nothing but an insult. The king and his group were obviously going to have to go much further in their attempts to negotiate with the Commons of England.

Another meeting occurred on the night of 13 June at the house of Thomas Farringdon, an ally of the Essex army, to draw up the rebels' four key demands: first, that each man should be beholden only to himself and that no man should be bonded to his lord; second, that none of the rebels should be punished for their actions in the rising for they acted in the name of justice, and right was on their side; third, that the peasant be granted the right to sell his produce in the fairs and markets and in whichever town and borough he chose; and fourth, that land rent should be set at four pennies an acre. The winning of these demands would have forever undermined the foundations of feudal oppression. The king had already agreed to meet with the rebel leaders the following morning at Mile End outside the walls of the city. The confidence of the rebel leaders was now at its highest.

On the morning of the meeting with the king, around 100,000 serfs and Londoners had gathered at Mile End. In the fourteenth century, Mile End was a small village surrounded by open spaces, allowing this huge assembly to occur. The meeting had been set for seven in the morning. As the king and his group approached Mile End on horseback, peasants on either side of them began shouting out their demands and grievances. As the commotion rose, the royal entourage became agitated. As the king moved forward, petitioning hands grabbed at the reigns of his horse. At one point, Thomas Farringdon intercepted the king to request the head of the traitor Hales. The king replied they 'might work their will on any traitors who could be proved such by law'.[10] Farringdon now rode off to the tower to make sure that their quarry did not escape. As Richard reached the meeting point, the rebel army knelt to greet the boy-king they believed would be their salvation. Wat Tyler now proceeded to put forward the peasants' demands, and Richard agreed to every one of them. This was the moment of victory, and once again, there was work to be done. Thirty lawyers were brought from the Temple to Mile End and some also sent to St. Pauls in the city. All day long, they received delegations from every part of the country and drew up charters in the king's name. Each document was a charter of freedom granting all of the Mile End demands for even the smallest village.

Tyler himself rode to the tower to dispense justice with the king's authority. John Legge, the devisor of the third poll tax, went to the block. Hales and Sudbury had been preparing for death in the tower chapel from soon after the king's departure. Their escape plan had not succeeded, and although the tower was a rabbit warren of secret passages and hiding places, they knew that they could not trust the guards not to have given them away. They now awaited their fate with stoicism. After they were executed, their heads were displayed on London Bridge. Sudbury suffered the eternal indignity of having his mitre attached to his head with a large nail to keep it from falling off. Retribution at the hands of the rebels was by now sweeping all over London. Richard Lyons, the most important merchant in London and one who had opposed the Good Parliament, was beheaded at Cheapside. The lawyers who had escaped the previous day were not so lucky now. Tax collectors were also singled out, as were profiteers and unjust landlords. On 14 June 1381, an episode occurred that illustrates the separate agenda of the Londoners in the revolt. This was the massacre of the Flemish weavers who had long been the object of inter-guild rivalry and resentment.

Whilst the rebels took their revenge on those who had oppressed them for so long, the survivors of the royal group were reassembling at the Wardrobe – a fortified building in Carter Lane near the Lud Gate. At this point, they could have been forgiven for giving all up as lost. As the king and his advisors gathered at Carter Lane, however, Salisbury's plan was taking effect. As each of the village and town delegations had received their charters of freedom, they had begun to pack up and begin the long walk back to their homes. The 30,000 or so peasants who remained were mainly, though not exclusively, from Kent where there had been a high proportion of peasants who were already free. For them, the rising had been about more than simply an end to *villeinage*. They were concerned with much greater freedoms, and their ideas went much further. It was amongst these peasant rebels that Ball's egalitarian ideas held sway and from whom calls came for the property of the Church to be taken from it and distributed to the poor. Nonetheless, a division was opening up between the most advanced and leading elements of the rising and the peasants who did not think much further than their fields.

Wat Tyler requested a second meeting with the king, this time at Smithfields. The clique around the king at Carter Lane was plotting again, but now with murderous intent. They sent word that the king would again meet Tyler. As they rode out that evening, however, their appearance belied their true purpose for their robes concealed the armour they wore underneath. On arriving at Smithfields, the king and his group saw the massed ranks of the remaining rebels, still around 30,000 in number. After taking up their position on the far side of the fields, away from Tyler's army, they sent Walworth over to the rebels to request that Tyler accompany him to meet with the king. On meeting Richard, Tyler stepped down from his horse, knelt before the king and, holding his hand warmly, pledged to him the loyalty of the commons. He now rose to present the king with a new set of demands. These went much further than the demands that had been put only the previous day at Mile End. They called for a repeal of all the oppressive laws enacted since the Plague of 1348, the abolition of the status of outlaw, an end to lordship and *villeinage*, an end to the power of the manor and for the stripping away of the wealth of the Church. The king, according to the plan devised by Salisbury, conceded every one of the demands put to him.

Tyler, happy but exhausted, called for beer to wet his throat and toast the new order of things. The nobles now moved to make their kill. A page had been primed to goad Tyler. He shouted out that he knew Tyler to be a rogue and a thief. Tyler, already back on his horse, span around at this impudence to see who it was who had spoken. Furious, he ordered one of his attendants to dismount and behead the page and, perhaps sensing the sudden change in the atmosphere, drew his own dagger. The drawing of Tyler's dagger in the king's presence was the pretext for which the nobles had been waiting. They descended on him, stabbing wildly. Seeing Tyler's horse breaking away from the band of murderers around the king, with their dying leader across it, the rebel army realized what had happened. There are moments when history turns on the point of a needle, and this was such a moment. As Tyler fell from his horse, the rebels, outraged at what had occurred, began to bend their bows to the sky, aiming at the royal group. But now Richard made a frenzied gallop across the fields to where the rebels stood and cried out that they should trust him. Bewildered at the loss of their leader, they now listened to Richard, in whom they had always placed their hopes, and began to move towards Clerkenwell fields from thence to disperse and go home. In truth, they had been tricked. Even whilst Richard was conceding the demands at Smithfields, Sir Robert Knowles had been mustering a force of perhaps 8,000 since the executions at the tower. With Tyler dead and the rebels beginning to drift back to their fields, the back of the peasants' revolt in London had been broken.

The revolt repressed

Around the country, the rising was still in full flow. Risings were now underway across Essex and the East Anglian counties. Suffolk and Norfolk were also ablaze. At Cambridge, the rebels had taken control of the city. Despite this wave of revolt spreading outwards from the South East, the counteroffensive of the ruling group around the king was already in full swing. On 15 June 1381, Walworth had presented King Richard with the head of Wat Tyler. Richard now granted dictatorial powers to Walworth to win back control of the city. Walworth was invested with the authority to dispense retribution for the impudence of the peasants either within the law or by any other means. If the rebels who had followed Tyler and Straw had any lingering illusions in the king as their friend, they were soon to be dispelled by the beheadings, torture and mutilation, which characterized Walworth's terror in London over the months of July and August. The tide had turned and was now running powerfully against the rebels.

King Richard led his army into Essex on 22 June and stopped at Waltham. Here a delegation of peasants from Essex came to speak to Richard to ask that he honour the promises that he himself had made to them regarding their freedom and also to request that they no longer be obliged to attend the king's courts. Richard's answer expressed all the contempt, then and now, of the rich for the poor. In the same way that the words of John Ball ring down to us over the centuries as a clarion call of freedom, so do Richard's words ring down to us as a warning to all who suffer the delusion that there are 'friends of the people' amongst the rich and powerful in society. Coldly eyeing the peasants kneeling before him, he uttered these words:

> O most vile and odious by land and sea, you who are not worthy to live when compared with the lords whom ye have attacked; you should be forthwith punished with vilest deaths were it not for the office ye bear. Go back to your comrades and bear the king's answer. You were and are serfs, and shall remain in bondage, not that of old, but in one infinitely worse, more vile without comparison. For as long as we live, and by God's help rule over this realm, we shall attempt by all our faculties, powers, and means to make you such an example of offence to the heirs of your servitude as that they may have you before their eyes, as in a mirror, and you may supply them with a perpetual ground for cursing and fearing you, and fear to commit the like.[11]

The rebels now gathered at Billericay. Reinforcements came from Great Baddow and Rettenden, south of Chelsmford. On 28 June 1381, Richard sent a large cavalry of heavily armoured soldiers against the rebels, and they were routed in a short time. Five hundred died at Billericay, and yet the rebels fought on. They retreated to Colchester and Huntingdon where they attempted to rally the townsfolk. But news of the death of Tyler and the repression in London had dampened the tinder that had originally ignited the revolt. The Essex rebels had hoped to join forces with the Suffolk army led by John Wraw. Unbeknown to them, however, Wraw had already been defeated. Richard pursued them now into Colchester where on 2 July he issued a proclamation revoking all of the promises he had made at Mile End as well as all of the manumissions conceded as a result of the revolt.

The judge appointed by Richard as his Lord Chief Justice to exact punishment from the rebels was Robert Tressilian, who was notorious for his harshness. Every accused person brought before him was condemned and swiftly dispatched at the gallows and the block. So zealous was he in his given task that sometimes nine or ten rebels were hanged at the same time. Tressilian moved his assizes from one place to the next, and in each place he stopped, the wealthy of the area came forward to form juries and to point the finger of accusation – and, in effect, of death – at whomever they chose. In the royal reaction that followed the revolt, the chroniclers tell us that 7,000 perished by the axe and the noose. Reliable estimates since have reckoned the final toll to have been less than this – probably more in the region of 3,000 to 4,000.[12] This figure is still more than ten times the number of people killed in the revolt itself.

The legacy of the revolt

In 1381, the peasants of England made a leap of consciousness marking the beginning of a wave of revolt that was to sweep eastwards into central Europe. Crucial to this new way of thinking was the idea of freedom. The manorial system had been breaking up for 30 years before the revolt and with it the particular relation between the lord and his serfs. The labour shortage created by plague, the escape of serfs and the increasing importance of money and waged labour meant that the individual peasant was no longer beholden to an individual lord. The feudal system was breaking down, though the capitalist system that was to follow had not yet really begun. These changes spelt the end of the old relations of patronage and personal duties and obligations. This in turn created the objective potential for a more generalized consciousness of opposition between wealthy rulers and those 'who are more like us'.

All of this had taken the fetters off the imagination of the peasant. Whereas previously peasants had been unable to look beyond the boundaries of the manor, now they looked far beyond them. The highest expression of this new consciousness was found in the idealism of John Ball and his closest followers. The radicalism of Ball's vision of freedom and of the new society is breathtaking for the age. This was a vision rooted in the experience of class if not yet in the theorization of class that the proletarian politics of a very different period was to make possible. It is best described, perhaps, as a radical egalitarianism and a desire to sweep away the power of the lords, cleanse society of corruption and establish a federation of communes. There are the first notions here of equality, freedom and justice in their political aspects. Those peasants who had already experienced the economic dislocation of the fourteenth century were also those who were the most receptive to the most radical and inspired ideas of the age. It is no coincidence that Ball found his most enthusiastic support amongst the Kentish rebels where *villeinage* was already a hated memory. It is also no coincidence that it was mainly the Kentish army that stayed after the granting of the Mile End charters to push the revolution further.

What freedom means, of course, changes from one historical period to the next. The demands and aspirations of social movements and revolutions have a social content that is particular to the time. For the peasants of 1381, freedom meant the right to sell their labour power, the right to sell their surplus and the right to move about without harassment from the sheriff. This was the social content of the demands at Mile End and Smithfields. But we are inspired today by this revolt of more than six centuries ago because of the desire for freedom in a more trans-historical sense. The peasants demanded that their relationship with society be one based on complete equality. It is a desire, often suppressed but sometimes apparent, which spans the whole of human history and which we recognize in ourselves. This is the reason why the Peasant Revolution of 1381 – really the first revolution – has been important for the revolutionary tradition ever since. The Levellers debated the revolt in the seventeenth century, and Paine defended it against Burke in the eighteenth century.

In the end, the rebels of 1381 were not so different from ourselves. Of course their lives were very different. But as human beings, they yearned for lives that were radically freer and more equal than the ones they had. They were able to make that leap of imagination from 'things as they are' to 'things as they might be'. They wanted lives of free association and free expression – as do we. It is in this spirit that we should never allow the memory and the stories of Wat Tyler, John Ball and the peasant armies of 1381 to fade.

Notes

1. For a fascinating insight into the trials and tribulations of daily life in the medieval village, see R. Hilton, *Class Conflict and the Crisis of Feudalism* (London, 1990), pp. 19–40 and R. Hilton, *Bond Men Made Free: Medieval Peasant Movements and the English Rising of 1381* (London, 1993), p. 31. Other sources of information regarding daily life include C. Dyer, *Everyday Life in Medieval England* (London, 1994), pp. 133–65 and C. Coulton, *Social Life in Britain from the Conquest to the Reformation* (Cambridge, 1918), p. 308.
2. Quoted in B. Wilkinson, *The Later Middle Ages in England* (Harlow, 1969), p. 202.
3. For a useful description of the impact of trade on the 'borough economy', see C. Platt, *The English Medieval Town* (London, 1979), pp. 93–114.
4. Quoted from a chronicle known as *The Brut* by M. Prestwich, *The Three Edwards: War and State in England 1272–1377* (London, 1980), p. 260.
5. Charles Oman, in his history of the revolt, says that the population of England had, according to the census records, fallen from 1,355,291 in 1377 to 896,481 by 1381. C. Oman, *The Great Revolt of 1381* (Oxford, 1906).
6. This portrayal of events was given by the Elizabethan historian, John Stow. Quoted by P. Lindsay and R. Groves, *The Peasant's Revolt 1381* (London, 1950), p. 82.
7. N. Saul, *Richard II* (New Haven, 1997), p. 63.
8. Quoted by Lindsay and Groves, *The Peasant's Revolt 1381*, p. 102.
9. For an account of the rivalries and tension between the London aldermen that led to the city being left unsecured, see R. Webber, *The Peasants' Revolt* (Lavenham, 1980), pp. 62–63.
10. Quoted from the chronicles by M. McKisack, *The Fourteenth Century* (Oxford, 1988), p. 411.
11. Quoted from John Stow's account by H. Fagan, *Nine Days that Shook England* (London, 1938), p. 252.
12. This figure comes from Lindsay and Groves, *The Peasant's Revolt 1381*.

2
Riot and Religion in Sixteenth-Century France

Penny Roberts

The Protestant Reformation led not only to ideological difference, but also to political discontent and social unrest. In France, it resulted in decades of confessional conflict and civil strife known as the Wars of Religion (c.1562–98). On the Protestant side, having rejected many aspects of Catholic devotion, the Huguenots sought to establish rights of worship in the face of widespread Catholic opposition. The crown's decision to uphold a policy of religious toleration in order to bring an end to the conflict was controversial and divided Catholic opinion. The ultimate manifestation of this was the emergence of the Catholic League, which opposed any compromise with the Huguenots and, in particular, the accession of their leader, Henry of Navarre (r.1589–1610). Although there was violence on both sides, and it was the Huguenot minority that was frequently depicted as the more subversive group, in practice, it was Catholic activities that proved most disruptive and bloody. Rioting ensued when confessional sensibilities were challenged or offended by a word, gesture or deed.

In the context of a broad comparative study of riot, sixteenth-century France exhibits both familiar and peculiar characteristics. The violence that Protestant actions provoked was ritualized; it could sometimes be spontaneous, at others highly organized; it involved attacks on both individuals and congregations. Its peculiarly brutal nature has been carefully analyzed by historians, drawing on lurid and dogmatic contemporary accounts. The crown's pretended neutrality convinced neither side, especially after the murder of the Huguenot leadership at the time of the Saint Bartholomew's Day massacres in 1572 and the assassination of the league leaders, the Guise, in 1588. Later in the wars, popular protest against other aspects of royal policy, principally increased taxation at a time of subsistence crisis, added traditional socioeconomic discontent to the mix. The French religious wars thus provide an important backdrop to the exploration of riot in the context of confessional upheaval, contested loyalties and popular unrest. They demonstrate how riot was but one stage in the contested dialogue between groups in a state of opposition to, or dispute with, one another.

Religious riot shares many characteristics with other forms of disorder, involving a violent or active disturbance of the peace. The closest equivalent French words used in the sixteenth century are *émeute, tumulte* or *émotion*. Religious riot was aimed at people or objects on the basis of confessional allegiance or association. 'Disturbers of the public peace' was a common accusation levelled against opponents in contemporary sources, playing to the principal concern of the authorities. It is, however, the unusually violent aspects of the disturbances and clashes between the faiths that took place during the French religious wars that have inevitably attracted most historical comment and interest to date. The debate regarding the systematic and seemingly gratuitous use of violence during the confessional conflict has proved, nevertheless, far from conclusive.

Our discussion of religious riot in sixteenth-century France has been dominated for the last 40 years by Natalie Davis's seminal article, 'The Rites of Violence'. For Davis, what distinguishes religious riot is its targets. In the opening section of her essay, she defines it as 'any violent action, with words or weapons, undertaken against religious targets by people who are not acting *officially* and *formally* as agents of political and ecclesiastical authority'.[1] Thus, she argues, the crowd assumed clerical and magisterial roles because it believed that local officials were failing in their duties to uphold the Catholic faith.[2] In contrast, the Saint Bartholomew's Day massacres of Huguenots in 1572, which were anyway on a much greater scale, involved a belief that the perpetrators were carrying out the royal will.[3] Above all, discussion has focused on Davis's analysis that Protestants were 'the champions in the destruction of religious property' whilst 'in bloodshed, the Catholics are the champions'.[4] Denis Crouzet's two-volume study of violence during the wars built on Davis's thesis to construct a more thorough-going analysis of the mentality of both faiths throughout the wars.[5] For Crouzet, Catholics sought to eradicate the threat posed by the Protestant 'heretics' to the well-being of the kingdom, by performing what they perceived to be their sacral duty by killing them. Protestants, meanwhile, sought to de-sacralize Catholicism, by attacking what they saw as its idolatrous trappings and the priests who peddled them, in the interests of establishing a new providential order. A more prosaic note is struck by Mark Greengrass in his study of confessional violence in the city of Toulouse in 1562. He recognizes ritualistic elements, but also 'familiar elements of civil war', 'shaped by *rights* as well as by *rites*' in the struggles within local communities.[6] Janine Estèbe and Henry Heller have respectively challenged the Davis thesis by concentrating on what they see as the overwhelmingly socioeconomic concerns of those participating in sixteenth-century riots.[7] Although pillage and social antagonism played a part in many incidents, notably the murder of the baron de Fumel in Guyenne by both Catholic and Protestant peasants in 1561, such views have not prevailed amid a renewed focus on the religious aspects of the wars.[8]

Not only written sources but also printed images have shaped and reinforced our perception of confessional violence in France, such as those of the massacres at Cahors, Vassy, Sens and Tours drawn by the Lyon Protestants Jacques Tortorel and Jean Perrissin.[9] A series of snapshots, they reinforce the depiction of Huguenots as hapless victims and martyrs for their faith whilst endeavouring to be true to eye-witness accounts. On the other hand, studies of the most notorious massacre of Catholics by Protestants at Nîmes in 1567, the so-called Michelade – also depicted by Tortorel and Perrissin – have challenged the presumptions lying behind the supposed contrasts between the faiths, or 'how Protestants behaved when they were not restrained by their minority status'.[10] Allan Tulchin asserts that, 'Protestant and Catholic massacres were more similar than different, probably because they stemmed from similar anxieties', and religious violence was 'a common medium' by which to communicate very different messages to opponents.[11] Yet these common categories and this shared 'repertory of actions' by the faiths were also acknowledged by Davis in her earlier debate with Estèbe.[12] Nevertheless, the contrast between Huguenot and Catholic experience of riot in sixteenth-century France persists.

It is, above all, the exceptional nature of the violence witnessed in France that still commands most historical attention. Mark Greengrass has recently noted the cultural context of Davis and Crouzet's contributions, but also points out that these are 'complex events with a large "hinterland"', encompassing a variety of pre-existing and contingent factors that influence the outcome of any dispute.[13] In particular, he highlights the importance of political context: 'the politics of violence, played out on a local stage with a national backdrop', supported by the valuable yield from the many regional studies of the wars.[14] Benjamin Kaplan observes with regard to France that 'none of the other religious wars of the early modern era saw neighbour commit violence against neighbour...on such a scale', which he chiefly attributes to 'the rule of law' and 'charity and neighbourliness'.[15] These factors may have acted as a restraint in some circumstances, even in France, but were clearly outweighed in others by a mixture of hatred and fear. In her comparative study of violence in France and the Netherlands, Judith Pollmann emphasizes the role of radical clergy, the religious orders and the use of aggressive vernacular print in France.[16] She asserts: 'Even in the sixteenth century it took more than the existence of religious difference to make people start lynching their neighbours'.[17] In the Netherlands, she argues, confessional animosities were internalized, whereas in France the clergy encouraged the laity to act in open defiance of the authorities.[18] The determination of the crown and its officials to calm confessional tensions through temporary concessions to the Huguenot minority, although the policy ultimately backfired, is explicable in this context.

Thus, religious riot was destabilizing to the community and, therefore, worrisome to the authorities. Confessional division and sensitivities heightened the likelihood of disturbances and violence. The authorities' concern to maintain peace and tranquility made them intolerant of any disorderly acts whatever the motivation or justification. This was especially the case following the outbreak of the religious wars. The increased threat posed to local security, combined with pressure from the crown to uphold its edicts, made 'disturbers of the peace' of either religion the focus of official concern. Both faiths used this phrase to denigrate their confessional opponents as seditious and untrustworthy. In 1568, the Catholic estates of Languedoc called for action against 'rebels and disturbers of the public repose' in the region.[19] Likewise, among the demands to the crown by the Huguenots of Saintonge in 1581, was that those who assaulted or provoked them should be duly punished as 'infringers of the edict and disturbers of the public peace'.[20] The 1598 Edict of Nantes, often seen as the last act of the wars, reiterated this prohibition in its second article, which itself repeated the wording of earlier legislation:

> We forbid all our subjects...from...attacking, resenting, injuring, or provoking one another by reproaches for what has occurred...from disputing these things, contesting, quarreling, or outraging or offending by word or deed...under the penalty of being punished as infractors of the peace and disturbers of the public repose.[21]

Such declarations demonstrate that it was not private beliefs but public actions that attracted most official opprobrium and, not coincidentally, generated the popular violence that the authorities were so keen to quell. Just as with any other acts of affray, perpetrators could be brought before the courts to answer for their actions, providing a powerful incentive for those determined to discredit their enemies.

In his study of toleration in early modern Europe, Kaplan argues that, 'riots required specific sparks as well as underlying causes'; the flashpoints he identified in the case of religious riot were the public provocation caused by, 'processions, holiday celebrations and funerals'.[22] Likewise, Andrew Spicer, in his account of confessional disputes in Orléans, asserts that, 'the public veneration of religious images or relics, liturgical processions or rites of passage could all give rise to tension and sometimes lead to rioting and violent outbursts'.[23] Although certain feasts, such as Corpus Christi, were volatile occasions, it seems that it did not take much to spark a riot in sixteenth-century France whatever the season. Accusations, however tenuous, that there was a 'heretic' or 'Lutheran' in their midst resulted in many an assault by Catholic crowds.[24]

Yet, in 1559 in Troyes, a woman who cried out to this effect was arrested and imprisoned for making a public disturbance.[25] In 1560, in a bid to avert further bloodshed, nationwide legislation was issued banning the use of the provocative or pejorative terms, 'Lutheran', 'Huguenot' and 'Papist'. Despite official efforts to curb the violence, confrontation between the faiths resulted from many other actions and deeds.

Tensions arose, for instance, in the early 1560s over the practice of baptism and burial, as in the case of a rebaptism and subsequent violence at Nemours resulting in the death of the baby's mother.[26] When an infant at Bordeaux died during the Protestant baptismal service and was taken to be buried in the cemetery of one of the town's churches, it resulted in an explosion of Catholic anger; 14 were subsequently arrested for affray.[27] The brutal murder of a weaver at Chateauneuf near Orléans led to his murderer being sentenced to death. But despite legal injunctions forbidding any public demonstrations, he was honoured with a lavish funeral and upheld as a Catholic martyr.[28] Trouble was only avoided, the Protestant account claims, because Huguenots stayed quietly in their homes.[29] Nevertheless, it is clear that both faiths were capable of provoking violence. Protestant acts of iconoclasm acted both as a cause and result of riot; as too did incitement to violence by Catholic preachers and priests. Failure to doff a hat or to decorate a house for the passing of a religious procession, or the open singing of psalms, was a direct affront to Catholic devotions and could provoke an attack. The participation of children (and women) in these acts is worthy of note, as too are aspects of 'popular justice', as victims were given a mock trial, sentenced and executed. Although it can sometimes appear that to walk down particular streets or to express an opinion might, depending on the situation, land either members of the Huguenot minority or Catholic priests in trouble, such incidents were a sporadic rather than daily occurrence, however much they dominate contemporary accounts. Nevertheless, the details of such incidents can still prove shocking.

In particular, we have the characteristically macabre descriptions provided by a major Protestant source, the *Histoire Ecclésiastique des églises réformées au royaume de France*. The gratuitous mutilation of bodies that it depicts has fascinated and repulsed commentators at the time and since. Huguenot victims were ritually disembowelled and body parts, such as ears, taken as trophies.[30] In Draguignan in Provence in 1559, nobleman Antoine de Mouvans was targeted by children who had been encouraged to act by priests and a local *parlementaire*. A hostile crowd gathered who, despite Mouvans surrendering himself to justice, killed him in cold blood. Most barbarically of all, they tore out his guts, dragged them around the town and threw them in a ditch. Finally, 'his heart and liver were removed, stuck on sticks and carried around the town in triumph'. When a piece of his liver was presented to a dog, the chronicler reports, the animal turned out to be more humane than these assailants by refusing to eat it, and was mockingly accused of Lutheranism.[31] A similar scene was reported from Villeneuve d'Avignon in 1561. Here a Huguenot prayer meeting was broken up by papal soldiers who, having committed many murders, paraded the liver of one victim on an iron rod and offered it for sale.[32] Other accounts tell of Huguenot hearts or livers being bitten or eaten, as by the executioner at Carcassonne, having shown off his expertise by skinning five of the victims after a riot.[33] Alongside gratuitous violence, deliberate provocation by priests and the involvement of children were common in Huguenot accounts, as was the resilience and courage of the victims.[34]

Unsurprisingly, confessional bias colours the allocation of blame for the initiation or provocation of confrontation and responsibility for the first act of violence. Thus, the priest Claude Haton claimed that the Huguenots of Sens deliberately set out 'to dispute with and provoke the Catholics to riot' prior to the massacre in the town in 1562, a month after that at nearby Vassy.[35] He further claimed that 'at the start the Catholics offered no violence since they had only their books of hours in their hands while the Huguenots had pistols ready to draw'.[36] One of the most famous 'riots' of the wars took place in the Paris suburb of Saint-Médard in December 1561, when there was a clash between the Catholics of the parish and Protestants worshipping nearby.[37] According to a Protestant account, trouble began when Catholics maliciously rang their bells so loudly that it drowned out the Protestant sermon, and when they were asked politely to desist, the Protestant congregation was set upon with stones and other missiles. The author emphasizes the premeditated nature of the act whilst claiming that his coreligionists acted only in self-defence. In contrast, Catholics claimed that the Protestants were so incensed by their bell-ringing that they attacked their church and helpless local parishioners, killing several and deliberately desecrating the Host. Thus, the identification of the victims who acted only in self-defence was reversed. Clashes between congregations in close proximity with one another, forced to share space, were a common cause of religious riots.

The royal edicts of pacification which attempted to lessen tensions by offering concessions to the Huguenots established official locations at which those of the so-called reformed religion could worship. However, Huguenots knew that the journey to and from these sites, often through town gates into the surrounding suburbs or countryside, left them vulnerable to assault. At Orléans, they requested that the governor, 'provide them with an appropriate and nearby site for worship where they will not be attacked, that they can freely come and go to the site' already granted.[38] Reported attacks on Huguenots and their children as they went to and from services were common. In Provence, in 1562, it was claimed that 'the seditious (people) of Grasse assemble daily on holidays and Sundays ... to murder and kill those who live according to the confession of faith'.[39] In January 1564, governor Tavannes reported from Dijon in

Burgundy on Huguenot complaints of 'injuries and excesses that they say take place daily...both coming and going to services'. He had consulted with the municipal authorities and forbidden the inhabitants 'from insulting, provoking or attacking' the Huguenots 'by word or deed' and throwing mud or ordure at their houses, but to 'let them live peacefully in freedom of worship'.[40]

Such slurs and acts of degradation were typical of Catholic attempts to discredit the moral status of the Huguenot minority. The importance of defending one's honour was at the heart of many interpersonal slights that came before the courts in the early modern period. The preservation of a woman's sexual honour, in particular, was crucial to her and her kin. In Amiens in 1580, the Catholic authorities even took action to provide protection for Huguenot women returning from services after a series of aggressive approaches by young men of the town.[41] Verbal and physical abuse of this sort was part of the steady drip of vexatious episodes and victimization that the Huguenots faced on a daily basis in many communities. Such incidents were unavoidably tinged with the threat of violence that might eventually result in a riot. Yet sometimes the tables were turned. There were also reports of Protestant violence against Catholics as they went to and from services, for example at Auxerre and Blois in 1568. In this last instance, at least, the intimidation was reciprocal with the burning down of a barn used at the site for reformed worship.[42] The destruction of meeting places, pulpits and even private houses, was commonplace, as when a bookseller in Nantes hosted a Huguenot prayer meeting in August 1560.[43] In Dijon in October 1561, clashes between the faiths (including the pelting of Huguenot women with mud as they emerged from a service) escalated into several days of full-scale armed rioting.[44] Riot was a manifestation of the uneasy relationship that existed between two groups who feared and distrusted each other.

Catholic complaints about the siting of worship frequently focused on previous seditious acts by local Huguenots that revealed the potential for further trouble if concessions were granted. At Nantes, it was declared that if services were allowed in the town there would be 'sedition' and 'division'; Huguenots in Rennes had been refused a site in 1561 because of the risk of 'trouble and popular unrest'.[45] Such fears were compounded by the threat posed to public order and security if those attending services were carrying weapons. In view of the incidence of confessional violence, it is unsurprising that Huguenots felt the need to be able to defend themselves. It is also easy to comprehend Catholic nervousness about the coming and going of armed groups. In 1570, the municipal authorities in Dijon were anxious about those of the 'new opinion leaving town in troops with swords and daggers and going to the suburbs... [to] hold assemblies and dangerous services'.[46] Meanwhile, the Huguenots at Lyon pleaded that it was the danger and distance of the route they had to take which forced them to go armed to services.[47] The combination of weaponry with existing tension and mutual suspicion was explosive and was bound to result, sooner or later, in violence.

Yet the account of the *Histoire ecclésiastique* and other such sources also reveals that tensions arose not only between the faiths but between the faithful. This is demonstrated by the local Huguenot leadership's condemnation of the actions of drunken iconoclasts at Agen who did not wish to tarry for the consistory, and were 'impossible to restrain'.[48] They were assisted in their endeavours by the town's executioner who declared it his duty to set fire to the wooden images piled up in the churches. Here, as in the earlier account in Carcassonne, the executioner becomes a symbol of the most brutish, but also sometimes humane behaviour, in keeping with his liminal role in a dishonourable trade.[49] His restraint in other cases is used to highlight the contrast with the behaviour of the perpetrators of violence. Animals, like the dog in Draguignan, play a comparable role in underlining the inhumanity of Catholic foes. The similarities between such accounts suggest a shared cultural repertoire of storytelling rather than verifiable actions. Tales of cannibalism, the inversion and mockery of religious ritual, such as the baptizing of a child in the blood of her parents or the arrangement of body parts in the shape of a cross, conjure parallels with contemporary accusations against witches and other deviants.[50] The symbolism of such accounts is redolent with meaning in a way in which the facts are now (as largely then) unrecoverable.

Not all communities encountered such a bloody experience, as Elizabeth Tingle has argued for Nantes, notable for its 'relatively low number of large-scale incidents and the small amount of bloodshed', which she attributes primarily to the municipal council's 'distaste for disorder'.[51] As already noted, the authorities, both royal and municipal, were primarily concerned with the instability caused by confessional tensions and the subsequent risk of riot. They were more successful at controlling events in some communities than in others. One of the most infamous episodes of internecine strife during the wars, catalyzed by traditional carnival celebrations but also incorporating a power struggle between local political factions, occurred in the small town of Romans in Dauphiné in 1579–80.[52] Religion was only one of the factors at work in the dispute. Indeed, it is the case that religious division was not at the heart of all uprisings in France during the sixteenth century, as William Beik asserts elsewhere in this volume. The religious wars resulted in political division within as well as between the faiths, primarily that between royalist and leaguer later in the wars. As the wars progressed and the tax burden to pay for them increased in the 1570s and 1580s, there was also a growing incidence of traditional socioeconomic discontent in local communities that was only loosely connected with national religious and political divisions.[53] As the confessional map of France hardened, as the number of Huguenots in the north dwindled, so religious riot became a less frequent occurrence after 1572, which here as in so many other ways represented a watershed. Yet the Saint Bartholomew's massacres themselves were the result of increased tensions and unresolved grudges generated in the 15 or so years before.

Amid the individual tales of brutality and inhumanity, the Huguenot seizure of many towns at the beginning of the wars in 1562 stand out as episodes that shaped a generation. They entered the collective memory, reinforcing the interconfessional discourse of division and deceit. The events would not be forgiven or forgotten, especially when they involved the ransacking and desecration of churches and shrines, the scattering and destruction of relics, saints' statues and other objects of local devotion, as at Orléans and Le Mans. The capture of major towns including Lyon, Rouen and Toulouse, established the Huguenots as betrayers of the community who could never again be trusted. Repeats of these assaults later in the 1560s, as occurred in Orléans and Mâcon, strengthened this view. The atmosphere of suspicion fed directly into the willingness to carry out St Bartholomew's Day massacres in several communities in 1572.[54]

A notable incident occurred in Paris in 1571, when the so-called Cross of Gastines, which had been erected on the site of a razed house where Huguenots had clandestinely assembled, was removed by officials in accordance with an edict of pacification.[55] A Catholic crowd had torn the house down and subsequently erected the cross, and another now sacked and torched Huguenot properties. Outbreaks of rioting between the faiths followed, and the tensions continued well into 1572. At least a dozen other communities that experienced ongoing clashes, occasional violence and disputes over sites for worship and burial, would also witness echoes of the St Bartholomew's Day massacre up to two months after the violence in Paris.[56] Riot could result from minor tensions and lead to major unrest. No wonder then, that the authorities were anxious to clamp down on manifestations of discontent before they reached a stage beyond their control. Yet, faced by a determined crowd, and without external assistance from the troops of a royal governor, they were hardly ever in a position to resist the popular will.

Religious riot can thus be seen as a necessary preliminary to more extensive bloodshed and as playing a key role in ramping up the tensions between confessions within a given community. The relatively minor but cumulative acts of vandalism and brutality on both sides from the mid-1550s on are significant indicators of ongoing belligerence between the faiths. Catholics and Huguenots found themselves participating in a drama that had real and sometimes fatal consequences for those involved. Religious riot drew on an existing repertoire of retributive justice, but it also departed from it in striking ways. Due primarily to the faiths' understanding of their relations with one another as confessional rivals and estranged neighbours, conditions were tense, and provocation all too easy. Ultimately, 'religious violence was meant both to restore the divine order and to allay divine anger'.[57] Yet, it also had much to say about social relations. Religious riot signalled the breakdown of the shared values of community, emphasizing difference and dissent through acts of exceptional destruction, whether of persons or of property.

The tit-for-tat antagonism between Catholics and Huguenots in sixteenth-century France created the conditions for riot. Protestant attacks on aspects of Catholic devotion – statues and images of the Virgin and the saints, holy relics, desecration of the Host and disruption and mockery of the Mass – struck a visceral blow to Catholic sensitivities, which resulted in certain circumstances in acts of bloody retaliation. Priests contributed to this, both by stirring Catholic hatred and attracting Protestant hostility. Yet, like Nirenberg's 'communities of violence' in medieval southern France and Aragon, sixteenth-century France witnessed periods of relative calm into which underlying tensions could, and did, spill out.[58] Episodes such as the seizure of towns during the first and subsequent wars, which were often accompanied by the most blatant and provocative acts of iconoclasm, reinforced a sense of suspicion and betrayal, a simmering grudge that could boil over as it did in many communities in 1572. Religious riot has many peculiar features that distinguish it from other acts of protest. Yet the fact that it (or the remembrance of it) is ritualized through the selection and treatment of targets, and that it is ideologically driven, is unexceptional. It encompasses individual and collective grievances and a sense of injustice that needs to be corrected, as well as a desire for retribution for past actions or present circumstance. The violence that accompanied it is remarkable, but we have seen how problematic its interpretation can be. It needs to take into account a wider cultural context of hostility to deviance and difference that permeated social relations in many different sorts of communities beyond those of sixteenth-century France.

Notes

1. Natalie Zemon Davis, 'The Rites of Violence: Religious Riot in Sixteenth-Century France', *Past and Present*, 59 (1973), p. 52.
2. Ibid., pp. 65, 70.
3. Philip Benedict, 'The Saint Bartholomew's Massacres in the Provinces', *Historical Journal*, 21 (1978), pp. 205–25.
4. Davis, 'Rites of Violence', p. 77.
5. Denis Crouzet, *Les Guerriers de Dieu: la violence au temps des troubles de religion (vers 1525-vers 1610)*, 2 vols. (Paris, 1990).
6. Mark Greengrass, 'The Anatomy of a Religious Riot in Toulouse in May 1562', *Journal of Ecclesiastical History*, 34 (1983), pp. 389–90.
7. Janine Estèbe, 'The Rites of Violence: Religious Riot in Sixteenth-Century France: A Comment', *Past and Present*, 67 (1975), pp. 127–30; Henry Heller, *Iron and Blood: Civil Wars in Sixteenth-Century France* (Montreal, 1991).

8. On the debate regarding the Fumel incident, see Kevin Gould, *Catholic Activism in South-West France, 1540–1570* (Aldershot, 2006), pp. 51–55. On the wider debate on the role of religion, see Mack P. Holt, 'Putting Religion Back into the Wars of Religion', *French Historical Studies*, 18 (1993), pp. 524–51, and Henry Heller, 'A Reply to Mack P. Holt', *French Historical Studies*, 19 (1996), pp. 853–61.

9. These prints have received extensive treatment recently in Philip Benedict, Lawrence M. Bryant, and Kristen B. Neuschel, 'Graphic History: What Readers Knew and Were Taught in the *Quarante Tableaux* of Perrissin and Tortorel', *French Historical Studies*, 28 (2005), pp. 175–229; and esp. Philip Benedict, *Graphic History: The 'Wars, Massacres and Troubles' of Tortorel and Perrissin* (Geneva, 2007).

10. Allan A. Tulchin, 'The Michelade in Nîmes, 1567', *French Historical Studies*, 29 (2006), p. 2.

11. Ibid., pp. 34–35.

12. Natalie Zemon Davis, 'The Rites of Violence: Religious Riot in Sixteenth-Century France: A Rejoinder', *Past and Present*, 67 (1975), p. 134.

13. Mark Greengrass, '"La Grande Cassure": Violence and the French Reformation', *Historische Zeitschrift*, 45 (2007), pp. 74–75.

14. Ibid., p. 90.

15. Benjamin J. Kaplan, *Divided by Faith: Religious Conflict and the Practice of Toleration in Early Modern Europe* (Cambridge, MA and London, 2007), pp. 75–76.

16. Judith Pollmann, 'Countering the Reformation in France and the Netherlands: Clerical Leadership and Catholic Violence', *Past and Present*, 190 (2006), pp. 83–120. The role of Catholic preachers was also emphasised by Denis Richet, 'Sociocultural Aspects of Religious Conflicts in Paris during the Second Half of the Sixteenth Century', in *Ritual, Religion and the Sacred: Selection from the Annales*, ed. R. Forster and O. Ranum (Baltimore, 1982), pp. 190–91.

17. Ibid., p. 119.

18. Cf. Greengrass, "La Grande Cassure", pp. 89–90.

19. Archives Municipales de Toulouse, AA 127, fol. 1–67r (Dec. 1568).

20. Bibliothèque Nationale de France [hereafter BNF] Manuscrits français [hereafter MS fr] 15564, fol. 81–82 (1581).

21. Quotation from Richard L. Goodbar (ed.), *The Edict of Nantes: Five Essays and a New Translation* (Bloomington, MN, 1998), p. 42. This article was directly copied from earlier edicts of pacification stretching as far back as that of Saint-Germain in 1570.

22. Kaplan, *Divided by Faith*, pp. 76, 78.

23. Andrew Spicer, '(Re)building the Sacred Landscape: Orléans, 1560–1610', *French History*, 21 (2007), p. 248.

24. See Barbara Diefendorf, *Beneath the Cross: Catholics and Huguenots in Sixteenth-Century Paris* (Oxford, 1991), pp. 53–54, 69.

25. Penny Roberts, *A City in Conflict: Troyes during the French Wars of Religion* (Manchester, 1996), p. 43.

26. G. Baum, E. Cunitz, and E. Reuss (eds), *Histoire ecclésiastique des églises réformées au royaume de France*, 3 vols. (Paris, 1883–89; rpt. 1974) [hereafter *Hist.ecc.*], I: pp. 833–34.

27. Ibid., I: p. 871.

28. On another similar case, see Roberts, *A City in Conflict*, p. 45.

29. *Hist.ecc.*, I: pp. 821–22.

30. On ears taken as trophies, see Crouzet, *Les Guerriers de Dieu*, I: p. 335, and Roberts, *A City in Conflict*, p. 113. In a League engraving of the 1567 massacre at Nîmes, a Protestant soldier is depicted wearing a necklace of priests' ears.

31. *Hist.ecc.*, I: p. 420.
32. Ibid., I: pp. 977–78.
33. Ibid., I: p. 964. See also on a similar incident in Troyes, Roberts, *A City in Conflict*, p. 113.
34. On more examples of children's involvement in violence, see David Potter (ed.), *The French Wars of Religion: Selected Documents* (Basingstoke, 1997), pp. 53, 62–63; and Richet, 'Sociocultural Aspects of Religious Conflicts in Paris', pp. 194–95.
35. Quoted in Potter (ed.), *The French Wars of Religion*, p. 51.
36. Ibid., p. 52.
37. Translations of both faiths' accounts are provided in Potter. See ibid., pp. 41–42.
38. BNF MS fr 3189, fol. 8 (1563/64).
39. Archives Départementales des Bouches-du-Rhône (annexe), B 3328, fol. 718v-20; also B 3329, fol. 390v-3r (May 1565).
40. Archives Municipales de Dijon, D 63 (Jan., Mar. 1564 and May 1565); also B 200, fol. 166r, 167r, 216r (Mar.–June 1564).
41. Olivia Carpi, *Une République imaginaire: Amiens pendant les troubles de religion, 1559–1597* (Paris, 2005), p. 86.
42. BNF MS fr 15545, fol. 178r, 196r (Apr. 1568); 15546, fol. 279–81, 287 (June 1568).
43. Elizabeth C. Tingle, *Authority and Society in Nantes during the French Wars of Religion, 1559–98* (Manchester, 2006), p. 63.
44. J.R. Farr, 'Popular Religious Solidarity in Sixteenth-Century Dijon', *French Historical Studies*, 14 (1985), pp. 192–96.
45. BNF MS fr 15879, fol. 6r (Jan. 1563); 15875, fol. 287, 289.
46. Archives Municipales de Dijon, B 207, fol. 62v-3r (Sept. 1570).
47. Archives Municipales de Lyon, GG 78, no. 21 (May 1572).
48. *Hist.ecc.*, I: p. 889.
49. On this point, see Kathy Stuart, *Defiled Trades and Social Outcasts: Honor and Ritual Pollution in Early Modern Germany* (Cambridge, 1999).
50. Mark Greengrass, 'Hidden Transcripts: Secret Histories and Personal Testimonies of Religious Violence in the French Wars of Religion', in *The Massacre in History*, ed. M. Levene and P. Roberts (New York and Oxford, 1999), p. 81, citing the Huguenot martyrologist Jean Crespin; Roberts, *A City in Conflict*, p. 113.
51. Tingle, *Authority and Society in Nantes*, pp. 70–72.
52. Emmanuel Le Roy Ladurie, *Le Carnaval de Romans* (Paris, 1979). Later English translation as, *Carnival*.
53. For a fuller account of such revolts, see Penny Roberts, 'Urban Conflict and Royal Authority: Popular Revolts in Sixteenth-Century Troyes', *Urban History*, 34 (2007), pp. 190–208. Also see J.H.M. Salmon, *Society in Crisis: France in the Sixteenth Century* (London, 1975), p. 312.
54. For one example, see Penny Roberts, 'Calvinists in Troyes, 1562–1572: The Legacy of Vassy and the Background to St Bartholomew', in *Calvinism in Europe, 1540–1620*, ed. A. Pettegree, A. Duke, and G. Lewis (Cambridge, 1994), pp. 100–118.
55. On this event see, Diefendorf, *Beneath the Cross*, pp. 83–88.
56. Benedict, 'The Saint Bartholomew's Massacres'.
57. Potter, *The French Wars*, p. 37.
58. David Nirenberg, *Communities of Violence: Persecution of Minorities in the Middle Ages* (Princeton, NJ, 1996).

3
Protest and Rebellion in Seventeenth-Century France

William Beik

France is an ideal place to study protest because there was so much of it. In the seventeenth century, during the period of so-called royal absolutism, there were no threats to constituted authority as serious as the English uprising of 1381, the 1525 German Peasants' War or the outbreak of revolution in 1789. No coalitions of elite and popular forces ever successfully overthrew the government as they did in the English Revolution or the Dutch Revolt. Nevertheless, France's numerous protests, riots, rebellions and everyday instances of resistance, provide a virtual laboratory to study the range of possibilities for political violence in a premodern European society.[1]

Indignation, defence of honour and the desire for retaliation were the emotions that lay behind most confrontations between individuals or demonstrations by groups. Such confrontations played an important part in the give-and-take of French daily life. The general population, having little access to legal remedies against exploitation, kept a watchful eye on the authorities. Knowing this, the authorities modified their behaviour in response to apprehensions over what might occur if they antagonized the crowd. In face-to-face confrontations, men proudly defended their autonomy by responding belligerently towards anyone perceived as challenging their honour. Collectively, crowds reacted in a parallel manner to counter perceived violations of their customary 'rights' either by attacking and humiliating the agents carrying out the orders, or by destroying property associated with the perpetrators. On a larger scale, powerful leaders with followings of clients and vassals raised armed rebellions against the persons in power at the royal court, enlisting along the way the allegiance of town governments and popular crowds with slogans promising 'freedom' or reduction of taxes, or preservation of ancient rights.

We can arrive at an idea of the nature of this undercurrent of resistance by reciting a long list of small incidents. In 1648, a man in Carcassonne throws rocks down from an upper window onto the inspectors who were investigating his violation of quarantine rules during the plague. In 1598, the leading villagers of Peyruis organize a plot to assassinate their lord and burn his papers. In 1624, another village that was quarrelling with its lord over water rights for irrigation raises an armed force and destroys the lord's canals and sluices. In 1603, the villagers of Signe murder in cold blood their lord, who also happens to be the bishop of Marseille. In 1626, some nuns and their female relatives revolt against a reform of their convent and torture a resistant priest by pulling out his beard. Rioters in Agen in 1635 demolish the barn of a local notable and burn his carriage in the public square. They stop just short of burning his horses alive. The same fate awaits the horse and carriage of the king's agent in Bordeaux in 1675. In 1669, a collector of the church tithe is beaten, and in the night his horse's tail and ears are cut off. Already these random events suggest focus and purpose. The angry are taking out their frustration on property, animals or subordinates always with an understandable symbolic connection to the perpetrator of the detested measure.

In many incidents, angry crowds adapted behavioural motifs borrowed from rituals of church, royal justice or holiday festivities and redefined them for use in rallying support and attacking enemies. The custom of dancing around a maypole created an object that could be used to acclaim a leader or express solidarity with a cause. Apparently setting up a maypole was a joyful ritual whose significance got transformed into a way of honouring dignitaries by 'planting a mai' outside their residence. Rebels in Bordeaux in 1652 'planted a maypole' in front of the house of the prince of Conti who was supporting their revolt. Rebels in Angers in 1630 did the same thing to honour a popular mayor who supported their cause. In Perigueux, in 1635, rioters reacted against an unpopular mayor who supported the new taxes by removing the 'may' bearing his coat of arms from in front of his door. This practice was transformed during the revolution into the planting of 'liberty trees'.[2]

A step beyond insulting or rejecting the offending authorities was for a crowd to depose then symbolically and assume their functions. They might storm *en masse* to council meetings, shout out their contempt, occupy the chairs reserved for the city officials or force through deliberations in favour of their cause. They might hold mock trials to acquit fellow travellers who had been freed from prisons or to condemn culprits they had captured. They might parade through their town in the manner of the regular magistrates, following the accustomed itinerary. The crowd's treatment of victims could be rough. They sometimes punished scapegoats in a crude imitation of official justice, cutting off ears, gouging out eyes, disemboweling corpses. However violent, these actions were still caricatures of official state punishments. Criminals were routinely sentenced to be publicly paraded through the city, forced to beg forgiveness at key locations and, in extreme cases, attached by the feet to a team of horses and dragged. Even one of the most common activities of crowds, demolishing the enemy's residence, was an echo of the official punishment of having one's dwelling razed to the ground and replaced by a sign proclaiming the eternal shame of the guilty individual and his whole family.

A mere listing of incidents like these conveys the flavour of popular retribution, but proves little about the frequency of these events or their significance. It does hint at the most important point concerning early modern crowds: that they were not random or uncontrolled. They sought to humiliate and punish men with power who abused the common good or introduced unfair novelties into the community. Their actions were a combination of violent retribution and ritual shaming on the part of local communities with no other channel for the expression of their fears and hatreds. When all the right ingredients came together, a trivial incident might escalate into a serious popular uprising. To take just two examples, in 1630 in Dijon, mixed crowds of men and women roamed through the streets, threatening elegant townhouses owned by judges of one of the king's sovereign courts because they believed the court was going to register a mandated change in the Burgundian tax system that was seen as a threat to the poor. There were meetings all night on walls and ramparts, and early the next morning, an all-male armed force emerged bearing pikes, swords and muskets. While drummers rallied support in the neighbourhoods, this popular army pillaged the mansions of seven major officials, burning their luxurious possessions in great bonfires in the streets, to cheering crowds. When the city finally persuaded a citizen's force to fire on the crowd, killing seven or eight demonstrators, the rebels barricaded the streets of the popular Saint Philibert quarter, creating a stronghold of opposition, with neighbours on every rooftop throwing rocks. On the third day, the uprising gradually subsided. Recriminations reached all the way to the crown, and the city was subjected to extensive repressive measures.[3]

In Rennes, in 1675, crowds angry at a shortage of tobacco caused by new taxes stormed and pillaged the tax bureau and went on to sack four other tax offices, making a bonfire of official records and generally causing havoc. A group of noblemen fired on the crowd, killing 13 and wounding nearly 50. This stopped the agitation, but anger among the population continued and murmuring continued about the need to burn down the houses of rich merchants. Later, when the governor arrived with three companies of infantry to subdue the city, his forces were met with derision and rock throwing. In response to the occupation, the bishop's palace, where the governor had established his headquarters, was besieged by 300 angry women who insulted him to his face, calling him a 'fat pig, fat beggar' and complaining 'that he had come to enrich himself at the expense of the province, that this was a fine dog of a governor'. Meanwhile half of the town's militia companies sided with the rebels and took over the streets. For 12 days, Rennes was split into two camps.[4]

When uprisings like these occurred, it was because an abuse had struck a responsive chord in the community. There would have been talk for weeks or months in advance about an anticipated offense. The initial outcry by someone in a public place – 'here comes the tax man' – rang like a self-fulfilling prophecy in the ears of the bystanders. Often the term used was *gabelle*, which technically meant the salt tax, but the word was widely used to mean any new, oppressive tax. The news would spread that the long-dreaded abuse had arrived and that a certain individual was the bearer of a threat to everyone's well-being. A crowd of angry citizens would form, determined to eliminate the abuse in the most simple and direct way possible, by tearing up the authorizing documents and chasing away the bearer of the bad news. They would begin by targeting the individual himself and then go on to attack property or persons connected in some way to the abuse or the abuser.

Uprisings like those in Dijon and Rennes were major events, noted all over the country. In this sense, they existed on a higher level than the petty everyday incidents. There were many comparable poplar uprisings, each with its own particular story. How do we evaluate the significance of these extended urban riots? The whole subject of popular revolt was debated in the 1960s when a Soviet scholar, Boris Porchnev, argued that the popular uprisings of the first half of the seventeenth century constituted a class struggle against a late feudal state that was defending the interests of the noble ruling class. Roland Mousnier, a noted French scholar and conservative defender of the royalist monarchy, challenged this view vigorously. He claimed that protest represented not a popular challenge from below, but rather a struggle of the various social orders to defend their corporate advantages against the central-izing and levelling tendencies of the absolute monarchy. Popular crowds were just followers doing the bidding of such elite leaders.[5]

At stake in the debate were two issues: whether France was best understood as a society of classes or as society of corporate orders; and whether popular crowds acted autonomously or only when led by elites. On the second, which concerns us here, researchers found that the issues were more complicated than this simple formulation and that there was evidence for both sides. Despite much controversy, two important conclusions have emerged. First, that protests constituted a form of communication between crowds and authorities. In terms of any sort of program of reform, the demonstrators always lost because they had neither the power nor the broader knowledge to change the system. They could rally and take over quarters of cities temporarily or occupy whole rural provinces, but they could not survive when confronted with regular troops. Still, riots were extremely disruptive for business and government, given the precarious public consensus on which law and order depended. Protests could make a big impact by disrupting local life for days or weeks, forcing the king to divert armed forces from other priorities and causing immense damage to the property of hated local authorities. Their indirect impact was enormous. Second, there was logic to the behaviour of the rioters, and our superficial impressions, especially the impression that crowds were governed by rampant violence, need to be re-examined. The crowd generally attacked individuals who happened to be accessible. Their victims usually bore some connection to the real perpetrators, even if they were not the real guilty parties. Envoys of municipal governments or detested tax collectors were besieged, stoned, chased out of town. If property was targeted, it was because of an association of the owner with evil.

These larger, more dangerous revolts impinged on the consciousness of local populations and worried authorities. Large city revolts made a big impression because they caused dramatic damage to the property of important dignitaries. They insulted and humiliated the officers of the town, including the highest royal officers, and they led to deaths and executions and spectacular punishments like the razing of town walls, the exile of royal courts and occupation by oppressive troops. But how many of these major riots were there? A rough guess is that in the seventeenth century there were some 40 or 50 urban revolts that lasted more than a day and caused serious disruption. They made a lasting impression on the public and were remembered long after. But they did not happen frequently enough to be worth plotting on a map or measuring their frequency.

Popular revolts were directed at a variety of objectives. A comprehensive study carried out by Jean Nicolas and a team of researchers came up with 8,528 known incidents from 1661 to 1789. The majority of these recorded events were brief mentions of minor disturbances. Only a few were major revolts of the sort alluded to above. Nevertheless, these 8,528 riots give an indication of the scope of protest and the range of grievances: 39 percent were protesting state taxes; 17 percent were about subsistence; 14 percent concerned the legal system; 5 percent involved labour issues; 5 percent were against seigneurs and 3 percent concerned religious belief. The other 57 percent attacked noble privileges, the clergy, notable individuals, municipal authorities, regional particularities and state efforts at reform.[6]

The incidence of revolt is often analysed in terms of the abuses being attacked and their relationship to the conditions of a certain era. In the sixteenth century, a great deal of spectacular violence came from conflicts between Catholics and French Calvinists, the so-called Huguenots. It is thus easily explained as a product of the Wars of Religion. In the seventeenth century, the predominant objective of protesters was opposition to new taxes and other fiscal intrusions on local affairs by royal officials. This fiscal pressure was necessary to pay for the massive cost of France's involvement in the Thirty Years War from 1635 to 1648 and its continuation against Spain until 1659. Not only were articles of common consumption that people needed being taxed, but many fees were assessed on specific groups for the renewal of their privileges and on royal officers who were being coerced into coming up with money for forced loans to the crown. Even worse, in the popular eye, was the perception that tax farmers were siphoning off much of the money for their own profit and pouring it into ostentatious palaces and luxury furnishings. The local agents of the tax farmers fitted perfectly the expected description of the exploitative outsider. And it was the victims' misfortune that if they wanted to collect an excise or sales tax, they would have to set up an office in a prominent public place. They proceeded from shop to shop in plain view of the neighbourhood to mark the merchandise. Such activities, associated in the popular mind with oppression, made the agents an easy target for angry demonstrators. After 1661, Louis XIV faced fewer popular protests, but there were nevertheless some very serious ones. In the eighteenth century, we tend to think primarily of riots against the high cost of grains in the markets. The most famous example is the Flour War of 1774.

But while it is perfectly correct to connect sixteenth century with religion, seventeenth century with taxes, eighteenth century with grain, we should remember that there were popular protests of all kinds in every century. A famous grain riot in Lyon, the 'grand rebeine', took place in 1529. The eighteenth century saw people rioting over religion. The inhabitants from the village of Quernes near Saint Omer, for instance, chased a Jansenist priest out of their church and all the way to the edge of the village, tearing his cassock into tatters. When the bishop came to the village a few days later to calm things down, he was met by about a hundred women and girls, 'armed with rocks, clubs and pitchforks, who blocked him from entering the church', calling him 'beggar, filthy Huguenot, heretic, damned to Hell, Jansenist'. The crowd chased the bishop from the village, demolished his litter with rocks and wounded his assistants.[7]

Who participated in all these riots? It is hard to know specific details, but the crowd was usually a cross-section of the middle to lower classes from particular neighbourhoods. Participation was not uniform. Some neighbourhoods might remain untouched while others joined in. When rioters are identified, they are usually a mixture of craftsmen from various trades, sometimes bringing along their shop employees. Then there were day labourers and petty professionals, such as legal functionaries, process-servers and clerks. There was always a large contingent of women, and they were usually the most vociferous, partly because they were functioning as moral guardians of the community, egging on the men by screaming that 'this isn't right'; partly because they were less recognizable to the authorities and less subject to serious prosecution. Young men and children (boys, rarely girls) were frequently mentioned. They would be apprentices or school boys from the local college. Peasant bands from the surrounding villages might pour into town if the riot lasted long enough. Absent from the crowd were the more eminent city leaders: royal officers, merchants, resident nobles. The desperately poor might participate, but they were in the minority, contrary to official statements blaming the 'scum of the people' or outside agitators. Participation was never unanimous. There were probably just as many people who did not participate, as those who did, either because they did not approve, or were busy, or did not want to take the risk.

When an uprising was becoming serious and expanding to a whole city or stretching into a second or third day, people from the crowd, usually women, would march through neighbourhoods beating on a drum to rally the population. As there were minimal forces of order, crowds could storm through the streets and attack individuals or buildings with relative impunity, at least until the reluctant civic guard could be mobilized. Prominent city officials could go to the scene and command the rioters to desist, or arrest isolated individuals, usually not the most deeply involved, but they were relatively helpless to stop a mass movement until a real armed force could be brought in. At that point, the lightly armed crowd was easily subdued by soldiers on horseback with superior weapons. Still, until that stage, it was possible to join a revolt with good odds that you would not be caught. When an uprising reached the stage of actually occupying a city, the women and children would disappear, and an improvised military force of men with weapons would appear, no doubt using experience from the militia. Some riots were led by workers from particular trades, such as the unemployed journeyman weavers and wool combers in Amiens in 1628 and 1636. Boatmen on the Garonne raised the alarm in Agen in 1635. The revolt in Bordeaux in 1675 began in the shops of pewter makers.

How disruptive was crowd violence? Crowds were certainly dangerous, but they were usually semi-spontaneous, loosely organized movements with simple grievances. There was much real violence, but it is important to understand that French crowds, like private citizens, expressed much of their anger in formulaic terms borrowed from face-to-face encounters. The crudest, bloodiest threats were expressed that way in order to insult the honour of the enemy all the more effectively. But they should not be taken literally. An attack on honour was at least as effective as a physical assault, and maybe more so. Crowd violence was also narrowly focused on specific individuals. The perpetrators might be stoned to death, or their mansions razed, without harm coming to other bystanders or neighbouring houses. There was always a reason why a certain party was targeted, and those not implicated were left alone unless the protest evolved into a more general attack on the rich. Especially explosive were situations where the forces of order seized a few individuals or fired on a crowd. Such counterattacks invariably aroused the crowd further and set off a second wave of attacks on all the authorities or the rich.

Still, French seventeenth-century riots were relatively benign by modern standards, in that the rioters rarely had guns and their offensive was largely limited to throwing rocks and attacking doorways and roofs. The repression was also primitive. Soldiers could do little against rebel forces if they were massed in numbers in narrow impassible streets, where sympathizers could dump heavy objects onto the troops from windows and roofs. The usual procedure was to corner the rebels in one section of the city and wait for their tempers to cool. Firing on the crowd was effective, but it tended to escalate the conflict. Arresting the leaders, if indeed there were real leaders, was difficult because they were hard to identify. A more common response was to grab several unfortunate demonstrators from the edge of the crowd and throw them in prison. Later they might be tried and hung as examples, even though this tactic often enraged the crowd further at the injustice of executing the innocent or mildly guilty.

The riots we have been discussing involved self-motivated urban inhabitants. Other disturbances were organized from above. A typical episode was the seizure of control of a town by an ostracized faction of the local elite. In the process they might enlist the support of common citizens, making their coup look like a popular uprising. They might also join forces with a noble rebellion going on outside, adding support for their cause, but at the cost of losing the initiative to noble leaders. Municipal battles between the in-group and the out-group had the negative effect of polarizing all the local bodies such as sovereign courts, town councils, royal agents and town officials, compromising law and order; stalling legal cases and paralyzing local business as each body seized the opportunity to extend its jurisdictional claims by challenging the others.

In the Provencal cities of Aix and Marseille, factional conflicts took the form of semi-permanent rivalries between clans of urban nobles led by powerful patrons who viewed local politics as an eternal struggle between clientèles. In Marseille, sides formed around the Valbelle family and the Glandèves-Félix group that opposed them. The memoirs of Antoine de Félix convey the way these self-confident aristocrats manipulated a crowd of fishermen angered by a rise in salt taxes that they blamed on the consuls:

> We went in a troop as far as Saint Jean where my brothers had some power, and after the party had been expanded by adding Gressy and some fishermen who carried oars and poles and those long rods that they call *grapes*, we were shouting 'Vive le Roy' and the group that was at Saint Victor was shouting that those people were thieves and that we should go and attack them; then we withdrew into the fortress of Notre-Dame de la Garde.[8]

Félix and his fisherman allies were shouting slogans to get a riot started. He noted with satisfaction how the crowd they stirred up had besieged the hôtel de ville, where the consuls spent the night barricaded against 'certain unknown persons who appeared with axes and hammers to go and break down the doors and pillage the houses of the consuls allied with Cosme de Valbelle'.[9] This sort of rabble-rousing would not have worked if the crowd had not already been angry. Stirring up revolt was a dangerous business. Crowds could get out of hand. A month later, when royal guards arrived to implement the rise in salt taxes, Félix describes how the soldiers were besieged in the house of the second consul and how his brothers had to come and decoy the crowd away from the building so that the besieged *gabeleurs* could escape over the roofs.[10] This was a typical factional situation. The partisans of Félix enjoyed stirring up a riot against their enemies, but the demonstrators tended to have minds of their own and might go farther than the instigators really wanted. Armed rivalries and near confrontations continued to characterize conflicts in Marseille throughout the seventeenth century.

Many towns experienced similar clashes between two factions of upper-class citizens, each with a popular following. Sometimes the split was strictly local, but often it was linked to a larger issue that gave the two sides an intellectual justification for their differences, which might in reality be more a conflict of personalities than a fight over issues. For example, during the religious wars of the sixteenth century, the split between radical Catholic Leaguers, moderate Catholic royalists and Calvinists tore many towns apart. Factions formed in the earlier part of the seventeenth century over differing forms of taxes, local leadership struggles and legal disputes. In addition to confrontations between individuals over honour and power struggles between urban factions mobilizing popular followings, the most dangerous rebellions were those led by dissident nobles with regional followings. They gave focus to a rebellion, and they had the capacity to redirect popular anger towards political objectives. These rebellions were led by grandees with significant regional power bases. Such men could mobilize networks of followers and soldiers capable of actual battles. If they ostentatiously withdrew from the king's presence, their departure was likely to split those attending the king into several camps, as they weighed their loyalties and private obligations. Royal ministers and agents take sides, producing contradictory rulings.

Meanwhile, in the rebellious regions, members of the secondary nobility would also take sides, as would the towns or factions within the towns. The noble rebels would be tempted to link up with popular movements in towns under their influence because doing so was an easy way to gain popularity. Popular protesters might be seduced by the illusion that linking up with a larger movement would get results. This was a bad move for the local protesters because their noble leaders would inevitably sell them out when a peace was negotiated. It was also a dangerous strategy for the noble commanders, because popular anger could get out of hand and lead to unintended consequences. The prince of Condé found this out during the Fronde, when he used the city of Bordeaux as a base from which to oppose the regime of Cardinal Mazarin. His allies, the so-called party of the Ormée, took over the city and welcomed the rebellious princes. But they also threatened and expelled leading judges from the Parlement of Bordeaux, established a sort of emergency city government, terrorized the opposition and fought several pitched battles against the usual leaders of the community. The Ormée was a creative attempt to reform the power structure of Bordeaux in favour of the middling citizens, but it was an embarrassment to Condé, who could not control the violence or the attacks on persons of importance.[11]

So far we have been examining urban forms of protest. Even more serious than popular uprisings or noble rebellions were the large regional peasant uprisings. Many peasant revolts have left their mark, including the Jacquerie (1358), the Pitauds of Aquitaine (1548), the Gautiers of Normandy (1589), the Nu-Pieds of Normandy (1639), the Sabotiers of Sologne (1658), the Tard-Avisés of Quercy (1707) and the Great Fear of 1789. They presented a nasty problem for the king. Putting them down would require a military campaign. If rebel nobles got involved as commanders, the problem would be even worse. Militant peasants were perfectly capable of courageous battles and eloquent appeals when sufficiently aroused, although they were no match for an organized army.

Peasant revolt came in two forms. One consisted of separate disturbances occurring in waves over a whole region in response to a common grievance. An example was the so-called Bonnets Rouges movement in Brittany in 1675. In response to the news that the province's two leading cities, Rennes and Nantes, had risen up against the stamped paper and other excise taxes, peasants in small towns and villages all over the province challenged the rights of their lords, attacked and burned castles and blockaded the roads. Taken collectively, these riots produced a serious regional crisis. On 23 July 1675, the bishop of Saint Malo wrote despairingly to Louis XIV's finance minister, Colbert:

> The [tax] agents in all the little towns around here do not dare to use [stamped paper] any more, and most of them have abandoned their houses or been expelled from them by the owners for fear that the houses will be burned down. Almost all the nobles of Lower Brittany and the surrounding districts are leaving their country homes and taking refuge in the principal cities, bringing along what they can of their most precious furnishings and all their papers to keep them from being pillaged or burned, which is what happened at the Chateau of Kergöet, one of the best fortified of Lower Brittany.[12]

Another well-known example of proliferating, autonomous local disturbances is the Great Fear of 1789. As rumours of approaching armies of anti-revolutionary forces passed from village to village, the villagers responded by attacking castles and burning records.

A second kind of peasant war was a coordinated military confrontation in which peasants formed armed units and confronted the forces of order. In 1578–80, Dauphiné was faced with widespread anger at heavy, wartime taxes levied illegally on the province by marauding troops, along with outrage at the unfair distribution of the official taxes. Peasants were feeling the pinch, while urban bourgeois were angered by a tax system that enabled nobles to remove new land purchases from the tax rolls. Action took place on three fronts. There were urban uprisings from below, including a famous case in Romans.[13] There was a more constitutionally informed legal movement by middle-class reformers in the Estates of Dauphiné, a regional assembly of nobles and towns, to restrict the nobles' *taille* exemptions. This effort gave leaders from different towns some experience in collaboration with one another. There was, thirdly, a Peasant League in which towns joined with rural villages to create an armed force to defend themselves from the destruction caused by marauding troops. By 1580, 4,000 peasants had been mobilized, led by village lawyers and notaries. They were seizing strongholds and opposing troops. Encouraged by the discussions in the estates, they also began to oppose the idea of noble privilege itself. On 26 March 1580, about 1,000 peasants were killed by royal forces in a bloodbath at Moirans, and the rest were defeated by royal troops in September. This combination of separate but parallel levels of agitation had some impact on the future of the *taille* in Dauphiné.

Some of the most renowned peasant armies were the *Croquants* of the southwest. This term was loosely used to describe peasant rebels. It was a term of opprobrium meaning roughly 'hayseeds' or 'bumpkins'. The peasants never used it, referring to themselves rather as 'the communes'. In 1636, deluged with heavy taxes and troop exactions, the peasants of Angoumois and Saintonge began ringing the tocsin and forming local forces to defend the villages from tax collectors and the soldiers backing them up. Meetings of men from all the communes in a traditional district called a châtellenie were held in the central market town to coordinate their efforts. The use of the familiar feudal districts indicates that they were modelling their organization on traditional structures. Word of a meeting would be passed around three or four days in advance. Messengers were sent from place to place, notes were exchanged and a rendezvous point would be announced. On the appointed morning, the tocsin would ring for miles around and an army would emerge of 'around four thousand men armed with arkbusses and pikes, divided into twelve to fifteen companies led by their priests, all marching in good order accompanied by the sounds of fifes and violins, for lack of drums'.[14] There were local community contingents acting pretty much on their own. They formed in the late spring when the crops were in and disbanded at harvest time. Their demands were all about taxes: insufferable rates, distorted assessments, violent collection by guards, excessive seigneurial dues and tithes and the diversion of church

revenues to distant owners. They did not question the existence of the traditional *taille* and tithe, only their misuse.

They spoke in the name of 'the people' or 'the communes'. They expressed
a total contempt for measures coming from Paris, and the term 'Parisian' was
almost as detestable to them as 'gabelleur'. Besides the local curés, the leaders
of the movement were petty local judges from seigneurial or royal courts with
their clerks and subordinates. They took command of the troops by haranguing
them from a makeshift platform built out of barrels. There were incidents of
cruelty against cornered individuals, but the movement was without extraordinary violence. In mid May 1636, a large force decided to invade the city of
Angouleme during the annual fair, but the city got wind of the plan and blockaded the streets. The peasants withdrew and agreed to send an appeal to the
king instead of further military action. The king sent an agent to investigate
their demands, and that process seems to have quieted the situation.[15]

If the 1636 movement had been a somewhat reasoned, armed appeal to the
king, the 1637 Croquants of nearby Perigord set the record for militancy and
made the term 'croquant' a feared household word. In that year, special levies
increased the *taille* by a third and took unconventional (therefore suspicious)
forms. The response astounded the authorities. When an archer who was
delivering the tax commissions was asked by an old woman in the village of
Notre-Dame des Vertus what he was carrying, he replied, jokingly, that it was
'the gabelle'. Seemingly out of nowhere, the tocsin rang out, and an army of
5,000 men appeared. They besieged the city of Périgueux, which was considered the tax collectors' base of operations. They demanded that they be given
the city's cannons and that the *gabeleurs* be turned over to be killed. In class
terms, this was a conflict between the town, associated with tax collections
and government agencies, and the suspicious, overtaxed countryside. When
the city closed its gates, the peasants proceeded to lay waste the rural homes
of known *gabeleurs* and held a great rally in a prairie outside the city. There
they elected Antoine du Puy, sieur de La Mothe La Forêt, as their 'general'
and sent messengers throughout the province to summon more men. Two
other nobles, Antoine de Ribeyreix, 'the Turk', and Léonde Laval, baron de
Madaillon, emerged as leaders. All three were from the genuine local nobility.
Ribereix was the spokesman for the rebels. Madaillon was an old, experienced
soldier. La Mothe La Forêt, 55 years old, seems to have believed that when the
king learned of the distress of the people, he would moderate his demands. He
reported that the Virgin Mary had told him in a vision that their cause was
just.

On 8 May 1637, 30,000 men gathered in the forest of Vergt. La Mothe La
Forêt picked 8,000 of the best of them to form 60 companies armed with
pikes, pitchforks and muskets. Of his appointed captains, six were noble, six
were artisans, 14 were judicial personnel, many others were farmers. The

army maintained strict discipline and taxed some 400 parishes for revenues, each for the upkeep of its own soldiers. On 10 May, the army marched on Bergerac, which was undefended, and occupied the city for 20 days. Their movement issued a 'Protest by the Assembled Communities' that announced their existence and issued regulations for their meetings and a 'Request of the Insurrectionary Communes of Périgord to the King' in which they demanded punishment for the *gabelleurs* and a return to the olden days by a revival of the estates of Perigord, which had been abolished in 1611.

They treated the people of Bergerac mildly except for those reputed to be *gabeleurs*. The offending tax had been apportioned by Jay d'Ataux, lieutenant-general of the sénéchaussée, and the orders distributed by his greffier André Alesme. Ataux was arrested by the peasants and would have been executed except for the intervention of La Mothe La Forêt. Alseme had his townhouse pillaged, and his suburban house burned down, his garden ruined, his grape vines pulled up and his well filled in. He and his family went into hiding until October. Six other officials connected to tax collections received similar treatment. Here we can see that the peasants spoke the same language of retribution as the city rioters. The peasant army under its two noble commanders made plans to advance on Bordeaux while sending for more recruits from all the communes of the province. They moved towards the Agenais, occupying small towns along the way, but when the duc de La Valette approached with a small royal army, they barricaded themselves in a small walled town called La Sauvetat and stationed 3,000 peasant soldiers inside. In a fierce two-hour battle, La Valette's men assaulted the town, overthrew barricades and set fire to houses where the Croquants had taken refuge. The result was 'a bloody butchery because they refused the quarter offered to them and defended themselves with an obstinate rage, street by street, from shed to shed, in the church and in the houses'. The result was a death toll was 200–800 royal soldiers and 1,000–1,500 Croquants. The whole country was amazed at this dogged resistance by mere peasants. The remaining forces fell back on Bergerac, where LaMothe decided to accept a truce on condition that there be no reprisals against the rebels.

The Croquants of 1637 had managed to raise the hopes of hundreds of villages, and they had effectively expressed the utter contempt felt in the countryside for the king's oppressive tax measures. But they had focused only on taxes. They had no program of reform beyond the absolute destruction of new taxes and the total elimination of anyone who dared to be involved with them. It had been a genuine peasant war, despite the leadership of La Mothe and Madaillon. The regional nobility wanted no part of it, and the towns were unanimously opposed. The only people who were impressed were the peasants in neighbouring regions, who continued to carry out similar uprisings throughout the 1640s.

The French experience shows that common people were not powerless and that their many forms of complaining and fighting back enabled them to pull some weight in the struggle over legal advantages and resources. Seventeenth-century France was full of protest and rebellion, but there was no revolution because the society was still characterized by a disjunction between those with power and vested interest and those with grievances but no legal way to assert them. Ordinary people in their various communities – peasant village, urban neighbourhood, parish, guild, confraternity – were cognizant of the way the system disadvantaged them, and they often struck back using the cultural tools available to them – crude defence of personal and collective honour; reprisals against those held responsible for oppressive innovations or attacks on persons and things associated with those individuals. They used symbolic justice meted out in traditional ways; armed rebellion applying skills learned in urban militias; experiences in the army or rural campaigns against wolves and intruders.

The crowd did not think abstractly about law and government. Their sense of legality was commonsensical: they acted in self defence to protect what they knew was right and what was customary. Their objective was to eliminate the abuse, but more than that, to express outrage at the humiliation of being treated in this way and to retaliate by humiliating the offending party. In increasingly violent steps, depending on the degree of indignation and the way the events unfolded, crowds threw rocks at an agent, beat him up, killed him or destroyed his property. Very few crowds were violent enough to reach these final stages. More often they threatened the offender, who quickly made himself scarce. More developed crowds turned on the local authorities either because they had counterattacked or because they had arrested some demonstrators who needed to be liberated from prison. In extreme cases, the crowd would attack the rich because they were seen as complicit in the abuse or simply because they were unjustly rich and ostentatious. Peasant armies rallied whole districts, fought courageously against impossible odds and created legends that persisted long after.

But the crowd was always local, and the peasant army was regional. They lacked the weapons, the programs and the unified purpose that would be needed to confront the government effectively. And despite the occasional expression of revolutionary objectives, they did not have a vision of a different world. Their vision was of the present world, with novel taxes and offensive outsiders eliminated. Meanwhile the persons with the power and the broader vision were beneficiaries of the growing royal state. They were royal officers and great nobles, arbiters of regional client networks and landed influence. All had grievances against the state, and sometimes they enlisted the aid of ordinary citizens in rebellions, using the pretext that they had common griev-ances. But such leaders also had personal ties and vested interests on the side of the royal state, and they only rebelled long enough to gain concessions for themselves. These never included the needs of their lesser followers, the ones with the awareness of grievances but little ability to pursue them. It would take some major changes before people who had resources and broader perspective would discover that they had common interests with the popular majority, against the royal establishment. The people in the crowd would have to learn how to apply their ritual indignation to larger goals, in alliance with national leaders.

Notes

A different version of this essay appears in William Beik, *A Social and Cultural History of Early Modern France* (Cambridge, 2009), pp. 237–54.

1. Major studies are Yves-Marie Bercé, *History of Peasant Revolts: The Social Origins of Rebellion in Early Modern France*, trans. Amanda Whitmore (Ithaca, 1990), which is an abridged translation of Yves-Marie Bercé, *Histoire des Croquants: Étude des soulève-ments populaires au XVIIe siècle dans le sud-ouest de la France* (Paris, 1974); René Pillorget, *Les mouvements insurrectionnels de Provence entre 1596 et 1715* (Paris, 1975); Jean Nicolas, *La Rébellion française: mouvements populaires et conscience sociale, 1661–1789* (Paris, 2002); Charles Tilly, *The Contentious French: Four Centuries of Popular Struggle* (Cambridge, MA, 1986); William Beik, *Urban Protest in Seventeenth-Century France: The Culture of Retribution* (Cambridge, 1997).
2. These incidents are described in Archives départementales de l'Aude BB5, 16 September 1648; Pillorget, *Insurrections*, pp. 156, 243–45; Emmanuel Le Roy Ladurie, *Les Paysans de Languedoc*, 2 vols. (Paris, 1966), I: p. 504; Bercé, *Histoire des Croquants*, p. 319; Yves-Marie Bercé, *Fête et révolte* (Paris, 1975), p. 60; Tilly, *Contentious French*, p. 88.
3. Beik, *Urban Protest*, pp. 126–33.
4. Ibid., pp. 146–57.
5. Boris Porchnev, *Les Soulèvements populaires en France de 1622 à 1648* (Paris, 1975); Roland Mousnier, 'Recherches sur les soulèvements populaires en France avant la Fronde', *Revue d'histoire moderne et contemporaine*, 5 (1958), pp. 81–113.
6. Nicolas, *La Rébellion française*, p. 36.
7. Ibid., p. 530.
8. Aix-en-Provence, Bibliothèque Méjanes 939 (RA 25), 'Mémoire d'Antoine de Félix', 23–25.
9. Ibid.
10. Ibid.
11. Beik, *Urban Protest*, pp. 219–49.
12. Jean Lemoine, *La Révolte dite du Papier Timbré ou des Bonnets Rouges en Bretagne en 1675* (Paris, 1898), pp. 194–200.
13. Emmanuel Le Roy Ladurie, *Carnival in Romans*, trans. Mary Feeney (New York, 1979).
14. Bercé, *Histoire des Croquants*, I: p. 369.
15. Ibid., I: pp. 364–402.

4

The Politics of Protest in Seventeenth-Century England

John Walter

An earlier tradition of writing about early modern English protest conceptualized the early modern crowd as 'pre-political' and its objectives as instrumental and backward-looking. These conceptualizations reflected in part a silent re-definition of the political as concerned with high politics, and they failed to recognize that in a period of accelerated social and economic change what we might term 'the politics of nostalgia' could offer a radical threat. More recent work, drawing on a re-conceptualization of the political in social theory as concerned with how power was constituted and contested in social spaces from the family outwards, has emphasized that early modern protests were necessarily political.[1] Early modern English protesters demonstrated a sometimes surprising depth of knowledge of the political system within which they operated and the way the transcripts of the state and a social elite might be appropriated to fashion and legitimize protest.

All periods of history might be said to be transitional. But the seventeenth century clearly registered some important shifts in the pattern of protest. A century in which social and economic change suggested to government and contemporaries alike that there was a growing threat of protest witnessed the decline and ultimately failure of rebellion. Agrarian protest triggered a number of large-scale protests in the first half of the seventeenth century but, with the exception of the Midlands Rising in 1607, none were comparable in scale with those that had occurred in the sixteenth century or to those large-scale rebellions that continued on the European continent. Paradoxically in England, the very changes that produced higher levels of poverty and growing social tension ultimately were also responsible for a decline in large-scale collective protest. Discontent, in as far as this can be measured, certainly increased, but its expression in open protest did not. However, this process was geographically uneven. Changes in the geography and typology of collective protest meant that while the period saw the apparent 'pacification' of some regions, it registered an increase in others. Within what might be termed a *politics of subsistence*, protest shifted from the claim for access to land that agrarian protest represented to access to a properly regulated marketplace.

At mid-century, grievances over political and religious changes produced a political revolution in which monarchy and key political institutions were abolished. This created a political space for new and precocious forms of popular political association and protest. But these protests failed to mesh with the discontent within a politics of subsistence, and here underlying social and economic changes helped to explain the defeat of the radical revolution within the mid-century revolution. The post-revolution politics of state and Reformation was in the second half of the seventeenth century to register new forms of political organization and expression and to become a major source of collective protests into the eighteenth century. But Monmouth's rebellion in 1685 registered the final collapse of rebellion as an expression of political and religious grievance; the Glorious Revolution of 1688 (despite widespread attacks on Catholics) was 'glorious' in part because it was achieved with the aid of a foreign army and without the need to mobilize the people and so risk a further episode of political radicalization and upheaval.

All of these judgements suffer from the benefits of hindsight. Seventeenth-century governments believed that more, not less protest, was the threat they faced. Like a generation of historians writing in the mid-twentieth century, early modern elites believed that popular protest was directly caused by economic crisis. In the context of the state of information-gathering in the early modern state, it was difficult for the government to comprehend and, more aware of their perceived consequences, all too easy to misjudge, a series of demographic and economic transformations. Of these, the most obvious was the growth in poverty and social tension. Rapid population growth had prompted increasing regional specialization and had promoted the further penetration of agrarian capitalism into the English countryside. The expropriation of a peasantry had begun well before the seventeenth century and only partly as a consequence of seigneurial pressures applied by the English landed class. The failure to adjust inheritance customs to a new demographic regime had also played their part in making smaller landholdings vulnerable, while market involvement had brought vulnerability to those whose surpluses were too small in years of harvest failure to benefit from higher prices and again too small to cope with the lower prices that years of plenty brought. Indebtedness allowed engrossing of smaller holdings by yeoman farmers, which contributed to a process of social polarization within rural communities.

The resulting landlessness and land poverty of a growing proportion of the population had seen a sharp growth in the labouring poor. For this group, demographic growth had brought under-employment and unemployment, and a sharpening vulnerability to the short-term crises of harvest failure and trade depression and to the longer-term price inflation that drove down real wages. Rural industrialization, where mercantile capital had challenged arti-sanal independence, and urbanization added to levels of vulnerability, pro-ducing concentrations of labouring poor dependant on the market both for employment and for the supply of their subsistence needs.

It was this growth in the scale of harvest-sensitive poverty that led govern-ments to expect increasing protests. This perception also drew upon com-monly held ideas about the nature of the people in early modern England. Like the landed elite from which they were drawn, governments subscribed to the image of the poor as a 'many-headed monster'.[2] In this representation, the people were seen to be animated by class hostility and with an appetite for violent and disorderly riot. This was a characterization of the people for which government and elite found confirmation in their Renaissance readings of ple-beian turbulence in the classical world and of popular risings in the medieval English chronicles. The reality of protest in seventeenth-century England was, however, rather different to that projected by the fears of the landed class both in form and number. Collective protest was seldom the first response of the poor, and when it did occur it often took forms that defied the easy stereotype of riot.

A culture of obedience

With the significant exception of protests during the English Revolution and the 1685 rising, collective protest in seventeenth-century England was not usually directed against the government. A popular monarchism saw royal government as an ally of the people and constructed an alliance between the monarch, as fount of justice, and its supporters, the 'true commons', against those whose self-interested and selfish actions threatened the interests of the commonwealth: depopulating enclosers, corrupt middlemen in the grain trade, covert Catholic conspirators. Thus, the monarch's authority was often invoked as a source of legitimation for protest and the monarch seen as a potential ally in punishing the enemies of the people and in remedying popular grievances. This strategic construction of a political alliance – we need to be careful not to assume that it accurately reflected universal popular political attitudes – was in part a direct, if unintended outgrowth of a deliberate policy on the part of early modern governments.

Early modern English governments were very conscious of the threat riot and rebellion posed to the social and political order. This was primarily because of the limited forces of repression that they had at their disposal. The absence of a professional police force and standing army meant that they were dependant on the locally raised and irreducibly amateur-trained bands for a military force and, at the local level, on policing by locally chosen constables. As the government had discovered, when rebellion did break out members of the trained bands, drawn from the region and sharing the grievances of their communities, might use such military training as they had on behalf of the protest, thus forcing the landed class, as in the 1607 Midlands Rising, to draw on a hybrid force of household retainers and others to suppress the protest.[3] And the nature of the constables' temporary and elective office made them as much brokers between the local community and the state. In regions where there was a widespread consensus about perceived injustices, constables often proved reluctant to arrest protestors and sometimes willing to head the crowd, using their staff of office to lead and legitimize the protest.

To respond to this perceived threat, early modern governments had passed a series of laws prohibiting and punishing protest. By statute and by judicial construction, they had sought to bring protest, both by word and action, within the laws of treason.[4] At moments of crisis the government was capable of executing protestors either under the summary 'justice' of martial law as a response to rebellion or of condemning them to the barbarous punishment of being hung, drawn and quartered as traitors. The reality was, however, that most 'riots' continued to be prosecuted under far less draconian medieval statutes as misdemeanours rather than capital felonies. But episodes of judicial repression were intended to emphasize that popular protest was illegitimate within the early modern polity. To the duty of the subject to obey was added the Christian obligation on subordinates to accept their superiors' authority. Again, this was a message assiduously preached, both as part of the Church's annual cycle of worship and from the pulpit in sermons directly commissioned by the government in an exercise in 'tuning' the pulpits in the aftermath of larger-scale episodes of protest. Patience and prayer in the face of earthly hardship were prescribed for the poor. Would-be protestors were told that an omniscient and all-seeing God could detect even unspoken thoughts against authority and that, if not before, then at death, he would punish such disaffection with the denial of salvation. In a society where arguably what mattered most to men and women was what was to be their fate in the after-life, a belief in the physical reality of Hell offered early modern government a powerful prop.

Obedience was an ideological message powerfully reinforced by the belief that saturated the early modern world: that God was directly responsible for its creation as a series of hierarchies in which superiors ultimately derived their authority over subordinates from God. Receiving frequent expression in a variety of media, physically re-enacted in quotidian and ceremonial social space, and literally inscribed on the body through a gestural code emphasizing dependence and deference, this might be seen as underwriting a form of cultural hegemony. Although early modern historians have yet to establish the depth (and limits) to the purchase this had on plebeian culture, its naturalizing of authority was undoubtedly important both in the internalized constraints within which much protest operated and, therefore, in the ability of a sometimes solitary magistrate to negotiate with crowds of protestors. If then early modern authority lacked the forces of repression available to the modern state, it had ideological resources with which it sought to compensate in the propagation of what might be termed a culture of obedience.

Given the strength of these sanctions against protest in early modern England, it might be thought more difficult to explain how men and women were in fact able to protest. A traditional answer to this conundrum has been to privilege the economic in explaining protest. Within the 'pressure-cooker' or hydraulic models of politics people were driven to protest by the depth of their suffering, and drawing on another explanatory model that saw them denied the right of political participation, they were seen as being forced to articulate their grievances through riot. There is, of course, a residual truth in this reading of protest as the ultimate weapon of the powerless. But this will not do, and certainly not for seventeenth-century England, where there was a discrepancy between the anticipated and actual levels of protest. This was signalled at the very end of the sixteenth century in the fact that successive years of harvest failure in the so-called hungry nineties, interacting with longer term immiseration, did not produce rebellion on the scale of what had occurred in England earlier in that century or in a contemporaneous roll call of major rebellions, numbering support in the thousands, across much of Europe in that difficult decade.[5] But it was another response of early modern government to fears of the 'many-headed monster' that undercut its own prohibitions on protest, afforded legitimacy for the expression of dissent and encouraged its own officials to negotiate with, rather than to repress, crowds.

Public transcripts and popular protest

Faced with the possibility that it would not be able to suppress large-scale protest once crowds had assembled, royal government had sought to anticipate discontent and to ameliorate grievance. In doing so, it followed a double policy. First, it sought to secure acceptance of its exercise of royal power as legitimate authority to which its subjects gave their consent. To that end, it stressed the divine nature of royal power and, as an inescapable corollary, the responsibilities that the ruler had for his or her subjects. Second, in pursuit of that responsibility, it passed legislation and initiated administrative measures designed to police pressure points within the economy. Identifying, not altogether accurately, enclosure (especially when associated with the conversion of arable land to pasture), as the primary cause of dearth, inflation, depopulation, landlessness and increasing rural poverty, it passed laws criminalizing certain methods and forms of enclosure. Similarly, confronted with the periodic threat of famine following harvest failure, the government had codified measures to regulate the grain market, to police transactions by middlemen and to mitigate the impact of harvest failure by ordering the crisis provision of grain at subsidized prices to poorer consumers.

Thus, formal weaknesses in the ability of authorities to repress large-scale protests and acute apprehension (even moral panic) about the potential threat posed by their image of the people as 'the many-headed monster' had made royal governments in this period anxious publicly to be seen as fulfilling their role as protector of the people. They had developed a public discourse in which monarchs repeatedly stressed their responsibilities to their subjects and advertised the measures they were taking. Lacking a professional bureaucracy, royal government depended heavily on royal courts of law as centres of administration as well as criminal law. In a system of what has been called 'self government at the king's command', an awareness of the potential clash of interests that might arise from requiring an unpaid magistracy, drawn from the landed class, to enforce laws that could contradict their interests as landlords made royal governments eager to enlist popular support in the administration of laws designed to protect their subsistence. Government invited the people's cooperation in the detection, presentment and prosecution of offenders against those laws in a system of policing from below. To that end, the monarchy employed a variety of media to enter into a dialogue with its subjects. For example, royal proclamations read from the pulpit and at the market cross, and the charge read out at the opening of meetings of provincial royal courts provided both often detailed reference to the laws in force and, especially in years of crisis, highlighted particular problems the government wanted addressed, sponsoring discussions of laws against popular grievances like enclosure and the hoarding of grain or, in a different context, the political and religious challenges represented by the threat of popery. That much of this state-sponsored education necessarily took place through the agency of the law and the arena of local law courts helps to explain the sometimes surprisingly sophisticated popular legalism deployed in early modern English protest.

Central to the dialogue between prince and people was the concept of the commonwealth, a conceptualization of polity and society that moralized social and economic relationships and that made defence of the common good the responsibility of everyone. In a world created by God, princes and those who exercised authority on their behalf had a duty to prevent the harm that the selfish pursuit of private interest might produce. Property holders, from aristocratic landholders to dealers in grain, were expected to exercise a stewardship in the enjoyment of their property that recognized the consequences of their economic actions for those tenants and consumers dependant on them for their living. Thus sermons in the period, in times of crisis commissioned by the government, reminded magistrates of their responsibilities to protect the poor, landowners of the sinfulness of over-exploiting their tenants and controllers of grain stocks of their God-given duty to place poor before profit.

This was – of course – a normative order, and one increasingly at variance over the seventeenth century with the reality of social and economic relationships and, after mid-century, even with changed government policy. But, within the concept of commonwealth lay the springs of what for a later period E.P. Thompson has called the 'moral economy' of the crowd.[6]

Despite, then, a political culture that proscribed protest and (literally) preached patience, government policy created a space for a popular politics that could extend to collective protest. In the face of the culture of obedience, a selective and strategic appropriation of the concept of commonwealth and a knowledge of government laws and policies provided protesters with legitimation for their protests. This gave rise to a politics of subsistence in which disputes over access to food, land and, to a lesser degree in this period, the proper rewards of skilled labour produced conflicts in which crowds often sought to involve authority as arbiter and ally. But, it should also be remembered that in their concern for legitimation, early modern English protests also reflected a strategic knowledge of the penalties for those whose protests the authorities chose to prosecute as crimes against the state and, accordingly, a desire not to allow their opponents to rebrand them as disorderly rebels and to escape the sometimes draconian punishments this might incur. There was a double conditioning of protest in fear of repression and appropriation of legitimation in the relationship between people and government. When in the revolution of the mid-century, the legitimacy of the godly prince was called into question by the policies pursued by the Stuart monarchy and compromised by a seeming collapse in its authority, then it becomes possible to see another and more radical face to early modern English protest, hitherto only to be found in the evidence of popular sedition for which individuals found themselves being examined and tried.[7]

The politics of subsistence and agrarian protest

Within the politics of subsistence, two forms of popular crowd action predominated in the seventeenth century: protests over access to land and over access to food. Both occurred throughout the period. Before the mid-century, protests over enclosure predominated, but after a zenith within the space created by the English Revolution these became more regionally confined in their geography, and in number they had by the end of the century given way to crowd actions over food, presaging what was to become the dominant pattern in the eighteenth century. 'Industrial' protests were also to be found, though not in any substantial number until towards the end of the century. Given the concentration of manufacture in urban workshops and rural cottages, these did not take the form of later strikes, but involved conflicts over the customs of the trade. Evidence for their occurrence is easier to find in mining communities where the struggle to defend 'ancient' customary rights produced large-scale and often long-running episodes of collective protest.[8] But the opacity of the urban workshop hides evidence of episodes of disputes between masters and journeymen, and urban guilds were also sites of contest over the customs of the trade. Attacks on immigrant labourers and early examples of machine-breaking were also to be found.[9] But that, for example, it was far more common for groups like clothworkers to stage collective protests over food might suggest that their politics continued to reflect a powerful belief, flying in the face of a shifting reality, in their identity as economically independent artisanal producers, for whom prices, not wages, were thought to determine their well-being.

Because of the prohibitions on 'riot', collective and open protest was not the immediate response to popular grievance within the politics of subsistence. There were other methods of articulating dissent, less spectacular but perhaps more continuous, in what James Scott has called 'the infrapolitics' of the poor.[10] Given the existence of a public transcript, prescribing protection of the weak and prohibiting actions that oppressed them, appeals might first be made to that transcript that ran from deferential petitioning (that nevertheless managed to convey a threat of retaliation), through public grumbling to anonymous threatening letters in which the threat of popular violence was made explicit. Given a context in which government feared popular violence and was unable to offer effective protection locally to those threatened, these tactics might enjoy some success in forcing those against whom the protests were directed to enter into negotiation, especially in years of crisis where the authorities could be prodded into intervening directly to address popular grievances and, as in years of harvest failure, to introduce remedial measures. The success of these 'weapons of the weak' helps to explain the relative absence of some forms of collective protest in this period.[11]

Where individual lords sought to change tenures and to increase rents and fines, protest might take subtle forms of resistance within the politics of contested custom. Where open protest occurred, it usually defied the stereotype of unpremeditated violence. Often considerable planning had gone into fashioning protest. But, given the knowledge transmitted through a tradition of riot and the ability of protesters to appropriate and adapt other forms of gathering, such planning did not necessarily require weeks to achieve. Crowds borrowed, sometimes directly, from occasions in either the calendar of state, church or festive culture to fashion their protest. The experience of mustering in the trained bands, and associated communications network of beacons and meeting places, were drawn on by enclosure protesters, especially in the north where border conflict with the Scots remained a recurring threat. The military hierarchy of popularly elected colonels and captains under whose command enclosure protesters marched to destroy hedges and fences had a similar origin. That the forms and days chosen had resonances for the nature of protest underlines the fact that the act of borrowing was not simply a pretext to assemble a crowd. Thus, for example, given that protesters against enclosure were protesting against both the loss of access to common rights over land and against the moral failings implied in this act of possessive individualism, the Rogationtide ceremony provided an apt occasion to stage a protest. An annual event within the church calendar that was designed to define both the community's physical and moral boundaries, which began with the minister denouncing in church those who removed their neighbours' landmarks and involved a crowd processing around the parish bounds, provided a perfect text for the destruction of enclosing hedges.

Popular culture, with its festive occasions marked by large crowds and inversionary humour, offered similar possibilities. May Day required the young men and women to go out into the surrounding area the night before and to select branches of greenery with which to decorate the parish church and village. Not surprisingly, this provided an opportunity for discerning decorators to pull down whole enclosures in pursuit of perfection. This helps to explain why the largest protest of the period against enclosure, the Midlands Rising of 1607, began on May eve. Shrove Tuesday was another day of popular licence still retaining medieval memories of a belief that law was said to be suspended on that day. 'Camping the ball' on that day involved large, boisterous crowds of men, drawn from different villages, competing for possession of a football, often over distances several miles long. It was no surprise then that camping the ball should become the occasion for the destruction of the enclosures associated with the hated large-scale drainage of thousands of acres of the fens of eastern England in the 1630s and on in repeated episodes into the eighteenth century.[12] The playful and inversionary humour that crowds exhibited reflected the psychic charge they got from reversing – however temporarily – the structures of power.

In striking contrast to much continental violence at this period, violence was usually directed against property and not persons. In the case of protests over enclosure for game, an unproductive use of land symbolizing aristocratic privilege and one therefore popularly detested, that protest might involve acts of mass slaughter of deer and rabbits, as happened in the early stages of the English Revolution.[13] Despite often dominating public space, crowds almost without exception never killed their victims (and only then in exceptional moments like the killing of several officers in the early stages of the English Revolution).[14] Within the sheer threat posed by the assembly of large numbers, crowds often contented themselves with deploying a rhetoric of violence, threatening but not inflicting the violence implied in, for example, the common boast to cut any who resisted them 'as small as herbs to the pot'. For the most part, the authorities might show a similar tact. But needing to repress large-scale protest, they showed no such restraint. Faced with rebellion on the scale of the Midlands Rising of 1607 where crowds numbering several thousand had toured the region attacking enclosures and had denied request to disperse on the promise of a royal pardon, then some 50 or more protesters were either killed in the battle that ended the rising or hanged under martial law immediately afterwards.[15]

Agrarian protest could, as in the case of the Midlands Rising where the impact of enclosure was concentrated, involve crowds numbered in hundreds or thousands or where enclosure, as in the northern uplands or in south-western forest and eastern fen royal-backed schemes of drainage and disafforestation, threatened many communities simultaneously with loss of common rights.[16] But agrarian protests usually involved crowds in much smaller numbers.[17] Crowds were composed of men, women and children, or destruction might be the act of unisex crowds either of men or, for reasons discussed below, of women. Such protests might take place over a number of days or even years, with some long-running disputes drawing impressively on a social memory of lost rights that stretched back over centuries. In these cases, dislocations in the local power structure with the death of the lord of the manor or at a national level with the death of the monarch, with whom laws were popularly held temporarily to die, might explain the recurrence of destruction.

Collective rural protest focussed on enclosure as both symbol and initiator of agrarian change. But despite differences of scale, the tactics deployed in acts of collective protest were often very similar. These focussed on enclosure as both the symbol and cause of economic change. Thus, at the heart of such protests was the physical destruction of the hedges and ditches preventing commoners from claiming contested common rights. Destruction might be conducted under the cover of night, but often it was done with considerable publicity. The day of the destruction might be announced in advance. Crowds, called to assembly by the blowing of horns or ringing of bells, processed formally to the disputed land, accompanied by the beating of drums and, at a prearranged signal, destroyed the enclosure, sometimes symbolically destroying only a part, and reclaiming common rights either by ploughing up crops being grown there or by depasturing it with their own livestock. Food and drink might be brought to those destroying the enclosures or the day end with the lighting of bonfires, for which the enclosures provided combustible material, and more feasting and dancing. Here 'riot' represented a physical restatement of communal rights and as such a literal enactment of community. The control of public space the crowd claimed and the commensality they enjoyed in feasting and drinking represented a claim to speak for the community of the manor, parish and commonwealth. Considerable efforts thus might be expended in trying to achieve unanimity, with protesters swearing oaths and issuing by-laws threatening those who failed to support them with fine or loss of common rights. Labourers brought in to enclose the land or tenants of the new holdings often became the targets of threatened and actual physical violence, while the encloser might be depicted in libellous verses and threatening pictures posted in sensitive sites like the local church or alehouses of the district or either hanged or buried in effigy. Such deliberate and public acts of destruction and physical intimidation were clearly intended to persuade the encloser to stop.

Despite the tactical sophistication that agrarian protesters might show, it is difficult to know how successful they were. In regions like the royal forests and eastern fens where disaffection with externally imposed schemes of large-scale 'improvement' might infect even some of the local magistracy and where the terrain often made the capture of protesters anyway difficult, open conflict, backed with a guerrilla campaign, made successful enclosure something still not entirely achieved by the end of the century. Opposition in some of these areas continued intermittently on into the nineteenth century. In the case of larger schemes of enclosure, for example those promoted by members of the aristocracy or city financiers, acts of destruction might be accompanied by appeals for intervention by the government to halt enclosure it was popularly believed to oppose, the protesters drawing up and sometime circulating petitions to be presented to the monarch or to what were thought to be favourable magistrates. The Midlands Rising may have ended in repression, but it was followed by a pardon and the issuing of a royal commission to investigate the extent of illegal enclosure as a prelude to the initiation of special prosecutions of enclosers by the government. Here, as elsewhere, opposition certainly acted as a drag on the rate of enclosure.

But, in terms of success, a distinction partly in terms of class and tenurial differences might be made between those crowds who intended to pressure the encloser to renegotiate the terms of enclosure and those who opposed the very act of enclosure. The defence of common rights might then involve commoners – those who claimed common rights, who were also socially members of the commons. But 'commoner' might also embrace wealthier farmers and even members of the gentry. Enclosure protest cannot always, therefore, be rendered in terms of class politics. In many episodes of agrarian protest, large and small, the physical act of destruction and trespass was also intended to initiate parallel legal action in the courts, with the commoners collecting a common purse to fee lawyers while seeking to use violence on the ground to counterbalance the power and wealth of the encloser. In the case of negotiation, where wealthy farmers and gentleman freeholders were more likely to be involved, compensation was often what was aimed at and often what was secured. But the law offered no protection to those squatters and commons without legal rights to common. For these groups, enclosure remained something to be resisted outright.

Over time, agrarian protest probably became less successful. It certainly became less common. A number of factors help to explain this. Attitudes to

enclosure began to shift. It had always had those willing to argue its benefits for the commonwealth in enhanced productivity (and – significantly – in
increased labour discipline for those who would now find themselves deprived
of the semi-independence offered by common rights). Enclosure remained
a contested process, but its advocates now began to outweigh it opponents.
Government policy remained inconsistent, with renewed commissions issued
against enclosure in the 1630s at the very time the crown was becoming the
leading encloser. But, after mid century, government policy became permissive,
not prohibitive.[18] While the royal courts offered more effective protection for
the property rights of manorial tenants with a legal estate in the land (or at
least those who could meet the legal costs of initiating legal action), they had
began to dismiss common rights less securely defined through claims of local
custom. Over time, these changes denied protestors the legitimation afforded
by the public transcript of commonwealth.

After mid-century, enclosure protest was no longer the dominant form of
popular protest it had once been. In reality, its decline had been occurring
for some while. Protests triggered by large-scale, crown-sponsored enclosure
of forest and fen in the 1620s and 1630s had increased sharply with the temporary paralysis of authority in the English civil war so that the early 1640s
saw widespread riots on a scale perhaps not seen since the so-called Peasants'
Revolt of 1381. But by contrast, the Midlands, which had seen in 1607 the last
major agrarian rising, remained (with the exception of a few royal forests and
aristocratic parks) remarkably quiet. Historians of protest sometimes find it all
too easy to ignore the evidence of the absence of protest. But the silence here
points to a more insidious process of social change and recasting of social alli-
ances that was undermining from within the community the ability to engage
in large-scale protests. This helps to explain the failure of those radical groups
who paid attention to the problems of the rural poor – not all did – to mobilise
them and why the cry of land and liberty did not characterize the English
Revolution.

The emergence of an increasing number of wealthy farmers – what contemporaries termed the middling sort – able to profit from the demands of a rapidly
growing population saw them hungry for more land and willing to enter into
acts of enclosure by agreement with manorial lords. In turn, members of this
landed class had been frightened off pursuing traditional seigneurial tactics
of expropriating a growing share of a diminishing peasant surplus by earlier
agrarian rebellion; they came increasingly to see the benefits of sharing in the
growing profits brought by agrarian capitalism. The classic tripartite structure
of (absentee) landlord, farmer and landless labourer this promoted helped to
explain a shift in the locus and form of agrarian protest. Middling sort farmers,
those with considerable standing and experience of local office-holding, had
often been important in leading and coordinating earlier protest. Now they

became willing to use their wealth and power to discipline the labouring poor, using a developing poor relief and the 'dull compulsion' of labour discipline to try to mould the 'respectable poor'. This was not a straightforward process. Open opposition to enclosure in forest and fen could continue as long as wealthier farmers there stood to benefit more in pursuit of agrarian capitalism by regional specialization in animal husbandry from their (over-) exploitation of waste and commons. But, especially in lowland arable England, collective protest became a luxury that a labouring poor vulnerable to victimization in loss of employment and poor relief could ill afford. By the end of the century, protest here, where it survived, resorted more frequently to E.P. Thompson's crime of anonymity: anonymous threatening letters, sometimes accompanied by night-time acts of destruction and animal-maiming.[19]

Food 'riots': from commonwealth to moral economy

Food riots had occurred since the Middle Ages, but they began to increase in number towards the end of the sixteenth century, and by the end of the seventeenth century they had become the dominant form of protest within the politics of subsistence. But such 'riots' were, until the very end of the period, apparently never numerous. To the extent that within a highly governed realm like England the government was able to secure enforcement of its policies to police the market helps to explain why food riots were always exceptional. Certainly, it is striking how London was free from such episodes in the seventeenth century. But it was the government's understandable willingness to privilege the capital by licensing against its own prohibitions the movement of grain from a rapidly widening hinterland that was one of the major causes of protests over food in much of southern and eastern lowland England. The other was the growing vulnerability of regions where economic specialization had seen the symbiosis between pastoral specialization and rural industrialization produce dense concentrations of vulnerable land-poor or landless populations dependent on the market both for employment and access to grain that they were no longer able to grow and sometimes living in areas of pastoral woodland where magistrates were not to be found. In these areas of pastoral woodland, the impact of harvest failure on consumers' purchasing power meant that dearth and trade depression often coincided, while the absence of a resident gentry made the resort to riot a necessary device to trigger relief policies.[20]

In a society where harvest failure was the heartbeat of economy and where famine remained a regional reality, early modern government took the threat of dearth very seriously. From the later sixteenth century, it had codified earlier policy in Books of Orders that required increasingly elaborate action from provincial and local authorities to police the market and grain trade. At the heart of this policy was a belief that it was manipulation of the markets by farmers hoarding, merchants exporting and middlemen inflating prices that caused dearth and suffering. Government policy thus called for the control of exports, the policing of grain markets and the privileged access of vulnerable consumers to grain at under-prices and, for the very poor, cheap or free distribution within towns and villages.[21]

As with agrarian protest, food protesters had other tactics available to them that stopped short of the need to riot. Reference to the public transcript developed by the government in response to the threat of famine offered the possibility of securing relief without 'riot'. Petitioning authority to implement its own policies and to prevent malpractices in the market might then be the first step taken by those facing the threat of starvation. But petitioners might also introduce an element of threat into their pleas by delivering the petition *en masse* and referring to the threat of violence; as the contemporary proverb ran, 'hunger will break through stone walls'. Or they might as dutiful subjects warn the authorities of plans by a supposedly unknown other – 'the poor' – to rise and seize grain. And anonymous threatening letters might employ the same tactic. 'NOTE.The. PORe.TheRe.is.More.Then.Goes.from.doore.to.dore' 'Be,fore. We .Arise.les[s]e will Safise', advised one such libel. Public grumblings in the market or threats in the alehouse to stick the heads of grain dealers on poles before their doors served a similar role.[22] Wise magistrates took the hint.

Men, women and even children might be found in crowds protesting over food. But many crowds were entirely feminine. This reflected women's crucial role in the provisioning of their families, their regular presence in the market place and their ability to manipulate contemporary concepts of women's supposed lack of reason, and, crucially, ambiguities in the law about the culpability of married women, protesters claiming women were not answerable at law.

Crowd actions defied the stereotype of collective theft with violence implied in the lazy shorthand of the 'food riot'. Protesters often shaped their actions by reference to government policy. For example, crowds protesting against the export of grain might, as in an episode in the early 1640s at the eastern port of Harwich, content themselves with removing the ship's sails, an action mimicking that taken by the king's customs official to impound vessels suspected of smuggling.[23] Similarly, when crowds attacked grain, it was almost without exception after it had been sold and was being moved out of the area. The grain seized was either subjected to a policy of *taxation populaire* – sold at a popularly determined price – or as in the West Country in 1614, the sacks of grain were pointedly returned and dumped outside the houses of local officials as physical exclamation marks punctuating the crowd's anger at the officials' inactivity in the face of the movement of grain out of the region at a time of threatened starvation.[24]

That crowds often did not take the grain they seized reflected their concern to distinguish their actions from simple theft. While those transporting the grain might be physically threatened and on occasion assaulted, the aim of the protesters was to avoid the label of riot and to secure the intervention of central and local government on their behalf. Since the most frequent protesters were either clothworkers or the urban poor of generally smaller towns and ports, their actions in defence of the moral economy nevertheless reflected their understanding of their dependence on the market economy and its agents for their regular supply of grain. Frightening away the dealers in grain upon whom they depended would prove self-defeating. The politics of the food riot was, therefore, necessarily triangulated: crowd actions had as their immediate target those manipulating the grain trade, but they were intended to prompt action by the magistrate.

Within this strand of the politics of subsistence, it is possible to be more confident about the success of the protesters. In all but the worst years, dearth was a temporary crisis and one therefore which government policy could act to contain. The ability of government to meet a short-term crisis was helped by two further aspects of the food riot. Crowds only attacked grain when it was being removed from the local economy and not when it was being hoarded. Appeals to the poor in years of scarcity to rise and rob the rich made by individuals subsequently prosecuted for seditious talk met with no success. Second, what caused a problem in most regions was not absolute shortage but a collapse in the 'exchange entitlements' over food that groups like the labouring poor or rural clothworkers experienced in periods of dearth and trade depression.[25] Crowd actions over food were often the necessary trigger to prompt central government to criticize the local authorities and to reissue the Book of Orders. The evidence suggests that in many regions action by regional and parish authorities might meet the problems of what was always a temporary crisis. Action to police the grain market, whatever its real success, also offered symbolic evidence of the authorities' concern for the poor. And there is evidence to suggest that the tradition of riot served sufficient warning to ensure the continuation or temporary re-instatement of a 'social economy of dearth' and the valuable access to food this gave the harvest-sensitive.[26]

But, as with enclosure, change after the mid-century altered the picture. While accelerating urbanization and regional industrialization increased the numbers of those dependent on the market, the increasing penetration of a national market saw local markets increasingly becoming bulking points for the onward movement of grain for export or to the larger cities and, above all, London. Against a background of increased agricultural productivity, royal government abandoned the policies of the Book of Orders that was no longer re-issued when the harvest failed and actively encouraged the export of grain. It abandoned its policy of policing the grain market at the point when an increase in buying crops in the field or 'at pitch' (from samples of grain) began to sidestep the market as the primary site for dealing in grain. But, in reality, both central and local government remained inconsistent; at moments of crisis triggered by harvest failure either or both might reintroduce aspects of an earlier regulative policy, thus keeping alive popular knowledge and expectations of how authority should behave in the face of threatened famine. All of these changes help to explain why, as the reality of famine receded, crowd actions over food had become by the 1690s the most common form of collective protest within the politics of subsistence. By then, the geography of the 'grain riot' had shifted further west and north reflecting the increasing demands of London and other large cities like Bristol and Norwich. A set of attitudes that had previously been the shared possession of both Crown and crowd was well on the way to becoming 'the moral economy of the eighteenth century crowd', with protesters now proclaiming that 'they were resolved to put the law in execution since the magistrates neglected it'.[27]

Early modern English protests were then never simply 'knife and fork' protests. There was a politics to the politics of subsistence. Within this tradition of direct action, crowds also sought to enter into a dialogue with authority. In the way that crowds shaped their protests, in the ideological justifications they offered for their actions and in the legitimation they claimed in the public transcripts of government, church and landed elite, crowds were capable of demonstrating an astute political awareness. Riot necessarily was an exercise in direct action, but it might be preceded by other forms of political activity and was usually intended to initiate a process of negotiation in which the role of the local magistrate and central royal government was envisaged as ally or arbiter. This is not to claim that all protests conformed to this model, nor that all those involved in protest subscribed to these aims. There was a darker side to protest. Physical intimidation by crowds was intended to remove popular grievance, but even here it was usually accompanied by a willingness to initiate action in the courts or to negotiate directly with the crowd's opponents. Nor was protest without a more radical potential. That the crown under Charles I became a major encloser in the seventeenth century challenged popular notions of the good king, while the threat to English liberties that Charles' political and religious policies were thought to bring draws attention to another strand of popular politics: the politics of the freeborn Englishman (and woman).

The politics of the free-born Englishmen (and women)

In the middle of the seventeenth century, England experienced civil war and a political revolution that (temporarily) abolished monarchy, episcopacy and the House of Lords. The popular political mobilization that these events required, first to fight the war and then to settle the peace, created a new political space for popular politics. An earlier, Marxist-informed analysis of popular movements within the revolution privileged economic and social grievances and the politics of class as the motivation for popular participation in these events. The early 1640s certainly saw a sharp increase in traditional forms of agrarian protest against enclosure by the landed classes, and also the innovation of attacks on the houses of some of the gentry and aristocracy.[28] But the decline in such attacks before the emergence of radical groups in the later 1640s was one of several factors weakening their appeal and impact. A more precise examination of the targets attacked in the early 1640s suggests that most crowds were attacking the estates of those bishops and courtiers now labelled as so-called enemies of the state by Parliament. Of course, some within these crowds certainly seized the legitimation this offered to settle local scores (later in royalist-controlled areas the landed estates of those supporting Parliament became similarly vulnerable to attack), but there is evidence to suggest that these crowds also had political and religious reasons for their protests.[29]

In many ways, popular politics within the revolution represented a working out of the political and religious tensions that can be traced back to England's incomplete Reformation. By 1600, England might have become a Protestant nation, but a nation of Protestants still had to contend with the fact that Catholicism remained a real presence. The black legend of popery, with its key dates of 1588 and 1605, symbolizing the double threat of foreign invasion and conspiratorial fifth column, was a key component of popular political culture. Developments in church and state were viewed through the distorting lens of a powerful anti-popery, and even before the civil war of mid-century, this had occasioned occasional, but powerful, demonstrations of support for a protestant regime in the face of perceived threats.[30]

A similar analysis might be made here of the relationship of this popular political culture and the structures of the early modern state. The installation of the monarch as supreme head of the church should have underwritten more strongly the emphasis on obedience, and it did. But the incomplete nature of the Reformation left the state to cope both with the problems of Catholic dissent and continuing criticism from those godlier Protestants who wanted a more thorough reformation. A confessional state, much as it tried to avoid it by a policy of accommodation, had then to confront the problems of dissenting consciences. That the state made the pulpit the site for political pronouncements about the nature of authority and political obligation made the parish church a potential site for political contest, a potential fully revealed in the religious conflicts of the English Revolution. That the state was also forced to rely to some extent on parishioners locally to police the boundaries of the confessional state, presenting Catholics and nonconformists to the church and criminal courts, might encourage the belief that the purity of the church as a local site of worship was the responsibility of the laity as well as the minister.

When, in the 1630s, Charles I and his bishops appeared to be introducing a religion that challenged the Calvinist orthodoxy that some thought defined the English church, and which many more feared would let popery back in, the result was a series of protests in the early 1640s in which crowds carried out acts of popular iconoclasm in parish churches and attacked Catholics, actions continued into the civil war by the people in arms in Parliament's armies.[31]

A second development, whose potential was again revealed in the early 1640s, was the growth of a popular political culture informed both by popular participation in the state – in terms of local office-holding and occasional, but widening, involvement in parliamentary elections – and by a rapidly developing print culture. The temporary collapse of censorship in the English Revolution saw an explosion in cheap print and newsbooks aimed at a popular audience. These developments were again registered in changes in the pattern of popular political protest within the English Revolution: nationwide popular petitioning campaigns and political demonstrations at their presentation to Parliament.[32] The requirements introduced by Parliament for universal (male) subscription to a series of state oaths led to their appropriation to legitimize independent acts of popular protest behind which lurked notions perhaps of citizenship, not subjecthood.[33] Subordinated groups, women as well as men,[34] found legitimation for a more active political role. The extent to which these changes, long in train, transformed the nature of early modern English protest was to be signalled by the emergence of radical political movements. Never parties in any modern sense, groups like the Diggers and Levellers, who had their origins in religious dissent and the struggle for religious toleration, exploited print and petitioning to advance radical social and political programmes.[35] For complex reasons, the revolution within the revolution for which these groups fought was stillborn. The ideas they advanced did not marry with an earlier tradition of agrarian protest, and in the case of the Digger programme for the common cultivation of wastes and commons as the first step towards a more general collective cultivation, directly clashed with a tradition of protest protecting common rights as the basis for individual holdings. More familiarly, their opponents were able to exploit print to misrepresent radical ideas of personal and sexual liberty as presenting a threat to the patriarchal structures of society from which all males might be said to benefit to some degree.[36] Moreover, the precocious ability of popular movements to advance radical ideas through the creation of textual communities ran well ahead of their ability to organize on the ground in rural society where the co-option of the middling sort saw the creation of a group committed to agrarian capitalism and willing to use their wealth and local office to discipline, as well as to relieve, the labouring poor. Finally, the army created by civil war, purged of support for the radical groups, could be used to address an earlier weakness of the early modern state and to suppress protest. By the end of the century, there was now an army with which to suppress protest, though its use by the civil magistrate remained controversial and might prove counterproductive.

The revolution failed, and monarchy was restored in 1660. But the new political space created by events in mid-century had produced changes in patterns of protesting that would continue to develop in the later seventeenth and following centuries. The restoration of monarchy saw the emergence of church and king 'mobs'. With Parliament's permanence secured by the fiscal needs of the state and elections more frequent, religious conflict, political partisanship and political parties lay at the heart of an enlarged public sphere. Petitioning and popular mobilization became even more organized, and a popular political culture developed in which competing crowds periodically demonstrated and fought, on appropriate political anniversaries and during political crises like the Popish Plot and Exclusion crisis of the 1670s for Church and king or the liberties of the freeborn English.[37]

The politics of seventeenth-century crowds

Riot in seventeenth-century England was both an immediate attempt to defend what were seen as rights and an attempt to impose and defend popular conceptualizations of the correct ordering of relationships in society, economy and polity. Early modern protest therefore involved both conflicts over material goods, popular rights – liberties if not liberty – but also over symbolic and linguistic meanings. Over time, this struggle became more difficult. The public transcript of state and elite no longer offered the same potential legitimation and leverage for crowds to exploit. The paternalistic model of the good lord that the English landed class had earlier in the century continued to uphold as a defining ideal proved even less of a guide to landlord policy by the end of the century. At the same time, the fault line in conflict in the English countryside shifted increasingly from lord and tenant to farmer and farm labourer, leaving the labouring poor ever more vulnerable to the denial of poor relief and employment and increasingly forced, therefore, to adopt the anonymous threatening letter to protest. After the mid-seventeenth century, government policy became more accepting of economic change and accordingly permissive in its ordering of enclosure and the grain market. Moreover, memories of 'the many-headed monster' in the English Revolution meant that within the politics of state and religion, even republicans and others regarded popular participation with some suspicion. We might have expected these changes to have radicalized an earlier tradition of protest. They certainly caused increasing resentment. But the willingness of government, particularly at the local level, to continue to negotiate with crowds and, for example in times of harvest failure, to reintroduce selectively aspects of an earlier social policy meant that there was no permanent fusion between the politics of subsistence and the politics of state and religion. Although social and economic discontent some-times found classed expression in the politics of the freeborn Englishman in the English Revolution and, after the Revolution, in support of the Good Old Cause in Monmouth's rebellion of 1685, there was to be no radicalization of the politics of subsistence.[38]

Despite George Rude's legacy, early modern English historians no longer speak of *the* crowd, recognizing that there were a variety of crowds whose social com-position could vary with the objectives sought.[39] Popular and class, therefore, did not always enjoy a straightforward relationship in popular protest. But an analysis of crowd actions that classifies them according to a typology of riot (food, enclosure, and so on) threatens to fracture what they have in common and almost inevitably produces an analysis that emphasizes their instrumental nature and limited objectives. The emphasis here has been on the inherently political nature of all early modern English protest. This is not to claim uni-versal subscription to such an idea from all those engaged in acts of protest. And it needs to be remembered that what English crowds did and said was to some extent constrained by the possible threat of punishment under a culture of obedience and perhaps by the ideological limits imposed under the par-tially realized cultural hegemony of the English landed class. Both help to explain the otherwise puzzling discrepancy between the class hostility voiced in individual acts of sedition and the more muted reality of crowd protests. But, as we have seen, all protests carried within them a potential critique of the obligations attendant upon the exercise of power and possession of property. Disputes over access to food or land or the customs of the trade or confessional identities could raise more fundamental questions over the nature of rights and obligations, the role of the people in church and polity, and the proper exercise, even provenance, of authority.

Notes

1. J. Walter, 'Reconstructing Popular Political Culture in Early Modern England', in *Crowds and Popular Politics in Early Modern England*, ed. J. Walter (Manchester, 2006), pp. 1–13.
2. C. Hill, 'The Many-Headed Monster', in his *Change and Continuity in Seventeenth-Century England* (London, 1974), pp. 181–204.
3. J. Nichols, *The History and Antiquities of the County of Leicestershire*, 4 vols. (London, 1795–1811; rpt. 1971), IV, pt. 1: p. 83.
4. J. Bellamy, *The Tudor Law of Treason: An Introduction* (London, 1979); K.J. Kesselrig, *Mercy and Authority in the Tudor State* (Cambridge, 2003).
5. J. Walter, '"A Rising of the People"? The Oxfordshire Rising of 1596', in Walter, *Crowds*, pp. 73–123.
6. E.P. Thompson, 'The Moral Economy of the English Crowd in the Eighteenth Century', *Past & Present*, 50 (1971), pp. 76–136.

7. A. Wood, '"Pore Men Woll Speke One Daye": Plebeian Languages of Deference and Defiance in England, c. 1520–1640', in *The Politics of the Excluded, c. 1500–1850*, ed. T. Harris (Basingstoke, 2001), pp. 67–98; A. Wood, 'Fear, Hatred and the Hidden Injuries of Class in Early Modern England', *Journal of Social History*, 39 (2006), pp. 803–26; J. Walter, '"The Pooremans Joy and the Gentlemans Plague": A Lincolnshire Libel and the Politics of Sedition in Early Modern England', *Past & Present*, 203 (2009), pp. 29–67.

8. A. Wood, 'Custom, Identity and Resistance: English Free Miners and Their Law, c. 1550–1800', in *The Experience of Authority in Early Modern England*, ed. P. Griffiths, A. Fox and S. Hindle (Basingstoke, 1996), pp. 249–85; A. Wood, *The Politics of Social Conflict: The Peak Country 1520–1770* (Cambridge, 1999).

9. T. Harris, *London Crowds in the Reign of Charles II: Propaganda and Politics from the Restoration until the Exclusion Crisis* (Cambridge, 1987), pp. 189–204; J. Walter, *Understanding Popular Violence in the English Revolution: The Colchester Plunderers* (Cambridge, 1999), pp. 243–56, 266–72.

10. For the concept of infrapolitics, see J.C. Scott., *Domination and the Arts of Resistance: Hidden Transcripts* (New Haven, 1990).

11. J.C. Scott, *Weapons of the Weak: Everyday Forms of Peasant Resistance* (New Haven, 1985); J. Walter, 'Public Transcripts, Popular Agency and the Politics of Subsistence in Early Modern England', in *Negotiating Power in Early Modern Society: Order, Hierarchy and Subordination in Britain and Ireland*, ed. M.J. Braddick and J. Walter (Cambridge, 2001), pp. 123–48.

12. M. Beloff, *Public Order and Popular Disturbances 1660–1714* (London, 1938), pp. 79–80; B. Bushaway, *By Rite: Custom, Ceremony and Community in England 1700–1880* (London, 1982), pp. 251–52.

13. D. Beaver, 'The Great Deer Massacre: Animals, Honor, and Communication in Early Modern England', *Journal of British Studies*, 38 (1999), pp. 187–216.

14. I am preparing an article on this exceptional episode; see M.C. Fissell, *The Bishops' Wars: Charles I's Campaign Against Scotland 1638–1640* (Cambridge, 1994), pp. 271–72.

15. J. Martin, *Feudalism and Capitalism: Peasant and Landlord in English Agrarian Development* (Basingstoke, 1983), pp. 172–74; Huntington Library, San Marino, California, Hastings Papers, HA 4169, 5423.

16. K. Lindley, *Fenland Riots and the English Revolution* (London, 1982), pp. 253–58; B. Sharp, *In Contempt of All Authority: Rural Artisans and Riot in the West of England 1585–1660*, (Berkeley and London, 1980); R.B. Manning, *Village Revolts: Social Protest and Popular Disturbances in England, 1509–1640* (Oxford, 1988).

17. What follows draws largely on my as yet unpublished research on early modern agrarian protest.

18. Joan Thirsk, 'Changing Attitudes to Enclosure in the Seventeenth Century', in *The Festschrift for Professor Ju-Hwan Oh on the Occasion of His Sixtieth Birthday* (Taegu, Korea, 1991), pp. 517–43.

19. E.P. Thompson, 'The Crime of Anonymity', in *Albion's Fatal Tree: Crime and Society in Eighteenth Century England*, ed. D. Hay et al. (London, 1975), pp. 255–344.

20. J. Walter, 'The Geography of Food Riots, 1585–1649', in Walter, *Crowds*, pp. 67–72.

21. P. Slack, *From Reformation to Improvement: Public Welfare in Early Modern England* (Oxford, 1999), pp. 53–76.

22. TNA, PRO SP 16/175/81.

23. TNA, PRO SP 16/497/6.

24. Wiltshire & Swindon History Centre, Q/S Gt. Roll, Trinity 1614/108, 112–14.
25. For the concept of grain entitlements, see A. Sen, *Poverty and Famines: An Essay on Entitlement and Deprivation* (Oxford, 1982).
26. J. Walter, 'The Social Economy of Dearth in Early Modern England', in *Famine, Disease and the Social Order in Early Modern Society*, ed. J. Walter and R. Schofield (Cambridge, 1989), pp. 75–128.
27. Beloff, *Public Order*, pp. 56–75 (quotation at p. 64).
28. B. Manning, 'The Peasantry and the English Revolution', *Journal of Peasant Studies*, 2 (1975), pp. 133–58; B. Manning, *The English People and the English Revolution* (London, 1976), pp. 112–227; J. Walter, 'The English People and the English Revolution Revisited', *History Workshop Journal*, 61 (2006), pp. 174–77.
29. See, Walter, *Understanding Popular Violence*.
30. R. Clifton, 'Fear of Popery' in *The Origins of the English Civil War*, ed. C. Russell (London, 1973), pp. 144–67.
31. J. Walter, 'Abolishing Superstition with Sedition? The Politics of Popular Iconoclasm in England 1640–1642', *Past & Present*, 183 (2004), pp. 79–123; Walter, 'Popular Iconoclasm and the Politics of the Parish in Eastern England, 1640–1642', *Historical Journal*, 47 (2004), pp. 261–69; I. Gentles, *The New Model Army In England, Ireland and Scotland, 1645–1653* (Oxford, 1992), pp. 109–10.
32. D. Zaret, *Origins of Democratic Culture: Printing, Petitions and the Public Sphere in Early-Modern England* (Princeton, 2000); D. Underdown, *A Freeborn People: Politics and the Nation in Seventeenth-Century England* (Oxford, 1996); J. Walter, 'Politicising the Popular? The "Tradition of Riot" and Popular Political Culture in the English Revolution', in *The English Revolution c. 1590–1720: Politics, Religion and Communities*, ed. N. Tyacke (Manchester, 2007), pp. 95–110.
33. D.M. Jones, *Conscience and Allegiance in Seventeenth Century England: The Political Significance of Oaths and Engagements* (Rochester, NY, 1999); E. Vallance, *Revolutionary England and the National Covenant: State Oaths, Protestantism and the Political Nation* (Woodbridge, 2005).
34. P. Crawford, '"The Poorest She": Women and Citizenship in Early Modern England', in *The Putney Debates of 1647: The Army, the Levellers and the English State*, ed. M. Mendle (Cambridge, 2001), pp. 197–218.
35. B. Manning, *Aristocrats, Plebeians and Revolution in England 1640–1660* (London, 1996); J. Gurney, *Brave Community: The Digger Movement in the English Revolution* (Manchester, 2007); G.E. Aylmer, *The Levellers in the English Revolution* (London, 1975).
36. J. Walter, 'The Impact of the English Civil War on Society: A World Turned Upside Down?', in Walter, *Crowds*, pp. 181–95.
37. Harris, *London Crowds*; M. Knights, *Representation and Misrepresentation in Later Stuart Britain: Partisanship and Political Culture* (Oxford, 2005).
38. Walter, *Understanding Popular Violence*, pp. 266–84; R. Clifton, *The Last Popular Rebellion: The Western Rising of 1685* (London, 1984).
39. G. Rudé, *The Crowd in History: A Study of Popular Disturbances in France and England, 1730–1848* (New York, 1964).

5

Provisioning, Power and Popular Protest from the Seventeenth Century to the French Revolution and Beyond

Cynthia A. Bouton

France, from the sixteenth century to the revolutionary era, witnessed increasingly widespread, violent food rioting as hungry consumers struggled with producers and merchants, and both sides invoked protection and support from their rulers. Those who needed food and those who controlled it clashed over transports on highway and river, over supplies stored in farms and urban granaries, over sacks displayed for sale in markets, over flour in mills and over bread in bakeries.[1] This overview considers three eras in the history of food rioting in France. It looks first at the period from the end of the sixteenth to the mid-eighteenth century – a 'formative era', when overt clashes over access to food displayed an *ad hoc* and diverse character and occurred less frequently than clashes over religion or taxes. It continues through the eighteenth century and early years of the revolution – a second, 'classical period', when food riots became one of the most dominant forms of protest and assumed characteristics, such as popular price fixing, that historians have often cited as exemplifying subsistence movements. Food riots ultimately became an important formal constituent of the political fabric in the pre-revolutionary and revolutionary cauldron because commercialization took place within a political context that facilitated bargaining between rioters and rulers. This classical period provoked a briefer third period, when the revolutionary government instituted the *maximum* of Year II (1793–94), which fixed maximum prices on essential consumer goods, especially grain and its products: for some, a consumer paradise *manqué*, for others, an ill-fated, pragmatic attempt to feed and pacify desperately needy and politically dangerous citizens. Juxtaposing the crisis of 1794–96 that followed, the *maximum* reveals the extent to which the social and political relations of subsistence of both the *ancien régime* and the earlier revolution had changed. Although this essay ends with the revolutionary era, the tortured road of the politics of subsistence led not just to the

80

French Revolution, but through and beyond it. A brief conclusion will consider this nineteenth-century trajectory to mid-century, during which successive governments had not only stripped needy consumers of their formal political powers but also attempted to de-politicize subsistence issues and de-legitimize the people's claim that need took precedence over property rights.[2]

Over the course of three centuries, France experienced massive changes in its economic and social structures, its government and its culture. The problem of feeding the people loomed throughout these centuries, as an economic problem and as a major political issue. The origins of food riots lay beyond the short-term fluctuations associated with shortages. Rioters invoked long-standing communal norms to respond to larger economic, social and political changes that menaced and outraged them. The French 'grain war'[3] contributed substantially to the fall of *ancien régime* ministers, the desacralization of the monarchy and the fate of revolutionary governments. Despite the existence of market relations in early modern Europe, the assumption had widely prevailed, even among elites, that in times of food crises popular subsistence needs took precedence over property rights and local needs came before more distant ones. This 'moral economy' or right to existence (as revolutionaries and nine-teenth-century socialists often called it),[4] was embedded in religious and cultural norms as well as local and royal consumer safeguards that had enveloped the production and distribution of food since the late Middle Ages. Although never consistently implemented or entirely successful in stabilizing prices and supply – and sometimes vitiated by royal, seigneurial or guild privileges – these regulatory policies had sought to mitigate some of the worst effects of widely fluctuating prices, to supply markets emptied by hoarding and speculation or to impede the departure of grain to other markets. They also indicated political commitment and sensitivity to local welfare dictated by the knowledge that public order required feeding the people.

Food riots emerged as a pre-eminent expression of the people's displeasure with the provisioning system. Indeed, the proliferation of food riots coincided with the growth of regional and national grain markets in France, a development that brought tectonic dislocations in its wake. The contours of this protest (its geography, protester behavior, their targets, crowd composition and relationships with authorities) changed over these centuries in response to transformations within France itself: changes in economic and social geography, structures of production and distribution, demand, the political economy itself, as well as shifting structures and strategies of relief and repression.

The formative period to the 1750s

The 1560s marked a turning point in the fortunes of France.[5] Surging Protestantism and a weakening monarchy that followed the death of Henry

II in 1559 instigated a century of wasting war. Population growth, inflation, an increasingly polarized society and mounting pauperization and vagrancy combined into an economic and social crisis. In these straitening circumstances, subsistence crises erupted more frequently and carried more serious consequences than previously. Prior to the 1690s, the more prevalent religious riots or anti-taxation riots often had subsistence concerns intertwined with them. However, ever greater numbers of food riots erupted during the crises of 1585–87, 1625–26, 1642–44, 1652–53, 1660–62, but they remained largely isolated, vindictively violent, and *ad hoc*.[6] The 'ethic of public responsibility'[7] prevalent among municipal magistrates catalyzed an interventionist approach to subsistence crises. By the mid-seventeenth century, *parlements* and the crown increasingly involved themselves as well. Food riots usually took the form of protests against grain 'exports' (what rioters called any shipment out of or through their locale). Popular price fixing occurred rarely. Rioters came from diverse social backgrounds, sometimes including the bourgeoisie. Prosecution proved uneven, from severe exemplary punishments to general indulgence.

During this period, bad harvests and the ensuing distribution dislocations often ignited riots, for example, in Amiens in 1585–87, and in Troyes in 1625–26.[8] The trigger for these particular riots – grain export – provoked a shipment interception (an *entrave*);[9] rioters also assaulted merchants and other culprits. Confronted by such pressure, local authorities often banned outbound grain shipments, actions that from the sixteenth century on countermanded crown proclamations of freedom of circulation for trade, especially for army munitioners and shipments to Paris.[10] Authorities further responded to riots with mixtures of regulation, relief and repression. Experience taught them that a successful response must include not just a restoration of order, but also a means to address consumers' needs. In fact, food riots manifested rioters' expectations that authorities could do something – that there existed strategies and resources to alleviate their distress. In 1626, authorities in Troyes, for example, discovered, as many would in the coming centuries, that at first they could not rally an adequate force, for most of the militia companies and their captains refused to serve. The crowd raged unchecked for two days, sacked the houses of several of the town elite and threatened to torch all the so-called 'good houses' in town. Finally, the notables mustered 200 men, not of the militia, but from among themselves, confronted the rioters, dispersed them, made arrests, condemned 11 culprits to death and executed them on the grain market. Violent rioting having brought even more violent repression and a sullen populace, Troyen officials then coupled relief to repression, arranging institutional purchases of grain and distributions of reduced-priced provisions to the poor.[11]

By 1690, Louis XIV had strengthened the monarchy, built a centralized administration, manipulated a standing army and extended the royal reach into arenas once dominated by local authorities. Regional grain markets had developed, and

Paris, with a population of 480,000 by the end of Louis XIV's reign, had a provisioning network to match and had emerged as price setter in the Paris Basin.[12] However, the traditional relief systems, dominated by Church institutions and dependent on voluntary charity assumed a largely stable society, an assumption increasingly problematic by the end of the turbulent seventeenth century. In this context, the crown monitored and intervened more directly in subsistence matters. A series of bad harvests, beginning in 1691, triggered a crisis and rioting from 1691 to 1694. The War of the League of Augsburg, which put over 300,000 men under arms on four fronts, aggravated the situation, diverting money that could have offered relief, as well as grain and ships, barges and carts that could have supplemented distribution efforts. Moreover, war impeded access to foreign grain purchases, and endangered shipping channels.[13] The crisis became national (96 riots), exacerbated by dearth and by disruptions in trading patterns that resulted when merchants, munitioners and administrators scrambled to find supplies outside their normal networks.[14]

As in the past, desperate consumers reacted by rioting, mostly by resorting to shipment interceptions. Moreover, the crisis also witnessed the proliferation of bands of poor roving the countryside, demanding bread from cultivators and threatening violence against those who hesitated.[15] Although still infrequent, this phenomenon usually occurred in surplus-grain producing regions of France with rural populations polarized between producers and land-poor peasants and day laborers. Riots over bread, especially bread prices, showed that bread had become a contentious issue. As more consumers bought bread, more authorities turned to bakeries as a way to manipulate food prices to reduce hardship.[16]

From the crises of the 1690s, food riots became an increasingly dominant form of protest, and they erupted more widely throughout France. Important episodes occurred in 1691–94, 1697–99, 1708–10, 1725, 1737–40, 1747–48 and 1757.[17] Most rioting still featured shipment seizures rather than price fixing, but riots became less physically violent and involved more menacing 'demonstrations' by protesters before authorities. During this formative period, some characteristics associated with the next, 'classic' period of food rioting emerged, particularly in local and royal government responses. Indeed, the monarchy took a more aggressive interest in food riots and, until the 1760s, intervened actively with regulations as much as repression and relief. The three crises of the era from the 1690s to 1710 brought increasingly complex and frequently tense relations among the different levels of authority involving not only local authorities who had traditionally grappled with subsistence crises, but also *parlements* and monarchy. All addressed some dimension of the crisis: reissuing previous regulations on the grain trade, managing poor relief and privileging Parisian provisioning.[18]

Cities like Paris, Lyon, Marseille and Bordeaux opened public ovens, distributed bread, money and sometimes *soupes populaires*. They fixed the price of bread and banned baking certain types of 'luxury' loaves. Towns frequently resorted to institutional purchases, overseas if necessary. Warfare made such efforts difficult, but need drove French authorities to seek supplies far and wide. Southern France looked to the Mediterranean; northern France to the Baltic.[19] Local authorities found royal intervention most efficacious when accompanied by grants of money or resources. Patronage and clientage networks often proved central to effective relief strategies.[20] In general, in this formative period, the interests of a spectrum of people – from workers to bourgeois, peasants to large property owners and many local authorities – converged around the subsistence issue.

Collective action drew upon a prior sense of solidarity or community forged in such networks as neighbourhoods, workplaces, families and camaraderie. Both women and men played crucial roles, acting together and separately. For example, women seized grain in La Ferté-Imbault in 1692,[21] stopped grain traders in Rogin in 1693,[22] policed the market at Albi and Gaillac in 1694.[23] They predominated in Rouen 1693, where authorities explained that they had arrested two men 'for having mixed with the women' in the riots.[24] Children also participated, often alongside their mothers, as in Marseille in 1709.[25] Other protester came from the ranks of all-male trades such as construction and wood splitting.[26] Strikingly, local elites sometimes joined rioters. The crisis of 1708–9 struck deeply into the reserves of leisured as well as poor, and poor relief procedures that taxed or otherwise involved bourgeois imperiled their resiliency. Officials in Dieppe asserted that 'the excessive price of grain has made the majority of bourgeois unable to buy subsistence for their families'.[27] In 1709, observers reported that alongside the common people, 'bourgeois besieged houses known to contain grain and took it',[28] and in Marans, 'the principal inhabitants declared their solidarity, by public act, with all the pillage that might come in the future'.[29]

Between 1710 and 1760, several crises erupted, but none on the scale of the previous 15 years. Repression remained uncertain, although officials, local and royal, turned increasingly to the *maréchaussée* and the military for assistance. During the formative years, coping with such severe crises provided officials with experience they called upon repeatedly in later years, and inflicted the common people with enduring scars. A tradition of subsistence protest emerged that linked consumers, authorities, producers and merchants in an increasingly complex competition for control of grain and its products.

The classical period, 1760s to 1793

The last decades of the *ancien régime* brought changes such as the triumph of the Enlightenment, the culmination of the 'administrative monarchy', the rise of public opinion and an oppositional political culture and the desacralization of the monarchy. 1789 marked even more profound changes: debates and elections for the Estates General, the transfer of sovereignty from king to the National Assembly, the Declaration of the Rights of Man and the Citizen and ultimately the creation of a Republic, one and indivisible. Even in the arena of provisioning, the period saw more change than continuity, especially in state policy, where first royal then revolutionary regimes sought to dislodge traditional patterns of supply by decreeing free trade in grain and attempting to enforce it by *force majeur*.

The monarchy proclaimed free trade in grain with a declaration in 1763 and unhindered foreign export in 1764,[30] then reversed itself in 1770, returning briefly to a modified regulatory policy. A return to liberalization followed in 1774, with limited freedom of export in 1776. In 1776, liberalization gave way to greater control over the trade. Thus, four times in 13 years royal policy on the grain trade shifted. Then in 1787, the monarchy revived liberalization again, only to overturn it during the crises of 1789. By invoking liberalization, the monarchy, in effect, abdicated direct responsibility for the subsistence needs of its subjects. The crown, moreover, had traditionally favoured consumer over producer and, most especially, over merchant. Now, whenever it decreed liberalization, it switched sides. While claiming its first concern remained the people's subsistence, it emphatically aligned itself with producers and merchants. Injunctions not to interfere in the trade meant protection for those who sold grain and no longer for those who bought it. The frequent reversals and modifications only added to popular anxiety. Ultimately, in the people's mind, the 'King Baker' betrayed his subjects.[31]

These changes, however, confronted powerful continuities:[32] the people's need for subsistence, their expectations that the state, whether royal or republican, local or national would see to this need, and the escalating, if episodic, conflict between the common people's expectations and the state's willingness and ability to act on this issue. Crises provoked by bad harvest were thus aggravated by dislocations associated with changing market and political relations. Major episodes of food rioting occurred in 1764–68, 1770–72, 1773, 1774, 1775, 1784, 1788–89, 1790–91 and 1792–93.[33] The period prior to the outbreak of the revolution saw a major increase in the number of riots, which acquired their 'classic' contours: market-based disorders that demanded price fixing and evinced widening fissures between consumers and owners of grain and its products over issues of property versus social rights; rural incursions and attacks on granaries. By the 1760s and 1770s, food riots had evolved from episodes apparently concerned more with retribution than with procuring supplies to a more orderly, albeit angry, set of actions focused on the processes and products of provisioning. By the time of the revolution, rioters appeared 'already imbued with a sense of unjust institutions and not just unjust individuals'.[34]

Moreover, significant numbers of local officials remained opposed to or at least feared liberalization that, among other things, eroded their public powers. Faced with the crises of the 1760s and 1770s – high prices, market shortages, merchants pursuing their interests untrammeled, some blamed free trade for the menacing combustible populace around them. Sometimes local authorities worked out an 'accepted script' for free trade: 'no requisitions, no set prices, administrative "neutrality", and sellers who were ostensible "masters of the price"'.[35] Often, however, they invoked traditional strategies – fixing prices, forcing grain to market, prohibiting sales outside the market – sometimes after resisting, other times without much of a fight.[36] When authorities refused to respond in traditional ways, the situation often worsened into mounting violence.

Although the process had already gotten underway before 1789, the revolution further politicized subsistence as it did everything else. The 'October Days' of 1789 represents the quintessential example of a politicized subsistence movement.[37] While the women of Paris marched to Versailles to collect the 'Baker, the Baker's Wife and the Baker's Helper' (the king, the queen and the dauphin) to bring them to Paris, the capital's national guard absconded with 1500 *setiers* of grain held in Versailles granaries for local use and the people of Versailles tried to attack the local Paris granaries. Finally, on 16 October, women ignored the presence of national guardsmen and regular soldiers, rioted in the marketplace and forced producers to sell their grain at lower prices.[38] The revolution also helped recast the subsistence issue in a new vocabulary – of rights (individual and social) – and the subsistence issue contributed heavily to the charged debates around demands for transparency and fraternity.[39]

During the period between 1790 and the laws on the *maximum* in May and September 1793, revolutionaries crafted a new France. They created a republic and killed a king; they abolished feudalism; they reorganized how France administered and policed itself; they reconceptualized poor relief as a national obligation; they nationalized Church lands, suppressed religious orders, made clergy state functionaries and severely circumscribed their activities; they abolished guilds and prohibited strikes. France also deteriorated in significant ways: the paper money (the *assignats*) depreciated; the country confronted international war and counterrevolutionaries at home.[40] Amid all this, the Constituent and Legislative Assemblies, as well as the early Convention, adhered to free trade, while consumers in the provinces clamored increasingly for regulation. Although ongoing distribution problems created dislocation, tension and an occasional explosion, throughout 1790 and most of 1791, French people concerned themselves less with subsistence itself than with other issues: seigneurialism, taxation and religion, for example.[41]

Conditions deteriorated rapidly after the poor 1791 harvest. Prices rose and the *assignat* continued to depreciate. Producers increasingly refused to exchange grain for *assignats*. Moreover, the outbreak of war in April 1792 meant that munitioners once again competed with consumers, and since France fought the war on its soil, frontier departments felt the dislocations caused by blocked producers and transportation routes as well as the hungry ravages of enemy as well as French troops. Paris, now the pampered capital of the revolution, exerted a heavy influence on supply networks, and the map of rioting during this period reveals how provisioning Paris created dislocations. All these factors, together with the nationalization of the Church and the abolition of religious orders, crippled traditional relief efforts and ignited protests.

Faced with hunger, riots and dissident authorities, the revolutionary government proved no more able to maintain consistent policies than its *ancien régime* predecessor. Incessant decrees in 1790, 1791 and 1792 promised punishment to any who interfered in the free circulation of grain. Then, following the overthrow of the monarchy, the assembly in September 1792 granted amnesty to violators of grain trade laws.[42] In December, the Convention reaffirmed its commitment to free trade and vowed again to punish food rioters, especially those who interfered with the provisioning of Paris.[43] However, it reversed itself again, in February 1793 after the king's execution, with another amnesty that covered all rioting through January.

In essence, the revolutionaries, like the monarchy before them, found themselves caught among competing visions of human rights: the right to subsistence, as well as the right to protest and revolt, threatened rights to property. The revolution, united against tyranny, found itself splintered by conflicting economic theories and political philosophies just as had the monarchy before it. The revolution itself had legitimized the right to insurrection, but then found itself having to distinguish between legitimate revolt and criminal disorder. Food riots raised all these issues, thus revealing a wrenching political and economic schizophrenia.

During the 1760s and 1770s, the incidence of certain types of riot and the dominant behavior of rioters changed. Although interceptions of shipments remained the most common type of riot, they declined considerably relative to market riots, attacks on urban warehouses and storage areas and incursions into grain producing farms. Moreover, the balance between seizures and price fixing, the *taxation populaire*, had changed; rioters often set a strikingly uniform price. By the revolution, price fixing became even more common. For example, during the spring of 1792, bands ranging from 5,000 to 15,000 people carrying arms and preceded by drummers roamed from market to market in the Beauce to force officials to fix prices.[44] This rise in market riots and price fixing correlated with liberalization. As the crown instructed authorities to refrain from price fixing, the crowd took over. As the state's function in the marketplace changed, the market became increasingly central to popular concerns. In fact, the emergence of the marketplace as a focus of popular protest occurred late in the history of food riots.[45]

A largely original development of this period involved rioter incursions into the farms of surplus grain producers. Not until the 1770s did subsistence crises generate significant, rural disturbances conducted by rural residents them-selves.[46] The 1775 Flour War brought a new escalation, when rural riots erupted throughout the surplus grain-producing part of the Paris Basin. Most riots pitted local agrarian wage-laboring and small- and medium-sized property holders against surplus-grain producers.[47] This form of rioting continued as a common feature of the rioting of the revolutionary period as well as the nine-teenth century.

On occasion, rioters' growing political awareness encouraged them to seek legitimacy for their actions by writing petitions and getting local authorities' signatures. Written documents also suggested permanence, a desire that the fixed prices persist even after the riot had ended. In effect, rioters' written documents constituted new laws – laws that acknowledged the right to sub-sistence – that they, the people, now invested with sovereignty, thought they could invoke. Prior to the eighteenth century, subsistence movements had drawn from socially diverse sections of the French population. Bourgeois and property owners sometimes appeared among rioters or cheered from the side-lines; the *milice bourgeois* proved an undependable force for order when it came to repressing food riots. By the 1760s and 1770s, the social strata from which rioters came had narrowed. Workers, unskilled and semiskilled, urban and rural, constituted the backbone of more riots. Rural day laborers played important roles in the rural rioting of the Flour War, but the bourgeoisie and significant property owners had largely disappeared from the ranks. These developments mark both the growing numbers of wage laborers and vulnerable craftsmen by the second half of the eighteenth century and a defection of property owners from a culture of protest that did, indeed, attack property.[48]

By 1760s and 1770s, food riots had emerged with some fairly clear gen-dered characteristics. Market town riots constituted a favorite female activity (although wage-earning males increasingly joined in). For example, during a market riot in 1775 in Nemours, a husband tried to assist with confiscating sacks. His wife pushed him away from the fray, saying: 'Go away. This is women's business'.[49] By this period, even when women and men appeared in the same episodes of rioting, they often performed different acts. Attacks on urban warehouses, storage areas and shipment interceptions all involved more balanced proportions of men and women. By contrast, rural incursions into farms remained overwhelmingly male in composition. In the riots of the revo-lutionary era, these patterns largely persisted for the gender and social compos-ition of crowds as well.

For their part, authorities of the 1760s and 1770s, like their predecessors, did sometimes resort to repression, immediate or eventual. The unevenness of response also harked back to earlier periods and depended on such factors as the authorities' interpretation of the seriousness and illegality of the situation, the availability and reliability of the police, guard, or military, and the response of the rioters. However, during the 1760s and 1770s, authorities found themselves relying more frequently on the *maréchaussée* and especially on troops rather than local efforts. By the 1770s, troops had become a common feature of the environment, most comprehensively during the Flour War when 25,000 troops converged on the Paris Basin to re-establish order.[50] As Robespierre later observed, if the government wanted free trade in commerce, it would need 'bayonets to calm fears or to pacify hunger'.[51]

Although courts during the Flour War and revolutionary era sometimes sentenced rioters to death, prison, exile, the galleys or flogging, such severe sentences remained rare.[52] Moreover, although the convicted could not know at the time, as long as they avoided execution, their sentences usually proved shorter than anticipated. The king and assembly ultimately amnestied all participants. However, the presence of police and troops not only testified to the mounting intervention of the state in local affairs, but also to the failure of communities to solve their problems locally. While the revolution decentralized authority by investing local authorities with control over the forces of repression, in the years prior to the *maximum*, actions traditionally associated with food riots increasingly occurred at the instigation (or at least with the cooperation) of local authorities and the local forces of order.

Liberalization demanded a reconsideration of policies toward the ever-growing masses of poor.[53] In 1764, the crown launched an attack on the 'bad poor' – vagabonds and healthy beggars – designed to punish by confining them in workhouses and by handing out less bread and more jobs. Despite this activism, the central government nevertheless left to the cities, towns and villages of France the problem of coping with the poor and their most pressing need, food. These, in turn, had left it to the Church and private acts of charity; yet the problem of poverty ultimately overwhelmed them all because the system had developed to confront local problems, while poverty had grown into a national dilemma. In crises like that of 1788–89, the poor simply overwhelmed the system. Riots erupted, bands of poor roved the countryside, cities incurred ferocious debts and municipal governments collapsed under the stress. Relief efforts proved increasingly difficult during the early revolutionary years.[54] The revolutionary assault on the Church and municipal tolls throttled crucial sources of revenue that had funded *ancien régime* relief efforts. The Comité de Mendicité, established in February 1790, pronounced in its first report of June 1790, that 'all men have the right to subsistence', 'that poor relief is a social duty' and that 'the social organization is responsible to the best of its capacity to provide work for everyone'.[55] The Constitution of 1791 proclaimed the state's obligation to create 'a general establishment for public welfare to raise abandoned children, to care for the sick poor, and furnish work for the able-bodied poor'.[56]

A 19 March 1793 law on public assistance attempted to establish the contours of a national welfare system. The state assumed responsibility to provide work for the able-bodied and home relief for the ill and aged; however, little concrete occurred for quite some time at the local level, especially in rural areas, a failure that contributed to the tumult that engulfed the hungry populace in the years 1791–93. In summary, as John Markoff has suggested, 'when we consider that the economic liberalism that dismantled the Old Regime's controls in 1789–91 was succeeded by the most systematic price controls in the country's history, we might well see this greatest of subsistence movements as uniquely effective – if only temporarily – in obtaining policy shifts'.[57]

The era of the maximum, May 1793–December 1794

1793 began with the execution of Louis XVI on 21 January. The spring proved difficult: defeats by enemies within and without; an *assignat* worth half its original value; increasing radicalization of the common people, particularly in Paris; provisioning dislocations induced by the competing demands of armies, Paris and other consumers; the continuing desertion of markets by cultivators and merchants seeking safer and more profitable opportunities and chronic unrest over subsistence but also over religion and access to the land. The common people of France, increasingly supported by their local governments, pressured incessantly for fixed lower prices and more control.[58] The Convention dealt with the crushing subsistence question by finally abandoning its commitment to free trade and declaring the 'first *maximum*' on 4 May 1793. This, by attempting to create a consistent, ongoing national policy, marked the beginning of a truly revolutionary change in subsistence policy from the *ad hoc* policies of previous centuries. This first *maximum* of 4 May 1793 sought to force grain from granaries to the marketplace by requiring sales only on the market. This first attempt by a French national government to fix prices failed. In particular, its policy of price fixing by department created price differentials. Because producers could still choose their markets, they preferred higher priced ones. The central government quickly found itself grappling with blockades of shipments, hoarding and public protests. Disorders often erupted during this difficult summer, less often and with less emphasis on market riots because the markets often had no grain. As always, incessant demands of Paris provoked resistance throughout its provisioning zone, usually by rioters who tried to block grain from leaving their own region.[59]

Overall, however, rioting dwindled compared with the extraordinary violence of 1792. This decline during a period so difficult – with deserted markets, plummeting *assignats* and a considerable quantity of requisitioned grain in motion, coinciding with the classic *soudure* period – points to several factors. First, regardless of the outcome, consumers now had the satisfaction of seeing their administrators actually do something before, not just in response to, rioting. Price fixing, requisitions, public granaries and ovens and the promise of prosecution for hoarders contrasted sharply with previous refusals to do much to combat the provisioning crises of 1789–92. Despite the 1793 Constitution's proclamation that 'society owes subsistence to its needy citizens, either by procuring work for them or by assuring the means of existence to those unable to work',[60] through the summer of 1793 local governments wrestled to support a large population of poor with little assistance from the state. In fact, local authorities often collaborated more obviously with desperate consumers and refused to invoke repressive measures when riots erupted because many revolutionary municipalities shared assumptions of the common people they represented.[61]

In many places, angry rioters demanded more rigorous enforcement of the *maximum* and vigorous repression of hoarders. The Convention acquiesced by officially proclaiming terror the order of the day and ordering, among other concessions, the formation of an *armée révolutionnaire* to enforce grain requisitions and protect transports to Paris.[62] As the wars continued to go poorly, the Convention passed the 'Second Maximum' on grain and then the more far-reaching 'General Maximum' that fixed the prices of many other goods, as well as salaries.[63] Applying the lessons of the first *maximum*'s failure, the Convention declared a single price throughout France, rather than set prices by department. This new *maximum* showed that administrators had effectively renounced trying to supply French markets by trade and accepted instead the emergent trend to provision them by requisition.

Although the *maximum* never worked perfectly, the period between autumn 1793 and the fall of Robespierre in June 1794 did bring improvements for many consumers and a concomitant decline in food riots. The *assignat* gradually rose. Aggressive surveillance committees, 'revolutionary armies', local (and sometimes national) representatives ferreted out supplies and pursued evaders. Districts that traditionally suffered deficits found requisitions served them well. Hoarders faced the threat of harsh sentences. A few indictments led to the guillotine, and many more ended in prison sentences and fines. Those riots that did erupt exposed tensions produced by a system that relied so heavily on requisitions and the terror to enforce them. By the winter of 1793–94, the number of shipment interceptions rose impressively, particularly in the Paris Basin. Again, however, most of these represented the work of local officials who, together with their constituents, tried to resist the omnivorous power of Paris.[64] Price fixing rarely appeared as an issue, because the state had already established the *maximum*. Attacks on producers disappeared as a form of riot, for local authorities now performed searches legally. Riots during this period manifested social and gender profiles of rioters similar to past disorders. However, the heavy participation of local authorities in these movements does mark a shift in crowd composition, and shows what a hazy line separated illegal and legal actions. In general, the recognition that the government had committed to aggressive regulation, as well as the realization that little surplus grain existed to seize, made food rioting largely irrelevant for a time.

By winter and spring 1794, France's fortunes had turned on the war and counter-revolutionary fronts. In the meantime, supplies in granaries had dwindled despite aggressive requisitioning. Similarly, less grain appeared on the markets, and people waited in long bread lines for their rations. Authorities reported more resistance to the law and less success preventing violations of provisioning and price regulations. Nevertheless, food riots remained extremely rare until the winter of 1794–95. The fall of Robespierre in July 1794 accelerated the breakup of the *maximum*.[65] With the removal of the repressive threat of the terror, cultivators openly ignored the law, making off-market sales at prices well above the *maximum*. Some local authorities reported rebellious producers who refused to provision the market, even under requisition.[66] In Bordeaux, a traditional bastion of hostility to the *maximum*, authorities simply stopped enforcing it.[67] Finally, in December, the Convention formally abolished it.

From December 1794, the economic situation in France progressively decayed. The last months of 1794 and the spring of 1795 witnessed a massive upswing in food riots, particularly in the Paris Basin and Normandy.[68] Many manifested the intense politicization characteristic of many revolutionary (and counter-revolutionary) outbreaks. In Amiens, female rioters cried 'du pain, du pain. Vive le roi'.[69] Shipment interceptions and attacks on farms constituted by far the two most numerous forms of protest during this period, despite frequent military escorts. Although most rural rioting resembled that of the Flour War, large roving bands of poor also reappeared in some places, such as the region around Paris or the pays de Caux, to terrorize cultivators.[70] For the first time since the first half of the eighteenth century, rioters in late 1794 and throughout 1795 tended more to confiscate the grain, flour or bread they captured than to fix prices.

Many riots manifested a level of violence that resembled riots of the sixteenth and seventeenth centuries, except that rioters raged more frequently at authorities who refused their demands than at anyone else. By comparison, attacks on granaries and other storage areas and market riots seldom occurred. This behavior makes sense given the conditions the people confronted: deserted markets and resistance to requisitions drove desperate consumers to seek grain at the point of production; refusals of authorities to fix prices, or to fix them at affordable levels, encouraged people to protest their insensitivity. The gender and social patterns of participation continued to resemble those of earlier periods, and as in the past, considerable worker and artisan participation continued. The local situation deteriorated further when the Convention fundamentally altered its policy on poor relief. The Constitution adopted in August 1795 omitted the right to assistance and the state's obligation to provide work or relief. October brought a decisive withdrawal of the central government from public assistance and a decentralization and privatization of relief institutions.[71] Municipalities struggled to shoulder the new burden by throwing themselves on private charity, but most had already gone to that well so often that they could expect little now.[72]

With the breakup of the *maximum* came a new interpretation of food riots. Gradually, the central government terminated the legal and moral ambiguity that had traditionally surrounded subsistence movements. As it decriminalized more and more merchant behaviour, it criminalized consumer protest. Laws in March and June declared food rioters subject to repression. The Constitution of 1795 dropped the clause granting the 'right to insurrection'. Indeed, authorities pursued food rioters with greater ferocity than they had in years. The current of tolerance and support had clearly reversed. The Convention overcame its qualms about using the military to maintain domestic order and, increasingly, turned to troops of the line – regular army detachments containing troops from all over France and thus less squeamish about cracking down locally – to repress disorders and protect shipments. By the end of 1795, the government had forged a more aggressive, dependable repressive apparatus comprised of troops, gendarmes and national guard.

After 1795, food riots dwindled to insignificance or blurred with brigandage. The harvests of 1796 and 1797 proved excellent. By the second half of 1796, the government managed to return poor relief to a steadier institutional and financial basis at the local level. The government definitively abandoned paper money in February 1797 and returned to specie. In June, it declared unambiguously its commitment to free trade in grain. Finally, produce returned to the markets. A combination of improved harvests, more affordable grain prices, a lighter burden from war and counter-revolution helped spare France from more subsistence crises until the nineteenth century.[73]

Beyond the revolution

France entered the nineteenth century to confront regime change, war, periodic economic dislocations and popular claims for subsistence justice. Food riots erupted during the crises of 1801–02, 1811–12, 1816–17 (when the largest wave of rioting in France's history occurred), 1829–30, 1829–40, 1846–47 and only waned in the mid-1850s.[74] With exception of the Napoleonic experiment with a form of the *maximum*, the restoration and July Monarchy governments remained largely committed to liberalization backed by aggressive repression and tempered by some efforts to avoid the worst effects of provisioning crises. Thus, the Paris Reserve managed the grain supply for the capital. A mixture of institutional purchases, sliding scale tariffs that governed exports and imports, local controls on bread prices and charity offices, workhouses and bread, soup and rice distributions funded by a combination of some state and mostly private donations created a modest but often insufficient approach to relief. Although successive governments sought to depoliticize subsistence issues, the experiences of regime change, revolution and counter-revolution nurtured by emerging socialist and working-class politics had left their marks on some popular memories and behaviour.

The crisis of 1846–47 witnessed the last widespread eruption. The traditional hotbed of subsistence riots – the Paris hinterland and the industrial regions of Normandy and the North – remained relatively calm, while disorder spread widely in the west and centre. The last episodes of the 1850s manifested a similar geography, but proved less extensive. Only a handful of riots erupted during the crisis of 1867. By this time, France had experienced improvements in roads and railroad construction, which facilitated both provisioning and repression. Other important social, economic, institutional and political factors also contributed to the decline of rioting.[75] Protest had not disappeared of course; in the second half of the nineteenth century, it largely shifted from consumer-oriented food riots to wage- and workplace-oriented labour movements and the transposition of the struggle over subsistence to other realms: the National Assemblies and ultimately to the welfare state.

Notes

This work has received funding from the Council for European Studies, the National Endowment for the Humanities and Texas A&M University. I have presented portions of it to the George Rudé Seminar on French History, the Société des Etudes Robespierristes and the James Allen Vann Seminar at Emory University. It has benefited greatly from the helpful insights offered by participants at these conferences. Thanks also to John Bohstedt, Manfred Gailus, Martin Geyer, Judith Miller, Jeff Horn and my colleagues at Texas A&M University for their generous suggestions and useful critiques.

1. My essay relies on a combination of my own archival research and the work of other historians. The most important general studies of food riots during the early modern and revolutionary eras include George Rudé, *A Study of Popular Disturbances in France and England, 1730–1848* (London, 1967; rev. ed. 1981); Steven L. Kaplan, *Bread, Politics and Political Economy in the Reign of Louis XV*, 2 vols. (The Hague, 1976); Steven L. Kaplan, *Provisioning Paris: Merchants and Millers in the Grain and Flour Trade during the Eighteenth Century* (Ithaca, 1984); Charles Tilly, 'Food Supply and Public Order in Modern Europe', in *The Formation of National States in Western Europe*, ed. Charles Tilly (Princeton, 1975), pp. 380–455; Charles Tilly, *The Contentious French: Four Centuries of Popular Struggle* (Cambridge, MA, 1986); Judith A. Miller, *Mastering the Market: The State and the Grain Trade in Northern France, 1700–1860* (Cambridge, 1998); Jean Nicolas, *La Rebellion française: Mouvements populaires et conscience sociale, 1661–1789*; Anatoli Ado, *Paysans en révolution: Terre, pouvoir et jacquerie, 1789–1794* (Paris, 1996); John Markoff, *The Abolition of Feudalism: Peasants, Lords, and Legislators in the French Revolution* (University Park, PA, 1996); and my '"La Liberté, l'égalité,

et la libre circulation dès grains": le problème de l'économie morale sous l'Ancien Régime et pendant la Révolution française', *Annales historiques de la Révolution française*, 319 (2000), pp. 71–100. Other more specific works appear below.

2. Such periodization reflects my identification of certain attributes common to rioting during each period. However, this approach does not mean to suggest that either rioting itself or the responses riots provoked evolved in any neat, linear fashion. Unfortunately, this approach cannot do justice to the ways that historical contingencies of time, place and individual interests and behaviour shaped collective violence in specific ways, a specificity that the space allotted here does not permit.

3. A translation of the phrase 'la guerre du blé' featured in F. Gauthier and G.-R. Ikni (eds.), *La Guerre du blé au XVIIIe siècle: la critique contre le libéralisme économique au XVIIIe siècle* (Paris, 1988).

4. Nicolas Bourguinat has also called this the 'social contract on subsistence'. *Les Grains du désordre: L'Etat face aux violences frumentaires dans la première moitié du XIXe siècle* (Paris, 2002).

5. For the best brief discussion of this situation, see Mack Holt, *French Wars of Religion, 1562–1629* (Cambridge, 1995), pp. 193–201.

6. For example, I have identified five riots during the 1585–87 crisis, 15 riots during the 1629–31 crisis and 24 riots during the 1661–62 crisis. All attempts to 'count' riots are fraught with difficulties. Numbers supplied here are approximate and intended only for comparative purposes.

7. Robert Schneider, *Public Life in Toulouse, 1463–1789: From Municipal Republic to Cosmopolitan City* (Ithaca, 1989), p. 72; Barbara Diefendorf, *Paris City Councillors in the Sixteenth Century* (Princeton, 1983), p. 300.

8. On Amiens, see M.L. Pelus, 'Une Crise de subsistance à Amiens (1585–1587)', *Annales historiques compiégnoises*, 15 (1981), pp. 4–11; 'Marchands et échevins d'Amiens dans la seconde moitié du XVIe siècle: crise de subsistances, commerce et profits en 1586–1587', *Revue du Nord*, 44 (1982), pp. 51–71. On Troyes, see William Beik, 'Moral Economy, Violence, Retribution: The Motivations of Crowds in Seventeenth-Century France', paper presented to the James Allen Vann Seminar, Emory University, 1992, and William Beik, *Urban Protest in Seventeenth-Century France: The Culture of Retribution* (Cambridge, 1997). I would also like to thank William Beik for passing me his notes on the riots of 1586 and 1626 (correspondence of December 1992).

9. Authorities frequently referred to this form of riot as an 'entrave contre la circulation des grains'. Louise Tilly shortened this to 'entrave'. See 'The Food Riot as a Form of Political Conflict in France', *Journal of Interdisciplinary History*, 2 (1971), pp. 23–57.

10. Abbot Usher, *History of the Grain Trade, 1400–1700* (Cambridge, MA, 1913), pp. 235–36; and Patrice M. Berger, 'The Famine of 1692–1694 in France: A Study in Administrative Response' (PhD dissertation, University of Chicago, 1972), p. 193.

11. Some towns established public granaries (*magasins* or *greniers d'abondance*) filled with grain purchased by their administrations. During the sixteenth century, the monarchy and *parlements* also ordered grain purchases and public granaries. However, not until the seventeenth century did this practice spread.

12. Louise Tilly, 'The Food Riot as a Form of Political Conflict in France', pp. 36–42.

13. On the conditions, see Marcel Lachiver, *Les Années de misère: La Famine au temps du Grand Roi* (Paris, 1991), pp. 442; Berger, 'The Famine of 1692–1694 in France', pp. 4, 10–12, 20, 260; and Micheline Baulant, 'Réflections sur les mesures prises à

l'occasion des disettes de 1693–1709', *Proceedings of the 7th International Economic History Congress*, 2 (1978), p. 339.

14. The most heavily touched regions included northern France, the Paris Basin, the Pays de la Loire, the Massif Central and the southwest. Provinces such as Burgundy, while not suffering as terribly from dearth, became the focus of heavy grain exports for the army, in particular. Brittany, with a good sarazin harvest to sustain it, survived the crisis largely unscathed. Berger, 'The Famine of 1692–1694 in France', p. 4; Lachiver, *Les Années de misère*, pp. 196, 201–2.
15. For example, the intendant of Amiens signaled the presence of wandering groups of poor in the surplus-grain producing parts of Picardy. Pierre Deyon, *Amiens, capitale provinciale. Etude sur la société urbaine au XVIIe siècle* (Paris, 1967), p. 468.
16. For a slightly later period, see Judith A. Miller, 'Politics and Urban Provisioning Crises: Bakers, Police, and Parlements in France, 1750–1793', *Journal of Modern History*, 64 (1992), pp. 227–62.
17. The crisis of 1708–10 witnessed the most food riots. Jean Nicolas counted 228 for the period, 1700–1709; I found 166 for the period 1708–10 (with 148 in 1709).
18. See the lists of regulations in Nicolas Delamare, *Traité de la police*, 4 vols., 2nd ed. (Amsterdam, 1729), II: *passim*, and Kaplan, *Bread, Politics and Political Economy in the Reign of Louis XV*, pp. 1–95.
19. Lachiver, *Les Années de misère*, p. 336.
20. These relief subventions 'were most often the product of individual influence and local power rather than attempts at a just or efficient distribution'. Gregory Monahan, *Year of Sorrows: The Great Famine of 1709 in Lyon* (Columbus, 1993), pp. 3, 6.
21. Alain Bouthier, 'Un Episode de révolte frumentaire à Cosne-sur-Loire (Nièvre) en 1693', *Actes du 114e Congrès national des sociétés savantes* (Paris, 1990), p. 83.
22. Usher, *History of the Grain Trade, 1400–1700*, p. 310.
23. On Albi, see M. Arthur de Boislisle, *Correspondance des contrôleurs généraux des finances avec les intendants des provinces*, 3 vols. (Paris, 1879–97), I: #1319, p. 363; Lachiver, *Les Années de misère*, pp. 150–51. On Gaillac, see Lachiver, *Les Années de misère*, pp. 150–51.
24. Lettre de Montholon au contrôleur général (20 avril 1693), AN, G7 1632, n. 300.
25. AN, G7 1648; AHG A1 2188; René Pillorget, *Les Mouvements inusrrectionnels de Provence entre 1596 et 1715* (Paris, 1975), p. 975; and Nicolas, La Rébellion française, pp. 236–37.
26. Wood-splitters – a male job – dominated the bands of rioters who descended upon farms in the environs of Moulins-Engilbert in the Nivernais in 1694. Lachiver, *Les Années de misère*, p. 151.
27. Procès-verbal (7 juillet 1709), AD Seine-Maritime, C 105.
28. M. Arthur de Boislisle, 'Grand hiver et la disette de 1709', *Revue des questions historiques*, 73 (1903), p. 508.
29. Boislisle, *Correspondance des contrôleurs généraux des finances avec les intendants des provinces*, III: #346, p. 117.
30. This story had been told many times. See Kaplan, *Bread Politics and Political Economy in the Reign of Louis XV*, and most recently, Miller, *Mastering the Market*, pp. 43–46, 116–25.
31. Kaplan, *Bread Politics and Political Economy in the Reign of Louis XV*, II: pp. 700–702; Steven L. Kaplan, *Le Meilleur pain du monde: les boulangers de Paris au XVIIIe siecle* (Paris, 1996), p. 37. Liberalization altered the relationship of consumers and producers by legitimizing and facilitating behaviour hitherto perceived as morally

and legally ambiguous for producers: long-term grain storage in and direct sales from farm granaries, as well as active participation in the grain and flour trade. Liberalization also specifically prevented local authorities from invoking trad-itional strategies to force grain to market and into the hands of local consumers.

32. See P.M. Jones's attempt to draw out the common features of the period of the 1760s to 1791. *Reform and Revolution in France: The Politics of Transition, 1774–1791* (Cambridge, 1996).

33. Jean Nicolas counts 183 riots for the period 1760–69, 334 for 1770–79 and 335 for 1780–May 1789. I count 295 for the 1775 Flour War. For the revolutionary era, I count 277 episodes after May 1789, 259 from 1790–91 and 402 from 1792–93 (before the first *maximum*). John Markoff observes that 'if we were to regard the subsistence disturbances of 1788–93 as an aggregate, they would probably constitute the largest wave of food riots up to that moment in French history (and in Western European history for that matter)', in *The Abolition of Feudalism*, p. 242.

34. Markoff, *The Abolition of Feudalism*, p. 249.

35. Miller, *Mastering the Market*, p. 92.

36. For example, after a 'seditious' crowd of women with rocks in their aprons started a riot in the market of La Ferté-Gaucher in 1767, authorities gave in and fixed prices. Kaplan, *Bread Politics and Political Economy in the Reign of Louis XV*, I: p. 190. A riot that threatened the safety and property of several merchants in Châlons-sur-Marne in 1768 drove local authorities to issue a classic regulatory ordinance. It promised people distributions of rye bread and prohibited sales outside of the marketplace. Lettre du lieutenant général de police et procureur du roi au procureur général (25 juillet 1768), Ordonnance de police, BN, Collection Joly de Fleury, 1140, ns. 95, 98–99. At Roye, in Picardy, officials averted violence in May 1775 when they 'opened the reserves and [brought] the grain to market and fixed it at a moderate but reasonable price'. Lettre (8 mai), BN, Collection Joly de Fleury, 1159, ns. 227–28.

37. The bibliography on this is huge. See, for example, Darline Gay Levy and Harriet B. Applewhite, 'Women and Militant Citizenship in Revolutionary Paris', in *Rebel Daughters: Women and the French Revolution*, ed. Sara E. Melzer and Leslie W. Rabine (New York, 1992), pp. 82–85. For those historians who have looked at the local/Versailles subsistence side of the episode, see A. Defresne and F. Évrard, *Les Subsistances dans le district de Versailles de 1788 à l'an V*, 2 vol. (Rennes, 1921), I: pp. 245–48; Sukla Sanyal, 'Riots and Revolution: Food Riots in the Department of the Seine-et-Oise, 1789–1795' (PhD dissertation, University of Maryland, 1994), pp. 148–49, and Gustave Bord, *Histoire du blé. Le Pacte de famine: histoire et légende* (Paris, 1887), p. 82.

38. Defresne and Evrard, *Les Subsistances dans le district de Versailles*, I: p. 224.

39. William Sewell, 'The Sans-Culottes Rhetoric of Subsistence', in *The Terror. The French Revolution and the Creation of Modern Political Culture*, ed. Keith Baker (Oxford, 1994), IV: pp. 249–69; and Patrice Higonnet, *Goodness Beyond Virtue: Jacobins during the French Revolution* (Harvard, 1998).

40. The assignat depreciated 14% by September 1790 to 61% by August 1793.

41. See the graphs of various forms of riot over time by John Markoff, *The Abolition of Feudalism*.

42. The only people exempt from the amnesty were those who had received money to riot.

43. See Décrêt rélatifs aux auteurs, fauteurs, et complices des attroupements pour s'opposer à la libre circulation des grains et aux dénonciateurs (6 décembre

1792), AN, AD XI 69; Décrêt qui établit la peine de mort contre les personnes qui s'opposeraient aux libre accès des subsistances à Paris (6 décembre 1792), AD Tarn, L 344; Décrêt sur les subsistances (8 Décembre 1792), Pierre Caron, *Le Commerce des céréales: Instruction, recueil de textes et notes de 1788 à l'an V* (Paris, 1907), pp. 43–45.

44. On these bands, see Francis Évrard, 'Les subsistances en céréales dans le département de l'Eure de 1788 à l'an V', *Bulletin trimestriel de la Commission de recherche et de publication des documents relatifs à la vie économique de la Révolution* (Paris, 1909), pp. 42–43; George Rudé, *The Crowd in the French Revolution* (Oxford: Oxford University Press, 1959), pp. 110–11; Michel Vovelle, 'Les taxations populaires de février-mars et novembre-décembre 1792 dans la Beauce et sur ces confins', in *Ville et campagne au XVIIIe siècle: Chartres et la Beauce* (Paris, 1980), pp. 259–63; Guy-Robert Ikni, 'L'arrêt des bateaux de grains sur l'Oise et l'Aisne en février 1792', *Annales historiques compiégnoises modernes et contemporaines*, 5 (1979), pp. 13–36; Albert Mathiez, *La Vie chère et le mouvement social sous la Terreur* (Paris, 1927; rpt. 1973), pp. 62–63.

45. Of course, not all price fixing took place in the marketplace, in fact, rioters set prices at virtually every opportunity: in farms, at warehouse, in bakeries and during interceptions of shipments.

46. For example, in 1773, a band of 'peasants' roved the region around Libourne in search of grain. Julius Ruff, *Crime, Justice, and Public Order in Old Regime France: The Sénéchaussées of Libourne and Bazas, 1696–1789* (London, 1984), p. 151. In the Paris Basin, Steven Kaplan reports that in 1770 'throughout the Brie "considerable seditions" erupted in which "the people forced the laboureurs to sell them grain at a price they set themselves"', in *Bread Politics and Political Economy in the Reign of Louis XV*, I: p. 198.

47. For more on this see, Bouton, *The Flour War: Gender, Class, and Community in Late Ancien Régime French Society* (University Park, PA, 1993), pp. 141–46, 234–49.

48. As Colin Lucas has observed, 'property owners became more uncomprehending and more quickly frightened of the crowds'. 'The Crowd and Politics in France', *Journal of Modern History*, 60 (1988), p. 430.

49. Lettre du procureur du roi à Nemours (8 mai), BN, Collection Joly de Fleury, 1159, ns. 196–97; Information: déposition de Jean Héaron (8 mai), AD Seine-et-Marne, B 2957(1).

50. On the disturbances that continued to occur and the calls for troops to establish order see Bouton, *The Flour War*, pp. 95–96. Previous convocations of troops had been rare and focused locally and only briefly, as in 1709.

51. 'Sur les subsistances,' discours à la Convention, 2 décembre 1792, Robespierre, *Œuvres*, t. 9 (Paris, 1958), p. 111

52. On the repression during the Flour War see Bouton, *The Flour War*, pp. 99–109.

53. See, for example, Olwen Hufton, *The Poor in Eighteenth-Century France, 1750–1789* (Oxford, 1974); Robert Schwartz, *Policing the Poor in Eighteenth-Century France* (Chapel Hill, 1988), pp. 154–242; Thomas M. Adams, *Bureaucrats and Beggars: French Social Policy in the Age of Enlightenment* (New York, 1990), esp. pp. 39–52; Clay Ramsay, *The Ideology of the Great Fear: The Soissonnais in 1789* (Baltimore, 1992).

54. On what follows, see Alan Forrest, *The French Revolution and the Poor* (New York, 1981); Jean Imbert et al., *La protection sociale sous la Révolution française* (Paris, 1990); Isser Woloch, *The New Regime: Transformations of the French Civic Order, 1789–1820s* (New York, 1994); Bernard Allemandou and Jean–Jacques Le Pennec, *60,000 pauvres à Bordeaux: la politique d'aide sociale sous la Révolution* (Talance, 1995).

55. C. Bloch and A. Tuetey, *Procès-verbaux et rapports du Comité de Mendicité de la Constitution 1790–1791* (Paris, 1911), p. 388 ; and Allemandou and Le Pennec, *60,000 pauvres à Bordeaux*, pp. 126–27.

56. Titre premier: Dispositions fondamentales garanties par la constitution, Constitution du 3 septembre 1791 in *Constitutions et documents politiques: Textes et documents*, ed. M. Duverger (Paris, 1957), p. 20.
57. Markoff, *The Abolition of Feudalism*, p. 243.
58. On the era of the maximum see, for example, Mathiez, *La Vie chère et le mouvement social sous la Terreur*; Albert Soboul, *Les Sans-culottes parisiens en l'an II* (Paris, 1958); Richard Cobb, *Les Armées révolutionnaires, instrument de la Terreur dans les Départements*, 2 vols. (Paris, 1961–63), translated as *The People's Armies: The Armées Révolutionnaires: Instrument of the Terror in the Departments April 1793 to Floréal Year II*, trans. M. Elliott (New Haven, 1987), and *Terreur et Subsistances, 1793–1795* (Paris, 1964); Kare Tönnesson, *La Défaite des Sans-culottes* (Paris-Oslo, 1959, 1978); Gauthier and Ikni, *La Guerre du blé au XVIIIe siècle*; Dominique Margairaz, 'Le Maximum, une grande illusion libérale?' in *État, Finances et Économie pendant la Révolution* (Paris 1991), pp. 399–427; Jean-Pierre Gross, *Fair Shares For All: Jacobin Egalitarianism in Practice* (London, 1997).
59. Sanyal, 'Riots and Revolution', pp. 197–98.
60. Déclarations des droits de l'homme (24 juin 1793), art. 21 in *Constitutions*, p. 80.
61. Especially the revolutionary committees and clubs. See J.-P. Jessene, *Pouvoir au village et révolution, Artois, 1760–1848* (Lille, 1987), p. 95; Colin Lucas, *The Structure of the Terror: The Example of Javogues and the Loire* (Oxford, 1973), pp. 44–45, 235–40; Michael Kennedy, *The Jacobin Clubs in the French Revolution: The Middle Years* (Princeton, 1988), pp. 74–79.
62. For Paris, this meant a force of 6,000 men and 1,200 cannoneers. On the *armées révolutionnaires*, see Richard Cobb, *The People's Armies*. Revolutionary armies had emerged at popular or Jacobin initiative in a great many provinces even before the September days, but the Convention had never sanctioned them.
63. On the Second Maximum, see Mathiez, *La Vie chère et le mouvement social sous la Terreur*, pp. 299–306; Rudé, *Crowd in the French Revolution*, pp. 130–32; Guy Lemarchand, 'Maximum' in *Dictionnaire historique de la Révolution française*, ed. Albert Soboul et al. (Paris, 1989), pp. 729–30.
64. See the long list in Cobb, 'Le Ravitaillement des villes sous la Terreur: la Question des arrivages (septembre 1793, germinal an II)', *Bulletin de la Société d'histoire moderne*, 11e série, 53 (1954), p. 11. On laws, see Pierre Caron, *Le Commerce des céréales: Instruction, recueil de textes et notes de 1788 à l'an V* (Paris, 1907), pp. 180–81.
65. Miller, *Mastering the Market*, Chap. 7. For a recent look at an important aspect of this era for provisioning Paris, see Michel Biard, 'Contrainte ou liberté économique? Les représentants du peuple en mission et le ravitaillement de Paris en l'an III', *Annales Historiques de la Révolution française*, 339 (2005), pp. 35–53.
66. Sanyal, 'Riots and Revolution', p. 215.
67. Allemandou and Le Pennec, *60,000 pauvres à Bordeaux*, p. 110.
68. Counting riots proves extremely difficult for this period. However, I have so far counted over 226 for the period from the abrogation of the maximum to 1796.
69. Cobb, *Terreur et Subsistances*, pp. 263, 282–85; Bryant Ragan, 'Rural Political Culture in the Department of the Somme during the French Revolution' (PhD dissertation, University of California at Berkeley, 1988), pp. 138–39.
70. Sanyal has observed that this form of disturbance heavily predominated in the surplus-grain producing part of the Seine-et-Oise, Sanyal, 'Riots and Revolution', pp. 113, 127. Guy Lemarchand describes large bands of people from as much as ten communes uniting more than 500 men, women and children. *La Fin du Féodalisme*

dans le Pays de Caux, conjoncture économique et démographique et structure sociale dans une région de grande culture, 1640–1795* (Paris, 1989), pp. 516–19.

71. Forrest, *The French Revolution and the Poor*, p. 56.

72. The cases in eastern France are described by Robert Werner, *L'Approvisionnement en pain de la population du Bas–Rhin et de l'armée du Rhin pendant la Révolution, 1789–1797* (Strasbourg, 1951).

73. Of course, brigandage remained endemic until Napoleon finally succeeded in suppressing it. See especially, Howard Brown, *Ending the French Revolution: Violence, Justice, Repression* (University of Virginia Press, 2006).

74. Robert Marjolin, 'Troubles provoqués en France par la disette de 1816–1817', *Revue d'histoire moderne*, 8 (1933), pp. 423–60; Ernest Labrousse, *Aspects de la crise et de la dépression de l'économie française au milieu du XIXe siècle, 1846–1851* (La Roche-sur-Yonne, 1956); and Roger Price, *The Modernization of Rural France: Communications Networks and Agricultural Market Structures in Nineteenth–Century France* (London, 1982). Recent work by Judith Miller (*Mastering the Economy*) and Nicolas Bourguinat (*Grains du désordre*) as well as his dissertation, 'Ordre naturel, ordre public et hiérarchie sociale dans la France de la première moitie du XIXe siècle: Etat et les violences frumentaires' (Thèse de doctorat, Université Lumière-Lyon 2, 1997), and Denis Béliveau, 'Les Révoltes frumentaires en France dans la première moitie du XIXe siècle. Une Analyse des rapports de sociabilité, de la distribution des rôles sexuels et de leurs impacts sur la repression des désordres' (Thèse de doctorat, EHESS, Paris, 1992) contribute tremendously to our understanding of the era.

75. On the decline of food riots, see Price, *The Modernization of Rural France*, pp. 196–204, and Louise Tilly, 'The Decline and Disappearance of the Classical Food Riot in France', New School for Social Research Working Paper, n. 147 (1992), *passim*.

6
Food Riots and the Politics of Provisions in Early-Modern England and France, the Irish Famine and World War I

John Bohstedt

The politics of provisions gained surprising power from the common people's need for bread and their states' need for their orderly allegiance. Many societies acknowledged a *droit de subsistance*, a law of necessity that in emergencies gave human survival priority over individual property rights, an entitlement that paternalism viewed as charity and consumers, as a right.[1] But need alone did not generate effective protest; hungry people have often suffered and died unnoticed. As much or more than needs and norms, the politics of provisions was shaped by particular political cultures, economies, histories of conflict, social networks, policy decisions and wars. Sometimes that matrix of factors empowered food rioters to win relief; but sometimes hunger had no voice, and then corpses lined Irish or Chinese roads.[2] But when outrage inflamed hunger, given a 'political opportunity', people might risk a riot, declaring, 'We'd rather be hanged than starved!' If that risk was real, so were – sometimes – their rulers' measures to relieve them.

Such 'negotiations' comprising riots, repression and relief constitute the 'politics of provisions'. Using physical force to seize shipments, lower prices or compel authorities to act, rioters negotiated with local officials who anxiously tried to negotiate the frail raft of social order through turbulent straits. What critical ingredients could make such negotiations fruitful? In this essay, I will trace the evolution of English provision politics over three centuries of commerce and crisis, from paternalist controls to free markets enforced by arms. From that analysis emerge parameters that illuminate other key moments of provision politics, from the flawed ambitions of the French monarchy, to the failures of the Irish potato famine, to the decisive role of provisions-warfare in World War I.

England, c. 1550–1850: commerce and war, moral economy and provision politics

Provision politics in England arose in the Tudor regime when food supply and demand were both commercialized, making it possible to convert power into relief. Economic, political and social trends converged to shape three distinct 'centuries': 1527–1650; 1650–1739 and 1740–1820.[3] In the Tudor-Stuart century, both cities and manufacturing districts created jobs for a growing population. In an archipelago of regions, capitalist commercial economy emerged, so that a growing proportion of consumers bought their food via markets.[4] In response to those demands, plus the provisioning of the court, the fleet and the armies, British agriculture increased productivity, and producers increasingly moved their cereals through wholesale merchants to processors like bakers and consumers. Crown officials began to monitor corn supplies as early as Cardinal Wolsey's survey of 1527, while national policies to regulate grain traders evolved from municipal precedents. (During these three centuries, corn was the contemporary British term for bread grains, especially wheat, but also including barley, oats and rye). From the beginning, the shadow of riots was present: Joan Thirsk observes that government agrarian policies 'may be fairly summarized as a series of *ad hoc* measures to guard against any threat of turbulence and riot because of food scarcity'.[5] Royal proclamations conjured up customary villains – 'forestallers, engrossers and regraters' – who manipulated markets, but that was mostly lip service to a royal paternalism claiming to protect common folk from greedy middlemen. More substantial royal Books of Orders (1587–1631) directed magistrates in times of scarcity and high prices to supervise merchants and supplies of grain and to exhort or pressure farmers to supply marketplaces at moderate prices.[6] Official price fixing was not attempted after 1550, except for the Assize of Bread, by which magistrates linked the price of bread to fluctuating wheat prices.

Local food riots began to be a familiar response to harvest failures in the 1580s, as the older Tudor rebellions – religious, peasant and dynastic – receded.[7] Rioters were typically craftsmen and non-agricultural wage earners, endowed with sufficient social autonomy to engage in 'collective bargaining by riot'.[8] Working families' modest reserves might enable them to ride out one bad season, so it typically took a combination of either recurrent dearths or a coincidence of trade slump and bad harvest to provoke food riots.[9] The great majority of such riots intercepted food shipments in transit – especially when they passed through communities of consumers in manufacturing districts or ports and towns. Not much evidence of repression survives – certainly nothing to match the brutal punishment of the peasants in the Pilgrimage of Grace of 1536 or Kett's Rebellion of 1549. The unusually harsh example made by the execution of four rioters at Maldon in 1630 reflected the peacekeepers' weakness rather than strength; but that demonstration may have deterred some food riots even through the civil wars of the 1640s.

Importantly, food riots succeeded, not only by seizing shipments often without punishment, but also by wringing relief from the well-to-do. A political culture of reciprocity, headed by the royal father of his people, extended down through the landed gentry's patronage and configured paternalism and deference as two sides of the social fabric. Again physical supply was primary: Magistrates learned that riots were quieted, not by symbolic crackdowns on the old cardinal sins of forestalling, regrating and engrossing, but by officials' actions to 'stay' grain shipments for local use, and by export commissioners' enforcements of occasional royal bans on grain export.[10] In times of dearth, both rioters and relief efforts focused on supply. In the can-do spirit of Renaissance humanism, more than a dozen cities created emergency stores of foodstuffs for subsidized distribution to stave off starvation, topped by the London Livery Companies' grain reserve.[11] What we have then is a *politics of provisions*: food rioters in time of dearth risked being hanged or shot by challenging authorities to provide real food relief. They were not protesting to preserve a customary local economy of self-sufficiency and mutual exchange, as E.P. Thompson claimed, for the food trades had long since burst those bounds to create market economy in many times and places.[12]

In the second century of provision politics (1650–1739), popular protest receded following upon political and economic watersheds. As the high-political fractures of the Civil Wars healed, parliamentary governance assured the rule of landed gentlemen, the 'natural rulers', since land, patronage and power reinforced each other. Now central policies favoured producers rather than consumers, so bounties promoted exports and the Tudors' cardinal market sins were almost forgotten. The early capitalist improvement of English agriculture and transportation diverged from France's peasant farming, and mostly ended starvation crises in England after 1622.[13] Population growth stagnated, so that for a generation after the Treaty of Utrecht in 1713 agricultural surpluses made England the granary of Western Europe. That, together with the political tilt toward producers, lowered the pressure in provision politics and the relatively few food riots clustered chiefly in the war-ridden 1690s. When dearth did occur, however, the crown could no longer ban exports, since the royal prerogative had been curtailed by Parliament.[14]

In the third 'century' of provision politics, the most riotous phase occurred between 1740 and 1801, when nearly 700 food riots crackled in half a dozen waves across England. As manufacturing and trade increased, craftsmen, miners and petty manufacturers formed crowds to seize wagonloads and barges of corn, and attack mills and granaries. Increasingly after 1750, they sold out the goods at lowered prices in marketplaces and farmyards, and returned the proceeds to the owners. That seemed to be an attempt to reduce their legal liability, for England was becoming a more-governed society and exemplary hangings of rioters increased after 1750. Hungry and indignant men and women broke the peace at some risk, for rioters could be shot as well as hanged. With their trademark cry, 'We'd rather be hanged than starved!' rioters called on their rulers to relieve their necessity. By word and deed, the political theatre of food riot pressed magistrates – the natural rulers, landed gentlemen and municipal elites – to use their wealth and power to relieve the community.

E.P. Thompson's brilliant essay on the 'moral economy' opened up key areas of enquiry but did not resolve them. To begin with, at the core of the 'moral economy' is a more general 'law of necessity' that, in times of scarcity, human needs take priority over property rights and 'business as usual'. That 'right' to subsistence is widely recognized across world history; centred in the 'gut' where physiological need meets ethical reckoning to create 'justice', the right to food has been enshrined for the past 60 years in the United Nations Declaration of Human Rights.[15] To place that axiom in particular history, Thompson's 'moral economy' might connect particular variations and manifestations with English customs and practices. But Thompson's model does not fit either the particular economic history nor recorded rioters' words and actions in eighteenth-century England.[16] Food rioters were not protesting a commercial market transition; that had taken place centuries earlier. In their formative years, they chiefly sought out and seized food stores and shipments; their 'central action' was not marketplace price fixing, an implicit critique of commercial marketing, Thompson claimed, until later.

Second, Thompson showed how the moral pressures of such emergencies opened up a 'political space for bargaining' between common people and officials, in which the force of the people's needs made the magistrates 'prisoners', as did their claims to rule for the public good.[17] But the efficacy of provision politics depended not merely on shared moral norms, but on the varying structures and dynamics of community politics. In eighteenth-century Britain, a 'moral economy' of frequent, disciplined and successful food riots was not universal, but was sustained by the dense social networks of stable, medium-sized town communities.[18] Food riots were not made by the most desperate and often transient poor who lacked the communal ties and leadership to negotiate by riot (to act collectively or to speak for the community).[19] Instead rioters were usually established artisans and labourers of small to medium-sized towns who had the solidarity to act in disciplined fashion so as to maximize gains and minimize liabilities. Such bargaining by riot was also facilitated by 'veteran communities', perhaps of weavers or miners accustomed to bargaining collectively with employers and petitioning Parliament.

Vertical ties were even more crucial. Sometimes rioters parleyed directly with magistrates. More often both acted out a well-rehearsed political minuet. Weavers, colliers, butchers and other artisans had the patronage ties to local elites sprung from work, small property tenure, election mobs and militia corps that enabled them to invoke the claims of reciprocity and shared interests. Conversely, farm workers took almost no part in food rioting, unlike small French peasants who had to sell their grain in the fall and buy in the hungry spring. Why? Perhaps English farm labourers were inhibited by the potential losses of their annual wage-labour contracts, informal charity and formal poor relief entitlements, set by local Boards of Poor Law Guardians.[20] They were, Thompson argues, only too vulnerable to 'the revenges of village paternalism'.[21] Moreover, most of the subsistence crises took place during wars: 1740, 1756–57, 1782–83, 1795–96 and 1800–1801. Those wars stretched armed forces thin, anti-riot deployment strategies took decades to develop and village constables were no match for crowds.[22] So the balance of physical force usually favoured crowds, and the remedial powers of patronage and moveable wealth could still offer rioters some hope for success.

Both rioters and 'veteran' magistrates in town and country gleaned 'political learning' from successive waves of rioting. For instance, repressive strategy: in 1740 and 1756–57, royal judges on circuits of the Assize courts rendered harsh judgments on rioters – multiple transportations in 1740 and hangings in 1756. Partly distracted by the large wars during those two crises, military repression was haphazard. But, in 1766, widespread rioting occurred during peacetime and was systematically repressed: the secretary at war set up a military camp in the West Country epicentre, and Special Assizes made demonstrative hangings. The lesson took: only sporadic rioting occurred in succeeding dearths, until England was again embroiled in a large war in 1795. Major outbursts of rioting were contained by a combination of military force and targeted hangings, but especially by much more ambitious relief efforts. A similar crisis recurred in 1800–1801.

Such relief efforts were the finest fruits of the politics of provisions. Leading citizens learned to pool their purses to import foodstuffs from 'abroad', while larger towns erected soup kitchens. For the most part in England's 'golden age of riot' between 1740 and 1801, frequent and disciplined food riots won substantial relief at an acceptable cost in repression. Conversely, elites won a return to tranquillity, their authority ostensibly reconfirmed. The responses to dearth – the interactions of riot, repression and relief – comprised the 'politics of provisions'.

But even while the 'politics of provisions' delivered successful outcomes for rioters and magistrates – relief in exchange for order – several trends converged to bring its rapid demise after 1800. First, industrialization and rapid urbanization dissolved and swamped the horizontal and vertical networks of social patronage that had permitted accustomed negotiations among familiar players. In the new industrial 'towns of strangers', crowds became more violent, and authorities more anxiously retributive.[23] Second, big boom-towns like Manchester and Birmingham needed food supplies from a catchment area extending over hundreds of miles. Food riots in Manchester or Birmingham could cause distant wholesale food dealers to divert their food shipments to safer markets, leaving Manchester or Birmingham to starve. Hence both their officials and national governments could no longer tolerate food riots. They had to preclude them either by military patrols or soup kitchens or both. Third, to that end of protecting their markets, magistrates received an adventitious innovation during the long wars against the French Revolution and Napoleon. The yeomanry, local corps of volunteer cavalry, were formed from 1794 onwards, auxiliaries to the militia as home defence against invasion or insurrection. Local amateur corps of farmers and gentlemen's sons mounted on their own horses turned out to be the perfect antidote to food riots. Thus, rather suddenly, magistrates had both the motives and the means to suppress riots, and the viability of food riots – their prospects of success – petered out. Fourth, the dramatic and critical convergence in 1811 and 1812 of Luddism, Jacobin radicalism and transatlantic war brought savage reprisals and hangings that dampened the politics of provision for a generation. From the so-called 'Hungry Forties', food riots retreated to the peripheries of the national economy, to Devon, Cornwall and the Moray Firth, while the political spotlight was hogged by the more systemic Chartist campaign for household suffrage and the Anti-Corn Law League, agitation for international 'free trade' in corn. Chartists suspected the Manchester-inspired league of seeking cheaper bread as a means to lower wages. Political economy had emphatically replaced moral economy in the councils of government. Most important, food prices plummeted to such low levels over most of the nineteenth century that they disappeared from politics, until at the turn of the century Joseph Chamberlain's quixotic 'imperial preference' scheme was crushed by cries of 'bread tax!'. Edwardian liberals responded to both the rediscovery of poverty and a mobilized trade union movement with such measures as school meals, old age pensions and national insurance. Those roots of the modern welfare state derived, not from stigmatizing charity and Poor Law, but from the 'entitlements' won by a militant provision politics a century before.

The contrasting provision politics of early modern France

By October 1789, the revolution had fallen short by at least one essential measure, so the women of Paris marched to Versailles to bring back 'the Baker, the Baker's wife, and the Baker's son'. They meant thus to redeem the monarchy's ancient promise of provisions. The privileged demands of Paris and the incessant demands of war had left a growing population hungry, as France's half-improved economy failed to keep pace. The shortcomings of both policy and production generated a provision politics much more riotous than

England's. By 1789, the French monarchy's legitimacy was as bankrupt as its finances.

France's riotous provision politics had begun about the same time as England's. In a century of expanding population and early commercialization, harvest shortfalls in the mid-1580s occasioned a few food riots, overshadowed in their first century, as in England, by peasant revolts and civil war. By the 1690s, food riots predominated.[24] Like English food riots before 1750, the French were mainly *entraves*, blockages of food shipments especially to Paris, a pattern that recurred down to the 1840s, with the brief exception of the Flour War of 1775 and the intense politicization of 1791–93.[25] Marketplace price-fixing riots were rarer, as in England, but French rioters began to make assaults on merchants' granaries, a form little seen in England before 1750.[26] We do not hear of mills being attacked in France as they were in Britain, when millers became great wholesalers of flour. In contrast with England's pragmatic grain seizures, seventeenth-century French riots were much more violent, sometimes descending into disorderly brawls, and they were marked by moralistic over-tones. Rioters sought not only to procure grain but also to punish merchants for hoarding and selfish greed, sacking their houses and apartments, acting out William Beik's 'culture of retribution'.[27] France had many more food riots than Britain – 1,265 events compared with Britain's 380 between 1661 and the spring of 1789.[28] Because France was nearly four times as populous, England was somewhat more 'riotous' (per capita), but that greater number of food riots was politically more critical because of the centralization of provision politics in France's absolute monarchy.

After 1600, the political cultures of England and France increasingly diverged. The English king's late medieval persona as father of his people withered as seventeenth-century revolutions dispersed power through his constitutional partners: landed aristocrats and gentry and urban bourgeois elites. Paternalism was dispensed through their local patronage, so food rioters negotiated with them by riot to construct local 'constitutions' that included a politics of pro-vision. Like the fiscal power of John Brewer's 'fiscal-military state', provision politics were robust and stable because they were rooted in a dispersed political nation. By contrast, the French monarchy bore a huge and centralized burden; a cornerstone of absolute royal authority was its covenant to underwrite the people's subsistence. 'Though it was never inscribed in the fundamental laws of the realm', Steven Kaplan writes, 'the commitment to subsistence became, in the vernacular, a responsibility and an attribute of kingship'. The apologist for Louis XIV's divine right to absolute authority, Jacques Bossuet, asserted that the king's obligation to ensure subsistence was the 'foundation' of all his claims on his people. Some eighteenth-century commentators traced it back to Charlemagne. Like the Chinese Emperor's mandate of heaven, this was a social contract 'by which the people agreed to submit to taxation, military service and 'subjectly' fealty in return for the promise that the mythic nourishing prince, embodied in the state, would spare them from starvation'.[29] Above all was the state's 'intense concern for social stability'. As intendant Berthier de Sauvigny put it, the 'prerequisite' for order was 'to provide the subsistence of the people, without which there is neither law nor force that can contain them'.[30]

Instead of merely improvising reactive measures every decade once harvests had failed, experience, paternalism and pragmatism suggested advance preparation, the *Parlement* of Paris reminded the new king in 1776, in a variation of the 'law of necessity':

> A popular movement becomes a popular riot, and then the instruments of suppression must come into play to restore law and order. ... It was, Sire, because they had weighed these drawbacks that our fathers multiplied precautionary measures. ... One does not reason about necessity, for it involves one's own existence.[31]

Not surprisingly, such precautions focused on the capital. When rioters sacked a bakery in the Faubourg de Saint Antoine in 1725, it spurred the monarchy and city officials to provision Paris for half a century.[32] The capital's chief officials, representing the royal ministry, the *parlement*, the city guilds and the 'police', used their traditional jurisdictions and their financial networks far beyond the capital to procure grain at home and abroad ('the king's grain'), however much it might disrupt provincial markets.[33] Such centralized efforts were all too likely to trigger the latent popular suspicions of a *pacte de famine*, a famine plot wherein royal officials sought to profiteer at popular expense.[34] And, in the subsistence crisis of 1738–41, some intendants and city officials refused to cooperate with royal officials and blocked shipments to the capital – an 'administrative analogue to ... grain riot' – on the grounds that they feared local disorder.[35] Such conflicts between royal and local officials eroded the king's promises as royal provider.

Central officials rejected the notion of creating a large storage granary in advance of need as Lyons (a silk manufacturing centre) and Geneva had done; Paris was huge, and the problem of grain spoilage was formidable. But the lieutenant general of police did create a reserve network by requiring Parisian religious communities – monasteries and convents, hospitals and schools that already handled a lot of grain – to maintain reserve supplies of three years' consumption. For nearly half a century, that reserve gave ministers a breathing space of a few market days when dearth struck to reduce public fears and speculation.[36] Kaplan concludes that the state did not invest enough resources in these preventive measures,[37] although such efforts were far greater than any English attempts. England's only ministerial effort to procure grain came in 1795:[38] it was undertaken in secrecy, it failed and merchants had then to be promised in the next crisis that the crown would not get into trading. Local gentlemen preferred to donate to *ad hoc* relief subscriptions.

France was so much more riotous, and dangerously so, because the royal promise to provision confronted an economy in which demands were growing much faster than productivity. French agriculture had not boosted its productivity in step with growing French population, so the masses became increasingly immiserated. Olwen Hufton observes that by the eighteenth century, starvation crises were replaced by chronic malnutrition for a third of the population.[39] Moreover, royally privileged demands for the 'king's grain' for Paris were not the only burden on French agriculture. Foremost among these was war: throughout the seventeenth century, France had only the briefest interludes of peace and then, in the 'long eighteenth century' before Waterloo, France and Britain engaged in titanic struggles every generation: to 1713; 1740–48; 1756–63; 1778–81 and 1792–1801. While Britain fought with ships and sterling, France fielded large land armies that drained the kingdom's food supplies.

The overstretch of French provision politics helped to discredit the monarchy. Long before the free trade royal decrees of the 1760s and 1770s, the monarchy ceased regulating the grain trade and depended more on markets and merchants to supply its swollen needs.[40] Royal opposition to grain control by local officials while privileged commissioners were buying up available local supplies for Paris and the army did indeed provoke much riotous resistance.[41] In 1764 and 1773, when the Ministry decreed that free trade must replace paternalist regulation, it was the last straw: 'The Baker-King had betrayed his people!'.[42] The new policy required military enforcement. Just as in England where 'free trade arrived at the point of a bayonet', so in France, the 'invisible hand of Adam Smith had become the very visible hand of martial law'.[43] Gusts of rioting, climaxing in the great Flour War of 1775, failed to get the decrees rescinded.

In the next two decades as revolution and war disrupted politics, production and markets, the politics of provision remained critical issues. Food riots intensified popular mobilization in 1789 and 1791–93 and contributed to regime changes. Bourgeois Girondins tried to enforce free trade while Jacobins set a grain price *maximum* that gave subsistence ('the right to existence') priority over property rights ('the right to self-fulfillment').[44] The *maximum* ended food rioting for a year, but the cities' *armees revolutionaires* that requisitioned grain in the countryside were very like institutionalized food riots.[45] When market riots flared up again in 1812, the Napoleonic regime answered not only with harsh repression and executions but also with a massive campaign by the prefects to mobilize private charity to support soup kitchens in the cities.[46] 'Free' marketing of food – freed of provision politics – was hardly 'destined' to triumph; economic doctrine paled against the power of mobilized hunger.

Hundreds of food riots still occurred in the 1840s and 1850s: the majority still intercepted food shipments.[47] Judith Miller shows how, by the 1860s, the state gained strength and competency in deploying provision policies that balanced, without disrupting, a profit-oriented market trade. She concludes 'free trade in grain was not the result of the market but of the state's intervention'.[48] In other words, a politics of provision partly driven by riots was one bridge from early modern to modern political economy.

To sum up, French provision politics contrasts with England's at many points. Both agricultural productivity and industrial growth lagged behind Britain's. Rioters were different, France's including many more peasants who had to sell their harvest in the fall and buy in the hungry spring and summer. Central royal (and later imperial) policies bulked much larger in France, as did supply of armies and the capital. French punishments and deployments of the army seem fewer, partly because the armies were usually occupied in war. Otherwise authorities responded to riots with similar measures, albeit with more state control: communal granaries, rationing, charity, price setting and so on.[49] French provision politics helped bring down a monarchy staggering under other burdens. French rioters echoed the English in one central claim: 'They preferred to be hung, or killed, than to die of hunger!'.[50] That statement was about pride and entitlement – about the politics of provisions – as much as hunger.

The failure of provision politics in the Irish Famine

Our third case of provision politics is set in troubled Ireland. In the Irish Potato Famine of 1845–52, 1 million people died, and more than a million emigrated. Why did provision politics fail so badly to succor that part of the 'United' Kingdom? First, Ireland was a conquered land, England's first and oldest colony. From top to bottom, England's authority in Ireland lacked the legitimizing reciprocity that sustained the political nation and provision politics in England. Ireland's colonial status in the United Kingdom took palpable form in the Irish Executive in Dublin Castle, headed by a lord lieutenant and a chief secretary for Ireland, and backed by army units and an armed constabulary. Barracks glowered on Irish horizons and Protestant magistrates governed Catholic subjects, bitterly alienated by religious persecution but even more by Irish resentment of British land seizures. As Terry Eagleton puts it: 'British sovereignty in Ireland never succeeded in establishing hegemony, as opposed to that blunter instrument known as power'.[51] Not only was there no tradition of gentry paternalism, 'there was no political space (as in England) within which the plebs could exert pressure on their rulers'.[52] Ireland's protest tradition was dominated by 'agrarian outrages' – nocturnal destruction of cattle and hayricks by secret peasant societies, punished in turn by hangings and transportations – poles apart from English food rioters' noonday bargaining.

Moreover, the Irish Famine occurred in socioeconomic conditions very different from those of industrial England. English food riots had flourished in commercial and industrial communities rather than in agrarian districts. But the great majority (83%) of the Irish population lived in towns of fewer than 2,000, and Ireland had been significantly deindustrialised by Britain's industrial revolution.[53] Especially in the western half of Ireland, potato culture enabled population to grow dangerously, so that millions of farm labourers and peasants became fatally vulnerable to the blight that recurred from 1845 to 1852. Most farm workers were paid by conacre – the annual grant of a potato patch to grow a year's sustenance – so the blight devastated not only food supply but also incomes. On potato lands where the harvest was completely lost in 1846, there was no food left for rioters to struggle over; they did not protest at empty barns. Famine deaths and emigration hit hardest in that desperately overpopulated west. Had robust landlords resided there, they might have brought relief. Elsewhere, some resident landlords paid poor rates, helped raise relief subscriptions and provided extra employment on their estates in the first year of the famine.[54] But, in the poorer districts, landlords were likeliest to be absentee, to avoid claims on their wealth, to be made poorer by rent arrears and to be without voice in British political circles. Hence the politics of provisions was hollowed out; it lacked resources of local wealth and leadership to mobilise for relief. Even the middle classes who filled out relief committees elsewhere were missing.[55]

Hence a provision politics of bargaining by riot was largely absent from Ireland, being only one-tenth as strong (measured in riots per capita) as England's: we count eighteenth-century Irish food riots in dozens rather than hundreds. They clustered in 1729, 1740, 1756, 1782–84 and 1800–1801. Their narrow geography matched Ireland's partial commercialization: 90 percent of them occurred in the east coast ports from Belfast to Baltimore, plus Limerick and Ennis, Sligo and Galway in the west. They were most frequent at Cork (1729, 1740, 1756, 1783 and 1801), Dublin (1729, 1741 and 1756), Drogheda (1729, 1740, 1756 and 1778) and Dundalk (1740, 1756 and 1801).[56] Most took the form of crowds' intercepting food exports bound from Cork to Dublin, or else to England or the continent. Occasionally, crowds sold their confiscated food at lowered prices. While there are no hints of a paternalist moral economy, in the larger eastern ports such as Belfast, Dublin and Cork, endowed with commercial wealth from Atlantic trades, riots did move town officials to set up substantial relief depots and soup kitchens, and also prompted Dublin Castle to ban exports in 1784 and 1800.[57] Elsewhere much of Ireland lacked the sympathies, traditions and social networks, as well as the wealth and leadership, for provision politics.

In the early years of the famine, besides those eastern cities, hunger riots occurred in a belt of counties – Clare, Limerick, Tipperary, Cork, Kilkenny and Waterford.[58] They drew on traditions of Whiteboy agrarian protest not resembling earlier English patterns of disciplined and successful bargaining by riot. In counties Clare and Limerick, previous dearths had sparked endemic violence, in which small groups of five to 20 men, often armed, attacked larger farmers, beat them and forced them to lower their prices for potatoes in the upcoming summer. In 1842, a wave of riots intercepted food shipments.[59] In the famine summer of 1846, small groups began to assault public works' officers, attempting to keep up wages or prevent discharges, but stopping short of homicide. Andrés Eiríksson argues that the public works themselves actually facilitated solidarity for collective action by gathering together workers who had previously been scattered. Strikes, marches and demonstrations at relief committee meetings failed to prevent the change from daily wages to piecework rates. Next, violent opposition to food exports took the form of shooting shipping carts' horses. But from October 1846, large crowds of hundreds, sometimes thousands, gathered for months to block oats shipments, especially around Ennis and Limerick. In one case, hundreds of public works' labourers supported by fields of women and children blocked a grain convoy despite its military guard, declaring that they were ready to be shot and 'die on the spot' rather than to 'suffer the corn to go'. The police described this as 'a triumph of the people'.[60] That was a rare success permitted by the presence of food to control, and by the authorities' not ordering the troops to fire. In early 1847, violent protests failed to prevent the closures of the public works. When one Captain Ferguson was hit with a rock, the crowd shouted, 'Blood is better than starvation!'.[61] But the protesters could not reach the decision-makers in London. Crowds did on many occasions plunder flour and grain from stores and mills. Finally, in 1847, Clare and Limerick rioters protested the new soup kitchens. Crowds and smaller gangs tried to destroy the boilers – because the soup was repulsive, and because they wanted to be given an uncooked meal to cook at home. Being fed collectively resembled the workhouse, so it was demeaning. The resisters declared they 'abhor[red] the idea of being made beggars'.[62] Despite a few temporary successes, those riots ended because local relief committees took over the soup kitchens (where punishment might include exclusion), and when the famine's toll of exhaustion, death and flight demobilized protest.

In the famine, provision politics stood cruelly on its head for most of the period, denying any English obligation to relieve the Irish, though they had been incorporated in the United Kingdom since 1801. In the first year of the famine, the mildly paternalist British Prime Minister Robert Peel imported a stock of corn from America to reduce price increases, and launched public works to put wages into the pockets of the needy. But when Lord John Russell followed Peel as Prime Minister in 1846, his weak Whig ministry was dominated by harsh *laissez-faire* treasury dogma, upheld by permanent Undersecretary Charles Trevelyan and Chancellor of the Exchequer Charles Wood. In May 1847, the humane Irish Magnate who had been Ireland's Lord Lieutenant, Lord Bessborough, died. In Black '47, the worst year of the famine, the British government phased out the public works, and that autumn, five years too soon, declared the famine over, closed the soup kitchens and threw the whole burden of famine relief onto the struggling Irish landlords' local taxes paid under the motto: 'Irish property must pay for Irish poverty'.

How might we explain a rich nation's failure to relieve starving fellow subjects of the monarch? Provision politics broke down in the famine because the hungry could not bring effective political pressure upon their rulers, because of ancient British contempt for Irish landlords and peasants and because deliberate British abstinence from relief was mandated by powerful dogma. English officials critically failed to seek out and finance relief imports, as eighteenth-century English communities had done under pressure of bread riots. The temporary soup kitchens of 1847 fed 3 million people a day for nearly six months, showing what government could do when it willed. Quakers and other private charity organizations did import supplies to Ireland, but the scale of need far exceeded their efforts. Irish unrest only confirmed the British public's compassion fatigue in the election year of 1847 (also a year of industrial slump), when an industrial middle class, taught by the likes of *Punch* and the *Economist* to regard the Irish as treacherous beggars, insisted upon curtailing aid.

Irish suffering was far from invisible to British officials, for there were ample published and administrative reports at every stage in the unfolding tragedy. Rather the treasury's miserliness was deliberate, resting on *laissez-faire* dogma that markets and private merchants would meet demand, despite the fact that starving peasants generated none. To avoid perpetuating Irish pauperism, relief recipients must be paid only for work completed on the works, even as famished millions grew weaker. Grain exports to Britain could not be banned, or Irish merchants threatened to stop trading. Moreover, *laissez-faire* dogma was sanctified by a Victorian conviction of Providentialism, 'the doctrine that human affairs are regulated by a divine agency for human good', that the famine was part of a divine plan, perhaps even to 'improve' Ireland by clearing away feckless landlords and peasants so that British capitalism might blossom.[63] Charles Trevelyan summed up both the tone and doctrine of treasury thinking in October 1846 when he declared: 'The deep and inveterate root of *Social* evil remain[s in Ireland] and ... the cure has been applied by the direct stroke of an all wise Providence in a manner as unexpected and unthought of as it likely to be effectual'.[64] As the British Treasury continually overruled the Dublin Castle Executive's call for more aid, Edward Twisleton, Secretary of the Irish Poor Law, ultimately resigned, rather than be an 'agent of a policy ... of extermination'.[65]

Peter Gray concludes that Ireland's British rulers chose 'to pursue moral or economic objectives at the expense of human life'. They shared with the British middle-class public 'ideas of moralism, supported by Providentialism and a Manchester-school reading of classical economics' that sustained 'a dogmatic refusal' to provide effective aid. And that, 'in the Irish conditions of the later 1840s, amounted to a sentence of death on many thousands'.[66] In the final analysis, we cannot imagine such dogmas prevailing if starvation had threatened Dorset or Westmoreland. Practical politics from both popular protest and landed paternalists would have interceded. Ireland's colonial status – the deficit of provision politics – permitted English ideologues to abandon her, and the worst-hit districts lacked the local material and political resources to make up that deficit.[67]

World War I: total war and provision politics

Total war called forth exhaustive mobilization of civilian and military resources, and so belligerent nations could and must strike at home fronts to undermine their enemy's material capacity – and will – to keep fighting. In World War I, provision politics was a decisive factor in victory and defeat. Ultimately, governments had to align the whole production and distribution of foodstuffs with civilian needs and protests to sustain the popular morale crucial for survival. Jay Winter concludes that 'it was precisely on the level of defending civilian living standards that Britain and France succeeded whereas Germany and her allies failed... In Central Europe, the manifest inability literally to deliver the goods undermined the war effort, discredited ruling circles, and brought down governments that had entered the war with powerful and widespread support'.[68]

By 1914, modern improved nutritional standards required massive food imports: 60% of Britain's annual needs and 25% of Germany's came from abroad.[69] Britain's defence of both the empire and the shipping lanes that stocked her breakfast tables culminated in the Dreadnought battleship in 1906, and in planning for blockade by 1909. European geography permitted Britain to create a 'distant' blockade across the North Sea and the Channel that was too risky for the German High Seas Fleet to challenge. British strategy aimed squarely at civilians' food welfare as much as military consumers – Britain could try to starve Germany into submission, rather than defeating her on the battlefield.[70]

Germany had no corresponding strategic plan to protect her food supplies. The emperor and his army gambled everything on a short land war to be won by the 'miraculous' Schlieffen Plan before a volatile mass public cracked and rebelled[71] and before the British blockade could tighten its slow noose. From 1897, the German Tirpitz Plan raced to construct at least a credible naval counter-force, but the naval arms race only aggravated tensions with Britain, without creating enough power to overcome British naval supremacy in war. Nor did Germany stockpile food for a long war because to do so would signal doubt in the Schlieffen Plan.[72] In 1917, Germany took an even more desperate gamble, resuming all-out submarine warfare against Britain's Atlantic suppliers, knowing it would provoke the United States to declare war. In December 1914, Admiral Tirpitz had boasted, 'England wants to starve us into submission; we can play the same game, blockade England'.[73] In the winter of 1916–17, admiralty chief of staff Holtzendorff, his team of experts and his allies persuaded the kaiser that Britain's industrial economy could not survive U-boat interruption of its food supplies. Lacking the character and authority to implement rationing, they claimed, Britain would be crippled by food riots, labour unrest and a 'grip of fear'.[74] Once again, Germany got the worst of both worlds. She had not nearly enough U-boats to do the job, and she had underestimated the American mobilisation of credits, grain and troops.[75]

Although 'Germany was not starved into defeat',[76] food crises decisively undercut her war effort. On the home front, German Understate Secretary Delbrück later reflected, 'There can be no doubt that whether or not the government succeeded in provisioning the population...would have a decisive impact on the course of the war'.[77] Maintaining barely enough total calories meant that half the time, half the people went hungry, while the shortfall of meat and fats created 'a sense of deep deprivation'.[78] Germans struggled for food, rich against poor, in a vast black market that undercut both social solidarity and the government's 'legitimacy'.[79] The German government's clumsy military-style food controls were poorly designed from the beginning. Soldiers were served first: Freiburg's residents discovered that 'prince army has the last word' (*Fürst Feldherr bestimmt*), as army contractors scoured the countryside in the early months of the war.[80] After soldiers, munitions workers were the next priority, at the cost of alienating urban middle classes, bureaucrats and farmers. Germany's 1914 price controls wreaked havoc: they were separately imposed either by municipalities or generals of military regions, thus throwing both groups into bidding wars over farmers' prices and supplies. Before long, price controls fostered shortages of the critical commodities of potatoes and pork. Street battles broke out, as women and men queued for potatoes in long lines that generated a rudimentary form of community; police feared they could evolve into mobs. By mid-1915, 'fiery resentment' against suspected hoarders built up, and Berliners began to demand first government action and then peace.[81] By October, police reported more than fifty 'excesses' or riots over butter; some of the Berlin crowds reached thousands. The national Bundesrat created a new Price Monitoring Authority, but the press complained it lacked teeth.[82] Not long after, official tinkering with bread undercut morale for a bread-conscious people.

Provision politics only continued to darken. By mid-1916, shortages provoked food riots in large and medium-sized towns: 'Women looted shops, overturned market stalls' and spread bitter anger through food queues that portended a 'counter public opinion' for peace.[83] In response to riots and shortages, the imperial government set up the War Food Office to actually trade in and manage food supplies. But the harvest failure of 1916 created the dismal 'turnip winter', and Germany faced 'a food crisis in dimensions unknown ... for almost a century'.[84] War work dropped off, and strikes broke out in Hamburg and Berlin. The next year was even worse: by April 1918, squads of soldiers were sent to the countryside to seize grain and potatoes for the market,[85] as had the Jacobin *armeés revolutionnaires* in 1793. By summer, military governors reported that 'economic conditions, and primarily the food situation, were decisive for the general state of mind'. By October, War Cabinet ministers feared that soldiers returning from home leaves would depress the army at the front with stories of food shortages. General Ludendorff was told: 'That is a question of potatoes. We have no more meat. ... As long as this puzzle cannot be solved, it is impossible to improve morale'.[86]

Austria–Hungary was even hungrier. Flour-ration cuts in January 1918 triggered huge strikes in Vienna that spread to Berlin and then the industrial Rhineland. More cuts in June touched off a 'potato war' in Vienna. Gangs sortied into the countryside to pillage terrified farmers. Austria was 'falling apart'.[87] Hew Strachan concludes that the British blockade alone did not bring German defeat but that 'its interaction with the fault lines in German society and in the structure of the German polity' undermined national unity. Combined with even worse conditions in Austria–Hungary and setbacks on the western front, provision politics sent German morale into a tailspin. Ultimately, the allies maintained the blockade even after the armistice. 'The food blockade is what finally forced Germany to surrender and to sign the Treaty of Versailles in June 1919'.[88] General Erich von Ludendorff observed: 'The waning morale at home was intimately connected with the food situation ... Our enemies' starvation blockade triumphed, and caused us both physical and spiritual distress'.[89] The failure to master provision politics was a major factor in Germany's defeat.

By contrast, Britain had debated and analysed the problem of wartime food supplies since the Boer War, so that at least its parameters were understood. In 1911, the Seeley committee warned: 'If the government were not prepared to control food distribution in time of war, the country would face a severe domestic upheaval', so when the war started in 1914, a Cabinet Committee on food supply immediately began work. Britain's control of Atlantic shipping and access to world resources gave her some initial breathing space. Margaret Barnett shows that 'the state did not rush in with controls too soon, as in Germany, and in the process wreck both the supply flow and the chances of consumer co-operation'.[90] By the end of 1914, government had authorized state agents to purchase, import and stockpile wheat and sugar, though not to the exclusion of merchants' private trade. Government also created incentives that increased wheat production by 59%. By late 1916, the government bought and shipped the bulk of Britain's imported foodstuffs. In the spring of 1917, Britain stood nearly alone, with Russia crippled by food riots and revolution and Italy also beset by food rioting.[91] The admiralty was mired in black pessimism by the U-boat campaign.[92] In 1918, pessimism was further fed by war-weariness, crippling losses at Paschendaele, industrial militancy and food shortages.[93]

However, by mid-1917, the tide had already begun to turn, thanks in part to provision politics. America's entry into the war brought about an inter-allied trading system that developed into a monopolistic hold on world food supplies. More immediately, organized labour agitation finally won effective food control. In May 1917, the powerful Miners' Federation threatened industrial stoppages unless steps were taken to fix food prices. The government now took firm control: the Ministry of Food was expanded ten-fold, and came to manage 90% of all food sold. Yet domestic tranquillity was not easily won:

> Protest strikes and demonstrations rippled through the winter months in 1917–18 as the first effects of government price controls was to disrupt food supplies, especially in rural areas and munitions centers. Queues lengthened outside food shops, and ... women in Sheffield [threatened] in late November to raid stores unless provided with tea and sugar. ... Their menfolk downed tools to take their place in the queues ... Popular resentment was heightened by allegations of class discrimination and accusations of hoarding.

Three big strikes protested food prices, queues and distributions at the key munitions centres of Coventry, Manchester and Bedford.[94] Finally, compulsory food rationing was introduced in January 1918.

Barnett concludes that the major shift in food policy in mid-1917 succeeded just because it interacted with consumer protest. 'At the opening of the war ... the voice of the consuming public did not form part of the decision making process. ... [Later] compulsory price controls and rationing came about in direct response to popular demand and were effective because that demand existed ... and representatives of [organized] labour and of the "consumer" [took part in the management] of food supply'. The 'sharing of both resources and sacrifices' via rationing accounted for 'much of the success and popularity of Britain's domestic food policies'.[95] In most ways then, Britain's wartime politics of provisions – in geography, policy and outcome – were the obverse of Germany's.

The biggest casualty of World War I's provision politics was, of course, Russia. Food supplies played a critical role in the February revolution.[96] By 1917, the tsarist regime had lost its legitimacy in defeat after defeat on the battlefield, and food riots and strikes over the cost of living grew more intense. For weeks, St Petersburg's women froze in queues for necessities, bitterly complaining of traders' stealing, favouritism to rich families and police collusion with 'speculators'. As in Berlin, the Moscow police chief declared that the queues acted like 'tens of thousands of revolutionary proclamations'.[97] In the climactic crisis, the giant Putilov works lockout merged with hunger demonstrations and International Women's Day to pack the streets of Petrograd with crowds carrying red banners proclaiming 'Bread', 'Peace', and 'Down with the Autocracy'.[98] It was hard for soldiers to suppress them, and when the tsar ordered an army crackdown, the regime collapsed.

So, total war strained government capacities and needs to the point at which the combination of food scarcity and outrage packed a powerful political punch. Total war converted people's necessities to governments' necessity. How governments and peoples negotiated their way through the crises of total war had telling impacts on its outcome. Some regimes managed to provision the people and survived. But a failed provision politics could and did combine with other factors to bring not only defeat but revolution.

Conclusion

The 'free' market is not a natural phenomenon but a historical construction based on political choices and conflicts. 'Economic' markets have thus been embedded in 'political markets' consisting of transactions between common people needing food and both local and national governors that need their acquiescence. The politics of food was unique and surprising because it mobilised strong community pressure that enabled normally powerless people to get their needs met. It was thus more successful than any other form of popular politics. The popular force exerted by common people often had a surprisingly critical role in shaping their government's course. In the early modern West, 'free' markets came ultimately to be protected from popular interference, 'at the point of a bayonet'. That was hardly the 'destiny' of a universal evolution, but rather the result of converging choices in particular material and ideological contexts: in a Britain undergoing the many-faceted changes of urbanization and industrialization, in a France lurching from absolute monarchy through revolution and dictatorship, by contrast with an unrelieved Irish Famine, the all-out ordeal of total war and many other crises in world history.[99] Unlike other freedoms, a 'free' market is not an individual freedom, but a complex social construct. Before the 'free' market economies that neoclassical economics takes for granted, there was a 'law of necessity'. In many contexts, in emergencies, human rights to survive took precedence over property (and profit) rights. The conflict between the two is so elemental that a 'moral economy' has been found in every society from the time of the ancient Greeks.[100] And yet that 'law of necessity', that right to subsist, was not universal – its morality only had traction when and where ruler and ruled inhabited the same moral universe, when rulers could be held accountable – by norms embedded in Christian doctrine, in common law or in a Chinese 'mandate of heaven', and by the power that could be generated by the people, in protest and/or in the state's needs for soldiers and subjects. At times when authorities were not yet proof against a servile uprising, notably during wars, the most elemental level of human service must be compensated by subsistence.[101] No guarantee against starvation, no obedience; that is, no food, no peace. Thus the political slogan of countless English food rioters, 'We'd rather be hanged than starved'. In England, the free market was delivered by armed guards, and the rise and fall of provision politics (the interaction of food riots, repression and relief) was a historical process, not a prefigured destination. As I write these lines, food riots are again in the headlines, now triggered by the economics of energy in a global economy. That is not so surprising, but this time the riots appear to have spurred two global institutions, the United Nations and the World Bank, to address the crisis systemically. Action remains uncertain, but it appears the politics of provisions have at last arrived on the global stage.

Notes

1. C.A. Bouton, 'Les mouvements de subsistance et le probléme de l'économie morale sous l'ancien regime et la revolution', *Annales historique de la Révolution française*, 119 (2000), p. 74.
2. J. Becker, *Hungry Ghosts: Mao's Secret Famine* (New York, 1996), pp. 130–65.
3. J. Bohstedt, 'The Moral Economy and the Discipline of Historical Context', *Journal of Social History*, 26 (1992), pp. 265–84; R.B. Outhwaite, *Dearth, Public Policy and Social Disturbance in England, 1550–1800* (Basingstoke, 1991), p. 9.
4. A. Everitt, 'The Marketing of Agricultural Produce', in *The Agrarian History of England and Wales*, ed. J. Thirsk (Cambridge, 1967–85), IV: pp. 466, 586–88; E.A. Wrigley, 'Urban Growth and Agricultural Change: England and the Continent in the Early Modern Period', *Journal of Interdisciplinary History*, 15 (1985), pp. 123–68.
5. J. Thirsk, 'Agricultural Policy: Public Debate and Legislation', in *The Agrarian History of England and Wales*, V: p. 298, and Everitt, 'The Marketing of Agricultural Produce', p. 582.
6. The 'chief regulations' in the Books of Orders are summarized in N.S.B. Gras, *The Evolution of the English Corn Market: From the Twelfth to the Eighteenth Century* (Cambridge, MA, 1926), pp. 236–40.
7. For earlier scattered riots, see B. Sharp, 'The Food Riots of 1347 and the Medieval Moral Economy', in *Moral Economy and Popular Protest: Crowds, Conflict and Authority*, ed. A. Randall and A. Charlesworth (Basingstoke, 2000), pp. 33–54; and A. Charlesworth (ed.), *An Atlas of Rural Protest in Britain 1548–1900* (London, 1983), pp. 63–83. Riots of all sorts are examined in R.B. Manning, *Village Revolts: Social Protest and Popular Disturbances in England, 1509–1640* (New York, 1988).
8. B. Sharp, *In Contempt of All Authority: Rural Artisans and Riot in the West of England, 1586–1660* (Berkeley, 1980), pp. 3–5, 7, 13.
9. Ibid., p. 31.

10. J. Bohstedt, *The Politics of Provisions: Food Riots, Moral Economy, and Market Transition in England, c. 1550–1850* (Aldershot, 2010).

11. P. Slack, *From Reformation to Improvement: Public Welfare in Early Modern England* (New York, 1999); and Gras, *The Evolution of the English Corn Market*, pp. 82–91.

12. Everitt, 'The Marketing of Agricultural Produce', p. 466.

13. J. Walter, 'Subsistence Strategies, Social Economy, and the Politics of Subsistence in Early Modern England', in *Just a Sack of Potatoes? Crisis Experiences in European Societies, Past and Present*, ed. A. Häkkinen (Helsinki, 1992), p. 55; Outhwaite, *Dearth, Public Policy and Social Disturbance in England*, p. 32.

14. Ibid., p. 37.

15. Food and Agriculture Organization of the United Nations, *The Right to Food in Theory and Practice* (Rome, 1998), p. 47.

16. E.P. Thompson, 'The Moral Economy of the English Crowd in the Eighteenth Century', *Past and Present*, 50 (1971), pp. 76–136; Bohstedt, *The Politics of Provisions*.

17. Thompson, 'The Moral Economy of the English Crowd in the Eighteenth Century', pp. 79, 88; E.P. Thompson, 'The Moral Economy Reviewed', in his *Customs in Common* (London, 1991), p. 261.

18. J. Bohstedt, *Riots and Community Politics in England and Wales 1790–1810* (Cambridge, MA, 1983), pp. 202–3.

19. Ibid., pp. 37–40.

20. See Walter, 'Subsistence Strategies, Social Economy, and the Politics of Subsistence in Early Modern England'; A. Kussmaul, *Servants in Husbandry in Early Modern England* (Cambridge, 1981), pp. 49–51; and Steve Hindle, *On the Parish? The Micro-Politics of Poor Relief in Rural England c. 1550–1750* (Oxford, 2004).

21. Thompson, 'The Moral Economy of the English Crowd in the Eighteenth Century', p. 119.

22. J. Bohstedt, 'The Waning of the Moral Economy: Military Force and the Politics of Provisions 1740–1820', *Consortium on Revolutionary Europe: Selected Papers* (1999), pp. 143–52.

23. Bohstedt, *Riots and Community Politics in England and Wales*, chapter 5.

24. Bouton, 'Les mouvements de subsistance et le probléme de l'économie morale sous l'ancien regime et la revolution', p. 75.

25. Ibid., pp. 82, 90; R. Price, *The Modernization of Rural France: Communications Networks and Agricultural Market Structures in Nineteenth-Century France* (London, 1983), pp. 126–83, especially figures 5 and 6.

26. Bouton, 'Les mouvements de subsistance et le probléme de l'économie morale sous l'ancien regime et la revolution', p. 78. In England, in the period 1660–1750, comparable with Bouton's, 70 of 126 food riots were blockages. See Bohstedt, *The Politics of Provisions*.

27. Bouton, 'Les mouvements de subsistance et le probléme de l'économie morale sous l'ancien regime et la revolution', p. 78, citing W. Beik, *Urban Protest in Seventeenth-Century France: The Culture of Retribution* (Cambridge, 1997).

28. Bouton, 'Les mouvements de subsistance et le probléme de l'économie morale sous l'ancien regime et la revolution', p. 72, n. 3; Bohstedt, *The Politics of Provisions*.

29. S.L. Kaplan, 'Provisioning Paris, the Crisis of 1738–1741', in *Edo and Paris: Urban Life and the State in the Early Modern Era*, ed. J.L. McClain, J.M. Merriman and U. Kaoru (Ithaca, 1994), p. 175.

30. Ibid., pp. 176–77.

31. C. Bouton, *The Flour War: Gender, Class, and Community in Late Ancien Régime French Society* (University Park, 1993), pp. 255–56.

32. S.L. Kaplan, 'The Paris Bread Riot of 1725', *French Historical Studies*, 14 (1985), pp. 33–34.
33. Kaplan, 'Provisioning Paris', pp. 53–60.
34. S.L. Kaplan, 'Lean Years, Fat Years: The "Community" Granary System and the Search for Abundance in Eighteenth-Century Paris', *French Historical Studies*, 10 (1977), p. 204.
35. Kaplan, 'Provisioning Paris', p. 188.
36. Kaplan, 'Lean Years, Fat Years', pp. 197–230. For the small granary established at Corbeil on the Seine in 1760, see S.L. Kaplan, *Bread, Politics and Political Economy in the Reign of Louis XV* (The Hague, 1976), chapters 8 and 15.
37. Kaplan, 'Lean Years, Fat Years', pp. 209–10.
38. R. Wells, *Wretched Faces; Famine in Wartime England, 1793–1801* (New York, 1988), pp. 184–91.
39. O. Hufton, 'Social Conflict and the Grain Supply in Eighteenth Century France', *Journal of Interdisciplinary History*, 14 (1983), p. 305.
40. Bouton, 'Les mouvements de subsistance et le probléme de l'économie morale sous l'ancien regime et la revolution'', pp. 76–77.
41. C. Tilly, 'Food Supply and Public Order in Modern Europe', in *The Formation of National States in Europe*, ed. C. Tilly (Princeton, 1975), pp. 380–455.
42. Bouton, 'Les mouvements de subsistance et le probléme de l'économie morale sous l'ancien regime et la revolution', p. 82.
43. Ibid., p. 85, quoting Florence Gauthier, 'Robespierre, critique de l'économie tyrannique et théoricien de l'économie politique populaire', in *Robespierre: de la nation artésiene á la République et aux nations: Actes du colloque d'Arras, 1–3 avril 1993* (Lille, 1994), p. 237.
44. J.P. Gross, *Fair Shares For All: Jacobin Egalitarianism in Practice* (Cambridge, 1997), p. 205.
45. R. Cobb, *The People's Armies: The Armées Révolutionnaires: Instrument of the Terror in the Departments April 1793 to Floréal Year II* (New Haven, 1987).
46. R. Cobb, *The Police and the People: French Popular Protest 1789–1820* (Oxford, 1970), p. 116.
47. R. Price, *The Modernization of Rural France: Communications Networks and Agricultural Market Structures in Nineteenth-Century France* (London, 1983), pp. 126–83, especially figures 5 and 6.
48. Judith A. Miller, *Mastering the Market: The State and the Grain Trade in Northern France, 1700–1860* (Cambridge, 1999), pp. 295–300.
49. Bouton, 'Les mouvements de subsistance et le probléme de l'économie morale sous l'ancien regime et la revolution', p. 79.
50. Ibid.
51. T. Eagleton, 'Afterword: Ireland and Colonialism', in *Was Ireland a Colony? Economics, Politics and Culture in Nineteenth-Century Ireland*, ed. T. McDonough (Dublin, 2005), p. 330.
52. Thompson, 'The Moral Economy Reviewed', p. 296.
53. C. Ó Gráda, *Ireland: A New Economic History 1780–1939* (Oxford, 1994), pp. 213, 308.
54. C. Kinealy, *This Great Calamity: The Irish Famine 1845–52* (Boulder, 1995), pp. 51–52.
55. J.K. Lumsden, 'Emerging from the Shadow of Death: The Relief Efforts and Consolidating Identity of the Irish Middle Classes during the Great Famine, 1845–1851' (MA thesis, University of Tennessee-Knoxville, 2008).

56. J. Kelly, 'Harvests and Hardship: Famine and Scarcity in the late 1720s', *Studia Hibernica*, 26 (1991–92), pp. 65–105; D. Dickson, *Arctic Ireland* (Belfast, 1997); E. Magennis, 'In Search of the "Moral Economy": Food Scarcity in 1756–57 and the Crowd', in *Crowds in Ireland, c. 1720–1920*, ed. P. Jupp and E. Magennis (Basingstoke, 2000), pp. 189–211; J. Kelly, 'Scarcity and Poor Relief in Eighteenth-Century Ireland: The Subsistence Crisis of 1782–84', *Irish Historical Studies*, 33 (1992), pp. 38–62; R. Wells, 'The Irish Famine of 1799–1801: Market Culture, Moral Economy and Social Protest', in *Markets, Market Culture and Popular Protest in Eighteenth-Century Britain and Ireland*, ed. A. Randall and A. Charlesworth (Liverpool, 1996), pp. 163–93. Of course, the eastern urban concentration may be a function of reportage, and the shortage of local studies in many counties, that will be revised by further research such as Eiríksson's (below).

57. Sources in note 56.

58. These paragraphs are based on Christine Kinealy, *The Great Irish Famine: Impact, Ideology and Rebellion* (Basingstoke, 2002), pp. 123–30; and Andrés Eiríksson, 'Food Supply and Food Riots', in *Famine 150: Commemorative Lecture Series*, ed. C. Ó Gráda (Dublin, 1997), pp. 67–91.

59. Ibid., pp. 72–75.

60. Ibid., p. 83.

61. Ibid., p. 84.

62. Ibid., p. 86

63. P. Gray, 'Ideology and the Famine', in *The Great Irish Famine*, ed. Cathal Poirteir (Cork, 1995), p. 91; P. Gray, *Famine, Land, and Politics: British Government and Irish Society, 1843–1850* (Dublin, 1999).

64. Gray, 'Ideology and the Famine', p. 93.

65. Lord Clarendon, quoted in Gray, 'Ideology and the Famine', p. 102.

66. Gray, 'Ideology and the Famine', p. 103.

67. For further comparisons, see P. Gray, 'Famine Relief Policy in Comparative Perspective: Ireland, Scotland, and Northwestern Europe, 1845–1849', *Eire-Ireland*, 32 (1997), pp. 86–108; and E. Richards, 'The Last Scottish Food Riots [1847]', *Past & Present*, supplement 6 (1982), pp. 1–59.

68. J. Winter, 'Some Paradoxes of the First World War', in *The Upheaval of War: Family, Work, and Welfare in Europe, 1914–1918*, ed. Richard Wall and Jay Winter (Cambridge, 1988), pp. 11–12; M. Healy, *Vienna and the Fall of the Habsburg Empire: Total War and Everyday Life in World War I* (Cambridge, 2004), p. 12; A. Offer, *The First World War: An Agrarian Interpretation* (Oxford, 1989); B.J. Davis, *Home Fires Burning: Food, Politics, and Everyday Life in World War I Berlin* (Chapel Hill, 2000); H. Strachan, *The First World War* (London, 2003); I.F.W. Beckett, *The Great War, 1914–1918* (Harlow, 2001), pp. 265–72.

69. Ibid., p. 214.

70. Offer, *The First World War*.

71. M. Howard, 'World War One: The Crisis in European History – The Role of the Military Historian', *Journal of Military History*, 57 (1993), p. 130.

72. Offer, *The First World War*, pp. 326–28.

73. H.H. Herwig, 'Total Rhetoric, Limited War: Germany's U-Boat Campaign, 1917–18', in *Great War, Total War: Combat and Mobilization on the Western Front, 1914–1918*, ed. R. Chickering and S. Förster (Washington, 2000), p. 191.

74. Herwig, 'Total Rhetoric, Limited War', pp. 195–98, drawing in part on J. Winter, *The Great War and the British People* (London, 1986).

75. Herwig, 'Total Rhetoric, Limited War', pp. 200–201, 204.
76. Offer, *The First World War*, p. 53.
77. Davis, *Home Fires Burning*, p. 237.
78. Offer, *The First World War*, p. 66.
79. R. Chickering, *Imperial Germany and the Great War 1914–1918* (Cambridge, 1998), p. 9; and Offer, *The First World War*, pp. 218–21.
80. R. Chickering, *The Great War and Urban Life in Germany: Freiburg, 1914–1918* (Cambridge, 2007), p. 162; Offer, *The First World War*, p. 27. See also Gerald Feldman, *The Great Disorder: Politics, Economics and Society in the German Inflation, 1914–1924* (New York, 1993), p. 66. Jay Winter calls this 'one of the fundamental errors of the German war effort'. J.M. Winter, *The Experience of World War I* (New York, 1995), p. 178.
81. Davis, *Home Fires Burning*, pp. 70, 74–75.
82. Ibid., pp. 87–88.
83. Offer, *The First World War*, p. 28; Feldman, *The Great Disorder*, p. 63.
84. Chickering, *The Great War and Urban Life in Germany*, p. 142.
85. Offer, *The First World War*, p. 70.
86. Ibid., pp. 71, 76.
87. Healy, *Vienna and the Fall of the Habsburg Empire*, p. 4; Strachan, *The First World War*, pp. 287–99.
88. Offer, *The First World War*, p. 78; C.P. Vincent, *The Politics of Hunger: The Allied Blockade of Germany, 1915–1919* (Athens, 1985); Strachan, *The First World War*.
89. E. Ludendorff, *My War Memories, 1914–1918* (2 v., London, 1919), 1: pp. 349–55, quoted in M. Olson, *The Economics of the Wartime Shortage: A History of British Food Supplies in the Napoleonic War and in World Wars I and II* (Durham, 1963), p. 80; and Strachan, *The First World War*, p. 221.
90. L.M. Barnett, *British Food Policy during the First World War* (Boston, 1985), p. 213. This paragraph and the next follow Barnett, pp. xiii–xix.
91. Italy, having reluctantly entered the war on the Allied side, was then defeated at Caporetto in late 1916. By mid-1917, violent protest peaked, especially in Milan and Turin. Strachan, *The First World War*, p. 256.
92. Quoted in Herwig, 'Total Rhetoric, Limited War', p. 192.
93. B. Waites, *A Class Society at War, Britain, 1914–18* (New York, 1987).
94. J. Stevenson, 'More Light on World War One', *Historical Journal*, 33 (1990), p. 205.
95. Barnett, *British Food Policy during the First World War*, pp. xvii–xix.
96. J.L.H. Keep, *The Russian Revolution: A Study in Mass Mobilization* (London, 1976), p. 52; Orlando Figes, *A People's Tragedy: A History of the Russian Revolution* (New York, 1996).
97. Keep, *The Russian Revolution*, p. 52.
98. B.A. Engel, 'Not by Bread Alone: Subsistence Riots in Russia during World War I', *Journal of Modern History*, 69 (1997), pp. 696–721.
99. I hope to discuss these in a forthcoming article.
100. K. Polanyi, *The Great Transformation* (Boston, 1944–57); M. Adas, 'Moral Economy', in *Encyclopedia of Social History*, ed. P.N. Stearns (New York, 1994), pp. 513–14.
101. J.C. Scott, *The Moral Economy of the Peasant: Rebellion and Subsistence in Southeast Asia* (New Haven, 1976).

7
Nights of Fire: The Gordon Riots of 1780 and the Politics of War

Nicholas Rogers

The Gordon riots were the most dramatic of London's history, paralysing the forces of law and order for almost a week in early June 1780. Erupting at a time of imperial crisis and new reformist movements, the disturbances resonated with the resentments of war; they were the platform on which bitter political differences – about Catholics, about America, about the sovereignty of parliament – were played out. The riots also sorely tested the relationship between street politics and radical associations, prompting the question as to whether crowds and 'people' were interdependent or mutually exclusive; part of the same vector of popular remonstrance or wildly divergent. For these reasons, the riots were the most complex the eighteenth century had witnessed. They posed serious questions about the shape and future of popular politics in the decades to come.

The riots were ostensibly, and for many contemporaries and historians, emphatically about religion. Named after the Scottish aristocrat, Lord George Gordon, the president of the Protestant Association in England, the riots were protests against the refusal of parliament to repeal the Catholic Relief Act of 1778. In Scotland, where a similar act had been contemplated, the authorities had buckled to popular pressure. Hard lobbying by a wide range of social groups, from synods, borough corporations, right down to minor incorporated trades such as the Pollokshaws weavers and shoemakers from Preston Pans revealed that substantial portions of the Scottish political nation disliked the proposed concessions to Catholics. This mobilization of opinion, combined with attacks on Catholic chapels and residences in Edinburgh and other towns, compromised the attempt to replicate the 1778 act north of the border.[1] Gordon clearly hoped he could apply similar pressure in London, and as petitions deluged parliament calling for repeal, he mustered tens of thousands in St George's Fields, Southwark (some claimed 50,000) to march upon parliament to show that Protestants meant business.

The Catholic Relief Act was to all intents and purposes a modest measure. It simply removed some of the most punitive statutes against Catholics passed during the reign of William III. Under the new act, priests and schoolmasters were no longer subject to the threat of life imprisonment, and Catholics were no longer vulnerable to the designs of Protestant relatives upon their estates, provided they swore an act of allegiance to the crown. These concessions were justified on the grounds that persecuting loyal Catholics was manifestly unjust, especially with the decline of Jacobitism as a political force after the mid-century. Within the social elite and the more urbane sections of middling society, there was also a distaste for the kind of reward-mongering that the prosecution of Catholics had fuelled. The concessions were a response to the Catholic lobby, which solicited greater security for their brethren in return for contributions to the war effort. Although the Bishop of Peterborough warned that the act might precipitate 'alarms of imaginary danger', flames that the 'authority of the law' might find 'difficult to extinguish', the Act passed easily through both houses at the end of the spring 1778 session.[2]

The flames that burst around the Relief Act, however, were linked to other policies. In Scotland and England, the statute was seen as a disturbing sequel to the Quebec Act of 1774, one that commentators believed had aggravated the rebellion of the American colonies.[3] That earlier act was the culmination of years of agonising thought on what to do with the 65,000 Catholic *Canadiens* who inhabited the old colony of New France. The Acadian precedent of deportation was out of the question; the terms of capitulation upon the conquest of Quebec in 1760 and their subsequent endorsement in the Treaty of Paris of 1763 precluded that option. While ministers toyed with various plantation schemes to counteract the presence of the *habitants*, they eventually decided that the only sure way to ensure the loyalty of the Francophones was to recognize French civil law in non-criminal matters and to allow them to practice their religion. Contrary to popular belief, the Quebec Act of 1774 did not technically establish Catholicism as the religion of the frozen north. While recognizing that Catholicism would be the religion of the majority for some time, it offered opportunities for the growth of Protestantism and laid down safeguards that the government would control the hierarchy of the Catholic church and eliminate papal influences.[4] But the willingness of the government to set up a system of endowments for the Catholic clergy and allow them to take tithes from their co-religionists did represent a very significant shift of policy to a nation that virtually outlawed the Catholic church at home and had established strong constitutional precedents against a Catholic restoration.[5] To many Britons, the act compromised the nation's political heritage, violated the king's coronation oath to protect the Protestant faith and set a dangerous precedent. The fact that the act denied Quebec a popular assembly and extended its territories to the Ohio valley and Great Lakes confirmed, in the eyes of British radicals and many Americans, the authoritarian thrust of government policy. This was especially so given the timing of the bill, which occurred when the government was reasserting its authority over a rebellious Massachusetts. Although the timing of the bill was fortuitous,[6] the Quebec Act was viewed as part of the government's attempt to coerce the American colonists into submission and to subvert cherished political traditions of liberty. One London newspaper asked what the architects of the 1688 settlement would have felt about the Quebec Act? How would they have reacted to 'establishing the Roman Catholic Religion together with the tyrannical Laws of our Natural Enemies the French in a very capital and extensive Province of the British Empire'?[7] Passions ran so high on this question that when the king returned from parliament upon giving assent to the act, one witness reported: 'I saw nothing but contempt and indignation in every face; not even a hat pulled off, whilst my ears were burned with…the repeated cries of No French Government! No Popish King! Wilkes and Liberty!'[8]

Seen in the light of the Quebec Act, the Catholic Relief Act took on ominous overtones. At a time when the government was running into difficulties in the conduct of the American war, especially with the entry of France, Spain and the Netherlands on the colonists' side, the Relief Act seemed an untimely concession to Catholics, who might well sympathize with the Bourbons. In the light of Catholicism's older association with absolutism, it was also evidence of the government's hidden agenda to establish some sort of authoritarian rule in the face of mounting criticism of the war. Not all members of the opposition necessarily saw it quite this way. Many of their leaders were sympathetic to the quite limited concessions that the Relief Act offered, which fell well short of Catholic toleration let alone Catholic emancipation. Neither John Wilkes nor the radical Duke of Richmond, for example, protested against the Catholic Relief Act, believing in liberty of conscience. But both had severe reservations about the Quebec Act because it entrenched Catholicism as the dominant religion in Canada and denied Quebeckers the political liberties given to other colonies. In Richmond's eyes, and indeed in those of both Rockingham and Shelburne, who had both struggled with the problem of the Quebec religious settlement while in office, much of the animus against the Relief Act was derived from the 1774 initiative. Sympathetic to the Americans in their struggle against the ministry, they suggested that the repeal of the Quebec act could best placate both colonists and the members of the Protestant Association who campaigned for the repeal of the 1778 act.

Certainly there was an element of *schadenfreude* to the attitude of opposition politicians to the ministry's predicament in June 1780. Although they were ostensibly shocked by the violence of the mobs that crowded the passages to parliament on 2 June 1780, when Lord George Gordon presented his monster petition for repeal, they no doubt relished the embarrassment of the government that only a few weeks earlier thwarted their hopes for parliamentary reform. Certainly members of the opposition were quick to point out that just as the government had mismanaged the war, so now they were mismanaging the volatile situation that Lord George Gordon had created at the very doors of the parliament. Lord Shelburne, no enemy to the Catholic Relief Act, wondered why a government so vigilant about mass meetings for parliamentary reform two months earlier was so lethargic and diffident in dealing with the Protestant petition.[9] That diffidence stemmed, in part, from a growing paralysis of government. With the entry of the European powers into the war, the prospect of a rapid settlement of the American rebellion dwindled dramatically. Britain's vaunted supremacy of the seas was thrown into question; there was a growing fear that Britain's Atlantic empire would disintegrate, not only in the American colonies but also in the Caribbean; and in Ireland, amidst the sabre-rattling of 40,000 volunteers, there were demands for greater legislative autonomy and freer trade. For this state of affairs, which also disrupted British commerce and intensified recruitment into the armed forces, the blame was placed squarely on the government. In February 1779, the trial of the pro-American Admiral Keppel for failing to defeat the French off Ushant the previous summer revealed the parlous state of government support nationwide. In a court martial largely attributed to ministerial malevolence, Keppel's acquittal was celebrated in towns and villages up and down the country; his enemies at the admiralty were burnt in effigy, even in some government-dominated boroughs. In London, in particular, the mood of the populace was vociferously hostile to the men in power. The windows of the secretary at war's residence in Pall Mall were demolished; the admiralty was attacked, forcing Lord Sandwich and his mistress to abandon their apartments and mobs even attempted to break into Lord North's house in Downing Street. It took 500 troops to inhibit further demonstrations against the ministry in the vicinity of Whitehall, although the government had to tolerate the burning in effigy of Keppel's main opponent, Sir Hugh Palliser, in Southwark and the city.[10]

The jubilations in favour of Keppel registered a range of opinion about the American revolution, but they undoubtedly indicated a singular disenchantment with the ministry, not simply because of its seemingly vindictive attitude towards the admiral, but because of the magnitude of the crisis that confronted Britain. The government leader, Lord North, felt this keenly. After the news of Britain's first defeat on the American continent at Saratoga, North considered resignation and grew rather paranoid about plots to replace him at the helm. In November, he confessed to Charles Jenkinson that the fear of abandonment 'preyed on his mind so much as rendered him capable of anything, he had no Decision, he could attend to no business'.[11] North managed to fend off the challenge of Henry Grattan and company in Ireland by liberalising the rules of trade to the colonies and permitting the exportation of wool and woolen manufactures, but in March 1780, he was still confronted by petitions from 18 Irish counties for the repeal of Poynings law.[12] He also faced growing demands for parliamentary reform from the Associated Counties and Towns, including Westminster, the seat of parliament, where 8,000 inhabitants met in early April 1780 to endorse a programme of shorter parliaments and 'more equal representation' and to campaign for an end to the war in America.[13] A few days later, Dunning passed his famous motion about the increasing influence of the crown, and North once again considered resigning at the end of the session.

This was the political space in which the Protestant Association was able to operate. The association had radical resonances. It adopted radical forms to press for the repeal of the Catholic Relief Act. It held monthly general meetings, corresponded with other local associations, distributed handbills, advocated instructions to MPs and embarked on a strategy of mass petitioning. Although the association pronounced that it was 'not formed to promote the views of party, or to embarrass the measures of government at this important crisis' it did prey upon popular anxieties. Whereas the government had passed the Relief Act partially to bolster Catholic loyalty at a time when France entered the war, the Protestant Association questioned the sagacity of this policy, focusing upon the perfidy of both French and Catholics.[14] From this perspective, repeal was a manifestly loyal but nonpartisan measure, safeguarding British liberties from the Catholic threat at an important crisis in national and imperial politics. This explains why the association was able to attract figures across the political spectrum: from ministerialists, such as the London alderman Evan Pugh, to moderate opposition MPs like Charles Barrow of Gloucester, to city radicals like Frederick Bull. In effect, the Protestant Association was a protean, populist movement, stridently evangelical in tone, which cut across orthodox political alignments.

At the same time, the Protestant Association sailed close to the radical wind. Various supporters linked the Relief Act with the Quebec Act and with ministerial incursions upon British liberty in America. The Reverend Dr Bromley, for example, minister of the Fitzroy chapel and a Middlesex associator, called 'the Quebec bill a most wicked and pernicious piece of business' and thought the Relief Act was 'an arrow shot from the same quiver'.[15] Others agreed. 'The seas of Protestant blood, wantonly shed in this ruinous and calamitous war', wrote one, 'to strongly prove that the subversion of civil and religious liberty is the grand point where all operations centre'.[16] The campaign for repeal was thus projected as part of a larger struggle against ministerial oppression. This explains why efforts were made to annex the repeal of the Catholic Relief Act to the political agenda of the Middlesex Association in April 1780.[17] The attempt was thwarted. In view of the violent Scottish resistance to the Relief Act, some feared that Lord George Gordon's maverick manoeuvres might throw all popular associations into disrepute at a critical moment in the campaign for parliamentary reform. Such fears were not altogether unfounded.

Although Lord George Gordon was ultimately acquitted of high treason for fomenting the riots of June 1780, there is little doubt that he intended to apply as much popular pressure as he could to the campaign for repeal. One informant alleged that Gordon had declared that 'a petition without a rising as they had in Scotland would be of no service to the good cause'.[18] Whether or not Gordon actually said this, the decision to call a mass meeting on 2 June 1780 was controversial; it was only under the threat of Gordon's resignation that the motion passed. As a result, some 50,000 members of the Protestant Association mustered in St George's Fields in their respective divisions and marched to Westminster to present their monster petition.[19] Estimates vary, but probably around 17,000 remained to hear the outcome. The march on parliament was an audacious step. There was a Caroline statute against tumultuous petitioning, and the leading lights of the Protestant Association knew their plan was illegal. Earlier petitions had been presented by delegates, not by such overwhelming numbers. The numbers certainly overwhelmed the Westminster justices, who with 76 constables were quite unable to control the crowd. Before the commons, several MPs were forced publicly to swear that they would repeal the act. In the approaches to the upper house, their lordships were jostled, heckled and assailed with the cry of 'No Popery'. Lord Mansfield, who had denounced informers of Catholics publicly in the courts, had the panels and windows of his carriage smashed in; Lord Stormont, the secretary of state for the Southern Division was held hostage by the mob for half an hour, during which time he was pelted with mud and said to suffer 'the most insolent liberties'.[20] The commons' lobby became so turbulent that Lord George Gordon was invited to placate the crowd and urge it to disperse. Instead, he highlighted those MPs in opposition to repeal and reiterated his belief that only repeal would prevent violence. 'Lord North calls you a mob', he is said to have told the people in the lobby.[21] Faced with an intransigent commons, the message was clear. It only took a little prompting to generate plans for retribution. As a painter called Colin McCrea deposed, the crowd asked 'a tall man who appeared to be a leader what they were to do if they did not get the act repealed, whereupon he told them they would go to Sir George Savile's as he was the man who brought in the Popish bill, and the general cry among them was they would have redress, or else'.[22]

The mob did not immediately target the residence of Sir George Savile, but it quickly turned its attention to some of the more visible places of Catholic worship, remembering that it was the attack on Catholic chapels that had clinched the Scottish repeal campaign. On the first evening, the chapel of the Sardinian ambassador in Lincoln's Inn Fields was set alight; that of the Count Haslang, the Bavarian ambassador, was gutted. Crowds also attacked a chapel in Ropemakers' Alley, Moorfields, but the city marshal managed to intervene before it was destroyed.[23] The following day, however, the rioters returned to sack the chapel, ignoring the Lord Mayor and several aldermen who had brought in a file of soldiers from the tower. The mayor justified his refusal to read the Riot Act on the grounds that there were innocent women and children in the crowd, but the truth was he feared popular retribution. The houses of prominent Catholics were also threatened, including those of Bishop Chaloner, Lord Petre and William Mawhood, a wealthy woolen draper and personal friend of the Catholic bishop. But few private houses were in fact touched at this stage of the riots despite the alehouse gossip that they would be.[24] The principal targets remained chapels, including that of the Portuguese ambassador in South Audley Street. Aside from Count Haslang, whose residence joined the chapel, the only houses that were attacked by the mob were those of Sir George Savile in Leicester Fields, which was partially ransacked on 5 June before troops intervened, and those of two Westminster tradesmen, Sampson Rainsforth and Stephen Mabberley. They were responsible for the arrest and committal of fourteen rioters apprehended at the Sardinian chapel, and gave testimony against them at Bow Street. Their names were also noted in the newspapers, which increased their vulnerability. Rainsforth, a former high constable and tallow chandler, was in fact a member of the Protestant Association, but that did not stop a crowd of 5,000 people pulling down his house in Clare market and setting fire to his candles and stocks of fat.[25] Seven bonfires burned in the market to accommodate his effects.

In the early days of the disturbances, the crowd scarcely deviated from the original cue of the Protestant Association. To underscore its solidarity with Gordon, it sported the blue cockades of the association and paraded the Catholic relics of the Moorfields chapel before Gordon's house in Welbeck Street, burning them in the adjacent fields. Although some historians have suggested that the rioters were already inebriated and out of control, the activities of the crowd bespeak of calculated pressure upon parliament. People awaited the return of the commons on 6 June, when it was hoped the petitions against the Relief Act would seriously be considered. The commons, however, refused to bow to popular pressure. It deplored the intimidation, urged the crown to prosecute the rioters and promptly adjourned until 8 June. At this point, the riots escalated. After the crowd had dragged Lord George Gordon's chariot through the streets, it broadened its jurisdiction to include not only Catholics, but members of the political establishment. Lambeth Palace was threatened; so, too were the residences of the archbishops of Canterbury and York. Crowds also directed their anger to politicians known to be sympathetic to the act. These included members of the opposition such as Lord Rockingham, Edmund Burke and John Dunning, as well as Lord North and Lord Mansfield, the lord chief justice who had earlier discouraged the prosecution of Catholics and disparaged the efforts of constables such as William Payne to do so. The rage of the crowd was now directed towards the cosmopolitan hierarchy whose tolerant attitudes were subverting 'True Protestantism' and the necessary vigilance against Catholics. These included the king, who despite his hostility to Catholic emancipation, was now suspected of converting to Catholicism. 'No Popery. Down with it' exclaimed one handbill, 'George the 3rd is a Roman Catholick'. 'Dethrone him or else he will Massacre you all', suggested one paranoid handbill. To the 'True Protestant' who penned it, George III deserved to lose his head for abandoning his coronation oath to preserve the Protestant faith.[26]

If the anger of the crowd swung against the Anglican establishment, it also focused upon the law and its officers. In sheer defiance of the commons' resolution that the attorney general prosecute the rioters, crowds attacked magistrates who had examined and committed rioters to jail or had intervened to protect supporters of the Relief Act. Many had their houses pulled down; only those like Justice Charles Triquet, who pleaded with the crowds in Bloomsbury Square that 'he was as great an Enemy to Popery as they could be', had their houses spared.[27] Jails were also raided to frustrate the course of justice against 'True Protestants'. On the evening of 6 June, a crowd assembled before Newgate and demanded the release of the rioters who were confined there. Receiving no satisfaction from the keeper, Richard Akerman, the crowd broke in, released all prisoners and set fire to the building. From there, the assailants moved on to New Prison, Clerkenwell, where they again demanded freedom for the Gordon rioters. The keeper, Samuel Newport, told them there were none in his jail, but 'the Mob told him they were determined to take them out, and to break open all the gaols in London that night'.[28] Forcing open the gates, they released all but one murderer, whom they refused to set at large, being an 'improper object of their charity'.[29]

There were fears that other gaols where rioters were held would be attacked. The Lord Mayor actually released rioters from the Poultry Compter, one of the two city gaols under the control of the sheriffs, to prevent it being ransacked or burnt. That did not stop the rioters, who besieged both compters, Poultry and Wood Street, and also the Surrey Bridewell and King's Bench prison south of the river, where other rioters were being held. King's Bench prison was set alight, and so too was the other principal debtors' prison, the Fleet.[30] Indeed, on Wednesday 7 June, the riots clearly diverged from their original objectives and began to focus upon social grievances unrelated to Catholic relief. The attacks on the jails were not simply rescue operations; they connoted a long-standing contempt for the iniquities of the prison system, which was particularly hard on poor people who could not tip or bribe turnkeys and were vulnerable to their petty oppressions. Similarly, the destruction of sponging-houses, temporary lockups for debtors seeking to raise bail before their suit came to law, stemmed from the same kind of predicament. As Richard Holloway noted, a debtor often found himself 'marred in and surrounded by a set of wretches, whose daily bread depends on the misfortune of others'.[31] According to one account, no less than 20 sponging-houses were burnt down in the borough of Southwark on 8 June.

Rioters not only protested against the humiliations of poverty in prison and sponging-house, they also protested against war-time recruitment after a year in which the government had been quite ruthless in ignoring exemptions to impressments, and in which both army and naval recruiting parties had intruded deeply into the lives of poor people. Early in 1780, impressed men had killed an informer who had thwarted a mutiny aboard one of the Thameside tenders; there had also been an ugly affray between press gangs and seamen near the tower. In the aftermath of the riots, there was another mutiny aboard the tenders, with impressed men breaking open the hatches, confining the crew and officers in the hold and escaping ashore as the vessel made its way down the Thames to Sheerness.[32] Anger against recruitment spilled into the riots in the form of attacks upon crimping houses, pubs where landlords enmeshed seamen in debt and virtually sold them to the armed services.[33] Mob rage also turned on the tolls of Blackfriars Bridge, which the city had promised to remove in the 1770s but had retained in order to finance other projects. To small traders south of the river, they were a smoldering grievance, and the tollhouse was pulled down in the swathe of destruction that beset the prisons on 7 June.

Perhaps the most dramatic attack of Black Wednesday was upon the Bank of England. Certainly the *Remembrancer* thought so, claiming it was 'the most serious circumstance in the whole riot'.[34] Precisely why rioters chose this target is unclear: was it a symbol of war finance, a perfect target alongside the Pay and Excise Offices? Was it perceived as underpinning government policy? To what extent was the attack a product of misrule, for the parade before its gates was led by a man on a drayhorse, caparisoned with the fetters of Newgate? To what extent was it fuelled by purely mercenary motives? Speculation will no doubt continue on what prompted rioters to attack the hallowed walls of high finance, but to the many middling to rich inhabitants who were abandoning the city, this was a sign that anti-Catholic prejudice had given way to social anarchy. As the radical Duke of Richmond stated in parliament: 'Robbers, thieves, felons, and all the rabble which form part of the mob in great and populous cities, took an advantage of the large numbers of people who collected themselves upon that occasion, and under the pretext of religious reformation, committed the most horrid, criminal and daring outrages, not only against private property, but against the laws of their country'.[35] It is upon this kind of rhetoric that a degeneration thesis was built, one that saw 7 June as an emphatic turning point in the riots, when crowds deviated from the writ of the Protestant Association and, in increasing waves of intoxication, turned to arson, pillage and extortion.

Precisely how anarchic the riot became is difficult to determine. After the break-ins to the jails, contemporary accounts became quite alarmist, and sympathizers with the Protestant Association had a vested interest in distancing themselves from the disturbances. Looting undoubtedly took place. There are a handful of trials in the Old Bailey proceedings that illustrate this. Several street sellers were found with casks, wine and copper funnels from Langdale's brewery, which was broken into on 6 June, and witnesses testified that they had brought liquor home with them to their rooms.[36] Rioters seem also to have freely helped themselves to the clothes and effects of Lord Mansfield's residence in Bloomsbury Square. One servant, Laetitia Hall, who stole petticoats, an apron and a portrait, boasted 'she had loaded herself well'.[37] Chris Conner's pub, the Red Lion, in Black Lyon Yard, Whitechapel, was also sacked; Mary Stratton, who lodged across the street, came away with blankets, curtains, a silk cloak and a couple of aprons, all of which she hoped to pawn.[38] Incidents of looting were probably underrepresented in the legal record; the crown prosecution was more successful indicting people under the Riot Act than it was for stolen goods, which were sometimes left with innocent neighbours for safekeeping.[39] Even so, in view of the dimensions of this riot, which was seriously under-policed in the first five days, the looting was probably not substantial.

Contemporaries were closer to the mark in emphasising the amount of drinking that accompanied the riots. Quite apart from Langdale's distillery in Holborn, which became the scene of a drunken frolic as the clerk there attempted to placate the crowd with generous libations of gin, there was plenty of drink available. Pulling down houses was hard work. It took a crowd anything from one to four hours to pull off the tiles from the roof, rip out the windows, wainscoting and floorboards, and throw out the furniture, bedding and so on. The captains of the wrecking crews frequently requested beer to help the men along.[40] At the destruction of one pub in Southwark, a justice testified that he saw Oliver Johnson give 'liquor to the populace' and drink a lot himself. 'He leaned his head against the pump', the justice recalled, 'and puked a great deal: it came out of his mouth like water, half a pint, I suppose, or more'.[41] Riots were often conducted in a revelrous mode, and we should not exaggerate the sobriety and respectability of the rioters, as George Rudé was sometimes inclined to do. Francis Place recalled 'the lower order of people stark mad with liquor, huzzaing and parading with flags'. Place was not always a dispassionate witness of the drinking habits of plebeian Londoners, but some of the trials reveal men 'fuddled' with drink and flushed with adrenalin from destroying Catholic chapels and houses. One apprentice confessed to his master of the 'fine fun' he had been having pulling down the chapel of the Sardinian ambassador; another reveled at the memory of making 'no less than six fires'.[42]

This evidence does not imply that the riots lost all direction. For much of the second week in June, they stayed on course. When the crowd turned its attention to Catholic houses, which it did increasingly after 6 June, it did so with a strong sense of ritual and legitimacy. Crowds sometimes rang bells upon arrival. Following the statutory precedent of 1606, the local captains called for the Book of Common Prayer or a Protestant bible, and searched houses for Catholic books, rosaries or crucifixes.[43] Some care was taken to ensure that the resident was telling the truth about his or her religious allegiance. When Charles Lee learned that a crowd was coming to sack his house in Golden Lane, he displayed blue ribbons, the insignia of the Protestant Association and showed people his bible. 'I went into the street and held it up', he testified, 'and said, This is my religion; here is no Popery; for God's sake do not pull the house down; they made a ring and swore me to my religion'.[44] At the same time, crowds were alert to the possibility of malicious accusations by spiteful neighbours. For example, Elizabeth Curry of East Bermondsey, whose house was next door to a chapel and drew attention to herself by removing some of her effects, pacified the crowd by kissing the Book of Common Prayer. Even so, two of her neighbours claimed she had a crucifix hidden under the stairs, but the crowd dismissed their complaints and threw them out of Curry's house on the grounds that they were malevolent busybodies.[45]

In carrying out these procedures, crowds assumed the place of authority. In their eyes, they did what the Anglican establishment should have done; that is, immobilize the Catholic foe in their midst. These extra-legal forms of action were quite discriminatory. As the crown prosecutors themselves admitted, they were directed at Catholics, or those directly involved in upholding the Catholic Relief Act, or in frustrating resistance to it.[46] But if the riot was overtly anti-Catholic, did it have any clear social overtones? Was George Rudé correct in claiming that 'behind the slogan of "No Popery" and the other outward forms of religious fanaticism there lay a deeper social purpose: a groping desire to settle accounts with the rich, if only for a day, and to achieve some kind of rough justice'.[47] Could the Gordon riots be termed a social as well as a politico-religious protest? Rudé's arguments on this score require quali-fication, particularly with respect to his claim that there was 'a distinct class bias in the direction of the attack made by the rioters on the Roman Catholic community'.[48] It is true that the geographical incidence of destruction was weighted towards the wealthier areas rather than the parishes and districts in which the majority of Catholic workers lived. Part of the reason for this was that some prominent Irish plebeians, the coal-heavers of the East End and the chairman of St James and Covent Garden, threatened reprisals upon dissenting meetings houses if the houses in their area were touched, a threat that the government, at least, took seriously.[49] This may well explain why the riots in the East End declined somewhat after the initial attack upon chapels and schools in Virginia Lane and Nightingale Street. Another factor influencing the geography of riot was the disposition of military forces, whether regulars or volunteers. Some ambassadorial chapels were saved from the wrath of the crowd because horse guards were quickly moved in after the initial reprisals elsewhere.[50] St James Piccadilly had a large Catholic population, but it was too close to the Westminster barracks and the Horse Guards for comfort. On the other hand, Southwark was vulnerable until the South Hampshire regiment arrived from Lambeth, where it was stationed to guard the palace and until a hastily formed volunteer association geared up for action.[51] The area around Holborn and the City of London had accessible targets as well, partly because of its jurisdictional complexities and partly because the forces of law and order were either overextended, defunct or sympathetic to the aims of the Protestant Association. As one marshal told Thomas Gates, 'he would not come to protest any such Popish rascals' because he had sworn the oaths of allegiance, adjuration and supremacy upon taking office.[52]

All these factors influenced the geography of pillage. Over 60 percent of the houses or chapels destroyed in the Gordon riots were situated in Clerkenwell, Holborn and the city.[53] Relatively few, only 7 percent, came from Westminster, which was always well guarded throughout the riot, a matter that gave rise to some complaints about the discriminatory use of troops to guard the richer areas where MPs and the social elite tended to live. Nearly 16 percent of the destruction occurred south of the river, in Southwark, Bermondsey and Rotherhithe, and 22 percent in the East End, with the concentration in Spitalfields and Bethnal Green rather than the riverside parishes frequented by the coal-heavers. Most of the victims of the crowd's anger lived in middling property or better, although they were not necessarily well-off. Over half, some 58 percent, lived in houses rated between £10–29 per annum, and less than a quarter in more substantial residences rated at £40 or over. This meant they did not live in houses that were more prepossessing than a representative group of London liverymen, although it meant that they were indisputably richer than the rioters themselves. What is striking about the victims of the riots is not their wealth so much as their place in the Catholic community. Rioters attacked the houses of gentlemen and tradesmen who were likely to give financial support to the foundation of new chapels and schools, a troubling development to opponents of the Relief Act. They destroyed large distilleries such as Thomas Langdale's in Holborn because it was thought to harbour a chapel. Alehouses were also favourite targets of the crowd because they were centres of sociability and of religion. It was not unusual in the 1780s for alehouses to rent rooms for religious meetings. In other words, what is crucial about the victims is the role they played in servicing the Catholic community. Over a quarter were involved in the drink trade, principally as publicans.[54] A further quarter were food retailers, dealers or pawnbrokers. Five of the 124 victims, who were compensated for the destruction of their property or property they rented, were schoolmasters. One was a newsman. In other words, it was not the gentility or wealth of the victims that is striking, especially if one eliminates the parliamentary supporters of the Relief Act and the justices, but their intermediary status within the Catholic community as sources of information, sociability and credit.

These figures bolster the impression that the main aim of the rioters was to immobilize the Catholic community in a continuing dialogue with parliament. Religion not class was the central preoccupation of the rioters. Even so, as the riots progressed, they moved to other targets, culminating in widespread attacks or threats upon prisons and government institutions such as the Excise, Customs and Navy Pay Offices, upon the Inns of Court and the three great monied companies, the Bank, the South Sea and the East India Company, and even upon some private banks.[55] Some of these attacks were directed at specific people. The attack on the Temple, for example, was directed at its master, the Bishop of Lincoln, who was confused with the Bishop of Peterborough, the most outspoken supporter of the Relief Act; that upon Lincoln's Inn was fired by a desire to destroy the chambers of John Dunning, another supporter of the bill.[56] Even so, the attacks upon what rioters saw as a perfidious establishment of cosmopolitan lawyers, politicians and bankers had a very definite anti-establishment flavour. This was accompanied by intimations of social levelling. 'Protestant or not', the shipwright William Heyter is said to have declared, 'no gentleman need be possessed of more than £1,000 a year, that is money enough for every gentleman to live on'. Such comments were unusual, as the justice's comments on this case revealed, and indeed, there were some very real doubts whether Heyter actually voiced them.[57] Even so, rioters did reap the advantages of their superiority in the streets by extorting festive gratuities from richer people with a momentary contempt for rank. 'Oh God bless this gentleman', mocked rioters to an apothecary who had been forced to concede half a crown, 'he is always generous'. Others dispensed with such civilities. 'Damn your eyes and limbs', exclaimed discharged sailor William Brown to a well-to-do cheesemonger in Bishopsgate; 'put a shilling in my hat, or by God I have a party that can destroy your house presently'.[58] Not surprisingly, in the heady atmosphere of the riot, the houses of a few wealthy tradesmen were threatened, whatever their religion. Self-styled 'Lord' James Taylor brazenly stole a watch from a shop declaring to the proprietor 'there was no Law now, and that it was in his power to bring a thousand people to pull his House down, and that he did not doubt but he had good liquor in his cellar'.[59] Similarly, George Pettit, a private in Sir John Wrottesley's company of guards who found himself caught up in the rush of the crowd, swore there was now 'no King, no Government, every man for himself'.[60] In this topsy-turvy world of what Elias Canetti would call 'reversal crowds', rioters sought rough justice and some release from the hierarchies of rank. Yet there was nothing that quite resembled a jacquerie, a ritual pillaging of the privileged. Perhaps this was because troops dramatically intervened when the riots began to spiral into more ominous forms of social upheaval. Aside from the magistrates and politicians, the vast majority of the gentlemen, merchants and manufacturers whose houses were actually attacked were Catholic. One exception was Henry Thrale, the Southwark brewer, whose manager pacified the mob with £50 worth of meat and drink until troops arrived to keep rioters at bay.[61]

In the panic and confusion of the riots, rumours circulated as to whom perpetrated them. Although the evidence suggests that the crowds operated within well-established conventions of popular politics and retained some autonomy from the Protestant Association, there was a welter of speculation about the real authors of the riot. Many predictably blamed the Protestant Association, largely because of Gordon's flamboyant role and because crowds continued to cheer the president when he appeared during the disturbances and wore the blue cockades of his organization. Yet, as Thomas Erskine stressed in Lord George Gordon's trial, no member of the association was criminally implicated in the riots from start to finish. Various individuals believed Americans fomented the riot. Those Yankees in London with plausible affiliations to the continent, to Gordon or with revolutionary activists were closely watched. One spy pinpointed the auctioneer John Greenwood, whose rooms were sometimes used for the meetings of the Protestant Association. The same informer was also troubled by the presence of one William Bailston in the metropolis, purportedly one of the leaders of the Boston Tea Party, who was believed to be in contact with Benjamin Franklin in France and later visited Lord George Gordon in the tower.[62] Mr Justice Daines Barrington even believed that the most active rioters 'were lads well trained by some of Dr Franklin's people...in the diabolical practice of setting buildings on fire, and abetted by French money'.[63] These rumours may be discounted as hard evidence of conspiracy, but they are indicative of the degree to which the American war touched interpretations of the riot.

In fact, the Gordon riots were one of the sites on which the vituperative politics of war were played out. From the very beginning, the pro-American 'patriots' in Britain were quick to tarnish the ministry with failing in its foremost task, the preservation of property and order. One writer in John Almon's newspaper, the *London Courant*, argued that the riots were the product of a political malaise brought on by bad government. He attributed this to the rejection of the 'civil petitions of the people', the continuation of the American war and the consequent decay in trade and heavier taxes, all of which made people more desperate.[64] Many in the opposition, ever suspicious of the authoritarian thrust of the North ministry since the Quebec and Coercive Acts, quickly accused the government of letting the riots get out of hand for its own nefarious purposes.

This seemed to be confirmed by the rapid utilization of armed force on Black Wednesday after five days of relative inactivity. Whereas troops had simply guarded known targets and were not deployed to disperse mobs without magisterial direction, on 7 June they were informed they could by-pass the magistrates and suppress disorder in a civilian capacity. In effect, the commander in chief of the army, Lord Amherst, took almost complete control of the repressive machinery of the state, a state of affairs that radicals thought little more than martial law. On the London Common Council, where anti-ministerialists mustered in force, a motion was passed commending Justice Sir Henry Gould for his strenuous opposition to army rule in Privy Council.[65] It was only because of his reservations, claimed the *London Evening Post*, that the metropolis was saved 'from the insufferable tyranny of martial law'.[66]

In these circumstances, the mobilization of volunteer units in the city and Westminster took on a new urgency. These units surfaced after 7 June when the riots had reached alarming proportions. Organized principally for the self-defence of their institutions or neighbourhoods, they came to be viewed in many quarters as a civilian counterpoint to the army. As Sir Philip Gibbes insisted, when a volunteer association was mooted for Marylebone, the object was to 'get rid of the necessary, but much to be dreaded interference of the military'.[67] When Lord Amherst then advised that the volunteer regiments be disarmed, allegedly because it was difficult for the army to distinguish rioters from volunteers, there were vigorous protests in both the city and parliament, with radicals reminding the government that the right to carry arms was sanctioned by the Bill of Rights.[68] This proposal to disarm simply increased the radical suspicion of government intentions. Those suspicions surfaced again when it was proposed that the city thank the king for his military assistance during the riots. On this occasion, on 8 July, there was a furious debate in Common Council with Alderman Townsend charging that the establishment of martial law had long been the goal of the government. Along with Wilkes and Frederick Bull, he refused to be nominated to the committee submitting the address, with the result that this particular one was never delivered.[69]

The actions of the government, then, did little to allay fears among the London patriots that it was bent on coercion at home. On the other hand, the government accused the opposition of undermining respect for authority with their mass petitions of reform and misguided zeal for American rebels.[70] The *Morning Post* talked of a 'patriotic plan of mischief' to undermine order in the metropolis and believed the reservations expressed about the army's right to suppress the riots without magisterial direction were factitious protests designed to unleash 'a wicked internal banditti' on the public and totally undermine the war effort.[71] At the same time, the government furrowed hard to find evidence of patriotic involvement in the riots. Lord Amherst, the commander in chief of the troops, even received from one of his subaltern officers a list of the

Common Councillors of London and their purported political affiliations, so that any sign of patriot sympathy for the rioters could be quickly located and exposed.[72] The government found one patriot who was plausibly involved in the riots and pulled out the legal guns to prosecute him. He was Henry John Maskall, an apothecary of Oxford Street, well known for the opposition to the war and involvement in radical politics. In November 1773, he had chaired a meeting of the free and independent livery to nominate Frederick Bull as MP of London, and it was Bull who had seconded Lord George Gordon's motion to repeal the Catholic Relief Act on 2 July 1780. During 1775, Maskall had attempted to mobilize the London liverymen and the Middlesex freeholders against the government's American policy, denouncing 'those wicked and despotic Ministers who would drive the colonists to desperation'.[73] In the following year, he became the president of the London Association, a radical group that financially aided the Americans in their struggle with the government and dedicated itself to mustering support against the coercive policies of the North ministry.[74] If the government could implicate the high-profile Maskall in the Gordon riots, it would vindicate its claim that the patriots were responsible for the reprehensible rabble-rousing that had brought anarchy to the London streets and imperilled both crown and government.

Henry Maskall's trial was the most celebrated of all those implicated in the Gordon riots. It covered nearly two pages of the *London Chronicle*, hit the front page of rival newspapers and within a week was published as a separate pamphlet.[75] Maskall was charged with tumultuously assembling to demolish the dwelling of Lord Mansfield in Bloomsbury Square.[76] According to the prosecution, Maskall was not directly involved in the destruction of Mansfield's house, but he had certainly encouraged the rioters to burn Lord Mansfield's effects, warming them to their task with shouts of 'No Popery'. One witness, Sir Thomas Mills, the nephew of Lord Mansfield, testified that he saw Maskall on the steps of his uncle's house as he ferried his relatives to safety and pleaded with soldiers to prevent pillaging. Another, Richard Ingram, a former army surgeon and apothecary, claimed that Maskall made inflammatory remarks to the crowd, openly dismissing the possibility that parliament would repeal the Catholic Relief Act. Upon leaving the scene, he purportedly prompted rioters to consider attacking the Excise Office and the Bank. In the eyes of the prosecution, who organized their case with care,[77] Maskall was a seditious busybody who deserved to be indicted under the Riot Act.

Henry Maskall's trial lasted six, perhaps seven hours. It took up the great proportion of the proceedings on 3 July 1780, and it was distinguished by the fact that, unlike so many other defendants at this memorable session, Maskall had defence counsel. Two of his counsel, Dayrell and Peckham, were well-known circuit lawyers, noteworthy for their cross-examinations; the third was Thomas Erskine, who was beginning to make a name for himself as a defence counsel following his debut at Admiral Keppel's court martial the previous year. Together they demolished the testimony of the prosecuting witnesses, especially of Richard Ingram, who was portrayed as an untrustworthy, reward-mongering bankrupt set up by the ministry. The defence counsel wondered why the crown had not produced a third major witness, Charles Molloy, another former army surgeon on half-pay, especially since he had been named as a witness on the indictment. They charged that his evidence would have totally compromised Ingram's testimony. The presiding judge was sympathetic to this argument, and the jury found Maskall not guilty without even leaving the courtroom. Cheers broke out in the court and outside when the verdict was heard, much to the consternation of the judge.[78]

Maskall's acquittal compromised the government's attempt to implicate the patriots in the Gordon riots. Indeed, the patriot opposition arguably emerged from the riots with greater credit than the ministry. Although the government certainly won some support for suppressing the riots by short-circuiting the conventional relationship between army and magistracy, patriot politicians could point to their role as constitutional guardians of order during the riots, and remind the public that the government's response had been initially wanting and deviously authoritarian. John Wilkes, in particular, came away from the riots as a responsible man of order, rushing to the support of the bank, leading the volunteers of his ward in the London Foot Association and arresting troublemakers such as the journalist William Moore, who in the *Thunderer* arguably incited disorder through his relentless and inflammatory anti-Catholic rhetoric.[79] Indeed, Wilkes was openly critical of his erstwhile ally Frederick Bull for persisting with the City petition for repeal when the riots were in full swing, and damned the Lord Mayor Brackley Kennett for his pusillanimous conduct for the riots. If Kennett was in any way guilty of misconduct as mayor, Wilkes thundered in the city chamber, he should be made to pay for the repairs of Newgate from his own pocket.[80]

In looking at the aftermath of the riots, historians have universally suggested there was a significant backlash to the new-fledged radical movement in the interests of order and a concomitant decline in support for America. In fact, things were not quite so straightforward. That there was a disenchantment with mob politics can be admitted. Even on London's Common Council, long a critical forum of government, motions thanking the king for his military assistance during the riots finally passed by narrow majorities.[81] At the same time, a disenchantment with mob politics did not necessarily translate into a disenchantment with radicalism, especially since the radicals had quite explicitly distanced themselves from the disorders of June 1780.[82] Nor was radicalism necessarily tarnished by its affiliations with the Protestant Association, an organization that deployed the strategies of popular politics honed by Wilkes, but was a populist movement that cross-cut orthodox political alignments.

In fact, some radical newspapers went out of their way to differentiate the Protestant Association from the association movement of Christopher Wyvill and his urban allies, and even to suggest that parliamentary reform could free the British people from dark anti-Catholic prejudices and bigotry.[83]

Had there been any significant backlash to the radical movement, one would expect it to have been registered in the general election that took place but three months after the riots, in constituencies well known to be weathervanes of popular sentiment. Yet radical and reformist candidates fared well in the metropolitan elections. The verdict, at a time when the last defendants were being tried for the role in the Gordon riots, was a triumph for anti-ministerialism and for the association movement that had built its case for reform on a disastrous war. Issues relating to the Gordon riots certainly surfaced during the election. Candidates were cued for their role in suppressing the riots, and for their attitude to Catholics. John Sawbridge suffered for his toleration of Catholics, but it was probably strategic voting by the conservative White Hart Association that deprived him of the fourth seat in the City of London. Two well-known members of the Protestant Association, Frederick Bull in the city and Nathaniel Polhill in Southwark, secured their elections, but against this, John Wilkes in Middlesex and Charles James Fox in Westminster faced down their critics when questioned why they voted for the Catholic Relief Bill. They still emerged victorious. In the end, anti-ministerial reputations counted for more than differences over Catholic concessions. In Surrey, the county association, chaired by none other than Sawbridge, campaigned aggressively for the radical distiller Sir Joseph Mawbey and Admiral Augustus Keppel, the hero of 1779 who had been rejected as MP for Windsor on the king's orders. The Onslow interest in Surrey, dominant for decades, was decisively rejected by the voters. The only quasi-ministerialist to win in the metropolis was Admiral Sir George Brydges Rodney, who was represented at the hustings by his son because he was still chasing the French fleet in the Caribbean. As the celebrity of the hour, the saviour of the sugar islands, he was eagerly endorsed by all parties. At the victory dinner for the two victorious candidates at which his surrogate, Admiral Young, was present, toasts were given to the free and independent electors of Westminster, to Admirals Hawke, Keppel and Rodney and to a host of opposition-radical luminaries including Burke, Sheridan, Wilkes and Sawbridge.[84]

The fact is that the trauma of the Gordon riots was successfully accommodated into the mainstream of metropolitan politics; it did not seriously deflect the association moment for parliamentary reform from its course. In one respect, however, the riots marked a turning point in British politics. This concerned the future relationship of crowd and 'people'.[85] The riots disrupted the rapport between crowds and radicalism that had been a hallmark of the Wilkite era, when crowds helped create the space for libertarian politics and even tipped the political balance of forces in ways that helped amplify arguments about liberty and parliamentary reform. In the Keppel disturbances of 1779, this relationship looked decidedly shaky, but in 1780, it finally came unstuck. Progressive Enlightenment ideas about tolerating minority groups conflicted with a traditional anti-Catholicism made more virulent by the politics of war. The fear that liberty might give way to licentiousness seemed to be confirmed by the behaviour of the mob during the riots and threatened to discredit the radical platform that was beginning to emerge. Bourgeois radicals suddenly realized that crowds were not necessarily the shock troops of liberty but could express a reactionary populism that did not conform to their ideas about responsible political citizenship, open systems of governance or a respect for private property. Indeed, the spontaneity of the mob, especially its pursuit of social grievances unconnected with the repeal campaign, revealed very clearly to all men of property the dangers of mobilising passions that could be not channelled into programmatic political movements.

One final point needs to be stressed and that concerns the context in which the Gordon riots took place. Erupting at the time of imperial crisis, the riots fed off the resentments and disillusionment of war. Virtually every aspect of the crisis was influenced by the politics of war: the near paralysis of the government; the *schadenfreude* of the opposition impotent to stop the war but keen to embarrass the government; the ideology of the Protestant Association that fed off the anxieties of war-time concessions to Catholics at home and abroad; the temper of the crowd, disenchanted with war and highly susceptible to appeals for a Protestant united front against foreign enemies and a perfidious establishment; the reaction of the radicals, ever suspicious of the government's authoritarian intentions; even the politically over-determined, if not paranoid, explanations as to who inspired the riots and set in motion the plebeian commotions that overwhelmed London for a week. Historians such as George Rudé made important contributions to our knowledge of the Gordon rioters and their victims, and opened up a fruitful discussion as to why ordinary people in the metropolis acted as they did. But what he and others marginalized in their analysis was the politics of war, the discursive terrain that framed this extraordinary event one hot summer in 1780.

Notes

1. See accounts in the *London Chronicle*, 6–9, 25–27 February 1779 and 16–18 March 1779. The fullest account in is Eugene C. Black, *The Association: British Extraparliamentary Political Organization 1769–1793* (Cambridge, MA, 1963), pp. 134–47.
2. Ibid., p. 133.
3. *London Chronicle*, 25–27 February 1779.
4. 14 George III, c. 83. See also Hilda Neatby, *The Quebec Act: Protest and Policy* (Scarborough, Ontario, 1973), pp. 58–61, for Dartmouth's instructions as to how the act should be executed.

5. Colin Haydon, *Anti-Catholicism in Eighteenth-Century England c. 1714–1780* (Oxford, 1993), p. 171.
6. Philip Lawson, *The Imperial Challenge: Quebec and Britain in the Age of the American Revolution* (Montreal and Kingston, 1989), ch. 7.
7. *Public Advertiser*, 22 February 1775.
8. *London Evening Post*, 21–23 June 1774.
9. *Morning Chronicle*, 3 June 1780; *London Courant*, 3 June 1780.
10. Nicholas Rogers, *Crowds, Culture and Politics in Georgian Britain* (Oxford, 1998), ch. 4.
11. British Library, (henceforth BL) Add Ms 38,212 ff. 248–53, North to Jenkinson, 25 November 1778.
12. P.D.G. Thomas, *Lord North* (London, 1976), pp. 121–22. Poynings Law gave the Privy Council the right of veto over Irish legislation.
13. *London Evening Post*, 4–6, 6–8 April 1780.
14. *An Appeal from the Protestant Association to the People of Great Britain* (London, 1779), pp. 3, 55–58.
15. *London Evening Post*, 11–13 April 1780.
16. *Protestant Packet, or British Monitor* (Newcastle, 1780), pp. 167–68.
17. *London Evening Post*, 11–13 April 1780.
18. The National Archives, London (henceforth TNA) SP 37/20/264.
19. There were four divisions: London, Westminster, Southwark and the London Scots.
20. J. Paul de Castro, *The Gordon Riots* (London, 1926), p. 36.
21. Ibid., p. 39.
22. TNA, SP 37/14/189.
23. *Carrington and Payne's Law Report* (1833), 5: p. 286; see also de Castro, *The Gordon Riots*, pp. 42–47.
24. TNA, SP 37/20/41 and SP 37/20/47; *The Mawhood Diary*, ed. E.E. Reynolds (London, 1956), pp. 150–51; James Langdale, 'Thomas Langdale, The Distiller', *London Recusant*, 10 (1975), pp. 42–45.
25. TNA, SP 37/20/159.
26. TNA, WO 34/103/325, 368. See also *British Museum Catalogue of Prints and Drawings*, nos. 5534, 5669, 5680–81.
27. TNA, PC 1/3097.
28. TNA, PC 1/3097.
29. *A Narrative of the Proceedings of Lord George Gordon* (London, 1780), p. 33.
30. De Castro, *The Gordon Riots*, ch. 4.
31. Richard Holloway, *A Letter to John Wilkes Esquire* (London, 1771), p. 28; *A Narrative of the Proceedings of Lord George Gordon*, p. 45.
32. TNA, ADM 1/3681/194; ADM 7/300, no 90; *London Chronicle*, 8–10 August, 1780. See also Rogers, *Crowds, Culture and Politics*, pp. 117–18.
33. *The Autobiography of France Place*, ed. Mary Thale (Cambridge, 1972), pp. 34–35.
34. *Remembrancer* (1780) pp. x, 13.
35. *Gazetteer*, 20 June 1780.
36. See the cases of James Irons, Thomas Cabbage and Sarah Guy, in Old Bailey online, t17800628–67, t17800628–86, t17800628–87.
37. Old Bailey online, t17800628–81. See also the trials of Sarah Collogan, Elizabeth Grant and Elizabeth Timmings, t17800628–106, t17800628–107, t17800628–108.
38. Old Bailey online, t17800628–119.
39. George Rudé cites 15 people brought to trial for thefts during the riots, of which seven were found not guilty. See Rudé, *Paris and London in the Eighteenth Century* (London, 1970), p. 282.

40. Old Bailey online, t17800628–115, testimony of Charles Lee, cited in trial of Thomas Price, James Burn, John Thompson; *The Proceedings of the King's Special Commission of Oyer and Terminer for the County of Surrey, 10 July 1780* (London, 1780), p. 57.

41. *Surrey Proceedings*, p. 69.

42. BL, Add MS 27,828 f. 127: Old Bailey online, trials of William Brown, Thomas Crankshaw and George Simpson, t17800628–35, t17800628–78, t17800628–101.

43. TNA, KB/8/79/228; SP 37/20/289; Old Bailey online, trials of Thomas Chambers and Jonathan Stacey, t17800628–15, t17800628–116. The guiding statute was 3 James 1, c. 5.

44. Old Bailey online, trial of Thomas Price, James Burn and John Thompson, t17800628–115.

45. TNA, KB 8/79/199–201.

46. TNA, TS 11/33/1213.

47. Rudé, *Paris and London in the Eighteenth Century*, p. 289.

48. Ibid., p. 286.

49. TNA, SP 37/14/147–8.

50. TNA SP 37/14/ 146–8. The chapels saved by cavalry intervention included those of the Portuguese ambassador in Mayfair and the Neapolitan ambassador in Lower Brook Street.

51. *Surrey Proceedings*, pp. 44–45. For a detailed account of the disposition of the armed forces, see Tony Hayter, *The Army and the Crowd in Mid-Georgian England* (London, 1978), ch. 12.

52. Corporation of London Record Office, Repertories of the Court of Aldermen, 184 (1780), 209–10.

53. Derived from calculations of those who petitioned for compensation to property damaged during the riots, TNA, Works 6/110, 111.

54. TNA, Works 6/110,111. The breakdown of the 124 whose occupational status can be identified is as follows: esquires, gentlemen, 14.5%; professions, genteel trades, 9.2%; food and small retailers, 18.5%; drink trade, 26.6%; brokers and dealers, 7.2%; artisans, 16.9%; labourers and lodgers, 4.8%.

55. For a list of the institutional targets, see Hayter, *Army and the Crowd*, Table 12.3.

56. *Fanaticism and Treason, or, a Dispassionate History of the Rise and Progress and Suppression of the Rebellious Insurrections in June 1780* (London, 1780), p. 74.

57. *Surrey Proceedings*, p. 11. Two deponents, a boatbuilder and a ropemaker, both described as substantial tradesmen, denied that he did. Baron Eyre refused the jury's plea for mercy, stating to them 'the danger of extending mercy to the Person who had disclosed Principles so destructive to society'. Later it was thought Heyter had been framed, and he received a royal pardon. TNA, SP 37/212/275–6, 308–10; Haydon, *Anti-Catholicism in Eighteenth-Century England*, pp. 221–22.

58. *Morning Chronicle*, 30 June 1780; Old Bailey online, trial of William Brown, t17800628–35.

59. TNA, KB 8/79/ 147.

60. TNA, PC 1/3097, information lodged with the Solicitor General, 16 June 1780.

61. James Boswell, *Life of Johnson*, ed. R.W. Chapman (London, 1953), p. 1059. On 'reversal crowds', see Elias Canetti, *Crowds and Power*, trans. Carol Stewart (Harmondsworth, 1973), pp. 66–70.

62. De Castro, *The Gordon Riots*, p. 218; Marsha Keith Schuchard, 'Lord George Gordon and Cabalistic Freemasonry: Beating Jacobite Swords into Jacobin Ploughshares', in *Secret Conversions to Judaism in Early Modern Europe*, ed. Martin Mulsow and Richard

H. Popkin (Leiden, 2004) p. 203. I have found no evidence of a Bailston in histories of the Boston Tea Party, so it is conceivable that the British miss-spelt the name.

63. De Castro, *The Gordon Riots*, p. 220.
64. 'A.B.' in the *London Courant*, 4 July 1780.
65. *London Chronicle*, 17–20 June, 1780.
66. *London Evening Post*, 8–10 June 1780.
67. *London Courant*, 16 June 1780.
68. *London Courant*, 14 June 1780, 19 July 1780; *London Chronicle*, 17–20 June 1780.
69. *Morning Chronicle*, 10 July 1780, *London Courant*, 11 July 1780.
70. See especially *Morning Post*, 10, 12, 17 June 1780.
71. *Morning Post*, 10 June 1780.
72. For Colonel Twistleton's hopes of finding a patriot conspiracy behind the riots, see TNA, WO 34/104/123. For the list, see WO 34/104/351–357.
73. John Sainsbury, *Disaffected Patriots. London Supporters of Revolutionary America, 1769–1782* (Kingston and Montreal, 1987), pp. 110–11.
74. *London Evening Post*, 19 March 1776, 27 February 1777; *Gazetteer and New Daily Advertiser*, 30 December 1777.
75. As *The Remarkable Trial of Mr Mascall, the Apothecary* (London, 1780), price 6d., noted in the *Morning Chronicle*, 5 July 1780 and in *St James's Chronicle*, 1, 6 July 1780. As the latter reveals, there were advertisements for the trial before it was even held.
76. Old Bailey online, Henry John Maskall, t17800628-10.
77. For the documentation, see TS 11/1130/5968.
78. For accounts, see *London Chronicle*, 1–4 July 1780; *London Courant*, 4 July 1780; *Morning Chronicle and London Advertiser*, 4 July 1780; *London Evening Post*, 1–4 July 1780.
79. De Castro, *The Gordon Riots*, pp. 142, 191–93.
80. *Gazetteer*, 20 June 1780; *London Chronicle*, 17–20, 24–27 June 1780.
81. *London Courant* 11, 25 July 1780. The divisions were 67 in favour, 54 against, and 77 in favour, 67 against.
82. Certainly there were some who were disenchanted. George Cumberland, a director of the Royal Exchange Association, hoped the Gordon riots would transform city politics and eliminate magistrates with 'false patriotism, factious principles and contempt of Government'. BL, Add Mss 36,492, ff. 352–53.
83. *London Courant*, 8 August 1780.
84. London Courant, 25 September 1780.
85. See Nicholas Rogers, 'Crowd and People in the Gordon Riots', in *The Transformation of Political Culture. England and Germany in the Late Eighteenth Century*, ed. Eckhart Hellmuth (Oxford, 1990), pp. 39–58.

8

'Reformers No Rioters': British Radicalism and Mob Identity in the 1790s

Michael T. Davis

On 27 August 1794, Lydia Hardy – the wife of the founder of the London Corresponding Society (LCS), Thomas Hardy – died within hours of giving birth to a stillborn baby. Two days later, when the impending funeral of Mrs Hardy was discussed at a meeting of a central committee of the LCS, one prominent member – James Parkinson, a physician probably best remembered for first describing what is now known as Parkinson's disease – raised the question of whether or not the LCS should make an effort to be represented en masse at the mournful event. Another member opposed the idea, arguing that it gave 'an opportunity to our Enemies to observe upon our calling together so great a Number of people as would attend that it indicated the Society's inclination upon every occasion offer'd, to collect a Mob, and to renew the tumults and riots which had so lately prevailed'.[1] This apprehension about the potential for the LCS to be publicly perceived as a mob ultimately informed and shaped the LCS's official instructions for the funeral of Lydia Hardy. There was no call for a collective gathering of the LCS, and it was 'recommended to each Member who knew Citizens that meant to attend the funeral earnestly to recommend to them to behave peaceably and becoming the solemnity of the occasion'. When it was all over, the LCS wanted to avoid any risk of a disturbance and recommended those members who did attend should 'disperse each to his own home immediately after the funeral'.[2]

This episode clearly demonstrates the concern – perhaps even the obsession – of British radicals in the 1790s with cultivating a consciousness of civility and distancing themselves from an association with a mob identity. There is also something of an ironic subtext to the tragic narrative of Lydia Hardy's death. While the LCS avoided the potential for being viewed as a mob by not gathering as a group at Mrs Hardy's funeral, her death and that of her unborn child was allegedly caused by the enraged actions of a loyalist crowd. It is difficult to determine how far this account was real or constructed, especially since Lydia Hardy had five previous stillbirths and the risk of maternal mortality in this period was very real,[3] but it was nevertheless deliberately positioned by radicals as a powerful and emotive anecdote. Thomas Hardy recalled how 'his innocent and unprotected family was persecuted with the most dastardly and unmanly rancour' following his arrest in May 1794 on charges of high treason, ultimately leading to the death of his wife.[4] The fateful moment came not long after Admiral Howe had been victorious over the French fleet off Brest in June 1794, which inspired what has been described as 'ecstatic demonstrations of loyalism in the south of England and the Midlands'.[5] On 11 June 1794, Hardy's house was to be one focus of this loyalist ecstasy even though it was illuminated as part of the patriotic ritual:

> On that night, a large mob of ruffians assembled before his house, No. 9, Piccadilly, and without any ceremony began to assail the windows with stones and brick-bats. These were very soon demolished, although there had been lights up as in the adjoining houses. They next attempted to break open the shop door, and swore, with the most horrid oaths, that they would either burn or pull down the house. The unfortunate Mrs Hardy was within, with no other protector than an old woman who attended her as nurse. Weak and enfeebled as she was, from her personal situation, and from what she must have suffered on account of her husband, it is no wonder that she should have been terrified by the threats and assaults of such a crowd of infuriated desperadoes. ... Mrs Hardy called to the neighbours who lived at the back of the house, and who were in a state of great anxiety for her safety, in case the villains should have effected their purpose of breaking into the premises. They advised her to make her way through a small back window, on the ground floor, which she accordingly attempted, but being very large round the waist, she stuck fast in it, and it was only by main force that she could be dragged through, much injured by the bruises she received. ... On the 27th of August, 1794, she was taken in labour, and delivered of a dead child. ... About two o'clock of the same day she had parted with her husband, in as good spirits as was possible in her situation – took her last farewell – it was her last – for they were doomed never to see each other again in this vale of tears.[6]

As melancholic as this story was, for British radicals it was part of a strategic narration. On the one level, it allowed them to construct a martyrdom discourse and use it for political leverage at a time when many leaders of the reform movement – including Hardy himself – were being detained under the suspension of *habeas corpus* ahead of their trials for treason.[7] Richard Lee, on the cover page of his sentimental poem *On the Death of Mrs Hardy*, declares 'she died a martyr to the sufferings of her husband'.[8] Some newspapers also followed this line of thought.[9] The *Morning Post*, for instance, reported that it was no surprise the 'accumulation of afflictions' suffered by Lydia Hardy after her husband's arrest in May 1794 aggravated 'the pangs which nature has made the portion of her situation... [and] have hurried her prematurely out of the World; or that her dying breath should have pronounced these oppressive circumstances the cause of her dissolution'. Personal tragedy and national politics became inextricably entwined: 'Thus has an excellent woman, and an unoffending infant, already fallen victims to the suspension of the Habeas Corpus Act; and who shall venture to pronounce how many more innocent individuals may sink under the same accumulated burthen'.[10]

While radicals endeavoured to seize some immediate political advantage from Mrs Hardy's death in the context of the 1794 political trials, they can also be seen as attempting to remap the boundaries of a new moral world. By connecting the death of Lydia Hardy and her baby with the actions of loyalist mobs, radicals tried to shift the dominant civil discourse in relation to the civilized and uncivilized, the moral and the amoral, the orderly and the disorderly. The underlying message was that loyalists – not radicals – were the violent and unruly section of society. Changing social attitudes towards violence and disorderliness in the late eighteenth century rendered the actions of mobs 'increasingly unacceptable'.[11] And, as James Epstein notes, British radicals of the 1790s 'often contrasted the decorum of their own proceedings to the drunken spectacle of loyalist mobs'.[12] According to this dialogue, loyalist crowds were illegitimate actors within the normative mainstream, transgressing behavioural expectations by engaging in riotous activities and their actions (especially in the context of Lydia Hardy's death) disrupting one of the dominant social values of the time – family life. Radicals sought to marginalize the social location of loyalists, identifying their collective action as a form of deviance. In sociological terms, the normative outlines of society were being reconfigured: 'A human community can be said to maintain boundaries... in the sense that its members tend to confine themselves to a particular radius of activity and to regard any conduct which drifts outside that radius as somehow inappropriate or immoral.'[13] Through this process of locating loyalist crowds outside an acceptable 'radius of activity', a deliberate plan of subverting the so-called language of Aristocracy[14] and redefining the political nation was being engaged. The labelling of loyalist action as a form of deviance allowed radicals to identify themselves by reference to their binary opposite, distinguishing what they saw as the 'worthy' members of society from the 'unworthy' mob. This social polarity was addressed by the radical pamphleteer, Charles Pigott, when he defined the 'mob' as so-called Church and King loyalists: 'a species of regular militia, kept in pay by the ministry, for the protection of property against Levellers and Republicans. Some writers suppose that they are a constituted tribunal, to take a sort of summary cognizance of Jacobines, Dissenters, and Presbyterians; and that they form an important part of our happy Constitution. They were serviceable at Birmingham, Manchester, and other places; and they are, without doubt, the most loyal portion of his Majesty's subjects'.[15]

As Pigott gestures towards, there was substance and not just satire in this definition of the mob. Church and King actions were, as Alan Booth put it, 'perhaps the purest distillation of the "flag-saluting, foreign-hating...side of the plebeian mind"'[16] and the threat from this popular form of militant loyalism was very real in the 1790s.[17] Radicals faced bias-motivated vilification and physical assaults in a loyalist campaign of unofficial terror that would today be classified as 'hate crimes'.[18] A contemporary reformer reflected upon this tumultuous period of history as 'full of jealousy and violence'[19] and, as one scholar notes, loyalists 'aimed to pursue a sort of vigilante politics which they hoped would silence radical voices'.[20] For counter-revolutionaries, the actions of loyalist mobs were summary justice, but in reality, it was nothing more than a 'highly destructive force'[21] of reactionary conservatism. The first and most protracted outbreak of Church and King violence occurred in Birmingham in July 1791 in what is known as the 'Priestley riots'.[22] For several days, loyalist mobs traipsed the local streets, with *The Times* reporting how 'the loyal spirit of the numerous inhabitants' was expressed in chants of 'God save the King; Long live the King and the Constitution in Church and State; Down with the Dissenters; Down with all the abettors of French rebellion; Church and King; Down with the Rumps; No Olivers; No false Rights of Man'.[23] At the end of the rampage, the meeting houses of Birmingham dissenters had been destroyed, and the house of Joseph Priestley, the distinguished reformer and scientist famous for identifying oxygen, had been razed to the ground. But this was not to be an isolated incident. As Priestley himself observed, the 'same bad spirit pervades the whole kingdom',[24] and it did so for much of the 1790s. In Manchester, the properties of prominent reformers became the focus of a determined Church and King mob in December 1792, using brickbats and stones to damage the houses of Joseph Collier, Matthew Faulkner, William Gorse and Thomas Walker.[25] And the house of Thomas Hardy seemed to be a particular favourite of loyalist mobs in London, attacked in June 1794 and again on 13 October 1797. On the latter occasion, Hardy refused to have illuminations in his windows to celebrate a recent British victory over the Dutch fleet, and the large loyalist crowd that gathered outside his house was relentless well into the evening. But, on this occasion, reform sympathizers were able to thwart a disaster: 'about 100 men, chiefly members of the [LCS]...many of them Irish, armed with good shillelaghs, took post early in the evening in front of, and close to, the front of Hardy's house'.[26]

The damaging of property was symbolic of what David Mansley calls the 'old-style riot'[27] and represents a key part of the repertoire employed by loyalist mobs during the 'reactionary' phase of collective action identified by Charles

Tilly in the late eighteenth and early nineteenth centuries.[28] While property was 'undoubtedly a satisfying target' of Church and King crowds, physical violence was always a looming risk.[29] In fact, the 'pulling down of houses' and inter-personal assaults were often a therapeutic and mutually reinforcing part of loyalist collective action in the 1790s: 'In Church and King disturbances, perhaps more than any other type of plebeian protest, the victim risked serious personal injury as well as the destruction of his property'.[30] As one contemporary noted in a satirical letter published in 1794, the Lord Mayor of London – who was mocked as the Right Honourable Paul Stupid – should be praised for 'his *ready* calling out the Military in June last, when the houses of divers of the peaceable inhabitants of this city were destroyed, their windows broken, and their lives endangered by the *Church and King Mob*'.[31] Perhaps no one knew loyalist harassment more in the 1790s than the veteran orator and LCS member, John Thelwall.[32] He was regularly the focus of Church and King assaults, and at one point in 1797 had to raise a pistol before a militant loyalist mob, warning he 'would shoot any persons who molested him'.[33] Thelwall was so obsessed with the threat from loyalists that he became somewhat neurotic: 'If he went into an oyster house, or an *á-la-mode* beef shop, he would concede that one-half of the boxes in the room had government spies in them, whose especial business was to watch and report, as far as possible, all he said and all he did'.[34] In the streets, Thelwall consciously walked in the middle to lessen the chances of being taken by surprise by loyalist thugs, and he took 'special care never to go down back streets, for fear of assassins'.[35] But not all British radicals were as circumspect as Thelwall, and some experienced the full fury of loyalist mobs. George Shawcross, for instance, tried to escape a rampaging loyalist mob in Royton in 1794, but he was trounced:

> When I was gotten over the garden hedge, and set out running, before I had gotten half way over the field I was knocked down by some persons and kicked for so long that I could with difficult take my breath. When I had got up and had recovered myself a little I set out a running again as well as I could but before I reached the brook at the bottom of the field I was overtaken again and in attempting to get over the brook I was knocked down into it. Rising again I made another attempt to escape them but was still very much abused – and as I could not go up the side of the brook from them, I offered to go up the brook when I was again knocked into a deep pool of water in the brook in which I expected to be drowned.[36]

In July of the same year, John Cheetham, the Salford radical, was ambushed by a loyalist mob while crossing the bridge to Manchester. As Cheetham fled, they threw stones at him and then dragged him by the hair for some distance.[37] The streets of towns in the 1790s were the site for loyalist mobs to humiliate radicals, transforming a public space into a venue for making popular political statements as well as dispensing what was seen as a form of exemplary communal justice. This transformation clearly took place in the market town of Macclesfield in September 1793 when a local silversmith was dragged from his house and physically abused in the streets to shouts of 'Jacobin' and 'Tom Paine'.[38] Perhaps even worse was the fate of a suspected radical named Thomas Whittacker of Failsworth, near Manchester, who was tied to the saddle of a horse and then tortured with pins to his legs in April 1794.[39]

While the violence and destruction perpetrated by Church and King mobs was both widespread and criminal, it is interesting to note that very few loyalist rioters were actually prosecuted. For Alan Booth, this anomaly is evidence of upper-class collusion: 'The sympathies of the authorities were plain'.[40] But the motivations of these activists was surely diverse: some would have been bystanders caught up in the hysteria of the moment; others would have been excited by the chance for a scuffle; while still more probably given to bravado under the influence of alcohol. And it 'would none the less be wrong to suppose that such crowds were always artificially contrived'.[41] As Malcolm Thomis and Peter Holt suggest, Church and King mobs were a genuine and spontaneous 'political response from the lower orders, albeit a crude, emotional and unreasoning reaction'.[42] Nevertheless, there is some evidence to support E.P. Thompson's claim that loyalist mobs were 'picked hooligans' and 'hired bands operating on behalf of external interests'.[43] If the local authorities did not provide active encouragement to loyalist rioters, at the very least they often failed to control them. Samuel Bamford recalled such a situation at Thorpe in April 1794, when the 'constables of the place had been called upon by the peaceably disposed inhabitants to act, but they declined to interfere, and the [Church and King] mob had their own way. Mr Pickford of Royton Hall, a magistrate, never made his appearance, though he lived within a few square yards of the scene of the riot, and was supposed to have been at home all the time during which the outrage was perpetrated'.[44] On another occasion, it is alleged that 'Sedition Hunters' in Winchester met – 'but having nothing to do – they ordered an effigy, for Tom Paine, to be made ... [and] caused the mob to assemble to carry this effigy about the City ... The Mayor and Alderman – being of the true Jacobite breed, gave money to the mob to Halloo – Church and King – and then to burn the effigy'. However, there was an interesting twist to the end of this gathering: 'when the mob got drunk, some few did cry out – Tom Paine forever – Tom Paine forever, but they were very drunk'.[45]

While Mark Philp interprets this as an incident contrived by radicals to 'tease' John Reeves about his loyalist endeavours as chairman of the Association for Preserving Liberty and Property against Republicans and Levellers,[46] it serves to highlight the point made by Thomis and Holt that crowds in the 1790s 'could and would be fickle in their political loyalties'.[47] It also indicates that collective action in this period was a contested space. As Adrian Randall notes, 'loyalists could not keep control of the streets for long'.[48] Although E.P. Thompson describes Church and King activists as the 'true *mobs*',[49] for most people in the 1790s it was British radicals that came to mind when they thought about the dangers of crowd action. And this was a mindset inflamed by conservative propagandists who were convinced – or, at least, tried to convince others – that British reformers were a real and dangerous threat to the status quo. William Cobbett, writing as a staunch anti-Jacobin in the 1790s, was one of the most virulent opponents of British radicals, and his reflections on 'the people' is indicative of the malicious stereotyping and victimization faced by reformers in this period: they were, at once, 'a boisterous host'; 'the ignorant multitude'; 'that many-headed monster, the versatile, venal, stupid, and ferocious mob'; 'a set of beings I cannot call men'; 'wretches; rough-headed wretches'; 'the stupid public' and 'two-legged brutes'.[50] But Cobbett's pejorative reflections do not imply a lack of power – in fact, quite the opposite. Cobbett believed that radicals and their affiliated crowds were a menacing manifestation from hell: 'Give me anything but mobs; for mobs are the devil in his worst shape'.[51] And, in dominant conservative discourse, it was Jacobinism and its revolutionary designs that possessed the politicized crowd. According to John Reeves, the 'new set of Reformers' in Britain were seeking 'the destruction of Monarchy...and a levelling Republic may then be substituted according to the imaginations and will of this rabble'.[52] *The Times* went so far as to describe members of the LCS as admirers 'of the murders and robberies committed in France' and believed the group were conspiring 'the same kind of massacres in England'. British radicals were 'internal Enemies', and the LCS was a wild and desperate 'Mob Club'.[53]

This association between British radicals and the mob violence of French Jacobinism was a very deliberate and potent political tactic engaged by conservatives, designed to cultivate a fear of political reform and its advocates. Some contemporaries of the 1790s would have memories of the devastation caused by the Gordon Riots of 1780, and it would not have taken much to arouse their suspicions of crowds.[54] Many more were being exposed to gruesome stories from France and the need for Britons to be alarmed. Not long after the September Massacres in France in 1792, some Londoners were reading sensationalized reports of the Parisian mob burning people alive and ghastly acts of cannibalism as pastry cooks prepared pies from the flesh of priests and emigrants.[55] Those who believed Edmund Burke would have seen an imminent threat of the same grim scenes being re-enacted on British soil. But this was more than just a dark performance. In Burkean terms, it was a disease that endangered 'the healthy habit of the British constitution': Jacobinism 'is such a plague, that the precautions of the most severe quarantine ought to be established against it'.[56] The British public were presented with only two options: the stability of Britain as it was or the anarchy that was symptomatic of the

Figure 8.1 James Gillray, *Promis'd Horrors of the French Invasion* (1796); British Museum Satires 8826

French disease. This polarity was reinforced in counter-revolutionary culture by graphic satire, which generated forceful images of the Jacobin threat in Britain. *The Contrast*, which was first printed by Thomas Rowlandson in 1792 as an etching and subsequently plastered on mugs and jugs, was perhaps 'the most widely disseminated design of the whole anti-radical campaign'.[57] The choice for Britons was clear and seemingly straightforward: on the one hand, the virtues of British liberty with its stability, morality, justice and security; on the other hand, the barbarity of French liberty embodied by a medusa hag that endorsed atheism, murder and anarchy.[58] Four years later, in the *Promis'd Horrors of the French Invasion*, James Gillray made it clear what would happen if Britain succumb to Jacobinism. On St James's Street in London, a French army marches through the city with an English Jacobin mob following close behind. Amidst the anarchical scene, a guillotine beheads government ministers; Prime Minister William Pitt is tied to a liberty pole and whipped; and the decapitated body of the Duke of Richmond lies in a pool of blood on the street.

As one scholar points out, 'caricature "Jacobinized" the English mob', and it 'gave Jacobinism, itself, and the exponents of reform in England a mob-like identity'.[59] More generally, there was fundamentally no distinction in the minds of many people in the 1790s between the 'mob' and a 'Jacobin'. Although the label of 'Jacobin' was a misnomer when attached to British radicals, it was nonetheless 'one of the most loaded terms in Britain's political vocabulary' in the 1790s and 'remained dangerously unfixed'.[60] It was indiscriminately applied to identify British reformers as a king-killing, bloodthirsty, unruly mob. One writer in 1798 emphasized the subjective and limitless application of the term: 'Whoever is an enemy of Christianity and natural religion, of monarchy, or order, subordination, property, and justice, I call a Jacobin'.[61] Jacobinism was, as Matthew Grenby notes, 'simply a label for all that conservatives found detestable within society'.[62] But 'Jacobin' was not the only well-used label in the loyalist lexicon in the 1790s. In fact, there was a bewildering and seemingly inexhaustible fluidity to the derogatory nicknames applied to British reformers: mob, Jacobin, democrat, rabble, leveller and republican were all synonymous. And this was name-calling with a political purpose. On one level, it was part of a cathartic process: 'Political slandering was a way of venting one's sentiments, a form of public expression that served as both tonic and therapy for vocal conservatives'.[63] As conservative propagandists attempted to nominate radicals as deviants in society, and distinguish between 'us' and 'them', between good and evil, nicknaming was also an identity-making exercise. A correspondent to the *Morning Chronicle* in July 1794 recognized the importance of this process, which they called 're-baptizing adults': '*Nicknames* are certainly useful to those who employ them. There is no necessity for argument, reason, inference, or conclusion: bestow the *nickname* and it is done; it cannot be shaken off'.[64]

One nickname that radicals could not dislodge in the 1790s was the trope produced by Burke when he referred to reformers as the 'swinish multitude'. These two words heralded a dire warning from Burke: if the common people were allowed to be politicized and the radicals have their way, then French-style anarchy would descend upon Britain as the status quo was 'cast into the mire and trodden down under the hoofs'.[65] While E.P. Thompson suggests 'no other words have ever made the "Free-born Englishman" so angry',[66] some radicals actually embraced this imposed porcine identity as the intended image of a vulgar and ignorant multitude 'was transformed by radicals in the 1790s into a banner of popular pride and assertiveness'.[67] Indicative of this transformation were journals like Thomas Spence's *Pig's Meat* and Daniel Isaac Eaton's *Hog's Wash*, with some contributions coming from writers using pseudonyms such as Pigabus, Spare Rib and Brother Grunter. However, the 'swinish multitude' phrase was meant to distinguish and belittle radicals by drawing on a long tradition of British iconography and discourse that represented the pig as brutish, mischievous and disruptive – just like the mob.[68] Charles Pigott – in typical satiric style – noted how Burke's epithet was synonymous with 'rabble' in conservative nomenclature, characterizing 'an assembly of low-bred, vulgar, and riotous people... [who] dare to grunt their grievances even at the foot of the throne'.[69] As one scholar argues, 'we need to read Burke as suggesting that the mob is not only mobile, ungovernable, swinish and all in all terrible – it is also monstrous'.[70]

Importantly, the homological and analogical use of terms like swinish multitude, rabble, democrat and the mob can be seen as part of a pathologizing discourse that used certain phrases and concepts to delegitimize and discredit reformers. According to conservatives in the 1790s, the pathological features of mobs – and, by implication, of radicals – supported a diagnosis of their inferior mentality and irrationality as well as their unruliness. The word 'mob' is an abbreviation of the Latin *mobile vulgus*, which translates as 'excitable crowd', and it was 'developed by the ruling class in the 18th century as a coda for the poor and thus the emergent working class. ... In particular, it became coda for *disorderliness*'.[71] From a crowd psychology perspective, 'mob' and its associated images served 'to convey a link between emotionality and collective "disorderliness"'.[72] Long before Gustave Le Bon – the nineteenth-century social psychologist – theorized about the 'popular mind' and argued that activists in crowds lacked reason and were governed by primitive instincts and emotions,[73] anti-Jacobinism in Britain was emphasizing the vulgar and mindless nature of the mob. When viewed from a loyalist perspective, these attributes were a menacing synthesis.

What made the mob especially dangerous in the eyes of conservatives in the 1790s was not only its indelible association with radicalism but also the vision that even a benign crowd collective could be affected by the malign influence of radical elements in the community. In part, this was explained as a symptom of the asininity of the mob. In recalling Burke, William Cobbett suggested there was 'no falsehood too gross for the swinish multitude to swallow'.[74] Moreover, as one scholar notes, when 'the collective is lacking in rational judgement, then it is susceptible to being directed by a powerful minority or demagogue'.[75] One report in *The Times* in August 1794 reminded 'all loyal subjects' to be alert 'to the Jacobinism of that multitude of French workmen, petty tradesmen, servants and adventurers, who... fled to this island to escape the punishment due to their bad conduct'. The report continues by noting a number of Frenchmen were among crowds that had recently gathered at Charing Cross and Whitcomb Street in London, and that their behaviour was troublesome and manipulative: 'several persons of the above description, were observed exciting the populace to insult the Guards, and behave disorderly; saying, that it was shameful to fly at the approach of the horses; and telling them of the conduct of the French in order to instigate the populace to resist the troops. It was even observed that shillings, eggs, gin &c. were given to the mob'.[76] Interestingly, when it came to the LCS, loyalists believed there was something of a double act being performed on the minds of the people. On the one hand, its members were looked upon as 'puppets whose strings were pulled by more intelligent, educated men'.[77] But, on the other hand, the LCS was seen as a puppeteer with crafty powers to rouse and exploit a crowd. For instance, following an outdoor meeting of the LCS at Copenhagen House on 12 November 1795, *The True Briton* warned of 'the danger of tolerating harangues of this nature' and highlighted the main threat arising from the way 'in which the most palpable *lies* are imposed on an ignorant multitude, as certain facts; and a spirit of discontent and disaffection excited in their minds (by an artful miscreant) from their inability to distinguish truth from falsehood'.[78]

The outdoor meetings of the LCS – of which the Copenhagen House gathering was one of seven staged between 1793 and 1797 – are, in fact, paragons of how radicals could seek to harness the power of crowds.[79] These meetings were hugely popular events, attracting thousands of spectators to each assembly. As one contemporary noted, the first open-air meeting of the LCS 'caused a great stir in London', and 'all the streets and avenues leading to the place where the society assembled were crowded with people'.[80] In a broad sense, the large crowds that collected at LCS outdoor meetings were part of what Charles Tilly has called 'cumulative scores', which 'signalled the presence of a disciplined force' and 'displayed worthiness, unity, numbers, and commitment to a cause'.[81] They were also useful public relations exercises. Thomas Hardy believed that many of the onlookers 'who came there to ridicule and abuse went away converted and afterwards joined the society and became zealous promoters of the cause'.[82] And, by staging the meetings in a public space, the LCS was seeking to invert and discredit allegations from their opponents that the society was secretive and clandestine.

Ironically, however, the popularity of the outdoor meetings of the LCS probably reinforced the association between radicals and the mob in the minds of conservatives – minds that some believed were inflamed by alarmist imaginings. A select few parliamentarians voiced their concerns about a ministerial conspiracy to raise a moral panic about revolutionary crowd actions: Charles James Fox believed there was 'a miserable mockery held out of alarms in England which have no existence', and the Marquess of Lansdowne denounced the government for sounding 'the alarm-bell, to terrify the people into weak compliances'.[83] Outside of parliament, in an *Address to the Nation* published in 1793, the LCS drew attention to 'the alarm of *Riots and Insurrections*' that had risen in London since November of the previous year, discrediting reports of tumult as 'groundless' and '*trumped-up falsehoods*'.[84] This was an important part of the counter-discourses constructed in the 1790s to de-amplify the panic about radicalism and to distance reformers from being connected to riotous behaviour. Similarly, radicals attempted to create a cultural identity that presented them as legitimate and normative actors in the mainstream of society, as peaceful rather than disorderly citizens. In the 1790s, respectability and civility were the keys to social inclusion. Presenting an image of being orderly and disciplined was central to any hope of achieving political reform. As John Thelwall stated: 'the way to attain liberty ... is not by being mad and desperate; but by calmly exerting your intellect in acquiring a just knowledge of the nature and causes of your oppressions. ... Let us cultivate reason and if violence comes, let it come from our oppressors'.[85] Thelwall was so convinced of the calm and rational character of radicals, that he teased government spies and informers in the crowd attending one of the LCS outdoor meetings in 1794 by directing them to report on their 'opportunity of learning good manners, order, and decorum from the Swinish Multitude'.[86]

Part of Thelwall's audaciousness was based upon the code of conduct imposed by the LCS on its members. The rules of the LCS were intended to cultivate civility and to dissuade those in the group from displaying excitable emotions. In 1794, a draft version of the LCS's new constitution included a section on 'Order': those members 'attempting to trespass on order, under pretence of shewing [sic] zeal, courage, or any other motive, are to be suspected. A noisy disposition is seldom the sign of courage, and extreme zeal is often a cloak of treachery'.[87] In the 1790s, quietness was respectable, and passion was the emotion of the mob. The LCS was acutely aware of this meaning behind self-restrained individual behaviour and the constructions that linked individual behaviour to that of the collective. Although the LCS's code of conduct was a functional and administrative policy, it also had a cultural purpose. Orderly practice 'had important symbolic connotations during the 1790s: in tumultuous times, the disciplined and ordered structures of the LCS not only provided a stabilised and normalised space in the micro-world of the meeting room, but those structures also supported the implication that the Society and its members were not given to transgressive behaviour'.[88]

The internal decorum of the LCS was intended to instil discipline in its members as well as to reflect more generally the peaceful, non-riotous nature of radicalism. In the first published address of the LCS in 1792, the society articulated 'their *Abhorrence* of Tumult and Violence, and that, as they aim at Reform not Anarchy, Reason, Firmness, and Unanimity are the only Arms they themselves will employ, or persuade their Fellow-Citizens to exert against Abuse of Power'.[89] Two years later, the LCS issued one of the clearest statements of the normative position of radicalism in a pamphlet, which captured in its title the underlying claim that there were 'reformers no rioters' among the ranks of British radicals in the 1790s. By this time, the LCS was 'accustomed to suffer from the misrepresentations and calumnies of those whose sordid interest can alone be promoted by the delusion of the people', and the group was not surprised by 'the unfounded assertion ... that this Society has been the agitators of the tumults, which ... disturbed the peace' in London during August 1794.[90] The LCS believed the 'ridiculousness of the accusation ... must be sufficiently apparent to everyone who is not disposed to become the credulous dupe of any state juggler, who may exercise his talent for the marvellous'.[91] Despite the 'great diligence' of government spies, only 'several persons have been apprehended', and the question was posed: 'are any of them members of this society?'[92] The answer was, no: 'What! the *London Corresponding Society*, the projectors and even the leaders of insurrection and riot, yet not one of its members carried off a trophy to magisterial vigilance!'.[93]

Reformers No Rioters, as part of the discursive contest for defining 'the mob' in the 1790s, positioned radicals within an acceptable and rational sphere outside of the margins of society. The message was explicit – radicals were not a dangerous mob: 'To take up ... *arms*, and revolt against the government of the country each time that every separate grievance might have been most gallingly felt, has neither been the *practice* nor one of the *principles* which guide' radicalism.[94] Even the title of this pamphlet itself constitutes a rebuttal and an alternative to the conservative classification of radicalism as unrestrained and disorderly. The term 'reformers' was intended to evoke images of self-control, and of change by gradual and constitutional means. Although *Reformers No Rioters* was a clear vindication of radicalism and a firm denunciation of riotous allegations made by 'pensioned alarmists',[95] loyalists inevitably viewed with suspicion the actions and intentions of radicals during the 1790s. Irrespective of what radicals said or did, there was no remorse from their opponents. Even saying nothing could make radicals culpable of misconduct, which was one of the factors that motivated the LCS to publish *Reformers No Rioters* in response to accusations of being riotous: 'as the evil genius of our accusers has prompted them (regardless of truth or decency) to bring against us this infamous charge, justice to ourselves demands that we should thus publicly meet the accusation, to prevent our silence being construed into an admission of guilt'.[96] It was, nevertheless, an impossible task for radicals of the 1790s. In a period of heightened sensitivity to crowd actions and the potential for revolution in Britain, the mob identity was firmly fixed: in the blurry vision of loyalists, radicals were rioters not reformers.

Notes

1. Report from William Metcalfe, LCS Committee of Correspondence, 29 August 1794, The National Archives [hereafter: TNA], Treasury Solicitor Papers, TS 11/956/3501.
2. Report from William Metcalfe, LCS Committee of Correspondence, 29 August 1794, TNA, TS 11/956/3501.
3. See Roger Schofield, 'Did the Mothers Really Die? Three Centuries of Maternal Mortality in "the World We Have Lost"', in *The World We Have Gained*, ed. Lloyd Bonfield et al. (Oxford, 1986), pp. 230–60; and Adrian Wilson, 'The Perils of Early Modern Procreation: Childbirth With or Without Fear?', *Journal of Eighteenth-Century Studies*, 16 (1993), pp. 1–19.

4. Thomas Hardy, *Memoir of Thomas Hardy, Founder of, and Secretary to, the London Corresponding Society* (London, 1832), in *Testaments of Radicalism: Memoirs of Working Class Politicians 1790–1885*, ed. David Vincent (London, 1977), p. 60.
5. Gerald Jordan and Nicholas Rogers, 'Admirals as Heroes: Patriotism and Liberty in Hanoverian England', *Journal of British Studies*, 28 (1989), p. 212.
6. Hardy, *Memoir of Thomas Hardy*, pp. 60–61. Also see the account in *The Tribune*, vol. 1 (1795), p. 137.
7. On the treason trials of 1794, see Alan Wharam, *The Treason Trials, 1794* (Leicester, 1992); and John Barrell, *Imagining the King's Death: Figurative Treason, Fantasies of Regicide 1793–1796* (Oxford, 2000).
8. [Richard Lee], *On the Death of Mrs Hardy, Wife of Mr Thomas Hardy, of Piccadilly; Imprisoned in the Tower for High Treason* (London, 1794), p. 1.
9. See *Lloyd's Evening Post*, 29 August 1794: 'Mrs Hardy, a few moments only before she expired, solemnly declared that the separation from her husband, and the uncertainty in which she was respecting the time of his trial, were the occasion of her death'.
10. *Morning Post*, 5 September 1794.
11. Robert Shoemaker, *The London Mob: Violence and Disorder in Eighteenth-Century England* (London and New York, 2004), p. 153.
12. James Epstein, 'Equality and No King: Sociability and Sedition: The Case of John Frost', in *Romantic Sociability: Social Networks and Literary Culture in Britain 1770–1840*, ed. Gillian Russell and Clara Tuite (Cambridge, 2002), p. 49.
13. Patricia A. Adler and Peter Adler, *Constructions of Deviance: Social Power, Context, and Interaction*, 3rd ed. (Belmont, 2000), p. 12.
14. Samuel Taylor Coleridge, *Conciones ad Populum*, in *Lectures 1795 on Politics and Religion*, ed. Lewis Patton and Peter Mann (Princeton and London, 1971), p. 52.
15. Charles Pigott, *A Political Dictionary: Explaining the True Meaning of Words* (London, 1795), p. 79. On Pigott, see Jon Mee, 'Libertines and Radicals in the 1790s: The Strange Case of Charles Pigott I', in *Libertine Enlightenment: Sex, Liberty and Licence in the Eighteenth Century*, ed. Peter Cryle and Lisa O'Connell (Basingstoke, 2004), pp. 183–203; and Jon Mee, '"A Bold and Outspoken Man": The Strange Career of Charles Pigott II', in *Cultures of Whiggism: New Essays in English Literature and Culture in the Long Eighteenth Century*, ed. David Womersley (Newark, 2005), pp. 330–50.
16. Alan Booth, 'Popular Loyalism and Public Violence in the North-West of England, 1790–1800', *Social History*, 8 (1983), p. 295.
17. See H.T. Dickinson, 'Popular Conservatism and Militant Loyalism, 1789–1815', in *Britain and the French Revolution, 1789–1815*, ed. H.T. Dickinson (London, 1989), pp. 103–25; and H.T. Dickinson, 'Popular Loyalism in Britain in the 1790s', in *The Transformation of Political Culture: England and Germany in the Late Eighteenth Century*, ed. Eckhart Hellmuth (Oxford, 1990), pp. 503–33.
18. On the 'unofficial terror' of loyalism, see Michael T. Davis, 'The British Jacobins and the Unofficial Terror of Loyalism in the 1790s', in *Terror: From Tyrannicide to Terrorism*, ed. Brett Bowden and Michael T. Davis (Brisbane, 2008), pp. 92–113.
19. Christopher Wyvill to Samuel Shore, 28 December 1792, cited in Jenny Graham, *The Nation, the Law and the King: Reform Politics in England 1789–1799*, 2 vols. (Lanham and Oxford, 2000), I: p. 434.
20. Eckhart Hellmuth, 'After Fox's Libel Act: Or, How to Talk About the Liberty of the Press in the 1790s', in *Reactions to Revolutions: The 1790s and Their Aftermath*, ed. Ulrich Broich et al. (Berlin, 2007), p. 139.

21. Adrian Randall, *Riotous Assemblies: Popular Protest in Hanoverian England* (Oxford, 2006), p. 316.
22. See R.B. Rose, 'The Priestley Riots of 1791', *Past and Present*, 18 (1960), pp. 68–88; G.M. Ditchfield, 'The Priestley Riots in Historical Perspective', *Transactions of the Unitarian Historical Society*, 20 (1991), pp. 3–16; David L. Wykes, '"The Spirit of Persecutors Exemplified": The Priestley Riots and the Victims of the Church and King Mobs', *Transactions of the Unitarian Historical Society*, 20 (1991), pp. 17–39; Stephen Bygrave, '"I Predict a Riot": Joseph Priestley and Languages of Enlightenment in Birmingham in 1791', *Romanticism*, 18 (2012), pp. 70–88; and Jonathan Atherton, 'Rioting, Dissent and the Church in Late Eighteenth Century Britain: The Priestley Riots of 1791', PhD. thesis, University of Leicester (2012).
23. *The Times*, 18 July 1791.
24. Cited in Graham, *The Nation, the Law and the King*, I: p. 238.
25. See Archibald Prentice, *Historical Sketches and Personal Recollections of Manchester* (Manchester, 1851), pp. 9–11.
26. John Binns, *Recollections of the Life of John Binns* (Philadelphia, 1854), pp. 42–43.
27. David R. Mansley, *Collective Violence, Democracy and Protest Policing* (New York, 2014), p. 30.
28. Charles Tilly, 'Collective Violence in European Perspective', in *Violence in America: Historical and Comparative Perspectives*, ed. Hugh Davis Graham and Ted Robert Gurr (Beverly Hills, 1969), pp. 4–42.
29. Booth, 'Popular Loyalism and Public Violence in the North-West of England', p. 307.
30. Ibid., p. 308.
31. *Politics for the People*, ed. Daniel Isaac Eaton, vol. 2 (1794–1795), p. 343.
32. See E.P. Thompson, 'Hunting the Jacobin Fox', *Past and Present*, 142 (1994), pp. 94–140.
33. *Annual Register for the Year 1797* (London, 1797), p. 16.
34. Binns, *Recollections of the Life of John Binns*, p. 44.
35. Cecil Boyle Thelwall, *Life of John Thelwall* (London, 1837), p. 144.
36. Cited in Booth, 'Popular Loyalism and Public Violence in the North-West of England', p. 308.
37. *Chester Chronicle*, 8, 15 and 22 August 1794.
38. Booth, 'Popular Loyalism and Public Violence in the North-West of England', pp. 307–8.
39. Ibid., p. 308.
40. Ibid., p. 301.
41. Malcolm I. Thomis and Peter Holt, *Threats of Revolution in Britain 1789–1848* (London and Basingstoke, 1977), p. 23.
42. Ibid.
43. E.P. Thompson, *The Making of the English Working Class* (London, 1963), pp. 81–82.
44. Samuel Bamford, *Early Days* (London, 1849), p. 47.
45. Original letters addressed to John Reeves, British Library, Add. MS 16928, fo. 5r.
46. Mark Philp, *Reforming Ideas in Britain: Politics and Language in the Shadow of the French Revolution, 1789–1815* (Cambridge, 2014), p. 81.
47. Thomis and Holt, *Threats of Revolution in Britain*, p. 24.
48. Randall, *Riotous Assemblies*, p. 317.
49. Thompson, *The Making of the English Working Class*, p. 81.
50. *The Country Constitutional Guardian and Literary Magazine* (Bristol, 1822), I: p. 468.

51. William Cobbett, *A Summary View of the Politics of the United States* [Philadelphia, 1794], in *Porcupine's Works: Containing Various Writings and Selections*, 12 vols. (London, 1801), I: p. 63.
52. John Reeves, *Thoughts on the English Government. Addressed to the Quiet Good Sense of the People of England* (1795), in *Political Writings of the 1790s*, ed. Gregory Claeys (London, 1995), VIII: pp. 249–50.
53. *The Times*, 17 October 1792. For a discussion of the ways in which the LCS constructed civility, see Michael T. Davis, 'The Mob Club? The London Corresponding Society and the Politics of Civility in the 1790s' in *Unrespectable Radicals? Popular Politics in the Age of Reform*, ed. Michael T. Davis and Paul A. Pickering (Aldershot, 2008), pp. 21–40.
54. On the Gordon Riots, see Nicholas Rogers' essay in this collection and Ian Haywood and David Seed (eds), *The Gordon Riots: Politics, Culture and Insurrection in Late Eighteenth-Century Britain* (Cambridge, 2012).
55. *The Times*, 12 September 1792.
56. Edmund Burke, *Reflections on the Revolution in France*, ed. William B. Todd (1790; rpt. New York, 1959), pp. 27, 107–8.
57. David Bindman, *Shadow of the Guillotine: Britain and the French Revolution* (London, 1989), p. 118.
58. For a discussion of this image, see Ibid., pp. 118–21.
59. Herbert M. Atherton, 'The "Mob" in Eighteenth-Century English Caricature', *Eighteenth-Century Studies*, 12 (1978), p. 55.
60. James Epstein and David Karr, 'Playing at Revolution: British "Jacobin" Performance', *Journal of Modern History*, 79 (2007), p. 495.
61. *Anti-Jacobin Review*, 1(1798), p. 223.
62. M.O. Grenby, *The Anti-Jacobin Novel: British Conservatism and the French Revolution* (Cambridge, 2001), p. 8.
63. Davis, 'The Mob Club', p. 23.
64. *Morning Chronicle*, 15 July 1794.
65. Edmund Burke, *Reflections on the Revolution in France*, ed. L.G. Mitchell (1790; rpt. Oxford, 1999), p. 79.
66. Thompson, *The Making of the English Working Class*, p. 90.
67. Robert Malcolmson and Stephanos Mastoris, *The English Pig: A History* (London and New York, 2001), p. 6.
68. On the political meaning of porcine imagery and discourse in the eighteenth century, see Carl Fisher, 'Politics and Porcine Representation: Multitudinous Swine in the British Eighteenth Century', *LIT: Literature Interpretation Theory*, 10 (1999), pp. 303–26.
69. Pigott, *A Political Dictionary*, p. 109.
70. Mark Neocleous, 'The Monstrous Multitude: Edmund Burke's Political Teratology', *Contemporary Political Theory*, 3 (2004), p. 82.
71. Ibid.
72. John Drury, '"When the Mobs Are Looking for Witches to Burn, Nobody Is Safe": Talking About the Reactionary Crowd', *Discourse & Society*, 13 (2002), p. 47.
73. See Gustave Le Bon, *The Crowd: A Study of the Popular Mind* (1895; rpt. New York, 2002); and David Waddington and Mike King, 'The Disorderly Crowd: From Classical Psychological Reductionism to Socio-Contextual Theory', *Howard Journal of Criminal Justice*, 44 (2005), pp. 490–503.
74. *The Country Constitutional Guardian and Literary Magazine*, I: p. 468.

75. Drury, 'When the Mobs Are Looking for Witches to Burn, Nobody Is Safe', p. 60.
76. *The Times*, 21 August 1794.
77. Barrell, *Imagining the King's Death*, p. 234.
78. *The True Briton*, 13 November 1795.
79. For a discussion of the LCS outdoor meetings, see my forthcoming article '"Humbug in the Field": The Outdoor Meetings of the London Corresponding Society, 1793–1797'.
80. British Library, Add. MS 27814, fo. 57.
81. Charles Tilly, *Popular Contention in Great Britain 1758–1834* (Cambridge, MA, 1995), p. 214.
82. British Library, Add. MS 27814, fo. 59.
83. *The Parliamentary History of England* (London, 1806–20), XXXII: p. 155.
84. [London Corresponding Society], *Address to the Nation, from the London Corresponding Society, on the Subject of a Thorough Parliamentary Reform* (1793), in Claeys (ed.), *Political Writings of the 1790s*, IV: p. 62.
85. Cited in Paul Keen, *The Crisis of Literature in the 1790s: Print Culture and the Public Sphere* (Cambridge, 1999), p. 166.
86. Frida Knight, *The Strange Case of Thomas Walker: Ten Years in the Life of a Manchester Radical* (London, 1957), p. 170.
87. [London Corresponding Society], *The Report of the Committee of Constitution, of the London Corresponding Society* (London, 1794), in *London Corresponding Society*, ed. Michael T. Davis (London, 2002), I: p. 339.
88. Davis, 'The Mob Club', p. 31.
89. [London Corresponding Society], *London Corresponding Society, Held at the Bell, Exeter-Street, Strand* (London, 1792), in Davis (ed.), *London Corresponding Society*, II: p. 327.
90. London Corresponding Society, *Reformers No Rioters*, in Davis (ed.), *London Corresponding Society*, I: p. 289.
91. Ibid., I: p. 290.
92. Ibid., I: p. 289.
93. Ibid., I: pp. 289–90.
94. Ibid., I: p. 293.
95. Ibid., I: p. 290.
96. Ibid., I: p. 289.

Part II
Riots in the Industrial Era

9
Machine-Breaking and the 'Threat from Below' in Great Britain and France during the Early Industrial Revolution

Jeff Horn

'Luddite'. 'Wrecker'. At once descriptive and accusatory, these terms have acquired a deeply pejorative connotation in the English-speaking world. They suggest a rejection of technological change by unruly and undisciplined workers who take a riotous approach to threats of unemployment. The implication is that such behaviour constitutes sabotage and is disruptive of the regular course of economic development. By weaving the Luddites into a narrative of progress, machine-breaking has acquired a certain romance along with a certain pathos that has obscured the ineffectiveness of the movement and thereby tarred the broader practice of machine-breaking during the Industrial Revolution with a tragic label for resisting the inevitable victory of the machine. Because the Luddites and their English compatriots did not achieve their goals, they deserve their tragic reputation; but, on the other flank of the channel, machine-breaking had a powerful effect on the course of the Industrial Revolution in France.

The place of machine-breaking riots in industrial relations came during the twin transformations that birthed modern society: the Industrial Revolution and the French Revolution.[1] In most of early modern Europe, riotous outbreaks of machine-breaking were recognized as an aspect of traditional popular protest. An acceptance of machine-breaking through popular action probably was most widespread in England. However, during the formative decades of the early Industrial Revolution, the state – on behalf of economic and political elites – came to regard machine-breaking as a fundamental threat to the perpetuation of the social order and the steady growth of the industrial economy. This re-categorization or re-conception of machine-breaking as rebellious or outside the bounds of acceptable popular action was a reaction to the 'threat from below' that emerged as part of revolutionary politics in France in 1789. The draconian measures undertaken in Great Britain to prevent or punish machine-breaking reveal that economic and political elites considered this form of riotous behaviour to be as a menace to their position. The relative success of state and society in dealing with the 'threat from below' embodied by machine-breaking riots explains much about the course of the Industrial Revolution in Great Britain and France.

The English Luddites remain the best-known incidence of machine-breaking. Despite their reputation, they are not the most important example of machine-breaking popular violence. Although machine-breaking and other forms of violence against property did not have the same deep roots in eighteenth-century France as in England, labour militancy was clearly on the rise in the 1780s, especially in industrializing regions.[2] Labour unrest directed at machines was particularly widespread in textile-producing centres hurt by the effects of the Anglo-French Commercial Treaty of 1786. The rapid diffusion of machinery patterned on those pioneered in England accentuated unemployment. These concerns were given voice in the *cahiers de doléances* (lists of grievances) drawn up in the spring of 1789.[3]

The events of the French Revolution are too numerous and too complex for a recitation here, but the Great Fear of July–August 1789 – a phenomenon sparked by concerns about 'brigands' – often desperate people on the tramp looking for food, and the possibility of an aristocratic reaction to the formation of the National Assembly, led rural folk all over France to sack noble châteaux and fire the property and debt records. Spurred by this massive popular action, on the frenzied night of 4–5 August, the frightened deputies in Versailles renounced most of the privileges that typified the *ancien régime* and accepted most of the key principles later incorporated into the *Declaration of the Rights of Man and Citizen*. In urban areas, popular agitation also led to municipal revolutions catapulting new individuals and different social groups to power. One element has been left out of this story of the first months of the French Revolution: machine-breaking. The largest outbreak of machine-breaking occurred in Normandy, the most industrialized of the French provinces.[4] Three days of determined food rioting on 11–13 July in Rouen, the capital of the province, required the intervention of not only the city's bourgeois militia, but also of the local garrison. As Parisian crowds stormed the Bastille, 200–300 infuriated woolen workers from Darnetal busted through a picket of royal troops and entered the manufacturing suburb of Saint-Sever. These hand workers destroyed or burned English-style machines in the district's warren of workshops and proto-factories. A crowd of 300–400 broke down the heavy front door of the newly formed establishment of Debourges and Calonne and Company and destroyed 30 machines before the firm's own workers repelled the mob with weapons distributed by the owners. A few feet away, led by the manager, another group of employees fired on the crowd, saving their stock of English machines from the flames. Despite such spirited defence, hundreds of spinning jennies and a number of newly built carding machines were wrecked. When the city's militia arrived to confront the crowds, five rioters were killed. In Rouen proper, another crowd ravaged the home of several public officials and the chief tax-collecting office before destroying machines in a number of the industrializing hamlets on the north side of the Seine River.

New incidents followed as part of a more generalized popular attack on the symbols of the *ancien régime*. Beginning on 14 July 1789, crowds attacked the residences or offices of authorities and destroyed labour-saving machinery that 'took the food out of workers' mouths'. On 19–20 July, machines were broken into pieces and then burned in Saint-Sever, Oissel and Rouen. The municipality attempted to smother this round of machine-breaking, but the volunteer militia sent to disperse the crowds joined them instead. In the midst of the Great Fear, on the night of 3–4 August, after sacking several public buildings, a crowd of 4,000 publicly burned an English-model carding machine taken from a nearby factory. Other crowds did the same in Darnetal and Saint-Pierre de Franqueville. A water-frame was dismantled, and its owner's shop looted on 19 September. Beginning on 17 October, a series of riots in Rouen and Sotteville, led by artisans, resulted in the declaration of martial law. Hundreds more spinning jennies were taken apart, and the pieces burned.[5] In other parts of Normandy, machine-breaking took place in Louviers, Argentan and in several places in the *pays de caux*. It also spread northward into Picardy. Machines were destroyed widely in and around the woolens centre of Abbeville where stiff English competition had agitated a formerly docile, rurally based manufacturing labour force.[6]

This wave of machine-breaking was impressive in scope. More than 700 spinning jennies, including nearly all the recently built models, were either broken or burned. The cost of crowd action on 14 July was high. One official source noted: 'in a single day, the misguided people have destroyed the benefit of nearly 100,000 *livres* of expense and more than 15 months of work undertaken on their behalf'.[7] Among those who lost their property were several industrial pioneers enticed from England to naturalize advanced textile machinery, including George Garnett and Nicolas Barneville whose machines imitated those of Arkwright and Crompton.[8] The smoking debris of several years of government investment and entrepreneurial activity played a role in shifting the attitudes of economic decision-makers in Normandy.

In July 1789, machine-breaking was linked to food shortages and to dissatisfaction with the local political leadership. However, by October, artisanal mobilization stemmed almost exclusively from hatred of 'the machines used in cotton-spinning that have deprived many workers of their jobs'.[9] The labouring classes objected not only to technological obsolescence, but also to how machinery lowered the cost of production thereby forcing hand-workers to sweat even longer hours to make ends meet. In the *pays de caux*, the workday reached 17–18 hours for the poorest families. Yet among the 182 (141 men, 41 women) arrested for machine-breaking in 1789, less than 30% (45 men, 8 women) worked in professions linked to textiles. The single largest occupational grouping was agricultural day labourers, while almost 30% of the women arrested for machine-breaking were prostitutes. Nor could the presence of 16 soldiers (9%) among the machine-breakers have comforted either the authorities or manufacturers. In 1789, the Normans' rage against the machine was inextricably linked to revolutionary agitation. Because of the political and social ferment, the authorities in Normandy – whether municipal, judicial, provincial or royal – could brake, but not halt, popular unrest.

In other parts of France, machine-breaking incidents continued earlier patterns of resistance to mechanization, but took on different meanings because of the revolutionary crisis. In Saint-Étienne, beginning in 1787, textile workers, miners and artisans in the metallurgical industries repeatedly and successfully used violence to deter the introduction of new machinery and to cast out foreign workers who brought new industrial techniques. On 24 July 1789, a large group of miners and artisans rioted at Roche-la-molière situated atop the Rives-le-Gier coal basin to prevent the opening of a new pit to be run with steam engines that would employ some German labour. After attempting to negotiate, the crowd smashed in the windows of the building and then broke all the machinery before covering their tracks by setting fire to the building.[10]

Through popular action, customary productive practice could derail innovation. Jacques Sauvade (1730–1806), a mechanic and entrepreneur, developed water-powered stamping dies imitating German processes to produce tableware, buckles, locks and bolts after six years of experimentation. On 1 September, a crowd of artisans specializing in the manufacture of forks gathered outside his workshop. Sauvade recognized the threat and promised the crowd that he would 'delay perfecting his establishment until the people believed it offered some hope of employing workers, and if not, then desisting [from his innovations]'. He even dismantled two key parts of his machine and gave them to the mayor for safekeeping. Appeased, the crowd dispersed. The cylinders disappeared, but that was not enough to save Sauvade. A crowd returned that night and dismantled the machines and waterworks, then burned the workshop. Nine companies of troops arrived too late to stop the riot. That evening, some fork-makers threatened one of Sauvade's mechanics with burning down his house if he helped to rebuild the hated machinery.[11] The effects of this wave of machine-breaking were devastating for the region. The exploitation of the rich coal seams of Rives-le-Gier remained crude, while the introduction of textile machines stalled for a decade. Sauvade fled the region, but not before he complained about his treatment and the lack of state support: 'The actions of this ungovernable group of unemployed workers would have been more justifiable if these machines, invented with such difficulty and perfected at such great cost, had been the true source of their unemployment. But you, Messieurs, you have knowledge to the contrary'.[12] Sauvade's patented machines were put to productive use in Alsace where he established a new industry that lasted for decades.

A final episode of machine-breaking in 1789 traumatized southern Champagne. Subsistence was a particular problem in and around the city of Troyes, sparking a violent municipal revolution punctuated by a series of food riots. Divisions within the urban elite sabotaged efforts to reassure the restive, unemployed textile workers. On 9 September, the royal mayor Claude Huez was murdered publicly and his corpse mutilated. According to placards posted all over the city before the riot, the major charge against Huez, beyond the general lack of affordable food, was that, 'he had favored machines'. The city's industrial entrepreneurs roused the ire of the mob by installing new cotton spinning machines. As the rioters sacked the homes of officials and notables, they also indulged their hatred of machines. The assaults penetrated the shop-front homes of several merchant-manufacturers who had workshops in their basements. The rioters successfully targeted a number of prototype textile machines recently purchased from Paris and Rouen or imported directly from England. All were destroyed.[13]

Although the number of machines destroyed in Troyes was minimal, the incident loomed large for the city's industrial entrepreneurs. The day after the riot, the Provisional General Committee that ruled the city banned mechanized spinning, hoping to prevent further unrest even though the ban would throw an additional 800 people out of work. Over the next few months, plans by several leading textile firms to purchase Arkwright machines or to invest in other new technologies were dropped. A group of industrial entrepreneurs explained why they had not followed up earlier investments in new machinery: 'These machines are often attacked during popular riots because those involved in hand-spinning fear that large machines will diminish their salaries, a fear which is frequently sustained by ignorance'. Recognising the intransigence of Troyes' militant labouring classes, the city's industrial entrepreneurs collectively decided not to proceed with investments in machinery begun in the mid-1780s. Instead, with the support of local administrators, they focused on maintaining total employment by shifting production to unmechanized sectors like linen and concentrating on satisfying the regional market. Troyes' manufacturers expanded the hand-weaving of high-end cotton fabrics thereby emphasizing quality not quantity, a major shift in their market orientation. These entrepreneurs hoped to avoid 'any anxiety on the part of the indigent worker'. To reinforce the lesson, hundreds of female spinners in Troyes demonstrated to protest against the introduction of jennies in 1791, success-fully preventing their installation.[14]

Continued machine-breaking further spread the attitudes exemplified by the Troyens. The carders of Lille destroyed machines in 1790. The following year, jennies were attacked in Roanne and at the critical experimental mechanical workshop housed in the Hôpital des Quinze-Vingts in Paris. At Vincennes, a pilot gun-making operation was heavily damaged in February 1791. The entrepreneurs of Troyes were not alone in fearing the recrudescence of machine-breaking riots. In 1792, local administrators in Amiens endorsed a plan to invest in production that would permit a 'progressive increase' in the number of workers employed through a 'limitation of the number of machines... at work in the textile industry of the department of the Somme'.[15] In the Revolutionary Year IV [1796], departmental administrators noted their inability to combat 'the prejudice in public opinion against machines because they limit the amount of work available to the poor. ... this prejudice against machinery has led the commercial classes... to abandon their interest in the cotton industry'.[16] According to these administrators and those who followed in their footsteps, fear of working class reprisal played a major role in this shift in industrial entrepreneurs' attitudes towards mechanization.[17]

Machine-breaking in 1789 was linked to the emergence of modern revolutionary politics. The inability of French authorities to reign in the 'threat from below' meant that industrial entrepreneurs could not invest with confidence in new machinery or count on state support in controlling their workers. This crisis of confidence undermined the impressive steps taken before 1789 to compete with the increasingly efficient producers of Britain. Machine-breaking riots played an important role in shifting the course of nineteenth-century industrialization in France away from the British model; this shift had spectacular consequences for the French economy in the nineteenth century.

Machine-breaking riots in France strongly effected the course of industrialization, but, despite their greater notoriety, the same cannot be said for the English Luddites. Throughout the early modern period, British labourers defended their interests with recurrent machine-breaking. A brief outline of the scope and scale of eighteenth-century English machine-breaking suffices to demonstrate the significance of riotous responses to mechanization. The colliers of Northumberland destroyed machinery at the pit head in the 1740s and again in 1765. The Spitalfields silk weavers rioted against the introduction of machines in 1675, 1719, 1736 and the 1760s. Charles Dingley's new mechanical saw mill was taken apart by a crowd of 500 sawyers in May 1768. James Hargreaves's first spinning jenny was dismantled in 1767; two years later more of his machines were destroyed. In 1776, the West Country experienced widespread popular sabotage of almost every form of machinery used in the woolen industry. Three years later, a mob around Blackburn demolished every carding engine and all the large jennies utilizing water or horse power. The same year, the water frames at Richard Arkwright's works at Chorley were destroyed along with several recently established cotton mills. Machine-breaking in Lancashire and the Midlands punctuated the era from 1776 to 1780. In the West Country, the introduction of the flying shuttle sparked riots at Trowbridge in 1785, 1792 and several times between 1810 and 1813. Joseph Brookhouse's attempt to utilize Arkwright's techniques provoked a violent response in Leicester in 1787. At Bradford, in 1791, three were killed defending a mill's machinery against a crowd of 500. In 1792, Manchester was the scene of an attack on a factory containing 24 of Edmund Cartwright's power looms; ultimately, the factory was burned by handloom weavers.[18] In Wiltshire and Somerset, the elite workers in the woolen industry, the shearmen, formed a powerful union. Associated with their counterparts in the West Riding district of Yorkshire, beginning from 1799 to 1802, West Country workers led a major campaign against the introduction of the gig mill and the shearing frame usually referred to as the 'Wiltshire Outages'. The shearmen resorted to violence only after repeated recourse to more peaceful forms of resistance had no effect.[19]

These events provide the context and set the stage for the Luddite movement of 1811–17. Named after a supposed Leicester stockinger's apprentice named Ned Ludham who in 1779 responded to his master's reprimand by taking a hammer to a stocking frame, the followers of 'Ned Ludd', 'Captain Ludd' or sometimes 'General Ludd', targeted this machine for destruction.[20] Early in February 1811, the movement began in the Midlands triangle formed by Nottingham, Leicester and Derby in the lace and hosiery trades. Protected by their communities, Luddite bands conducted at least 100 separate attacks that destroyed about 1,000 frames (out of 25,000) valued at £6,000–10,000. The riotous activities were aimed at special frames making cheap knockoffs that undermined the livelihood of skilled workers; these Luddites did not attack all machines or act indiscriminately. Luddism in the Midlands died down in February 1812, but it had already inspired the woolen workers of Yorkshire to take action, beginning in January 1812. These Luddites were more generally opposed to mechanization than their compatriots. A third outbreak took place in April among the cotton weavers of Lancashire where armed crowds attacked large factories. Thousands participated in these activities, including many whose livelihoods were not threatened directly by mechanization. Despite the occupational diversity of the crowds involved, the Luddites generally destroyed only those machines that were 'innovations' or that threatened employment. They deliberately and systematically left other machines alone. Collectively, these initial episodes of Luddism caused perhaps £100,000 of damage. Further waves of machine-breaking in the Midlands in which a few hundred additional stocking frames were destroyed took place in the winter of 1812–13, in the summer and fall of 1814 and in the summer and fall of 1816 that sputtered into early 1817.[21]

Machine-breaking did not disappear with the followers of Ned Ludd. Machine-breaking accompanied extensive rural rioting in East Anglia in 1816 and in 1822. In 1826, Lancashire endured a wave of machine-breaking more extensive than in 1811–12: 21 factories were assaulted, and 1,000 looms valued at £30,000 smashed. Three years later, power looms were targeted by Manchester's working classes. During the Captain Swing riots, which ran from 1829–32 with a high point in late August 1830, agricultural labourers relied on arson, but machine-breaking was an important means of expressing popular anger. As a result of more than 1,500 separate incidents, an impressive proportion of England's threshers were destroyed along with quite a bit of industrial machinery. The Plug Plots led by Staffordshire miners in 1842 concluded machine-breaking in Britain.[22]

Although the longevity, geographical scope and popular support for machine-breaking in Great Britain is impressive, the magnitude of government repression is astonishing. The Duke of Wellington began the Peninsular Campaign in 1808 with less than 10,000 troops, but the British state deployed 12,000 troops against the Luddites in 1812. On 14 February 1812, Parliament made frame-breaking a capital crime. George Rudé provided an approximation of English governmental response to all popular riots and disturbances. Against a grand total of two fatal victims of the Luddites and Captain Swing combined, British courts hanged more than 30 Luddites in 1812–13, and 9 'swung' in 1830 for machine-breaking among the 19 executed in the aftermath of Captain Swing. These figures do not include the casualties involved in the attacks themselves. For instance, in repulsing the Luddite attack on Daniel Burton's factory at Middleton in Lancashire on 18 April 1812, five were killed and 18 wounded. In addition to the dead and maimed, dozens more Luddites and 200-plus machine-breakers involved in Swing were sent to Australia. Nearly 650 were imprisoned. In the course of more than 20 major riots and demonstrations between 1736 and 1848, the English crowd killed no more than a dozen. The courts hanged 118 while 630 died from military action. Rudé concluded that machine-breaking was only one aspect – if the most spectacular – of the popular restiveness of the early industrial period.[23]

British state repression was also legal. To mention only those measures directly pertaining to the industrial work environment, new facets of state repression included: Pitt's Two Acts restricting individual liberties in 1795; the suspension of the Act of Habeas Corpus; the 1797 Administering Unlawful Oaths Act; the Combination Acts of 1799–1800; the final abrogation of paternalist industrial legislation in woolens in 1809 and the repeal of the Elizabethan apprenticeship statutes in 1814, eliminating the power of officials to regulate wages.[24] According to Nottingham town clerk George Coldham, the actions of the Midland Luddites, 'arise from the endeavours of the labouring Classes by terror to compell their Employers to increase the price of their labour and otherwise conduct the Manufactory in a manner more agreeable to the Interests or prejudice of the Artizan and their System must be kept down by Force before we can expect the restoration of Public Tranquility'.[25] Adrian Randall takes this view and makes it a general rule: he argues that in the aftermath of Luddism, the English state increasingly identified its interests with those of large-scale 'innovating' manufacturers at the expense of customary protections ignoring the desire to retain these protections among some segments of the elite and many small producers.[26]

The disproportion of British state response demands our attention. How successful were the Luddites and their riotous successors in defending custom and combating mechanization? A few limited but temporary successes lasted as long as the Napoleonic wars: after the Wiltshire Outages of 1802, the gig frame did not return until after Waterloo, and a 1787 attack on machinery in Leicester discouraged the introduction of mechanized spinning until after 1815.[27] The other major triumph of the machine-breakers was registered by the agricultural labourers who destroyed thousands of threshing machines during the Captain Swing outbreak; these machines did not return in anything like the same numbers to most of southern England for at least a generation.[28] In the industrial sector, outside of the city of Leicester, the only unequivocal success by English machine-breakers occurred in Wiltshire, an area that rapidly was becoming marginalized by the West Riding in an industry steadily being superseded by cotton. The contrast to the situation in France could not be more stark.

Machine-breaking popular action in Britain had little to no effect on the course of British industrialization. Over the course of the generation that lived through the French Revolution and the Napoleonic era, British entrepreneurs mechanized and disciplined their workforce. Unlike their continental competitors, they were able to do so because of the absence of a genuine revolutionary threat to their position. Innovative manufacturers in Britain could rely on the state to endorse their interests and assist them in the task of 'breaking' the British working classes.[29] This hope for state action was clearly justified; more than 60 acts of Parliament were enacted during the crucial 1793–1820 period to prohibit or repress working-class collective action.[30]

Having distinguished between the significance of machine-breaking riots on the two flanks of the channel, we must also move beyond the anecdotal to explore the place of the destruction of machines in labour relations and within the context of popular violence against property. This task has been made possible by Charles Tilly's groundbreaking statistical approach to what he calls 'popular contention'. Whatever qualms might be advanced about his research team's methodology, assumptions about the relationship of press coverage to events, and lack of attention to the effectiveness of state repression on the expression of popular public activity, Tilly has shown conclusively that violence against persons and property declined precipitously in the era from 1758 to 1834 in favour of less confrontational tactics. He has also demonstrated that machine-breaking incidents represented only a tiny fraction of the total of popular gatherings in England, even at the height of Luddite influence or during Captain Swing.[31] Yet even this tiny fraction dwarfed the incidence of machine-breaking riots on the other side of the channel. Tilly's exploration of 'how the development of capitalism and the rise of a strong national state impinged upon the contention of ordinary people' in France does not have an index reference to machine-breaking.[32] The greater incidence of machine-breaking riots in Britain and its inverse relationship to effective popular action are symptomatic of the greater powerlessness of the British labouring classes.

If British machine-breaking was so rare and so ineffective, how did it become such a significant part of the collective imagination of popular action? I would argue that the machine-breakers remain an important component of the historical record for two polar opposite reasons. On the one hand, the Luddites were a vital aspect of the efforts of ground-breaking leftist historians like Eric Hobsbawm, George Rudé and E.P. Thompson to provide a history of militant collective action by English labourers in the face of domination by the state during the rise of a capitalist industrial system. Whether focusing on the 'moral economy of the English crowd' or 'collective bargaining by riot', these pioneers demonstrated both the logic and the rationality of the English working classes during early industrialization. In keeping with their desire to provide a prehistory for the twentieth-century labour movement, these historians portrayed these sorts of riotous behaviour as relatively effective: they thought that, at the very least, the English labouring classes raised the spectre of revolution and forced elites – over the long term – to adjust their treatment of workers if they wanted to maintain their positions of dominance. Thus, machine-breaking and the Luddites especially, were portrayed as vital steps in the evolution of the contemporary labour movement.[33]

Such sympathetic treatments of machine-breaking riots represent one major strain of interpretation; a more common representation of the Luddites and the one that Thompson, Rudé and Hobsbawm and their successors like Maxine Berg, Adrian Randall and John Rule struggle against is the impression of brutal, destructive workers trying to hold onto a world of petty production made obsolete by technological change that could not survive the growing pains of industrial capitalism. Even so fine a historian as Peter Mathias argued that 'machine breaking which came in the worst years of distress, 1800, 1812, 1816, 1826–27, 1830, were not a new theme but the survival of a reaction characteristic of the pre-industrial world – the peasants' revolt'.[34] Gothic-tinged portrayals of the Luddites as a savage reactionary remnant of 'pre-industrial' attitudes have been far more common than those influenced by the left: such views perpetuate nineteenth-century elite fears of revolution.[35] In these hands, the actions of the Luddites facilitate a kind of demonization of collective action by workers that justified and justifies the paternalism of employers and legal and political restrictions on labour militancy and collective action. Taken together, these divergent uses of the tragic story of the Luddites have sustained their prominent position in the collective memory of labour action.

Although I would like to believe along with Thompson, Rudé and Roger Wells that there was a real possibility of revolution in Britain to mirror events in France, if not in 1811–17, then in 1830–31,[36] I am increasingly persuaded that this was not the case. The Luddite movement clearly had political overtones,[37] but the proper means of assessing the significance of riotous machine-breaking is through the effect of popular action on industrial entrepreneurs and on the behaviour of the state. The phenomenal scale and scope of government repression of the Luddites demonstrates that the British state would and could protect innovating industrial entrepreneurs from the wrath of the labouring classes. Thus, assured of thoroughgoing state support against the 'threat from below', British entrepreneurs safely and systematically developed efficient modes of production that made Britain the 'workshop of the world' throughout the first half of the nineteenth century.

Riotous machine-breaking had a completely different impact in France. There, because it was linked with the emergence of revolutionary politics in 1789, machine-breaking accentuated the concerns of industrial entrepreneurs who had to face not just massive political unrest and economic dislocation along with British competition, but also a 'threat from below' that – to their way of thinking – culminated in the Reign of Terror. The inability of the French state to control the working classes or enforce the laws already on the books left entrepreneurs to cope with their labour forces on very different terms than was the case on the other flank of the channel. Popular destruction of machines contributed significantly to retarding French industrialization and shifting its pattern away from one modelled on Britain. As a form of riot, therefore, machine-breaking had minimal impact in its most famous (infamous) outbreak: the English Luddites of 1811–17. Most historians reject the argument that the direct action of the working classes in destroying machines or in 'wrecking' more generally provided the chief impetus for the shifts in elite behaviour that furthered government reform of the workplace and the impressive long-term growth of the English electorate. Rather, the threat embodied by the French Revolution caused British elites to embrace a new form of politics.[38] At the same time, it was the intimate association with revolutionary politics that magnified the impact of machine-breaking on elite behaviour in France. Confident of the effective support of a powerful, repressive state apparatus, British entrepreneurs could innovate in ways that French economic elites could not. The lingering 'threat from below' experienced by Revolutionary France made machine-breaking a potent break on the emergence of industrial capitalism.

Notes

1. The arguments found in this chapter are developed fully in Jeff Horn, *The Path Not Taken: French Industrialization in the Age of Revolution* (Cambridge, MA, 2006), pp. 89–126.
2. George Rudé, *Paris and London in the Eighteenth Century: Studies in Popular Protest* (New York, 1970), p. 69, Steven L. Kaplan, 'Réflexions sur la police du monde du travail, 1700–1815', *Revue historique*, 261 (1979), pp. 35, 69–70; Michael Sonenscher, 'Journeymen, the Courts and the French Trades 1781–1791', *Past and Present*, 114 (1987), pp. 77, 81.
3. See Roger Picard, *Les cahiers de 1789 et les classes ouvrières* (Paris, 1910).
4. See Jean-Pierre Allinne, 'À propos des bris de machines textiles à Rouen pendant l'été 1789: émeutes anciennes ou émeutes nouvelles?', *Annales de Normandie*, 31 (1981), pp. 37–58. Unless otherwise noted, I rely on his account for Normandy.
5. Jean-Baptiste Horcholle, *Evenements de la Révolution française à Rouen de 1789 à 1801*, n.d. [1801], Bibliothèque Municipale [BM] Rouen Y128*, A.C. Poullain, *Analyses des délibérations de l'assemblée municipale et électorale du 16 Juillet au 4 Mars 1790 et du Conseil général de la Commune du 4 Mars 1790 au 25 Brumaire an IV, 16 Novembre 1795* (Rouen, 1905), *Journal de Normandie* 87 (31 October 1789), p. 397, *Jugement souverain prévôtal et en dernier ressort*, 20 October 1789, Archives Départementales [AD] Seine-Maritime 220 BP14.
6. Serge Chassenge, *Le coton et ses patrons: France, 1760–1840* (Paris, 1991), p. 190, Gay Gullickson, *Spinners and Weavers of Auffay: Rural Industry and the Sexual Division of Labor in a French Village, 1750–1850* (New York, 1986), pp. 89–90; Georges Ruhlmann, *Les corporations, les manufactures et le travail libre à Abbeville au XVIIIe siècle* (Paris, 1948), ch. 7.
7. *Rapport des Travaux de la Commission intermédiaire de Haute-Normandie depuis le 20 Décembre 1787 jusqu'au 27 Juillet 1790*, AD Seine-Maritime C 2114*, p. 200.
8. William H. Reddy, *The Rise of Market Culture: The Textile Trade and French Society, 1750–1900* (Cambridge and Paris, 1985), pp. 59–60.
9. Horcholle, *Evenements*.
10. Pétrus Faure, *Histoire du mouvement ouvrier dans le département de la Loire* (Saint-Étienne, 1956), p. 54; Jean-Baptiste Galley, *L'Élection de Saint-Étienne à la fin de l'ancien régime* (Paris, 1903), p. 58.
11. This paragraph is based on Ken Alder's account of this event. *Engineering the Revolution: Arms and Enlightenment in France, 1763–1815* (Princeton, NJ, 1997), pp. 214–15 (citation from these pages). Additional details are from Galley, *L'Élection de Saint-Étienne*, pp. 58, 74–75; Paul Tézenas du Montcel, *L'Assemblée du département de Saint-Étienne et sa Commission intermédiaire, 8 Octobre 1787 – 21 Juillet 1790* (Paris, 1903), p. 464; Jacques Schnetzler, *Les Industries et les hommes dans la région de St.-Étienne* (Université de Lyon II, thesis, 1973), p. 53; Jacques Sauvade, *Mémoire*, 2 July 1789, Archives Communales [AC] Saint-Étienne Ms 328 2 (2) [1 Mi 11].
12. Sauvade, *Mémoire*.
13. Lynn Avery Hunt, *Revolution & Urban Politics in Provincial France: Troyes and Reims, 1786–1790* (Stanford, CA, 1978); Jeff Horn, *"Qui parle pour la nation?": Les élections et les élus de la Champagne méridionale, 1765–1830* (Paris, 2004), chapter 3.

14. Albert Babeau, *Histoire de Troyes pendant la revolution*, 2 vols. (Paris, 1873–74), I: p. 243; Jean Ricommard, *La Bonneterie à Troyes et dans le département de l'Aube: Origines, évolution. caratèreres actuels* (Paris, 1934), p. 38; Bernhard Maudhuit, 'Recherches sur le textile troyen au XVIIIe siècle d'après le fond Berthelin et Fromageot', 2 vols. (Université de Reims: Maîtrise d'histoire économique, 1957), II: pp. 196–97; Jean Darbot, *La Trinité, première manufacture de bas au métier de Troyes* (Troyes, 1979), p. 16; *Pétition des Négociants et Fabricans de Troyes au Comités d'Agriculture et Commerce et Finances*, 12 August 1791; Archives Nationales [AN] F12 1342, Jacques-Edme Beugnot, 'Discours', 3 November, 1790, *Procès-verbal des séances du Conseil-général du département de l'Aube (1790)*, AN F1CIII Aube 2, [Louis-Ézechias] Pouchet, *Essai sur les avantages locaux du département de l'Aube, et sur la prospérité nationale, ou Adresse à Mes Concitoyens du Département de l'Aube*, 1791, AN F12 652, pp. 9–10.
15. Jacques-François Martin, *Circulaire*, 19 May 1792, AD Somme L496.
16. *Mémoire sur les Encouragements à accorder au Commerce par le directoire du département de la Somme*, 22 Floréal, Year IV [11 May 1796], AD Somme L496.
17. *La Décade du département de la Somme* 24: 2 (30 Fructidor, An VIII [17 September 1800]; Nicolas Quinette, *Lettre au Ministre de l'Intérieur*, 24 April 1806, AD Somme M80003.
18. Rudé, *The Crowd in History*, p. 71; Eric J. Hobsbawm, 'The Machine Breakers', in *Laboring Men: Studies in the History of Labour* (Garden City, NY, 1964), p. 14; Rudé, *Paris and London*, pp. 249–50; John E. Archer, *Social Unrest and Popular Protest in England 1780–1840* (Cambridge, 2000), p. 45; Maxine Berg, *The Age of Manufactures, 1700–1820: Industry, Innovation and Work in Britain*, 2nd ed. (London, 1994), p. 254; John Rule, *The Labouring Classes in Early Industrial England, 1750–1850* (London, 1986), p. 278; Ian R. Christie, *Wars and Revolutions: Britain, 1760–1815* (Cambridge, MA, 1982), p. 173; Malcolm I. Thomis, *The Luddites: Machine-Breaking in Regency England* (Hamden, CT, 1970), p. 16; Brian Bailey, *The Luddite Rebellion* (New York, 1998), pp. 11–12.
19. Adrian Randall, *Before the Luddites: Custom, Community and Machinery in the English Woollen Industry, 1776–1809* (Cambridge, 1991), pp. 249, 289.
20. Bailey gives a hard to swallow explanation of the origin of the name in his otherwise solid (although slanted toward Leicestershire) account of the Luddites. *The Luddite Rebellion*, pp. x–xi.
21. Rudé, *The Crowd in History*, pp. 79–80, 89; 'The Luddites in the Period 1779–1830', in *The Luddites and Other Essays*, ed. Lionel M. Munby (London, 1971), p. 39; Francis O. Darvall, *Popular Disturbances and Public Order in Regency England* (London, 1934), pp. 259–60, 209–10; Charles Tilly, *Popular Contention in Great Britain 1758–1834* (Boulder, CO, 2005), p. 348; Bailey, *The Luddite Rebellion*, p. 14.
22. 'The Luddites', p. 47; Archer, *Social Unrest and Popular Protest*, pp. 15–21, 54–55.
23. Rudé, *The Crowd in History*, pp. 83–90, 255; Rudé, *Paris and London*, p. 28.
24. James Moher, 'From Suppression to Containment: Roots of Trade Union Law to 1825', in *British Trade Unionism 1750–1850: The Formative Years*, ed. John Rule (London, 1988), pp. 74–97.
25. Cited by Bailey, *The Luddite Rebellion*, p. 22.
26. Randall, *Before the Luddites*, p. 248; Adrian Randall, 'The Philosophy of Luddism: The Case of the West of England Woolen Workers, ca. 1790–1809', *Technology and Culture*, 27 (1986), p. 15.
27. Hobsbawm, 'The Machine Breakers', p. 21; Randall, *Before the Luddites*, p. 289; Christie, *Wars and Revolutions*, p. 173.

28. Hobsbawm, 'The Machine Breakers', p. 21; Rudé, *The Crowd in History*, p. 90.
29. Moher, 'From Suppression to Containment', pp. 87–88, 90.
30. Archer, *Social Unrest and Popular Protest*, p. 86; Moher, 'From Suppression to Containment', p. 74.
31. Tilly, *Popular Contention in Great Britain*, p. 213.
32. Charles Tilly, *The Contentious French* (Cambridge, MA, 1986), p. 11.
33. See Hobsbawm, 'The Machine Breakers'; Rudé, *The Crowd in History* and *Paris and London*; E.P. Thompson, *The Making of the English Working Class* (New York, 1963), pp. 452–602; and E.P. Thompson, 'The Moral Economy of the English Crowd in the Eighteenth Century', *Past and Present*, 50 (1971), pp. 71–136.
34. Peter Mathias, *The First Industrial Nation: An Economic History of Britain 1700–1914*, 2nd ed. (London, 1983), p. 333.
35. See, for example, the influential views of Joel Mokyr, *The Lever of Riches: Technological Creativity and Economic Progress* (New York, 1990), p. 255 and David S. Landes, *The Unbound Prometheus: Technological Change and Industrial Development in Western Europe from 1750 to the Present* (New York, 1969), p. 123. For interesting reviews of the uses of the image of the Luddites, see Vincent Bourdeau, François Jarrige and Julien Vincent, *Les Luddites: Bris de machines, économie politique et histoire* (Paris, 2006), pp. 95–142; Nicolas Chevassus-au-Louis, *Les briseurs de machines de Ned Ludd à José Bové* (Paris, 2006), pp. 185–208; and Kirkpatrick Sale, *Rebels Against the Future: The Luddites and Their War on the Industrial Revolution: Lessons for the Computer Age* (Reading, MA, 1995), pp. 261–280.
36. Thompson, *The Making of the English Working Class*, pp. 807–8; Rudé, *The Crowd in History*, pp. 252, 264; Roger Wells, 'English Society and Revolutionary Politics in the 1790s: The Case for Insurrection', in *The French Revolution and British Popular Politics*, ed. Mark Philp (New York, 1991), pp. 188–226.
37. The best place to see these views in context is Kevin Binfield (ed.), *Writings of the Luddites* (Baltimore, 2004).
38. Tilly, *Popular Contention in Great Britain*, p. 143.

and culture. In this context 'militarization', a term with a fairly recent provenance, appears useful in describing the impact of war and the preparation for it on society and culture. Defined as 'less a thing than a process, one that does not depend on precise definitions of warlike values or even on distinctions like civilian/military' it carries far less baggage than the term 'militarism' and, if its fuzziness renders it too blunt a tool for social scientists, its flexibility ought to recommend it to historians.[5] Not least, it allows for the exploration of the militarization of forms and symbolic practices without necessarily implying that this signified the wholesale adoption of a military ethos or values. Rather, we can examine the *militarization* of certain aspects of society and culture, while still accepting persuasive arguments that the experience of war did not render Britons more enduringly *militarist*.[6]

In particular, it is useful in describing some developments within collective action after 1815. War has, of course, featured largely in accounts of collective action: as the creator of social and economic conditions in which action was encouraged and pursued; as providing opportunities whereby dissidents might attempt to shape the war aims of combatants; and as the vital plank in explaining government repression and the undermining of oppositional claims to patriotism.[7] The war, however, recedes out of view pretty swiftly in accounts of collective action after 1815, although there have been tentative attempts to link militarization to Ireland's precocious politicization in the early nineteenth century.[8] There is, of course, plentiful acknowledgement that the socioeconomic situation that nourished action was one created by the sudden lurch from war to peace and impressive work on the double-sided nature of the government's 'call to arms', which rallied unprecedented numbers in defence of the constitution, but carried the danger of politicizing them in the process.[9] Similarly, even the most cursory of glances at newspapers from the period confirms how far war and its legacies – in particular, the linked concerns of the income tax and fears of a standing army – continued to provide the framework for political debate into the 1820s. There is less recognition of the fact that collective action continued to respond to a society and political culture shaped, over the preceding 22 years, by the waging of war. This essay will offer an account of some key aspects of this relationship between militarization and collective action. First, it outlines, necessarily briefly, some of the principal ways in which preparation for war had impacted on society at large and how it maintained a presence after 1815. Second, it suggests that the physical presence of ex-servicemen was important in shaping the forms and strategies of collective action after 1815. Third, it explores how the complexion and activity of the mass platform, above and beyond those military personnel who participated, can be seen both as a creative and tactical response to those persistent accusations that radicals were a 'tumultuous mob' and as a legacy of militarization. It concludes by asking how these strategies altered and clashed with perceptions of collective action held by those whose job was to restrain or police it.

The impact of the long French Wars can scarcely be underestimated. In terms of the scale of participation of manpower and, indeed, womanpower, it was an unprecedented conflict, something in part conveyed by simple but striking figures. The participation rate of men of military age was 1 in 16 for the War of the Austrian Succession; 1 in 8 for the American Revolution; but rose to 1 in 5 or 6 at the height of the French Wars.[10] It was the largest war Britain had fought, and the scale of the lurch from peace to war was correspondingly striking. The peacetime army of 1789 stood at 40,000 – by 1814 it had reached 250,000. One of the most remarkable features of the period is the manner in which the British state proved capable of mobilizing manpower at those points at which French invasion seemed credible and imminent. In particular, the extraordinary mobilization of 1803–4, which saw volunteering on a huge scale, vastly increased the numbers of Britons with some military experience. While it avoided recourse to the novel French *levée en masse*, the British state nevertheless managed to create the 'armed nation'.[11]

While fruitful debates continue over the complex motivations for volunteering and the extent to which the French Wars thus bolstered an insurgent sense of national identity, the scale of the exposure to military spectacle and involvement in training under arms is undeniable. Visually, it would have been difficult to avoid the military. An extensive barrack-building programme had been initiated even before the war had begun, with new barracks strategically positioned near areas of popular unrest.[12] While local patriotic initiative was clearly of paramount importance, the notion that state-sponsored attempts to generate patriotism were somehow 'un-British' has been challenged in the past ten years by approaches that place such activity at the centre of Britain's war experience. Whether driven by the national or the local state, loyalist displays embodied an essential military component and increased in their scope, scale and sophistication during the war. Urban populations were encouraged to venerate military and naval heroes and to illuminate for famous victories as a British version of the French Pantheon was developed.[13]

The cultural impact of military spectacle was deep and sustained, even if there was no corresponding spread of military values. Military dress, especially among the royal family and political elites, enjoyed a long vogue, which outlived events at Waterloo. A dramatically expanded print culture was dominated by news of and comment on the wars, and after the cessation of hostilities, there was a new and popular market for eyewitness battle accounts written by and for the working classes. Military concerns suffused popular ballads and chapbooks and created new popular visual genres such as the 'panorama', designed to afford spectators an insight into the 'real' field of battle. Music and theatre, too, were dominated by militarized productions, often delivered to audiences of servicemen by actors in uniform. Nor, of course, was age any constraint and children played at being soldiers and with toy soldiers, could learn their *Army and Navy ABC*, or tinker with the commercially successful Waterloo model.[14]

No society could have snapped from a war demanding such a level of participation and commitment and return to the *status quo ante*. Britain's elite was faced with challenges common to the post-war experiences of other states and, indeed, other times.[15] First, new groups emerged with novel claims on the state or with old claims strengthened and given a new validity, while governments ran the risk of becoming victims of those rhetorical and political strategies they had employed to sustain the war effort. Second, the experience and impact of 'militarization' did not simply evaporate with the cessation of hostilities. Thousands of men with military experience were thrust back into a turbulent civilian life, and countless more people with exposure to years of military spectacle considered how best to promote and defend their interests in peacetime.[16] The physical impact of demobilized soldiers, in particular, was dramatic and formed an oft-stated anxiety of contemporary observers. The sheer numbers are worth recapitulating: between 300,000 and 400,000 ex-servicemen were demobilized in the years following Waterloo. In 1819, according to F.C. Mather, there were 61,397 out-pensioners registered at Chelsea, fully three times the 1792 figure. This continued to rise to a peak of 85,834 in 1828 and then steadily diminished after that point.[17]

Military recruitment, of course, had been strong in populous areas, and the army had been a destination for many from the manufacturing communities of the north of England and south of Scotland, as well as from increasingly landless and proletarianized rural communities. These men were thrust back into an economy that was contracting as it adjusted to post-war realities, with the predictable outcome of spiralling unemployment.[18] As Mather pointed out, to the ruling elites and nervous middle classes, these ex-servicemen represented at one and the same time a threat and an opportunity. The opportunity was slowly but, in the end, successfully grasped and men of military experience were co-opted into the peacetime law and order establishment. This was, however, a slow and uneven process with marked success only after 1819. Even if, as Cookson has argued, 'military service more obviously produced civil officers and "magistrates" men' than it did insurrectionists', it did create both and, before the 1820s, ex-servicemen were a threat to the social order as much as they were a guarantor of it.[19]

The basic contours of what E.P. Thompson famously dubbed the 'heroic age of popular radicalism' after 1815 are familiar.[20] Towards the end of 1816, the coalescence of Henry 'Orator' Hunt and metropolitan Spencean radicals around a strategy of mass meetings and petitioning signified the birth of the 'mass platform' agitation.[21] That it continued to coincide with other forms of collective action – the riot and the insurrectionary attempt – was amply demonstrated in the third Spa Fields meeting in December 1816, which appeared to be a composite of all three. The beginning of 1817 saw elite fears of large oath-bound insurrectionary networks and this, along with a shot purportedly taken at the Prince Regent, provided the rationale for repressive legislation including the suspension of *Habeas Corpus*. The closing down of constitutional protests saw both creative efforts to protest effectively within the letter of the law – most notably the march of the Blanketeers from Manchester – and desperate efforts to mount an insurrection at Pentridge in Derbyshire. 1819 saw both economic depression and, more importantly, renewed taxes on consumption, which confirmed the radical critique of old corruption. Mass meetings throughout Great Britain over the summer, culminating in the tragedy at Peterloo, marked the apotheosis of the mass platform agitation. Once again, legislative provisions, including the new Six Acts, limited radicals' constitutional room for manoeuvre and 1820 thus saw another flurry of insurrectionary attempts. First, the Cato Street conspiracy, with its ill-conceived plan to murder the cabinet while it sat down to dinner. Second, an abortive 'General Rising' in the north of England and the west of Scotland, which, in the event, convinced only small and uncoordinated groups of radicals to turn out in arms. The Queen Caroline agitation intervened to act as a salve to heal the body politic in the aftermath of these violent episodes, and one recent account has seen it as facilitating a crucial rehabilitation of constitutionalist popular politics.[22]

Militarization had a considerable impact on the personnel, strategies and language of this varied collective action after 1815. While Norman Gash is clearly correct that it would be 'absurd' to attribute all post-1815 social disorder to the presence of ex-servicemen, he did admit of their physical prominence during key episodes.[23] This had its most dramatic form in the leadership of and participation in insurrectionary attempts. Men with military experience had very obvious qualifications for this, and the phenomenon had manifested itself during the war, when the concerns of government for the loyalty of the armed forces both professional and voluntary had been acute.[24] The most spectacular occurrences were, of course, the mutinies of 1797.[25] Subsequently, Colonel Despard's conspiracy had thrown over 300 members of the guards under suspicion, and six of them had been executed alongside him.[26]

The tendency of military and naval men to be at the forefront of violent collective action after 1815 was marked. The leader of the Pentridge Rising, Jeremiah Brandreth the 'Nottingham Captain', was in all probability a man of military experience, and William Turner (executed alongside him) certainly was.[27] Arthur Thistlewood, a prime mover in Spencean insurrectionary circles, had experience as a lieutenant in the militia. Indeed, it was this military experience, along with his revolutionary credentials, that gave him considerable cachet with 'the unthinking of the lower orders' and doubtless helped to facilitate the Spencean strategy of attempting to recruit among the demobbed soldiers and sailors of London's underworld. One of the principal witnesses for the Crown against Thistlewood was one Robert Adams, who had been in the Dragoons and was approached by Thistlewood on this very basis.[28] In the abortive attempt at a general rising in April 1820, ex-military men were very much at the fore in both Scotland and England.[29] The leader of the band of radicals, which optimistically set out from Glasgow to seize the Carron Iron Works, was John Baird, a peninsular veteran, who was executed in September 1820.[30] James Clelland, who was also condemned to execution, but had his sentence commuted, was also probably a soldier.[31] So too was John Morrison, one of the leading figures in the Strathaven contingent, which also turned out, while Speirs and Smellie, who went around to make sure work had stopped at the cotton mills in Johnstone, had both been soldiers, Speirs a Sergeant in the 21st Regiment.[32] Many of these ex-soldiers must remain nameless, but turn up frequently both in depositions and in later accounts. For example, according to one deposition, when armed radicals arrived at Grange Moor near Huddersfield, 'a tall man in brown trousers from Lancashire who had been a soldier gave the words of command to the Barnsley men [and] wished to have put us into lines'.[33]

The qualifications of these individuals were obvious. As the appearance and role of the 'man in brown trousers' suggests they recommended themselves as being the most likely to be able to instil some kind of discipline and even genuine military strategy into largely untrained groups of men. One conservative newspaper sneeringly summed up the dynamic: 'Our people were promised leaders, but none having appeared, the command was usually conferred on the greatest boaster, particularly if he had ever been in the army'.[34] This *ad hoc* leadership could then act with tragic consequences: the Scottish radicals had marched in military step to Bonnymuir, and it was their military deportment in forming a square and facing the cavalry that allowed commentators quickly to describe it as a 'battle'.[35] Tactical leadership could be gleaned from ex-soldiers, and one deposition from March 1820 allows us an insight into how far insurrectionary strategies relied on the presence or at least the expectation of ex-servicemen as participants. In an intriguing discussion between Scottish radicals, the majority rejected a plan drawn up by one of their number and instead 'preferred the regular system established in the army & Sir David Dundas's plan was accordingly recommended, it being moreover thought that so soon as they did rise they would get plenty of their own numbers who had been in the Army & who were acquainted with these regulations to arrange them into Companies & Regiments'.[36]

Ex-servicemen might also have provided a degree of technological expertise in guerrilla warfare. Some level of military know-how must, for example, have lain behind the primitive hand-grenades that the Cato Street conspirators intended to use to liquidate the cabinet.[37] It would not be until 1832 that urban guerrilla tactics found systematic expression from Colonel Macerone, born in Birmingham to Italian immigrant parents, who fought in the Napoleonic wars and eventually became the aide-de-camp and envoy of Joachim Murat, King of Naples. His *Defensive Instructions for the People* was destined to become an 'underground classic', but similar information – in particular, how to repel cavalry with pikes – would most likely have been transmitted before this by individuals with some military experience.[38] Finally, in the absence of physical military leadership, idealized or imaginary leaders were cast in military guise, while massively optimistic projections were made about vast and supportive armies lying just over the horizon. The two most famous mythical leaders of the early nineteenth century were, of course, General Ludd and Captain Swing. Throughout the period under consideration, however, insurrectionists needed at least the belief that military expertise and experience would accrue if only enthusiastic amateurs struck the first blow. The radicals on Grange Moor believed that there were 'fifty thousand in a body armed in Scotland ready to come and join us'.[39] Meanwhile, in Scotland rumours circulated that the exiled 'radical laird' Kinloch of Kinloch would appear at the head of 50,000 men or, even more fancifully, that Marshal Macdonald would arrive with French troops to lead the rising.[40]

Those soldiers who drilled radicals between 1815 and 1820 were not, of course, universally sponsors of armed insurrection. Militarized symbolic action formed an important part of the strategies of the mass platform that emerged after 1816.[41] This was most obvious in the numerous reports of mass drilling in 1819, which so alarmed the authorities and of which Samuel Bamford has left perhaps the most memorable account:

> Our drill masters were generally old soldiers of the line, or of militia, or local militia regiments; they put the lads through their facings in quick time, and soon learned them to march with a steadiness and regularity which would not have disgraced a regiment on parade. ... We mustered, we fell into rank, we faced, marched, halted, faced about, countermarched, halted again, dressed, and wheeled in quick succession, and without confusion.[42]

Bamford's retrospective account is similar to many contemporaneous accounts, both hostile and friendly, which dwelt on the militarized nature of the mass movement. It was not only drilling, but the entire military panoply of fife, drums, flags and martial music that was remarked upon. It was, for example, a constant refrain in the diary of Charles Hutcheson, a private in the Glasgow Sharpshooters Volunteer Regiment between 1819 and 1820, who made frequent reference to the presence of 'flags, drums and fife' and the 'regular military step' with which radicals attended and left meetings.[43]

While Bamford undoubtedly overstated the novelty of ordered protest, which drew on a number of sources, the military inflection of the mass platform *was* something qualitatively new.[44] How should we account for it? The presence of ex-military personnel must clearly be a central part in any explanation. As Bamford's memoirs suggest, and in spite of Castlereagh's confident denial that any more than a few ex-soldiers were involved in the drilling of radicals, numerous accounts emphasized that it was ex-soldiers who rallied radicals into a 'military step'.[45] Part of the reason for the adoption of the 'military step' was certainly practical: it was the only way to move large numbers of people from one place to another without disorder. It was, however, the concern to avoid not only the actual occurrence but also the impression of disorder that provides the most convincing explanation for the militarized nature of the mass platform.

Developments within the historiography of popular politics and collective action in this period have made two things very clear. First, the exploration of popular radicalism as a set of strategies and aims directed at the 'state' ignores both the diversity of radicalism and the mutable and fast-changing political context in which it occurred. Following Mark Philp's advice that it ought to be seen rather as a 'developing political practice' that sought to fashion a 'logic of confrontation', exemplary work by Jonathan Fulcher has argued that radicalism after 1815 simply cannot be seen outside of its rhetorical engagement with government and with local loyalism.[46] Second, the work of James Epstein and others has vastly expanded our perceptions of what constitutes the 'political': symbolic practices and what might broadly be called the political culture of popular movements have become crucial and fruitful areas of inquiry.[47] Indeed, as one recent account, which focused on the complex range of meanings in the reformers' 'march to Peterloo', has pithily summarized these developments: 'the form *was* the argument'.[48]

With this in mind, the crucial question is what kind of rhetorical and symbolic purchase did militarized forms offer proponents of collective action after 1815? The first and the most important was that they allowed radicals definitively to reject the idea that they constituted a 'mob'. Militarized displays thus promised to defuse the principal rhetorical ploy of those who sought to delegitimize popular political action or, as Bamford expressed it, to 'disarm the bitterness of our political opponents'.[49] From the Gordon Riots of 1780, popular political action had been rendered synonymous with the excesses of the mob and all of its associated images of infantilism, popular licence, anarchy and bloodshed. Radicals had struggled against these charges in the 1790s, but to little avail, so that going into the postwar period 'the tumultuous mob was the spectre haunting the radical movement'.[50] The militarized display of the mass platform attempted to exorcise this spectre by echoing those spectacles of order and control with which Britons had become increasingly familiar in the early nineteenth century.

This was part of what Fulcher has called 'the rhetorical game', where radicals contested the language of patriotism and constitutionalism with armed loyalists and the government. In the aftermath of Peterloo, the strategy of peaceful, disciplined and ordered protest – and, in particular, the presence of women and children – allowed reformers not only to exorcize the demon of the tumultuous mob but set it loose among its begetters. The militarized mass platform staked out a powerful claim that it was the radicals whose ordered demeanour and respectable behaviour rendered them fit for citizenship. It was the loyalists, the Manchester Yeomanry and the regulars, who had rioted on St Peter's Fields and engaged in a wanton orgy of dehumanizing and Jacobinical violence.[51]

This was, perhaps, an unforeseen advantage, and there is no doubt that the militarized nature of collective action was not only intended to present radicals as orderly and disciplined, but also constituted a threatening and intimidating gesture. During the war, Luddite drilling had often been done consciously in full view of the authorities.[52] In spite of Hunt's regrets that weavers were 'playing soldiers' and Bamford's later attempts to sanitize such activity as simply an opportunity for healthy exercise and pleasant diversionary leisure time outdoors, drilling constituted both a challenge and an assertion of physical strength.[53] This consciousness of the effect of such activity on opponents was underlined by the openness with which radicals drilled and had their activities witnessed and even by such gestures as clapping in order to imitate the report of musketry.[54] If loyalists and the authorities sought to act against 'the people', they would not be suppressing a riot or quelling a mob, but facing an army. As a strategy, it was designed to play on elite fears current during the war that 'the armed crowd was the all too likely concomitant of the armed nation'.[55] It certainly exerted an effect on Lord Althorp, who argued in Parliament: 'The people had been taught to march in military array; they had been instructed to wheel, to form in column, and to go through other military evolutions in large bodies: and, would any persons say that, with arms in their hands, these men, though not capable of contenting with regular forces, would not be excessively formidable?'[56]

This leads us to the final area of inquiry: how did the militarization of collective action impact upon the perceptions of those whose role was to police it, to prevent it or simply to watch on aghast? Quite clearly, the organized mass platform continued to persist alongside other forms of collective action, and 1815 to 1820 was witness to numerous riots and turbulent industrial action, which ensured that the vocabulary of crowd perception might still be anchored in notions of the 'tumultuous mob'.[57] So too, the mass platform was far more than just a ritualized military display. The varied and, at times, apparently contradictory symbolic displays involved – military organization encompassing women and children, popular festivity accompanying the conscious display of order – were intended to produce a complex range of meanings and render the contextualization of particular episodes necessary to understanding them.[58]

As the legislative response to Peterloo in the shape of the Six Acts made clear, however, the mass platform was recognized as a qualitatively new type of collective action, some of the most alarming aspects of which were its militarized ones. It did not allow MPs and loyalists to dismiss it as a 'mob', and so existing legal and political strategies for dealing with it were insufficient. In the debates surrounding the Six Acts and, indeed, in the language employed by the measures themselves, it was these military features which were especially highlighted and attacked. The first measure to become law banned 'all Meetings and Assemblies of Persons for the purpose of training or drilling themselves, or of being trained or drilled to the use of Arms, or for the purpose of practising Military Exercise, Movements and Evolution'.[59] The act restricting meetings outlawed attendance even at a legally constituted meeting 'with any Flag, Banner or Ensign, or displaying or exhibiting any Device, Badge or Emblem or with any Drum or Military or other Music, or in Military Array or Order'.[60] In moving the legislation, Castlereagh dwelt on the militarized symbolic display of radicals and pursued the rhetorical strategy of the 1790s, claiming that the legislation would arrest 'a practice which had never been British, but was borrowed from the worst times of the French revolution'.[61] So too, at the trial of those involved in Peterloo, it was the militarized nature of the platform on which the crown focused. Convictions were secured for the defendants having assembled with seditious intent 'in a formidable and menacing manner and in military procession and array'.[62] The Tory periodical *Blackwood's* was explicit in December 1819 that the radical movement was now '*bona fide* an army, marching neither loosely nor weaponless'.[63]

The implications of these militarized perspectives had been apparent at Peterloo itself. This is not to suggest that the yeomanry, as civilian-soldiers, had a completely militarized outlook. How much weight, however, should be put on the idea that the armed force at Peterloo treated it very much as a military action and thought of St Peter's Field less as the site of an urban policing exercise and more as a battlefield? Famously, witnesses attested that the soldier's normal emotional investment in capturing the enemy standard translated at Peterloo into the obsession to take the radical banners and symbols: 'Have at their Flags' was the cry from the cavalry.[64] Even yeomanry with no extensive military experience, but mindful of the gleeful reporting of such incidents as the capture of the 'Invincible Standard' in Egypt, might have been apt to think in such terms. As on the field of battle, these captured 'standards' could then be used in ritualized display. One yeoman, for example, ostentatiously wore a captured radical banner as a sash thereafter.[65] After the events of Peterloo, hostile observers noted that radicals became even more markedly concerned to assign armed men as 'guards to the women and colours' and were 'determined that the flags should not be touched'.[66]

It was a process engaged in by both contemporaries and by posterity. The name by which the incident was recorded was coined shortly after the event as a barbed comment on the 'heroic' actions of the yeomanry on the day and, indeed, the presence of Waterloo veterans on both sides.[67] It also demonstrated an audience keenly aware of and still thinking very much in terms of the recent wars. Images of the Napoleonic Wars so suffused British culture that when graphic satirists came to represent the events of the day, they found their prototypes not just in atrocity images from the sixteenth and seventeenth centuries, but in the many recent images – circulated in engravings and cheap woodcuts – of Waterloo itself.[68] In this way, Peterloo and the response to it bear eloquent and poignant testimony to a process whereby collective action, the aims and strategies of its participants, and the perceptions and fears of its opponents had been militarized in the years after 1815.

Notes

I would like to thank the Leverhulme Trust for a generous Early Career Fellowship (ECF/2005/049), which made possible the research on which this essay is based.

1. 'Letter to John Murray Esqre. (1821)' in *Lord Byron: The Complete Miscellaneous Prose*, ed. Andrew Nicholson (Oxford, 1991), pp. 138–39.
2. Clive Emsley, *British Society and the French Wars 1793–1815* (London, 1979); David A. Bell, *The First Total War: Napoleon's Europe and the Birth of Modern Warfare* (London, 2007). See also N. Gash, 'After Waterloo: British Society and the Legacy of the Napoleonic Wars', *Transactions of the Royal Historical Society*, 5th Series, 28 (1978), pp. 145–57.
3. John Brewer, *The Sinews of Power: War, Money and the English State, 1688–1783* (1989); Linda Colley, *Britons: Forging the Nation 1707–1837* (London & New Haven, 1992); Lawrence Stone (ed.), *An Imperial State at War: Britain from 1689 to 1815* (London, 1994); Philip Harling and Peter Mandler, 'From 'Fiscal-Military' State to Laissez-Faire State, 1760–1850', *Journal of British Studies*, 32 (1996), pp. 44–70.
4. J.E. Cookson, *The British Armed Nation, 1793–1815* (Oxford, 1997).
5. John R. Gillis (ed.), *The Militarization of the Western World* (New Brunswick, 1989), p. 2; Colin Creighton and Martin Shaw, *The Sociology of War and Peace* (Basingstoke, 1987), pp. 1–13.
6. P. Woodfine, '"Unjustifiable and Illiberal": Military Patriotism and Civilian Values in the 1790s' in *War: Identities in Conflict 1300–2000*, ed. Bertrand Taithe and Tim Thornton (Stroud, 1998), pp. 73–93; Cookson, *The British Armed Nation*, pp. 244–45.
7. Charles Tilly, *Popular Contention in Great Britain, 1758–1834* (Cambridge, MA, 1995), pp. 249–54.
8. Thomas Bartlett, 'Militarization and Politicization in Ireland (1780–1820)' in *Culture et Pratiques Politiques en France et en Irelande XVIe-XVIIIe Siècle: Actes du Colloque de Marseille 28 Septembre – 2 Octobre 1988*, ed. L.M. Cullen and L. Bergeron (Paris, 1991), pp. 125–36.
9. Linda Colley, 'Whose Nation? Class and National Consciousness in Britain 1750–1830', *Past & Present*, 113 (1986), pp. 97–117. Though see the more skeptical line taken in Cookson, *The British Armed Nation*, pp. 246–52.

10. H.V. Bowen, *War and British Society 1688–1815* (Cambridge, 1998), p. 14; Cookson, *The British Armed Nation*, pp. 95–100.

11. Mark Philp (ed.), *Resisting Napoleon: The British Response to the Threat of Invasion, 1797–1815* (Aldershot, 2006); Linda Colley, 'The Reach of the State, the Appeal of the Nation: Mass Arming and Political Culture in the Napoleonic Wars' in Stone, *An Imperial State at War*, pp. 165–84.

12. Clive Emsley, 'The Military and Popular Disorder in England 1790–1801', *Journal of the Society for Army Historical Research*, 61 (1983), pp. 17–21.

13. Cookson, *The British Armed Nation*, pp. 237–43; Holger Hoock, '"The Cheap Defence of Nations': Monuments and Propaganda', in Philp, *Resisting Napoleon*, pp. 159–71; *idem*, 'The British Military Pantheon in St Paul's Cathedral: The State, Cultural Patriotism, and the Politics of National Monuments, *c*. 1790–1820' in *Pantheons: Transformations of a Monumental Idea*, ed. Richard Wrigley and Matthew Craske (Aldershot, 2004), pp. 81–106.

14. Philip Mansel, 'Monarchy, Uniform and the Rise of the *Frac* 1760–1830', *Past & Present*, 96 (1982), pp. 103–32; Scott Hughes Myerly, *British Military Spectacle: From the Napoleonic Wars through the Crimea* (Cambridge, MA, 1996), pp. 30–52, 139–50; K. Watson, 'Bonfires, Bells and Bayonets: British Popular Memory and the Napoleonic Wars' in *War*, Taithe and Thornton, pp. 95–112; Gillian Russell, *The Theatres of War: Performance, Politics, and Society 1793–1815* (Oxford, 1995).

15. See the introduction to Arthur Marwick (ed.), *Total War and Social Change* (Basingstoke, 1988), pp. x–xxi.

16. Emsley, *British Society and the French Wars*, pp. 169–82.

17. F.C. Mather, 'Army Pensioners and the Maintenance of Civil Order in Early Nineteenth Century England', *Journal of the Society of Army Historical Research*, 36 (1958), p. 110.

18. Tilly, *Popular Contention in Great Britain*, pp. 249–54; Gash, 'After Waterloo', pp. 152–57.

19. Mather, 'Army Pensioners and the Maintenance of Civil Order in Early Nineteenth Century England', pp. 111–24; Emsley, *British Society and the French Wars*, pp. 176–77; Cookson, *The British Armed Nation*, p. 207.

20. E.P. Thompson, *The Making of the English Working Class*, rev. edn (London, 1980), p. 691.

21. John Belchem, 'Henry Hunt and the Evolution of the Mass Platform', *English Historical Review*, 93 (1978), pp. 739–73.

22. Thompson, *The Making of the English Working Class*, pp. 660–780; Iain McCalman, *Radical Underworld: Prophets, Revolutionaries, and Pornographers in London, 1795–1840* (Oxford, 1988); F.K. Donnelly, 'The General Rising in 1820: A Study of Social Conflict in the Industrial Revolution' (PhD thesis, University of Sheffield, 1975); Dror Wahrman, 'Public Opinion, Violence and the Limits of Constitutional Politics', in *Re-reading the Constitution: New Narratives in the Political History of England's Long Nineteenth Century*, ed. James Vernon (Cambridge, 1996), pp. 83–122.

23. Gash, 'After Waterloo', pp. 150–52; Emsley, *British Society and the French Wars*, pp. 176–77.

24. Cookson, *The British Armed Nation*, pp. 182–95.

25. Roger Wells, *Insurrection: The British Experience 1795–1803* (Gloucester, 1983), pp. 79–109.

26. Marianne Elliot, 'The 'Despard Conspiracy' Reconsidered', *Past & Present*, 75 (1977), pp. 46–61; Myerly, *British Military Spectacle*, p. 122.

27. John Belchem, 'Brandreth, Jeremiah (1786/1790–1817)', *Oxford Dictionary of National Biography* [hereafter: *ODNB*] (Oxford, 2004); Emsley, *British Society and the French Wars*, p. 176.

28. Malcolm Chase, 'Thistlewood, Arthur (*bap.* 1774, *d.* 1820)', *ODNB*; Edward Aylmer, *Memoirs of George Edwards* (London, 1820), pp. 18. 77–78, 94–95.

29. Gash, 'After Waterloo', p. 151.

30. Peter Berresford Ellis, 'Baird, John (1788–1820)', *ODNB*.

31. Margaret and Alastair Macfarlane, *The Scottish Radicals Tried and Transported for Treason in 1820* (Stevenage, 1981), pp. 24–25.

32. John Stevenson, *A True Narrative of the Radical Rising in Strathaven* (Glasgow, 1835), p. 8; [John Parkhill], *The Life and Opinions of Arthur Sneddon: An Autobiography* (Paisley, 1860), p. 93.

33. 'Deposition of John Mitchell, weaver, Barnsley', The National Archives [hereafter: TNA], Home Office Correspondence: Disturbances, HO 40/12, f. 256.

34. *Glasgow Herald*, 7 April 1820.

35. John Macdonnell and John E.P. Wallis (ed.), *Reports of State Trials*, 8 vols. (London, 1888–98), I: pp. 697, 1351–52; Peter Mackenzie, *Reminiscences of Glasgow and the West of Scotland*, 2 vols. (Glasgow, 1875), I: p. 147; Edward Douglas to Lord Sidmouth, 20 April 1820, TNA, Home Office Correspondence: Scotland, HO 102/32, f. 469.

36. 'Deposition of A.B.', 7 March 1820, TNA, Home Office Correspondence: Scotland, HO 102/32, f. 235.

37. Aylmer, *Memoirs of George Edwards*, pp. 94–95.

38. Ian Haywood (ed.), *The Literature of Struggle: An Anthology of Chartist Fiction* (Aldershot, 1995), pp. 15–16. For an example of military tactics 'in action', see A.J. Peacock, *Bread or Blood: A Study of the Agrarian Riots in East Anglia in 1816* (London, 1965), pp. 50–51.

39. 'Deposition of John Mitchell', f. 256.

40. Mackenzie, *Reminiscences of Glasgow and the West of Scotland*, I: p. 130

41. The best account of the militarized nature of the platform so far is Myerly, *British Military Spectacle*, pp. 133–38.

42. W.H. Chaloner (ed.), *The Autobiography of Samuel Bamford*, 2 vols. (London, 1967), II: pp. 177–78.

43. 'Diary of C.H. Hutcheson, 1820–48', National Library of Scotland, MSS 2773, pp. 14–17, 24.

44. Thompson, *The Making of the English Working Class*, p. 746.

45. *Parliamentary Debates*, xli. 392 (29 Nov. 1819).

46. Mark Philp, 'The Fragmented Ideology of Reform' in *The French Revolution and British Popular Politics*, ed. Mark Philp (Cambridge, 1991), pp. 50–77; Jonathan C.S.J. Fulcher, 'Contests over Constitutionalism: The Faltering of Reform in England, 1816–1824' (PhD thesis, Cambridge, 1993); *idem*, 'The English People and their Constitution after Waterloo: Parliamentary Reform, 1815–1817' in *Re-reading the Constitution*, Vernon, pp. 52–82.

47. James Epstein, *Radical Expression: Political Language, Ritual and Symbol in England, 1790–1850* (Oxford, 1994); Paul Pickering, 'Class without Words: Symbolic Communication in the Chartist Movement', *Past & Present*, 112 (1986), pp. 144–62.

48. Robert Poole, 'The March to Peterloo: Politics and Festivity in Late Georgian England', *Past & Present*, 192 (2006), p. 116.

49. Chaloner, *The Autobiography of Samuel Bamford*, II: p. 177.

50. Ian Haywood, *Bloody Romanticism: Spectacular Violence and the Politics of Representation, 1776–1832* (London, 2006), p. 196. See also the essay by Michael T. Davis in this volume and his 'The Mob Club? The London Corresponding Society and the Politics of Civility in the 1790s' in *Unrespectable Radicals? Popular Politics in the Age of Reform*, ed. Michael T. Davis and Paul A. Pickering (Aldershot, 2008), pp. 21–40.

51. Ian Haywood, *The Revolution in Popular Literature: Print, Politics and the People, 1790–1860* (Cambridge, 2004), pp. 95–98.

52. Katrina Navickas, 'The Search for "General Ludd": The Mythology of Luddism', *Social History*, 30 (2005), pp. 290–91.

53. Donald Read, *Peterloo: The 'Massacre' and its Background* (Manchester, 1958), p. 123; Chaloner, *The Autobiography of Samuel Bamford*, II: pp. 177–78.

54. 'Diary of C.H. Hutcheson', p. 17; Kenneth O. Fox, *Making Life Possible: A Study of Military Aid to the Civil Power in Regency England* (Kineton, 1982), pp. 160–61.

55. Cookson, *The British Armed Nation*, p. 182.

56. *Parliamentary Debates*, xli. 528 (30 Nov. 1819).

57. Mark Harrison, *Crowds and History: Mass Phenomena in English Towns, 1790–1835* (Cambridge, 1988), pp. 168–91.

58. Poole, 'The March to Peterloo', pp. 109–53; James Epstein, 'Understanding the Cap of Liberty: Symbolic Practice and Social Conflict in Early Nineteenth-Century England', *Past & Present*, 122 (1989), pp. 75–118.

59. 60 Geo. III & 1 Geo. IV, c. 1.

60. 60 Geo. III & 1 Geo. IV, c. 4.

61. *Parliamentary Debates*, xli. 390 (29 Nov. 1819).

62. Cited in Robert Poole, '"By the Law or the Sword': Peterloo Revisited', *History*, 91 (2006), p. 275.

63. Cited in Fulcher, 'Contests over Constitutionalism', p. 245.

64. Epstein, *Radical Expression*, pp. 85–66.

65. Myerly, *British Military Spectacle*, p. 139.

66. 'Precognitions of George Webster and Robert Martin', National Records of Scotland, Crown Office Precognitions 1801–1900, AD 14/19/312, ff. 3, 17.

67. Read, *Peterloo*, p. vii; Joyce Marlow, *The Peterloo Massacre* (London, 1969), pp. 13, 55–56.

68. Diana Donald, *The Age of Caricature: Satirical Prints in the Reign of George III* (New Haven & London, 1996), pp. 189–92.

11

The Revolutionary Century? Revolts in Nineteenth-Century France

Peter McPhee

Three times within forty years – in 1830, 1848 and 1870–71 – popular revolt in Paris succeeded in toppling apparently well-established political régimes. Ever since, the dominant organising principle of narrative histories of nineteenth-century France has been the theme of revolution and reaction, as the ideological and social divisions of the French Revolution were fought out in a cycle of violent challenge from the heirs of the *sans-culottes* and its repression by post-revolutionary elites. This has thus been a history both of *Revolutionary France*, the name of a collection edited by Malcolm Crook, and of *The Bourgeois Century*, the title of Roger Magraw's history of nineteenth-century France. Only with the establishment of electoral democracy within a relatively stable Third Republic after 1877, in the words of François Furet's famous quip, did 'the French Revolution finally enter the harbour' and bring revolutionary upheavals to a close.[1]

The core of such a narrative is comforting in its simplicity and final reassurance, but is based on a series of assumptions that this chapter will question. First, popular revolt is assumed to be synonymous with the three revolutions of these decades. Second, it is assumed that this revolt was Parisian, and with much in common with the great revolutionary *journées* of 1789 and 1792; that is, that the Paris Commune of 1871 was the last episode of the French Revolution. Finally, it is assumed that revolt was the antithesis of organized political life, and necessarily ended when the ship of democratic republicanism entered the harbour of relative political calm after 1877; or, in the words of Quentin Deluermoz, with 'the dissociation of revolution and Republic'.[2] In contrast, this chapter uses the historiography of recent decades to challenge our understanding of the place in the political process of popular protest and rebellion. It then poses the question of what really changed in mass politics across the century. To follow Furet's metaphor further, did the ship of the republican state that entered the harbour in 1877 carry the same crew and ideological cargo as in 1792?

The outlines of the grand narrative of nineteenth-century French political history are long-established and well-known, as is the place of popular upheaval in Paris in this 'revolutionary century'. However, recent historiography has placed these revolutions in wider and longer-term contexts. Far from being examples of Paris once again seeking to impose its radical will on recalcitrant provinces, they are now better understood as national crises that were both profound and long-term. The first part of this chapter summarizes a new political narrative of the period 1814–77, one which places revolt in Paris within a wider context.[3] Like the victorious foreign coalition that overthrew Napoleon and restored monarchy in France, Louis XVIII regarded the years 1789–1814 as one revolution, and represented himself as a paternal figure who could build a bridge to older continuities. In the content of his Charter of 1814, however, he accepted that widespread acquiescence in the legitimacy of his royal authority had to be on the basis of an historic compromise with the French Revolution. Restored France was therefore to be a land in which would be recognized both the forms of constitutional, parliamentary rule and the paternalistic authority of the king; both the virtues of material success as the reward for talent and the honour traditionally due to the aristocracy; both the definitive abolition of seigneurialism and the power of great landed notables; and both the claims of a citizenry equal before the law and a hierarchy of power and status. Ultimately, Louis's compromise failed, both because of the attempt of his successor Charles X after 1824 to further roll back the revolution's legacy and because of resentment at the exclusion of all but the very wealthiest men from political life.

The vote was limited to the wealthiest 1 percent of males, but even within that narrow élite, there was liberal opposition to the autocratic pretensions of Charles X. After a decisive liberal electoral victory in July 1830, Charles introduced severe controls on the press and announced new elections on a franchise that excluded all but the 25,000 wealthiest men in France. Stung into action by Charles's attempted *coup* and pressure from angry working people with their own reasons for hostility to the régime, small groups of journalists and liberal deputies called for resistance. On 27 July 1830, barricades were erected in the streets of Paris, by their nature symbolizing resistance to authority in contrast to the direct invasions of palaces and parliaments in the Great Revolution. In the ensuing fighting, about 2,000 insurgents and soldiers were killed. The liberal Louis-Philippe d'Orléans accepted the crown as 'king of the French', and Charles was forced to flee the country.[4]

The Orléanist régime's revised charter was deliberately cautious. It offered only guarantees against infringement of press and religious freedoms, restored the tricolour as the national flag and reasserted the powers of the Chamber of Deputies. An electoral reform in 1831 slightly lowered the tax qualification for deputies, increasing the electorate from 100,000 to 167,000 (one adult male in 50). Not surprisingly, the Revolution of 1830 has often been seen as no more than a slight broadening of a landholding élite and a reassertion of constitutional rule: a revolution made by the people had quickly been 'stolen'. This is only part of the story. In fact, the Parisian Revolution of July 1830 had followed two years of nationwide economic crisis and popular – as well as parliamentary – discontent, and its implications were only to be resolved after four years of rapidly shifting conflict interrelated with protracted economic uncertainty and unemployment. Huge numbers of urban and rural working people organized and protested to push the régime in more populist directions before a new political élite finally succeeded in crushing such action in 1834.

Initially, there was little support for the small groups of republicans who had tried in July 1830 to push the workers' movement further than liberal reform. By 1832, however, a combination of disillusionment with the new régime, republican activism and the experience of political liberation and repression developed a new mass republicanism among skilled workers. This was not confined to Paris: in the Mediterranean department of the Pyrénées-Orientales alone, there were 300 members of the republican Society of the Rights of Man in Perpignan in 1832, and about 2,500 in the department as a whole. Provincial branches of the society were linked with the 50 republican papers still surviving across France in 1833. The experience of a protracted process of revolutionary liberation and repression was also to generate significant developments in the content of rural protest.[5] The collapse of royal authority in 1830 unleashed a wave of collective action: there were in fact many more instances of protest in 1832 than in 1830, including anti-tax riots, forest invasions and illegal land seizures.

In the process of the protracted struggle of the new élite to restrict the Revolution of 1830 to constitutional reform, huge numbers of rural people were alienated. Not all of them responded by commitment to a democratic or republican ideology. In parts of the countryside, notably the northwest and the Midi, a populist royalism re-emerged in response to the perceived Parisian and bourgeois nature of the new régime and the resurgence of republicanism. Seeking to capitalize on this, the duchess de Berry, mother of the young Bourbon pretender (the comte de Chambord or 'Henri V'), landed in Marseille in April 1832 and travelled clandestinely to the royalist heartland of the Vendée. The insurrection was larger and bloodier than historians have realized, requiring the government to place four departments in a state of siege and to quarter troops in some villages until 1845.[6]

Popular rebellion was also urban. In 1831, the anger of Lyon silk-workers (*canuts*) erupted over the *tarif*, a fixed minimum rate for finished cloth established by Napoleon, which the Restoration, and now the July Monarchy, had not respected.[7] For three days, bloody street-fighting raged between the bourgeois National Guard, and silk-workers ranged under the banner 'To live by working or to die fighting'. In February 1834, the Lyon master-weavers' Society of Mutual Duty called a general strike over rates of pay for finished cloth. In Paris, a rising in protest at the law of 10 April 1834, which required police authorization of all associations of more than 20 people, was summarily repressed, culminating in the 'massacre of the rue Transnonain', immortalized by Honoré Daumier's harrowing lithograph. The government's target was the Society of the Rights of Man: with the trial of 164 leading members of the society, and a new press law (9 September 1835) prohibiting insults to the king or calls for a republic and reintroducing strict censorship and bond-money, the revolutionary crisis of 1828–34 had been resolved.

In February 1848, as in 1830, a combination of political opposition, economic crisis and governmental ineptitude brought monarchy down in the capital.[8] On 23 February, nervous troops fired shots into crowds protesting at the government's crackdown on political meetings; barricades were erected all over the city, and Louis-Philippe fled. Crowds invaded the Chamber of Deputies and named a provisional government that proclaimed the Second Republic. The new government guaranteed subsistence to the urban unemployed through 'national workshops' opened in Paris, Marseille and other cities. It also introduced universal manhood suffrage, and freedom of the press and association. Like the Revolution of 1830, that of February 1848 stemmed in part from previous harvest failure and wider economic crisis. Food shortages after 1845 and a collapse of demand for manufacturers caused food rioting in rural areas and mass unemployment in rapidly growing cities. Once news of the Parisian Revolution reached the countryside, people in many regions took advantage of the collapse of authority. Conflict over control and use of forests was especially common in the Pyrenees and the east. Ultimately, the new republican régime had to mobilize more than 48,000 troops to reimpose forest regulations. Attacks were also directed at new techniques in agriculture and transport. Along the Paris-Orléans and Paris-Rouen railway lines, barge-workers, carriage-drivers and inn-keepers tore up lines and set stations ablaze. Threshing-machines, scythes and other labour-reducing machinery were destroyed, and recently sold common lands were restored to collective control or redistributed by household. Anger was also aimed at indirect taxes on essential foodstuffs and wine: tax offices were attacked and registers destroyed in southern towns such as Castres, Prades, Lodève and Bédarieux. Paralleling such attacks on the system of state taxation and the disproportionate wealth of some individuals were examples of violent protests against persons involved in usury. In the east, in many rural communes around Altkirch (Haut-Rhin), such protest became entwined with hostility to Jews.[9]

In Paris and many provincial towns, there was an unprecedented expression of a new political culture characterized by democratic clubs, workers' associations, a cheap and uncensored press and, in places, demands for women's rights. In most regions, however, those best placed to win the hastily called elections were well-known local notables. While a remarkable 84 percent of adult males voted in France and Europe's first elections by direct, universal manhood suffrage on 23 April 1848, the outcome was a conservative assembly dominated by landed proprietors, who wasted little time in targeting the radicalism of the capital. Social tensions were precipitated into insurrection by the assembly's decision on 21 June to close the National Workshops established for the unemployed after the February Revolution. For four days, an unprecedented civil war tore the city in two.[10] Both sides fought for 'the Republic', but between the battle-cries of 'family, property, religion' and 'the social and democratic republic' lay a bitter divide of class hostility, terror and desperation. The government lost about 800 troops in securing victory: at least 1,500 (and perhaps 3,000) insurgents were killed and up to 15,000 were arrested, of whom 4,500 were imprisoned or transported.

In the presidential elections of 10 December 1848, Louis-Napoleon won a staggering 74 percent of the vote. While popular opinion had often identified him with the promise of social change and national pride in the atmosphere of disappointment with the outcomes of revolution, it soon became apparent that he stood above all for social order. But many who had voted for him remained receptive to radical ideas. When France again went to the polls in May 1849, the party of Order won easily, but a strong rural constituency had emerged for the left-wing *démocrates-socialistes*, who won 35 percent of the votes, chiefly in parts of the centre and south. In 1850–51, provincial republicans went underground in an attempt to sidestep increasingly repressive restrictions on press and political freedoms by Louis-Napoléon's regime and a conservative parliament.[11] But republican hopes for electoral victory in 1852 were dashed by the removal of the right to vote from one-third of the poorest voters in May 1850, then by military *coup d'Etat* on 2 December 1851.

While Louis-Napoleon had engineered the *coup* in response to the provisions of the constitution preventing him from standing for re-election in May 1852, and quickly restored universal manhood suffrage as a sign of good faith, protest was immediate and widespread. Resistance in Paris was small-scale but bloodily crushed; however, in parts of the provinces, it exploded in the largest insurrection of the nineteenth century. The most striking characteristic of the resistance to the *coup* was that it was overwhelmingly rural.[12] Resistance occurred in 56 departments, although in 26 of these, it consisted only of unarmed demonstrations, and there were only relatively small-scale armed rebellions in 17 other departments. Armed resistance centred on four major areas: the centre, the southwest, the Mediterranean littoral and the southeast. About 100,000 people from 900 communes were involved in the resistance: perhaps 70,000 of these insurgents, from 775 communes, actually took up arms. In the week following 4 December, insurgents established revolutionary administrations in over 100 communes and seized control of an entire department (Basses-Alpes). Intrinsic to the incidence and style of such activity was the bedrock of republican secret societies, which had survived the crackdown of 1850–51 in anticipation of the re-imposition of democracy by force in the elections of 1852. In few areas were the insurgents able to hold out against the armed forces for more than several days: army units and the gendarmerie crushed pockets of armed resistance, killing about 100 rebels and imprisoning about 30,000 insurgents and their sympathizers. Now justified by Louis-Napoleon as an act of national salvation against looming socialist menace, the *coup* was endorsed overwhelmingly by popular plebiscite three weeks later. A year later, another plebiscite approved the proposition that Louis-Napoleon be president for life of a renewed imperial régime.

The mid-century crisis was over. It had been protracted and profound. Like the Revolution of 1830, from a national perspective, the Revolution of February–June 1848 appears less like another dramatic resurgence of 'revolutionary Paris' than the specific, régime-changing shock in a revolutionary process that was in fact more complex and protracted in both Paris and the provinces. Like the July Monarchy, the Second Empire was to last only 18 years and failed to outlive the man who had founded the régime. This time, however, historiography has long given priority to external military defeat as the reason for régime change. Napoléon III's need for imperial glory in 1870 found its pretext in Bismarck's challenge to French influence over the choice of the next Spanish monarch. Within a fortnight of the declaration of war (19 July), however, an entire French army had surrendered at Sedan, and the emperor himself had been captured. Once the news reached France, opposition groups rushed to proclaim the Third Republic.

The Revolution of August 1870 was result of military defeat, but the military misadventure of the summer needs to be understood in the context of Napoleon's desire to override internal social and political divisions by an appeal to imperial strength. In 1869, the freest elections for 20 years had stunned the régime for, while the emperor could still be guaranteed a docile legislature, opposition candidates won some 42 percent of the 7.8 million votes. The elections coincided with France's first major industrial economic crisis, in contrast to the harvest failures and food rioting that animated the electoral campaigns of 1829–30 and 1846. In June 1869, 15,000 workers were on strike in St-Etienne, followed by other major protests over the next year in industrial centres such as Aubin (Aveyron), Le Creusot and Mulhouse. By that time, however, the new freedom offered by the 'liberal empire' to organize and strike was facilitating other mass gatherings, as of 100,000 mourners at the funeral in Paris in January 1870 of the journalist Victor Noir, shot by the emperor's cousin. The use of troops to disperse demonstrators after Noir's funeral, and against strikers at Carmaux, Le Creusot, La Ricamarie and Aubin in 1869–70, suggested that there was an iron fist in the velvet glove of the liberal empire.[13] The belated decision to remove the right to strike fuelled the anger of more than 5,000 workers' representatives meeting in Lyon in March 1870, and in the following months, 30 workers' organizations affiliated to the international.

The combination of the liberation of political life after September 1870, the suffering during the Prussian siege until late January 1871 and anger at conservative national election results in February fuelled a vibrant culture of Parisian popular politics. The National Assembly's acceptance of crippling peace terms, including a huge indemnity and the cession of Alsace and parts of Lorraine to Prussia, created fury in the capital. When, on 18 March, soldiers were ordered to remove cannon remaining in Paris, popular resistance combined fierce patriotism with a yearning for political autonomy and radical social change. The hasty evacuation of Paris by the army created a power vacuum filled by the election of the Paris Commune a week later and the institution of a range of democratic and socialist reforms, particularly in the workplace. As in 1830, and to a lesser extent in 1848, religious and their institutions were particularly singled out for mockery, retribution and occasionally assault, even death, for their perceived role in entrenching the social order. By May, however, the National Assembly had assembled a conscript army from anti-socialist provinces, and in the 'bloody week' after 21 May, 130,000 soldiers ran riot through Paris, leaving 10,000 and perhaps as many as 30,000 dead. More than 40,000 were arrested, many of them deported to New Caledonia.[14]

The drama of the Paris Commune has obscured the parallels with other cities and towns where a programme of workers' control and participatory democracy had a deep resonance; indeed, Marseille and Lyon had established popular 'communes' before Paris. In March, further short-lived communes were established in Le Creusot, Narbonne, Toulouse, Limoges, St-Etienne and a score of other towns. Significantly, these were all urban centres that had grown rapidly during the Second Empire and where the 1860s had seen a vigorous popular participation in resurgent left-wing politics, culminating in 1871 in demands for national defence, municipal autonomy and socialist reform.[15] At a local level, particularly in the south, the years from 1871 to 1877 were a time of protracted conflict between the forces of order and republicans of various types over the nature of the new régime. As in 1830–34 and 1848–51, supporters of both sides combined electoral campaigns, popular festivals and political symbolism as they disputed victory through the ballot box and on the streets.[16]

This protracted and nationwide political process in 1868–77 paralleled those of 1828–34 and 1846–52. This time, however, a radically different resolution was reached on 20 February 1876 when, for the first time, a majority of Frenchmen clearly chose a republican régime as the best guarantee of civil liberties and social progress. Whereas in 1849 the *démoc-socs* had won more than 50 percent of the vote in just 16 of the 83 departments, now republicans polled a majority in 51. The west of the Massif Central, the east and the south-east remained their heartlands, but successful inroads had even been made into parts of the north-east and the west, where fewer than 20 percent had voted for the left in 1849. Parties of the right continued to dominate Brittany, Normandy, the west and south-west, and Bonapartist candidates continued to do well in some regions. The response of the government of 'moral order' was to counter-attack by dissolving the assembly (16 May 1877) and unleashing a punitive purge of local officials and associations, as in 1850–52. In 1877, 1,743 republican mayors were dismissed. The church organized huge pilgrimages to Lourdes and Paray-le-Moniol in an attempt to rally the forces of order. On 14 October, however, the republican victory of the previous year was repeated, one of the most significant turning points in French political history. In January 1879, even the Senate elections returned a republican majority. The *raison d'être* of the Republic – parliamentary democracy or socialism? – continued to divide republicans; nevertheless, in contrast to the aftermath of the repression of the insurrections of April 1834 or December 1851, this time a republican regime was able to maintain control of state institutions. In 1881, the first Bastille Day celebrations were held across the country.[17]

The durable establishment of the democratic republic was essentially the result of the consolidation of electoral politics and changes in ideology, even *mentalité*, among masses of French people. Historians agree that, in the century after 1789, a complex, regionally varied shift occurred in the relationship between the mass of French people and the state: in a word, they became 'politicized' in the sense of understanding their particular grievances within wider, particularly national structures and contexts. They disagree, however, about when this shift in political culture occurred, searching for an illusory moment of transition. The history of politicization, in fact, was not so unilinear: every generation relearns the meanings of public life. Michel Vovelle has seen the French Revolution as the moment of unprecedented popular participation in national politics, while Maurice Agulhon and many others have identified a mass political 'apprenticeship' during the Second Republic. For Eugen Weber, this was a process that only began after 1880 in the regions south of the Loire.[18] Sudhir Hazareesingh, in contrast, has emphasized the importance of the Second Empire, usually dismissed as an authoritarian hiatus in the republican narrative, in the use made, for example, of presidential tours through the provinces and, in particular, of the national festival of the 'Saint-Napoleon' on 15 August.[19]

The Saint-Napoleon was a deliberate link forged in 1852 by Napoleon III with the First Empire: in 1804, Napoleon Bonaparte had persuaded the Vatican to canonize a new saint whose celebration would coincide with 15 August, Napoleon's birthday. The festival was also deeply political. It gave authorities the occasion to increase surveillance of republicans, who in turn responded by ostentatiously absenting themselves from festivities or allowing a piece of red fabric to be visible on clothing. But, while the Second Empire certainly developed new forms of mass politics, it did not invent them. The cult built on earlier political celebrations – such as of the Fêtes de la Fédération held across the country in July 1790 and the public celebrations in November 1848 of the proclamation of the constitution of the Second Republic.[20]

Contemporaries no less than historians were struck by the changes and continuities in the articulated grievances and demands of insurgents in these three revolutions. And, just as popular understandings of why the world was as it was and how it might otherwise be reflected the realities of the historical moment, so did the precise ways in which riots were enacted. In each revolutionary crisis, the forms of collective protest reflected the changing society of which they were a product. On the basis of many years of studying and quantifying collective protest in France and elsewhere, Charles Tilly saw in the rich history of protest and revolt in nineteenth-century France the paradigmatic example of the interrelationship of changes in the nature of the state, society and protest. As he stressed, like the history of all societies, it was studded with examples of protest even in apparently peaceful years; unusually, however, three times in 40 years protest in France was powerful and radical enough to topple régimes.[21]

The focus of the most pressing material concerns shifted across these decades. In 1816, the Minister of the Interior reported on harvest failure and subsequent food rioting in many cities and towns in terms that could have been used during earlier crises, in 1775 or even 1709:

> This high price of corn [the highest for fifteen years] was the cause of the unrest which spread amongst the people and of the disturbances which broke out at the beginning of the winter. During the first few days of November there was quite a serious insurrection at Toulouse; people refused by buy corn at the price fixed and tried to steal it from the markets.

Two years later, a new type of protest erupted. In February 1819, the royal prosecutor in the town of Vienne, to the south of Lyon, reported a furious attack by textile workers on a new machine brought into the town by their employers. Cases of machinery were flung into the river Gère and smashed with the tools of trade, as weavers shouted 'We'll do for the machine all right', 'It's not the bloody machine that wants smashing' and 'Get rid of the machine'.[22]

By the 1850s, both forms of protest – which had also underpinned key elements of popular ideology in the first half of the century – had essentially disappeared. Tilly has argued that the years of the Second Republic were the time of critical transition in the forms in which political power was contested. The great wave of subsistence protests in 1846–47 and then the explosion of forest invasions, occupations and destruction of private property, and anti-tax rebellions in 1848 were to be the last great outbreak – at least on a large scale – of forms of protest described by Tilly as 'reactive' or 'parochial' responses to state centralization and capitalist economic structures. From 1848, they were juxtaposed with a remarkable proliferation of demonstrations, mass electoral rallies, organized political activity and coordinated insurrectional activity epitomized in secret republican societies and resistance to the *coup* in 1851: collective action he described variously as 'industrial', 'modern', 'proactive' or 'national'.

Fundamental to these changes in the nature and orientation of protest were transformations in urban and rural society. In Tilly's words, the decades before and after 1845:

> spanned the country's first great surge of industrial expansion and urban growth. They included the knitting together of the nation by railroad and telegraph. They contained the advent of universal manhood suffrage, the emergence of political parties, and the formation of trade unions. They even saw a crucial and durable switch from high fertility toward low fertility. ... It was a time of profound political transformations. The nature of collective violence changed in step with those transformations.[23]

The nature of urban work was also transformed in most trades. Small, artisanal trades in cities such as Paris, St-Etienne or Toulouse co-existed with large-scale industries, but were increasingly incorporated into their forms of production. The durability of artisan trades in France has led some social historians to question Marx's paradigm of the development of a large industrial working-class, arguing instead that the workforce remained a mixture of skilled artisans and disorganized, unskilled factory proletarians. Such an argument misses important changes in the average size of workplaces, in the division of labour within them and, most importantly, that wage-earners of whatever type of skill identified themselves primarily as workers.[24] As early as 1833, the Parisian shoemaker Efrahem was voicing a new meaning of 'association', that of a union of all trades as a basis for political power:

> If we remain isolated, scattered, we are feeble, we will be easily defeated and will submit to the law of the masters; if we remain divided, cut off from one another, if we do not agree among ourselves, we will be obliged to surrender ourselves to the discretion of our bourgeois. There must hence be a bond that unites us, an intelligence that governs us, there must be an *association*.[25]

Those over-represented among the arrested insurgents in June 1848 were from industries characterized by large workplaces (the metal, building and leather trades represented 31.7 percent of the arrests but only 10.1 percent of the workforce), and included 257 mechanics and 80 railway workers. While many insurgents sought to avoid punishment by pleading innocence or ignorance, others, such as the engineering worker Louis-Auguste Raccari, insisted his aim had been 'the organization of work through association ... to ensure that the worker receives the product of his labour'.[26]

Many historians have similarly contested Marx's contemporary assertion that the Paris Commune was an unprecedented revolution for a new socialist society in the hands of the working class and its allies. Instead, they have seen it as the last episode of the French Revolution, highlighting the constant appeals back to the revolutionary tradition, and the mixed, pre-industrial nature of the Parisian workforce.[27] It is true that huge numbers of Parisians remained in artisanal work; however, compared with 1846, the average workplace now had almost eight workers compared with five, and most workers were in far larger enterprises, such as the men and women in the building trades where the ratio of employees to employers was 13:1. Over 42 percent of those later arrested were labourers, wood-workers, stone-masons and metal-workers. The socialism of the commune was an expression of the workplace culture and experience of such workers, drawn from the tradition of 'republican socialism' developed by workers themselves since 1830. Workers at the huge arms workshop established at the Louvre compiled regulations that the workshop would be run by a revocable, elected manager and a council of delegates from each work-bench whose membership would rotate between workers each fortnight. As a stone-carver wrote to the Commission of Labour and Exchange, such cooperatives would result in the 'inevitable abolition of the class of employers and of the exploitation of man by man'.[28]

The subsequent consolidation of the Third Republic and parliamentary rule after 1877 did not, of course, render class-based protest redundant. Instead, working people in town or country were drawn to new political and social ideologies and their institutional forms. Between 1887 and 1902, for example, Bourses au Travail or labour exchanges were established in 94 towns and cities, and by 1907, there were 157 Bourses across the country. These were essentially run by workers themselves, and as the Confédération Générale du Travail advocated a 'syndicalist' program of direct action outside parliamentarism. Whereas unions had had a total membership of less than 200,000 in 1890, by 1914 there were about 1 million members; there were 47 strikes in the Paris building industry alone, and one strike in the underground railway lasted 11 months.[29]

Three times, in 1830, 1848 and 1870–71, large-scale, popular rebellion had succeeded in overthrowing political régimes; now, with the acceptance that popular choice was at last also republican, it could be concluded that the revolutionary century that had begun in 1789 was over. The republican ship had entered the harbour of power. Such finality is questioned by the ongoing existence of revolutionary political organizations and massive popular insurrections which, in 1907, 1936, 1944 and 1968, threatened or almost toppled governments. In 1907, for example, winegrowers on the Mediterranean coastline began a series of protests against the collapse in wine prices, caused (it was believed) by the flooding of the market by adulterated poor quality wines. From its origins in the village of Argeliers (Aude) in March 1907, a wave of demonstrations surged from 5,000 people at Coursan, 120,000 at Béziers, 170,000 at Perpignan, 220,000 at Carcassonne, climaxing at an estimated 500,000 at Montpellier on 9 June.[30]

Not surprisingly, people of means found collective protest terrifying and criminal, even barbaric. In contrast, from the comfort of hindsight, cultural historians have seen the occasional outbreaks of spectacular violence as ritualized displays of collective identity and values.[31] While it is certainly the case that violent acts were directed mostly towards property rather than persons, and that attacks on persons were most likely to be verbal and symbolic, the practice of collective violence and the few cases of deliberate cruelty by rioting crowds does need closer study. In some ways, these decades resemble a long civil war that occasionally erupted into horrific violence – as well as a long march towards institutional democracy.[32]

Most importantly, however, the victory of parliamentary democracy under the Third Republic was due more than anything else to deeply-held beliefs among working people that popular sovereignty implied manhood suffrage and electoral choice. When all adult males won the right to vote in April 1848, 84 percent used it. In the end, this was a victory won by revolution 'from below'. The collapse of the Second Empire lay not only in military defeat but also, as with monarchical régimes in 1789, 1830 and 1848, widespread resentment at its ruler's claims to personal power. Resistance to the practice of parliamentary democracy came from entrenched élites, not from insufficiently 'enlightened' working people with a predilection for violent protest. The fundamental transformations in collective protest and political culture in the nineteenth century were, however, neither sharp nor total: popular associational activity within a national political framework had proliferated in 1789–93, and the winegrowers' protests of the 1970s in Languedoc-Roussillon opposed state and European policies with symbols and tactics redolent of previous centuries. But the ways in which protesters understood the locus of power and the strategies necessary to influence it had changed definitively. The middle decades of the nineteenth century were the watershed of those changes.

Notes

1. Malcolm Crook (ed.), *Revolutionary France 1788–1880* (Oxford, 2002); Roger Magraw, *France 1815–1914: The Bourgeois Century* (London, 1983); François Furet, *La Révolution: de Turgot à Jules Ferry, 1770–1880* (Paris, 1989), esp. pp. 479, 516–17.

2. Quentin Deluermoz, *Le Crépuscule des révolutions* (Paris, 2012), p. 373.
3. This narrative draws on my *Social History of France, 1780–1914*, 2nd ed. (London and New York, 2004).
4. On the Revolution of 1830, see David Pinkney, *The Revolution of 1830* (Princeton, 1972); Pamela M. Pilbeam, *The 1830 Revolution in France* (London, 1991); Bertrand Goujon, *Monarchies Postrévolutionnaires 1814–1848* (Paris, 2012), chaps 4–5; and the path-breaking collection edited by John M. Merriman, *1830 in France* (New York, 1975).
5. Sylvie Vila, 'Une révélation? Les Luttes populaires dans le département de l'Hérault au début de la Monarchie de Juillet, 1830–1834', *Droite et gauche de 1789 à nos jours* (Montpellier, 1975), pp. 105–35; André Jardin and André-Jean Tudesq, *Restoration and Reaction, 1815–1848*, trans. E. Forster (Cambridge and New York, 1983), pp. 93–116.
6. Roger Thabault, *Education and Change in a Village Community: Mazières-en-Gâtine 1848–1914*, trans. P. Tregear (London, 1971), chap. 3.
7. Robert J. Bezucha, *The Lyon Uprising of 1834: Social and Political Conflict in the Early July Monarchy* (Cambridge, MA, 1974).
8. Surveys of 1848 include Maurice Agulhon, *The Republican Experiment, 1848–1852* (Cambridge and New York, 1983); Jill Harsin, *Barricades: The War of the Streets in Revolutionary Paris, 1830–1848* (New York and London, 2002), chaps. 13–15; and Roger Price, *The French Second Republic: A Social History* (Ithaca, 1972). Recent research is synthesized in Deluermoz, *Crépuscule des révolutions*, chaps 1–2; and Jean-Luc Mayaud (ed.), *1848. Actes du colloque international du cent cinquantenaire* (Paris, 2002).
9. Mary Lynn Stewart-McDougall, *The Artisan Republic: Revolution, Reaction, and Resistance in Lyon, 1848–1851* (Montreal, 1984), pp. 42–48; Peter McPhee, *The Politics of Rural Life: Political Mobilization in the French Countryside, 1846–1852* (Oxford, 1992), p. 85.
10. On the June Days, see Donald C. McKay, *The National Workshops: A Study in the French Revolution of 1848* (Cambridge, MA, 1933), chaps. 5–6; Mark Traugott, *Armies of the Poor: Determinants of Working-Class Participation in the Parisian Insurrection of June 1848* (Princeton, 1985); Charles Tilly and Lynn H. Lees, 'The People of June, 1848', in *Revolution and Reaction: 1848 and the Second French Republic*, ed. Roger Price (London, 1975), pp. 170–209.
11. On radical provincial movements and their repression, see Ted Margadant, *French Peasants in Revolt: The Insurrection of 1851* (Princeton, 1979); John Merriman, *The Agony of the Republic: The Repression of the Left in Revolutionary France, 1848–1851* (New Haven, 1978); Edward Berenson, *Populist Religion and Left-Wing Politics in France, 1830–1852* (Princeton, 1984); and McPhee, *The Politics of Rural Life*.
12. The best treatment of the *coup* remains Margadant, *French Peasants in Revolt*. See too, Maurice Agulhon, *The Republic in the Village: The People of the Var from the French Revolution to the Second Republic*, trans. J. Lloyd (Cambridge, 1970), chaps. 14–17; McPhee, *The Politics of Rural Life*; Sylvie Aprile et al., *Comment meurt une république. Autour du 2 décembre 1851* (Grâne, 2004); and Emile Zola's historical novel *La Fortune des Rougon*.
13. On Noir's funeral, see Roger Price, *The French Second Empire: An Anatomy of Political Power* (Cambridge and New York, 2001); and the innovative study by Avner Ben-Amos, *Funerals, Politics, and Memory in Modern France 1789–1996* (Oxford and New York, 2000).

14. See Roger L. Williams, *The French Revolution of 1870–1871* (New York, 1969); Jacques Rougerie, *Paris libre: 1871* (Paris, 1971); William Serman, *La Commune de Paris (1871)* (Paris, 1986); Laure Godineau, *La Commune de Paris, 1871* (Paris, 2010); and Robert Tombs, *The Paris Commune 1871* (London, 1999).

15. John M. Merriman, *The Red City: Limoges and the French Nineteenth Century* (Oxford and New York, 1985), chap. 4; Marc César, *Mars 1871. La Commune révolutionnaire de Narbonne* (Sète, 2008); Ronald Aminzade, *Class, Politics and Early Industrial Capitalism: A Study of Mid-Nineteenth Century Toulouse* (Albany, 1981), chap. 8; Jeanne Gaillard, *Communes de province, commune de Paris, 1870–1871* (Paris, 1971).

16. Maurice Agulhon, *Marianne into Battle: Republican Imagery and Symbolism in France, 1789–1880* (Cambridge and New York, 1981), chaps. 6–7; Tony Judt, *Socialism in Provence, 1871–1914: A Study in the Origins of the Modern French Left* (Cambridge, 1979), chap. 6.

17. See, for example, Sanford Elwitt, *The Making of the Third Republic: Class and Politics in France, 1868–1914* (Baton Rouge, 1975); and Philip Nord, *The Republican Movement. Struggles for Democracy in Nineteenth-Century France* (Cambridge, MA, 1995).

18. Michel Vovelle, *Les Métamorphoses de la fête en Provence, de 1750 à 1820* (Paris, 1976); Agulhon, *The Republican Experiment*; Eugen Weber, *Peasants into Frenchmen: The Modernization of Rural France, 1870–1914* (Stanford, 1976). The debate on 'politicization' is analyzed in Edward Berenson, 'Politics and the French Peasantry: The Debate Continues', *Social History*, 12 (1987), pp. 219–29; McPhee, *The Politics of Rural Life*, chap. 5; and Deluermoz, *Le Crépuscule des révolutions*, chap 2.

19. Sudhir Hazareesingh, *From Subject to Citizen: The Second Empire and the Emergence of Modern French Democracy* (Princeton, 1998); *The Legend of Napoleon* (London, 2004); and *The Saint-Napoleon. Celebrations of Sovereignty in Nineteenth-Century France* (Cambridge, MA and London, 2004). See also Alain Corbin's preface to Corbin et al., *Les Usages politiques des fêtes aux XIXe–XXe siècles* (Paris, 1994); Rosemonde Sanson, *Le 14 juillet: fête et conscience nationale 1789–1975* (Paris, 1976); Matthew Truesdell, *Spectacular Politics: Louis-Napoleon Bonaparte and the Fête Impériale, 1849–1870* (London and New York, 1997); Sylvie Aprile, *La Révolution inachevée, 1815–1870* (Paris, 2010), chaps. 10–11.

20. See Mona Ozouf, *La Fête révolutionnaire, 1789–1799* (Paris, 1976); Sheryl Kroen, *Politics and Theater: The Crisis of Legitimacy in Restoration France, 1815–1830* (Berkeley, 2000); Françoise Waquet, *Les Fêtes royales sous la Restauration ou l'Ancien Régime re-trouvé* (Geneva, 1981); Alain Faure, *Paris Carême-Prenant: du carnaval à Paris au XIXeme siècle* (Paris, 1978); Agulhon, *Marianne into Battle*; Olivier Ihl, *La Fête républicaine* (Paris, 1996).

21. Charles Tilly, 'Collective Violence in European Perspective', in *The History of Violence in America*, ed. H. Graham and T.R. Gurr (Washington, 1969), pp. 45–84; Charles Tilly, 'How Protest Modernized in France, 1845–1855', in *The Dimensions of Quantitative Research in History*, ed. W.C. Aydelotte (Princeton, 1972), pp. 192–255; Charles Tilly, *The Formation of National States in Western Europe* (Princeton, 1986); and Charles Tilly, *The Contentious French* (Cambridge, MA, 1986).

22. Irene Collins (ed.), *Government and Society in France, 1814–1848* (London, 1970), pp. 62–70. On the food riots of 1816–17, see Nicolas Bourguinat, *Les Grains du désordre. L'Etat face aux violences frumentaires dans la première moitié du XIXe siècle* (Paris, 2002), pp. 154–61 and *passim*.

23. Charles Tilly, 'The Changing Place of Collective Violence', in *Essays in Social and Political History*, ed. M. Richter (Cambridge, MA, 1970), pp. 139–64.

24. For a cross-section of different approaches to the nature of class formation, see Aminzade, *Toulouse*, chap. 4; Joan W. Scott, *The Glassworkers of Carmaux* (Cambridge, 1974); Rolande Trempé, *Les Mineurs de Carmaux, 1848–1914*, 2 vols. (Paris, 1971); Merriman, *The Red City*, chap. 3; Steven L. Kaplan and Cynthia J. Koepp (eds), *Work in France: Representations, Meaning, Organization and Practice* (Ithaca, 1986) chaps. 13–16; Gérard Noiriel, *Workers in French Society in the Nineteenth and Twentieth Centuries*, trans. H. McPhail (New York, 1990).
25. William H. Sewell, *Work and Revolution in France: The Language of Labor from the Old Régime to 1848* (Cambridge, 1980), p. 216; Eric Hobsbawm and Joan Scott, 'Political Shoemakers', *Past & Present*, 89 (1980), pp. 86–114.
26. Quoted in Roger Price (ed.), *1848 in France* (London, 1975), pp. 111–12.
27. Karl Marx, *The Civil War in France* (first published London, 1871); Jacques Rougerie, *Procès de communards* (Paris, 1964); Roger V. Gould, *Insurgent Identities: Class, Community and Protest in Paris from 1848 to the Commune* (Chicago, 1995); Ronald Aminzade, *Ballots and Barricades: Class Formation and Republican Politics in France, 1830–1871* (Princeton, 1993); David A. Shafer, *The Paris Commune: French Politics, Culture, and Society at the Crossroads of the Revolutionary Tradition and Revolutionary Socialism* (New York and Basingstoke, 2005).
28. Stewart Edwards (ed.), *The Communards of Paris, 1871* (London, 1973), p. 124.
29. An accessible summary of organized labour in these years is Roger Magraw, *A History of the French Working Class*, vol. 2, part V (Oxford and Cambridge, MA, 1992).
30. Félix Napo, *1907: la révolte des vignerons* (Toulouse, 1971); Jean Sagnes, 'Le Mouvement paysan de 1907 en Languedoc-Roussillon: révolte viticole, révolte régionale', *Le midi rouge. Mythe et réalité* (Paris, 1982), pp. 215–61.
31. Olivier Bosc, *La Foule criminelle, Politique et criminalité dans l'Europe du tournant du XIXe siècle* (Paris, 2007); Philippe Bourdin, Mathias Bernard and Jean-Claude Caron (eds), *La Voix et le Geste. Une approche culturelle de la violence socio-politique* (Clermont-Ferrand, 2005).
32. Jean-Claude Caron, *Frères du sang. La Guerre civile en France au XIXe siècle* (Seyssel, 2009). Note the analyses and commentary about examples of collective homicide in Alain Corbin, *The Village of Cannibals: Rage and Murder in France, 1870* (Cambridge, MA, 1992); Peter McPhee, *Revolution and Environment in Southern France: Peasant, Lords, and Murder in the Corbières, 1780–1830* (Oxford, 1999), chap. 8.

12
Red May Days: Fears and Hopes in Europe in the 1890s

Chris Wrigley

The early May Days of the 1890s aroused considerable alarm among the ruling classes in many parts of Europe, as well as expressions of considerable self-satisfaction among the British well-to-do, especially those of a Whig or Liberal outlook. In parts of Europe, the May Day demonstrations led to overreaction by the authorities, with loss of life in France in 1891. More generally, the early May Days revealed the nervousness of many of the propertied classes to coordinated campaigns by international labour and the emergence of the Second International. This essay examines the contrasting attitudes expressed about the early May Days, the outcomes and, as one way of judging the extent to which fears were justified, the composition of the demonstrations.

While the early May Days were a notable example of 'the invention of tradition', as Eric Hobsbawm has argued,[1] they also were notable for connecting with not only the labour movements' pasts but also with society's traditions, such as religious processions in Catholic countries. However, for the authorities in many countries, there were fears driven by past experience of demonstrations turning into riots or even revolutions. In an editorial written ahead of the first May Day demonstrations in 1890, the Liberal *Leicester Daily Mercury* expressed the confidence of British Liberals in British liberty and British institutions:

> It is difficult for the average Englishmen to understand why there should be so much uneasiness in the capitals of the continent at the labour demonstrations announced for today. In this country, in all large centres of population, demonstrations come and go, and in most cases the only business of the authorities is to see that the processions and meetings are undisturbed. On the continent matters are very different. Paris swarms with troops, as it has not done since the time of the Commune, Vienna is practically in a state of siege, pretty nearly the whole Austrian army being under arms in view of the emergencies, and in Berlin ball cartridge has been distributed to

the soldiers in case it should appear to the authorities wise to turn German troops against their brethren.[2]

There was further analysis of the backwardness of many continental European political systems compared with the British one in the Liberal Unionist *Economist*. The decision to call for international May Day demonstrations had been taken at one of two separate socialist conferences held in Paris to mark the centenary of the 1789 French Revolution. The calling of such demonstrations helped to rekindle ruling-class fears of the masses. The *Economist*'s editorial, probably written by John St Loe Strachey, commented on 'the suspiciousness of all continental governments which have never ceased to be influenced by the tradition of the French Revolution' and went on to observe:

> Even when fairly liberal in policy, and aware that in the end opinion governs, they never quite get rid of the feeling that they are menaced by a powerful enemy from below, and that the body of the people, if released from strict control, may indulge in the massacre of the upper classes. ... they cannot get rid of the idea that a mass meeting ends in a riot, a riot in a descent into the streets either in Revolution or civil war. ... They are, moreover, greatly influenced by the universal feeling of the Continent that clamour involves insult, which they are bound as self-respecting persons to avenge, on pain of losing all prestige among their own partisans and the soldiery, who, again, are, as a corporation, very easily roused. Soldiers on the continent will not endure the attacks, either verbal or physical, which are patiently borne in England, and their rulers, knowing this, are obliged to let them loose much sooner, and to take much more care that they are not defeated.

The editorial of the *Economist* went on to give a classic statement of the English sense of superiority over the wild continentals:

> The main cause of the disturbance is ... no doubt the temper of the people, which is much fiercer when they are excited than in the case of England. They are, to begin with, all – or nearly all – [ex] soldiers, they are much less accustomed to free discussion, and they are frequently much less civilised. The workmen of France are only just beginning to believe in peaceful combinations; those of Italy, though good-humoured, soon grow frantic with excitement; those of Germany include immense numbers of Socialists, who are avowedly at war with society; while those of Austria comprise a multitude of half-tamed men, Poles, Hungarians, Slavs, Czechs and Croats, who resort to force, through ignorance, upon the smallest provocation. It is almost impossible to reason with them, and when they are in the mood for riot, they shed blood. They hate the Jews, who they look upon as foreign

and unbelieving oppressors. ... They make up a terribly fierce crowd at all times.[3]

Hence, there was a widespread Whig-style satisfaction with the British political system and the way it was believed to train British working people to work within it to achieve social gains. More than that, liberals believed that the continentals would do well to adopt the British economic system. The British editorials did not hesitate to offer continental countries' working people the advice to be more like British workers:

The working men of the continent will probably find that there is no 'royal road' to improved conditions of existence, and that to effect what they desire they will have to follow the example of their English fellows and agitate peacefully and persistently till Reichstags and despotisms remove obstructions to their labour so that they may have a free course open to them to work out their own complete emancipation. If they were sharp they would soon make Protection impossible. That would be a big step forward.[4]

Such confidence in 'the soundness' of the great majority of the British working class led several British parliamentarians to witness the massive London May Day demonstration held on Sunday, 4 May 1890. William Gladstone, the Liberal leader, took care to check the mood of the marchers that day. He and his wife walked along Buckingham Palace Road as the marchers returning from Hyde Park headed towards Westminster Bridge. The Liberal *Manchester Guardian* noted with much satisfaction that the 'Liberal leader was cheered along the whole line of the procession'.[5] This was in spite of Gladstone having made clear his opposition to legislating for the eight-hour working day, the main unifying cause of the early international May Days.

While the liberals had cause to be reassured that the majority of working people shared their major political beliefs, conservatives were more wary of the mass politics represented by May Day. The *Edinburgh Evening News* in May 1891 observed that 'the sceptre of revolutionary thought has passed from France to Germany. Karl Marx is the Rousseau of the industrial revolution. He has imported and adapted to socialistic ends the teachings of the old English economists'. The editorial went on to argue that 'the revolutionists had better take to heart the lesson of the great French political revolution. It was expected that the millennium would follow the downfall of kings and priests. The millennium somehow failed to put in an appearance'. However, it also stated that for the authorities, 'the age of repression' was past.[6]

While in Britain there was far less anxiety about the early May Day demonstrations than in Austria or Germany, there were still some public order concerns. These were focused on the London anarchist and radical clubs, many of whose members were political refugees from Europe. On 30 April 1890, Sir James Munro, the Chief Commissioners of the Metropolitan Police, issued a proclamation banning any processions in London from marching other than from Victoria Embankment on a set route to Hyde Park. This was issued a few hours after Jack Williams, a leading figure of the Social Democrat Federation and the chief organizer of the National Federation of All Industries and Trades (composed of small 'New Unions' and centred on South West London, the organization behind the hard-line demonstration), had visited Scotland Yard to discuss plans for a rally in Hyde Park to be followed by a march to Clerkenwell Green and a torchlight meeting there. Williams denounced the proclamation, observing that he thought it 'a most unconstitutional proceeding and did not remember anything like it in his experience of labour movements. The men might as well be living in Russia, France, Germany or Vienna'. After questions in Parliament, the Home Secretary, Henry Matthews, confirmed that the chief commissioner had such powers to restrict demonstrations and indicated that he had given the chief commissioner specific instructions regarding at least a march on 7 June 1890.[7] While the ostensible reason for the proclamation was to avoid the general public being inconvenienced on other routes, it had the practical purpose of making policing easier.

There was firm policing on 1 May. The authorities had mounted Metropolitan and City of London police at the eastern end of the Thames Embankment near Blackfriars Bridge, the approved mustering point for the demonstrators. The police seized the black and red flag inscribed 'Vive l'Anarchie' of a group who tried to march from the Club Autonomie (which supported the German anarchist newspaper *Die Autonomie*) to the embankment, in defiance of approved routes.[8] While the reports of the *Times* and other national newspapers were not critical of the policing, the Socialist League's *Commonweal* included a more critical account by David Nicoll, soon to be one of its editors. This report added to the mounted police at Blackfriars Bridge '2,000 foot and horse [who] guarded the narrow hilly streets which lie between the Embankment and Fleet Street and the Strand'. He went on to write:

A procession of our East End comrades was broken up in Aldgate. Some of our friends from France were reminded that they were living in free and happy England by being set upon by the police in St Martin's Lane. These bullies kicked and cuffed the 'bloody foreigners', as they elegantly termed them, without mercy, and broke to pieces a flag they were carrying. On Clerkenwell Green our gallant police attacked the women who were on strike from Fenner's envelope factory in John Street, Clerkenwell, and knocked them about with the savage ruffianism with which we are now familiar. They didn't, however, frighten these plucky girls, who marched down to the Embankment and joined the procession.[9]

That this area was heavily policed is likely, even if the 2,000 figure seems high. According to the police and the press, the 1 May marchers numbered between 1,000 and 1,500. There were big crowds watching at the embankment, the *Times* reporting that Blackfriars Bridge and the pathways of the embankment 'were filled with working men, with their aprons on' during their lunch break. The *Star* blamed 'Munro's display of officious muddling' for the spectators and the throwing of the embankment into confusion for an hour. At the Reformers' Tree, Hyde Park, there were estimates of the size of the crowd between 200 and several thousands. There were larger numbers at the evening demonstration in Clerkenwell.[10] The huge demonstration estimated at between 350,000 and 500,000 people on Sunday 4 May was also well policed. According to the *Times*, there were 3,300 police on duty or in reserve. This was a substantial force as a precaution against unrest, not least given the police strength in the capital was 13,600 (or 12,189 when leave and average numbers ill are taken into account).[11] This suggests, rather like Oliver Cromwell's advice to pray to God but keep your powder dry, that in spite of the expressions of faith in the British constitution and British people, major precautions were taken in the capital. Other demonstrations in Edinburgh, Leeds, Bristol, Plymouth, Northampton and (a fortnight later) in Aberdeen also passed off without major incident.

In Vienna, the coming of the first international May Day caused alarm. A modern guidebook to the city bluntly notes that it 'frightened the wits out of the authorities and the middle classes'. The authorities in issuing ferocious warnings to working people not to stop work managed to add to the alarm of the propertied classes. A proclamation issued by a governor on 4 April 1890 warned that anyone refusing to work on 1 May would face severe consequences. On the 18 April, Emperor Francis Joseph chaired a meeting of his council to prepare measures to be taken against strikes on May Day. The respectable *Neue Freie* Press reported of Vienna on 30 April: 'The soldiers are alerted, the house-doors are bolted, people are laying in stocks of food at home as though preparing for a siege. The shops are deserted, women and children are afraid to go into the streets, all spirits are oppressed by heavy anxiety'. Others of the well-to-do fled the city. There were also accounts of a few fearful factory owners preparing cauldrons of boiling water to tip over any attackers.[12]

The military and the police were well-prepared in Vienna, and other Austrian cities. In Vienna, a socialist recalled: 'the Prater was heavily occupied by the infantry, cavalry and artillery. Every quarter of an hour infantry battalions and Hussar squads marched demonstratively through the park avenues. Here and there, behind bushes and trees, Uhlan bivouacs could be glimpsed. The whole police force was out on duty, but hidden, mostly on guard inside single houses'.

This account in the *Arbiter-Zeitung* also emphasized the peaceful nature of the crowds:

> Of the sixty meetings held in the morning, many were attended by three or four thousand people. ... A wonderful sight ... was the procession of over 100,000 Viennese workers in the Prater. ... Amid the loaded rifles and cannons, from one hundred thousand throats simultaneously, Lied der Arbeit [the Song of Work] rose to the sky.[13]

The special correspondent of the *Economist* in Vienna wrote on 6 May: 'In consequence of the unexpectedly peaceable course which events took on May 1, our bourse, by one sudden leap, recovered from the depression of weeks past'. In spite of further threats from employers and officials and also bans, May Day was successfully celebrated again in Vienna in 1891. By May Day 1892, the Austrian authorities were relaxed about the demonstrations, as were businessmen and financiers.[14]

In contrast with Austria, repression – or at least fears of repression – were effective in limiting the celebration of May Days in Germany and Russia. In Germany, the Social Democrats had won many Reichstag seats in February 1890, and the Anti-Socialist Law (1878–90) was running out, so the labour movement did not wish to provoke the renewal of the legislation. As a result, in 1890, most working people celebrated with rallies and festivities out of working hours. Where workers did stop working – with some 100,000 across Germany so doing – they avoided prosecution under the Anti-Socialist Law by mass walking in the countryside. Some 20,000 participated in this way in Berlin and about 12,000 in Dresden. The main exception was Hamburg, where 20,000 to 30,000 people who downed tools, ignored the ban on marches and the intimidation of police and employers. They subsequently faced an effective employers' lock-out, which succeeded in severely damaging Hamburg's labour movement. From 1891, the major German May Day rallies were held, as in Britain, on the nearest Sunday.[15]

In Russia and its empire in 1890, repression was highly effective, with May Day marked only notably in the Russian occupied part of Poland (with an unthreatening outing held in Helsinki, Finland). There some 8,000 to 10,000 factory and railway workshop employees went on strike in Warsaw, and several thousand did so in Lvov, holding a mass meeting in the city hall. Tsarist repression followed, with clashes against police and soldiers. Several Warsaw strikers received exemplary prison sentences. From 1891, there were underground celebrations of May Day in Russia itself. In 1891, some 70 to 200 people, apparently from the Putilov, Obukhov, Baltiisky and other factories and shipyards, attended the *maevka* in St Petersburg. This and later St Petersburg *maevka*, as well as those held elsewhere, were often held surreptitiously in the countryside. In the Volga cities, in the late 1890s, trade unions held secret meetings in working-class apartment blocks. Generally, tsarist repression was effective in minimising May Day observation. In 1891, a May Day strike of 8,000 textile workers at Zyrardow, was put down by an army regiment, and in 1892, a strike at Lodz of some 60,000 textile workers, linked to May Day propaganda, was put down by two infantry regiments. Police and troops were also used to put down May Day strikes in Riga in 1899. As the decade went on, there was more action by police, with troops deployed as back-up in Russian cities, with some 1,000 people arrested in 1897.[16]

In France, May Day was celebrated in between 160 and 200 places. In Marseilles, for instance, there was a peaceful march of some 50,000 people from the *bourse du travail*, led by a deputy and councillors. While a delegation was seen by the authorities, the path of the large crowd of supporters was blocked by the gendarmerie. In Lyon, the May Day celebrations attracted up to 40,000 people. The chief of police refused to allow a delegation of 12 men and three women to be received by the mayor in the police station. Instead, there was a big meeting in the *bourse du travail*. There were a few arrests in a street. Otherwise, the day passed peacefully. In Lens, some 23,000 miners and their families celebrated May Day, with proceedings becoming heated towards the 30 gendarmes present and reinforcements being sent from Arras. Other well-attended demonstrations included 35,000 at Roubaix; 20,000 at Lille; 15,000 at Calais and St Quentin; 12,000 at Bordeaux; 6,000 at Toulon and 5,000 at Troyes.

Yet France experienced fear on the part of the authorities somewhat similar to that shown in Austria, Germany and Russia. With fresh memories of the Commune, 1871, the French government feared unrest in the working-class districts of Paris, banned marches in the capital and had ready for action the 34,000 troops garrisoned in the capital, with further troops at Fontainebleau and Rambouillet and artillery at the ready at Versailles. Similar military and police preparations were made in other cities. In the Rhône valley, the police collected reports of many threats of violence and seizure of food made before 1 May 1890. One report claimed: 'Everyone is dreading the First of May because they are frightened of outbreaks of violence such as happened at the Theatre Bellecour. ... It is said that most of the silk mills have stored their stocks in a safe place, and two of the biggest mill owners have already left for Geneva'. In Lyons, many industrialists, bankers and shopkeepers requested the authorities to provide special protection. On 1 May, many factories closed. While the forces of law and order were deployed against crowds in Paris and elsewhere, there was no loss of life that year. There were violent attacks on factories in Marseilles, Vienne and Cette. In Marseilles, in the evening, the Jeansoulin oil works was wrecked by Italian workers and French youths, with the armed forces being brought in, and 76 arrests and prosecutions made. In Vienne, where anarchist influence was strong, weavers rioted and arrests and trials followed. During the unrest there, anarchists occupied a ruined chateau, where they flew black and red flags, and were dislodged by infantry.[17]

In 1891, there were lengthier preparations for May Day, and the leaflets advertising it at Fourmies and elsewhere placed much emphasis on the 'fête familiale' aspect of the celebration. With the killing of nine people including four young women (aged 16–20) and two children (aged 11 and 14), and the wounding of 35 others, by 54 foot soldiers at the Fourmies May Day demonstration, the authorities created martyrs who were to be commemorated at French May Day demonstrations thereafter. Fourmies was by far the worst May Day incident in France, though there were other clashes in 1891, notably at Clichy where a struggle over a red flag led to shooting, some people being wounded and two demonstrators receiving jail sentences. There were other clashes in subsequent years, as between police and artisans in Marseilles in 1893.[18] In France, the authorities were mindful of the revolutionary tradition, the Commune and the wildcat strikes of the 1870s and took a more hostile view of labour combinations than did most of their British equivalents. They were fearful of the labour movement, which was changing from the artisan-dominated one of the pre-1880s to one where there were more coal and rail workers, more employed in large industrial workplaces and more unskilled workers. They also claimed that some 4,000 to 5,000 foreign agitators were active.[19]

The success of the first May Days in the early 1890s owed much to the upturn in the international economy. This put labour in a relatively strong position in the labour market. The sheer scale of the London demonstrations held on Sundays owed most of their numbers to the burgeoning New Unionism (of unskilled workers) as well as the skilled trade unionists mobilized by the London Trades Council. The estimates varied, but figures of 250,000 to 500,000 in 1890, 1891 and 1892, seem reasonable, with those in 1893 and 1894 perhaps also of the lower end of the range. The big fall in the size of the Sunday demonstration came in 1895, with about 40,000 people present in Hyde Park. For a period thereafter, the London Trades Council did not organize a big central London demonstration, while the Social Democrat Federation from 1894 held its Hyde Park rally on 1 May.[20] The presence of New Unionism boosted numbers at May Day demonstrations around Britain and also explains the location of many of them. It was Tom Mann, a leader of the 1889 London Dock Strike and a socialist, who had convinced the older generation of trade unionists who dominated the London Trades Council, to participate in the great London Sunday demonstration of 1890 (and subsequent years). He got round their opposition to joining a demonstration calling for legislation for an eight-hour working day rather than securing it by collective bargaining, by proposing that they make their own arrangements and march to Hyde Park by a different route from the socialists.

Similarly, outside of London in places as far apart as Edinburgh and Northampton, trades council support turned May Day demonstrations into large events. In Edinburgh, in 1893, there were some 5,000 in the procession, and 'immense crowds lined the streets all along the route', with large crowds also in 1894, when the trades council gave its support whereas in 1890 and 1892 when it did not the Sunday rallies attracted 400–500 people. In Northampton in 1890, with the trade council's support, some 10,000 took part in the Sunday demonstration, whereas the following year, without its support, only 500 attended the meeting in the marketplace. Other places where trades council support appears to have been important include Norwich and Chatham in 1891, and Hull in 1892.[21] In many areas, New Unions were critical to large demonstrations. When the New Unions weakened in the mid-1890s, so did attendances at May Day rallies. The Gas Workers' Union played a major role in a lot of places, in some cases instigating the demonstrations. This was so in Northampton, where the local union leader George Green played the major role in arrangements, and also in Sittingbourne (Kent) and Leeds. In major ports, such as at Liverpool and Newcastle upon Tyne in 1891, the Sailors' and Firemen's Union took the lead. Local amalgamations of New Unions were also important, such as the Norfolk and Norwich Amalgamated Labour Union (with some 2,000 members) the Tyneside and National Labour Union and the Southern Counties Labour League, all of which were involved in 1891 May Day events.[22]

While the New Unionists were prominent, marching with new banners, there were also substantial numbers of members of older trade unions. Unsurprisingly, outside of London most demonstrations reflected employment in the areas. In Norwich, there were farm workers from the surrounding countryside and shoemakers from the city. In Liverpool, there were tugmen, and in Leeds, weavers and clothing workers. Bricklayers appear in many reports of May Days, as do bakers in some urban areas.

A feature of the early May Days in Britain, as elsewhere, was that often workers timed strikes to coincide with May Day or, if already on strike, joined the May Day demonstrations and publicized their cause. At the 1 May 1890 demonstration in London, 200 women on strike at the Clerkenwell envelope factory marched in the procession, with some carrying collecting boxes in support of the strike. In Norwich, shoemakers, who had just ended a dispute, participated in the 1891 demonstration as did bricklayers who were just starting a strike. The May Day demonstrations were also opportunities to express support for others engaged in industrial conflict. Thus, in 1893, at Huddersfield a crowd of 3,000, after passing a resolution on the eight-hour day, followed with another that condemned the Huddersfield Watch Committee for 'sending police to Hull to aid the Shipping Federation in their attempt to crush the Dockers' Union'.

In Edinburgh that year at the May Day rally, there was a collection of money for the Hull strikers.[23]

In France, in 1890, there were strikes spread across the country, but there was particular strength in the coalfields, the northern textile towns and the northern suburbs of Paris among gas workers and glass makers. These were areas marked by accompanying industrial unrest in May 1890 and later. Michelle Perrot's research has shown that May was a month notable for strikes in France, and in 1890, the levels were exceptional: 26 percent of all strikes and 58 percent of all strikers were recorded in that month, compared with 13 and 19 percent, respectively, as the May average over 1870 to 1890. The miners had been discussing an industry-wide strike and, working shorter hours than most in industry, the eight hours aim was attractive to other French workers. In France, the intended one-day May strikes were often extended into longer struggles.[24]

In both Britain and France, women participated as speakers as well as marchers. In London, Eleanor Marx was a key member of the Eight Hours Legal Working Day Committee, who organized the huge Sunday demonstration in Hyde Park in 1890. As well as Eleanor Marx, Annie Besant, Charlotte Despard, Annie Taylor and Mrs Hudson (Laundress's Union) were among several women who spoke from the platforms (and not only from the separate platform for women trade unionists) in the 1890s and after. In Glasgow, in 1895, the platform speakers included Enid Stacy and Katharine St John Conway, two of the leading women speakers of the Independent Labour Party. Louise Michel, the distinguished Communard and anarchist, spoke in Vienne just before 1 May 1890 as well as in London in 1892 and 1896. Women were prominent in the processions in London, Norwich and elsewhere. Some of the later reports suggest that more women were present, and like the Sozialdemokratische Partei Deutschlands (SPD) women in Germany, these were often wives of the artisans. In St George's Square, Huddersfield, in 1906, it was noted that 'women formed a considerable proportion of the audience'. They wore red rosettes and 'the children of the Socialist Sunday schools wore red sashes'.[25]

The great majority of the British trade unionists were moderate, as William Gladstone and the other liberal leaders recognized. The separate route and separate speeches of the huge London Trades Council contingent underlined the older trade union leaders' suspicions of the socialists and anarchists. While harbingers of more radical times, the younger socialist heroes of New Unionism, nevertheless, emphasized their respectability and their acceptance of the Parliamentary road to social change. The most popular speaker at the May 1890 mass meeting in Hyde Park was John Burns. The *Star* reported: 'He gave a digest of the reasons for the legal enforcement of the eight hours and he gave advice as to the means for obtaining it. 'What have you to do? Why, send me to Parliament'. 'Ay, ay', heartily came the answer from some of the Battersea boys'. The newspaper also reported Mann dealing with a drunken soldier who got on the platform beside him:

> He was head and shoulders higher than Tom, but the dockers' president calmly took him by the neck of his coat and lifted him over the edge, dropping him there. 'We want no drunken men here', said Tom, and the crowd loudly applauded.[26]

Burns, who was to move to the liberal party, had no time for the anarchists. At the start of 1894, he observed, 'the leaders are men of dreams, completely out of touch with the working classes, and their tools were the mentally deficient and the morally debased; the whole movement was a mere phase of criminality'.[27] Yet, men and women of dreams were a part of May Days, as Danielle Tartakowsky has emphasized (*La part due rêve:* The portion of dreams). In France, where hours of work remained very long, the 'eight-hour day demanded in 1890 was' as Michelle Perrot has commented, 'a very popular utopia'.[28]

The iconography of the May Day celebrations around the world expressed the hope and expectations of burgeoning labour movements. The end of feudalism and the rise of the working class, the rising sun of socialism and the renewal of life indicated in images of spring were recurrent themes. Also, many images of early 1890s May Days show garlands of flowers prominent. There was often music and a happy air of festivity to proceedings. The invented traditions were linked with much tapping into established ones, such as taking up the routes and even other aspects of the Catholic Church's public processions.[29] The May Day iconography conveyed powerfully the political aspirations of the organizers. Walter Crane's brilliant designs were used around the world.

The early May Days had substantial political impacts in several countries where the socialist movements were weak. In France, the massacre at Fourmies in 1891 was followed by the arrest and imprisonment of Marx's son-in-law Paul Lafargue on the absurd charge of having incited the crowd there when speaking several days earlier. That autumn he was elected in Lille to the *Chambre* by 6,470 votes to 5,175, marking the start of a breakthrough for the Marxist Parti Ouvrier Français in the northern region. In nearby Roubaix, a socialist council was elected in 1892, with Lille electing one in 1895. In 1893, Roubaix elected Jules Guesde, the socialist leader, to the *Chambre*, a seat he held until 1899. In Poland, May Day strikes and demonstrations contributed to the formation of the Polish Socialist Party and also to the Social Democratic Party of the Kingdom of Poland. Elsewhere, labour movements were given a boost as, for instance, Sweden, where the Social Democrat Party had been founded in April 1889. In Stockholm on 1 May 1890, some 20,000 people participated in the procession, with about 50,000 to 80,000 listening to August Palm, Hjalmar Branting and six other speakers.[30]

However, by 1892 or 1893, the fears aroused in parts of Europe in anticipation of May Day demonstrations had abated. In reviewing the changed attitudes, the leader writer in the *Economist* ascribed these, first, to the military preparedness of the authorities, who even in Paris 'could over-master any resistance in three hours'. As a result: 'The sense of the impossibility of victory if the conflict comes to blows weighs upon the spirits of the artisans who have worn uniform, and without their leadership, a mob is of working men is no more formidable than a mob of the bourgeoisie'. Second, it was argued, that the 'vote disinclines the masses to run the excessive risk now involved in insurrection'. Third:

> The Socialists deny it, but it is true, that they have recently grown milder, and that they are now rather Collectivists than Socialists – a material diffe-rence because the former wish to control the social machinery, rather than to break it – and that they are gradually ejecting the Anarchists who are assuming the position of Irreconcilables…and thirsting for an appeal to force for which, as they know, they have not the strength.

Fourth, it was argued that while wages were not much better, in other matters, such as hours of work, working people's conditions had improved and their sense of oppression lessened. In the editorial writer's view, as a result of these changes, 'May Day sinks from a day of magnificent demonstrations into a day of costly and useless ceremonial'.[31]

A further feature of the decline of fears of red May Days outside of Russia was a growing awareness of the distinction between, on the one hand, revolution-aries and anarchists and, on the other, trade unionists and democratic social-ists. In Britain, such misunderstandings are exemplified by Winston Churchill whose revolutionaries in his novel *Savrola* (1900) seems to owe much to popular images of the anarchists plus some English notions of the SPD while in *My Early Life* (1930) he mistook the anti-socialist trade unionist with whom he stood in a 1899 by-election for a socialist. Mark Sykes, en route to becoming a conservative Member of Parliament, took pains to assure a friend that he was politically not 'A Little Englander. An Anarchist. A Socialist'.[32] Concerns about 'socialism' remained, but the distinction between anarchists and others became clearer to most by the turn of the century. For the authorities, the mass turn-outs for May Day celebrations proved not to be a threat, and the London anarchists of 1890 and the Vienne anarchists of 1891 were a containable minority.

The belief that May Day had been accommodated within the systems of states was also given vivid expression regarding Austria-Hungary at the end of the 1890s. The *Economist*'s correspondent in Vienna wrote in May 1899:

> No disturbance happened in any part of Austria or Hungary in consequence of the very general celebration of May Day, although in Hungary, for the first

time, liberal principles have been followed, and processions and demonstrations were allowed within certain limits, and the workmen in Government concerns were allowed a whole holiday.[33]

The early red May Days had alarmed governments across Europe. Even in Britain, the authorities had taken the precaution of large police presences in case proceedings became violent. There were many ghosts behind the fears, not least those of 1789, 1848 and 1871 in France and 1848 more generally; as well as concerns about anarchist bombings and other assassinations. There was also the spectre of the First International, which threatened more than it achieved. The early red May Days had the feared masses on the march, yet generally the outcomes suggested that mass democracy might not match up to the wealthy classes' worst fears. Curiously, in Britain, in spite of several of the largest demonstrations in modern British history, the early red May Days have been invisible in the major histories of the period.[34]

Notes

1. E.J. Hobsbawm, 'Mass-Producing Traditions: Europe 1870–1914', in *The Invention of Tradition*, ed. E. Hobsbawm and T. Ranger (Cambridge, 1983), pp. 263–307, 283–86.
2. *Leicester Daily Mercury*, 1 May 1890.
3. *Economist*, 3 May 1890.
4. *Leicester Daily Mercury*, 2 May 1890.
5. *Manchester Guardian*, 5 May 1890; *Star* [London], 5 May 1890.
6. *Edinburgh News*, 4 May 1891.
7. *Times*, 1 May 1890; *House of Commons Debates*, 3rd Series, 344, 3 June 1890, cols 1845–48.
8. *Times*, 2 May 1890. The Club Autonomie, at 32 Charlotte Street, Fitzroy Square, was destroyed by fire in May 1893. On the anarchist background, see J. Quail, *The Slow Burning Fuse* (London, 1978); and H. Oliver, *The International Anarchist Movement in Late Victorian London* (London, 1983).
9. *Commonweal*, 10 May 1890. The French group were probably those from the Club Autonomie (believed, probably wrongly, by the *Times* to be mostly Italians).
10. *Times*, 2 May 1890; *Star*, 2 May 1890; *Commonweal*, 10 May 1890; E.P. Thompson, *William Morris: Romantic to Revolutionary* (London, 1955), p. 654.
11. *Times*, 5 May 1890; Parliamentary Papers (c7472), *Commissioner of Police of Metropolis Report, 1890*, p. A2.
12. Nicholas T. Parsons, *Blue Guide: Vienna* (London, 2002), p. 190; P.S. Foner, *May Day* (New York, 1986), pp. 48–49; Herbert Steiner, 'May Day in Austria', in *May Day Celebration*, ed. Andrea Panaccione (Venice, 1988), pp. 109–17; Harald Troch and Berthold Unfried, 'Austria', in *The Memory of May Day*, ed. Andrea Panaccione (Venice, 1989), pp. 345–64; Berthold Unfried, 'Il significato delle feste del 1 maggio nell'ambito della cultura politica della sociademocrazia Austriaca di lingua tedesca (1890–1918)', in *Ill 1 maggio tra passata e futuro*, ed. Andrea Panaccione (Manduria, 1992), pp. 193–211.

13. Quoted in Steiner, 'May Day in Austria', pp. 110–12. The Uhlans were Lancers (cavalry). Another estimate put the number of participants at 150,000.
14. *Economist*, 10 May 1890, 2 May 1891 and 7 May 1892.
15. Ulrich Borsdorf, Heinz Deutschland, Dieter Dowe and Horst Schumacher, 'Germany 1890/91', in *The Memory of May Day*, ed. Pannacione, pp. 225–44; Peter Friedemann, 'Il significato del 1 maggio nella cultura politica del movimento operaio del bacino industriale della Renania-Westfalia, 1890–1933', in *Il 1 maggio tra passato e futuro*, ed. Panaccione, pp. 111–22; Friedhelm Boll, 'Aspects internationaux du premier mai 1890: le cas de l'Allemagne', in *Fourmies Et Les Premier Mai*, ed. Madeleine Rebérioux (Paris, 1994), pp. 371–81.
16. Foner, *May Day*, pp. 49–52; Felixs Tych, 'Poland' and Vjaceslav Kolomiez, 'Russia/USSR', in *The Memory of May Day*, ed. Panaccione, pp. 497–506 and 507–59; Timor Timofeev, 'May Day Studies in Russia (Before and After the October Revolution of 1917)' plus bibliography in *May Day Celebration*, ed. Panaccione, pp. 27–53; anonymous, *May Day: A Hundred-Year History* (Moscow, 1990), pp. 29–31.
17. Maurice Dommanget, *Histoire du Premier Mai* (Paris, 1953), pp. 122–93; André Rossel, *Premier Mai* (Paris, 1977), pp. 106–19; Michelle Perrot, 'The First of May 1890 in France: The Birth of a Working Class Ritual', in *The Power of The Past*, ed. Pat Thane, Geoffrey Crossick and Roderick Floud (Cambridge, 1984), p. 143–71; Miguel Rodriguez, 'France', in *Memory of May Day*, ed. Panaccione, pp. 109–31; Madeleine Rebérioux, 'La tradizione del 1 maggio in francia in una prospettiva culturale e sociale', and Beatrix W. Bouvier, 'Tradizioni della Revoluzione Francese nelle cele-brazioni del 1 maggio della socialdemocrazia tedesca', in *Il 1 maggio tra passato e futuro*, ed. Panaccione, pp. 87–93, 95–109; Jean-Louis Robert, 'Autour des premiers premier mai en France (1890–1891)', in Rebérioux, *Fourmies Et Les Premier Mai*, pp. 65–75; Danielle Tartakowsky, *La Part Du Rêve: Histoire Du 1er Mai En France* (Paris, 2005), pp. 21–26.
18. Jean-Louis Chappat, 'La fusillade de Fourmies', in Rebérioux, *Fourmies Et Les Premier Mai*, pp. 23–48; *Economist*, 6 May 1893.
19. See, for instance, Roger Magraw, *A History of the French Working Class*, 2 vols. (Oxford, 1992), II: pp. 3–125.
20. On Britain, Chris Wrigley, 'Il 1 maggio del 1890 e del 1891 in Gran Bretagna', in *I luoghi e I sogetti del 1 maggio*, ed. A. Panaccione (Venice, 1990), pp. 137–66; Chris Wrigley, 'Great Britain', in *Memory of May Day*, ed. Panaccione, pp. 83–112; Chris Wrigley, 'Chi promosse le prime giornate dei lavoratori in Gran Bretagna?', in *Il 1 maggio tra passato e futuro*, ed. Panaccione, pp. 181–91; Chris Wrigley, 'May Days and After', *History Today*, (June 1990), pp. 35–41; Foner, *May Day*, pp. 62–64 and 69–69.
21. *Edinburgh Evening News*, 5 May 1890; *Times*, 5 May 1890, 4 May 1891, 8 May 1893 and 7 May 1894; *Northampton Daily Reporter*, 5 May 1890 and 4 May 1891; *Argus*, 4 May 1891; *Leicester Daily Post*, 2 May 1892.
22. *Argus*, 4 May 1891; Steven Cherry, *Doing Different? Politics and the Labour Movement in Norwich 1880–1914* (Norwich, 1989), pp. 32–33; *Newcastle Daily Leader*, 4 May 1891; *East Kent Gazette*, 2 and 9 May 1891.
23. *Leicester Daily Mercury*, 1 May 1890 (late edition); *Star*, 2 May 1890; *Argus*, 4 May 1891; *Times*, 2 May 1890 and 8 May 1893.
24. Perrot, 'The First of May 1890', pp. 146–47, 159 and 162–63; Jean-Louis Robert, 'Autour des premiers premier mai en France 1890–1891', in Rebérioux, *Fourmies Et Les Premier Mai*, pp. 63–75; Michelle Perrot, *Workers On Strike. France 1871–90* (Leamington Spa, 1987).

25. *Times*, 5 May 1890, 4 May 1891, 8 May 1893, 7 May 1894, 6 May 1895 and 2 May 1896; *Leicester Daily Mercury*, 1892; *Leeds and West Yorkshire Mercury*, 7 May 1906; *Eastern Daily Press*, 2 May 1904; *Glasgow Daily Record*, 2 May 1898.
26. *Star*, 5 May 1890.
27. Quoted in *Liberty*, 1, 2, February 1894, p. 12.
28. Perrot, 'The First of May 1890', p. 156.
29. The major work on imagery is *The Memory of May*, ed. Panaccione. Important interpretations include Eric Hobsbawm, 'Birth of a Holiday: The First of May', in *On the Move*, ed. C. Wrigley and J. Shepherd (London, 1991), pp. 104–22; and D. Tartakowsky et al., 'May Days', in *The Emergence of European Trade Unionism*, ed. J.L. Robert, A. Prost and C. Wrigley (Aldershot, 2004), pp. 141–65.
30. Felix Codaccioni, 'La presse politique et l'élection de Paul Lafargue à Lille en 1891', in Rebérioux, *Fourmies Et Les Premier Mai*, pp. 123–34; Patricia Hilden, *Working Women and Socialist Politics in France 1880–1914* (Oxford, 1986), pp. 174–75; Tychs, 'Poland', pp. 497–98; Martin Grass, 'Sweden', in *The Memory of May*, ed. Panaccione, pp. 269–96; *Social-Demokraten, 3 May 1890* (transcribed by Hal Smith; www.marxists.org/history/international/may-day-1890); Dommanget, *Histoire du Premier Mai*, pp. 130–31.
31. *Economist*, 6 May 1893.
32. On this aspect of Churchill, see C. Wrigley, *Churchill* (London, 2006), pp. 25–27; Shane Leslie, *Mark Sykes. His Life and Letters* (London, 1923), p. 205.
33. *Economist*, 6 May 1899.
34. This applies to the Oxford standard histories of the period, R.C.K. Ensor, *England 1870–1914* (Oxford, 1936); and Geoffrey Searle, *A New England? Peace and War 1886–1918* (Oxford, 2004) as well as to such a study of organized labour (in spite of its title), G.D.H. Cole and Raymond Postgate, *The Common People 1746–1946* (London, 1938).

Part III
Riots in the Modern World

13
1968: Politics Takes to the Pavement
Brett Bowden

You do not have to be of the 'baby boom' generation to appreciate that the year 1968 was not just another year, largely indistinguishable from those that preceded it or those that closely followed it. To the contrary, it is variously described as the year that: rocked the world; changed the world; changed history; shaped a generation; changed everything and the year of the barricades.[1] For some, it is remembered as an *annus mirabilis* or year of wonders, for others, it is an *annus horribilis*, the year the dream died.[2] I have no recollection of the 1960s. No, it has nothing to do with 'tripping' through an entire decade. I was not born until late May of 1968, on the same day that The Beatles headed into the studio to record 'Revolution' for their self-titled double album, also known as the White Album. At the time, some thought it an entirely appropriate theme song for a particularly volatile and troubled year. With the passage of time and the recent 40th anniversary of 1968, there is still much debate about the historical and ongoing significance of the year. Tariq Ali recently reminisced about a 'year that changed the world', a year that was 'remarkable' for the 'geographical breadth of the global revolt'. It was, he reflected, 'as if a single spark had set the entire field on fire. The eruptions of that year challenged power structures north and south, east and west. Each continent was infected with the desire for change. Hope reigned supreme'.[3] In response to Ali, Gerard Henderson has suggested that while '1968 was a big year for news', there is not much 'evidence to support the view that 1968 was the year that changed the world'.[4] It appears that views on the events and lasting impact of 1968 more generally, are, to a certain extent, dependent on the political and ideological leanings of those looking back on that turbulent time. Nevertheless, while 1968 might not have produced anything like a successful revolution, it did have more than its fair share of rioting and bloodshed; which is the primary concern of this book.

While this book is concerned with riots, rebellions and political protests more generally in Great Britain and France, and there were no shortage of these in both Britain and France in 1968, the significance of the year in question cannot be accurately gauged without an appreciation of the wider global context. That being the case, this chapter gives an account of some of the key dramatic events that shook the world in 1968. Central to the tensions running through the year was the war in Vietnam and the widespread opposition to it, the assassinations of civil rights leader Martin Luther King and Democratic presidential candidate Robert F. Kennedy, the general strike in France and the student uprisings that engulfed Paris and other French cities, the short-lived Prague Spring of political liberalization in Czechoslovakia under the government of Alexander Dubček and the Tlatelolco Massacre of protesting Mexican students on the eve of the Mexico City Summer Olympics.

In addition to these momentous events was a range of other headline grabbing moments throughout the year, including the Democratic People's Republic of Korea (North Korea) seizure of the American naval intelligence ship the USS Pueblo, claiming that it had strayed beyond international waters into Korean territorial waters. This event sparked what became known as the Pueblo crisis. Upon claiming gold and bronze medals, respectively, in the men's 200-metre sprint final at the 1968 Mexico Olympics, African-American athletes Tommie Smith and John Carlos controversially stood on the medal podium with their heads bowed and fists raised in a Black Power salute. Meanwhile, in western Africa, Biafrans continued to starve amidst the drawn-out Nigerian civil war. And at year's end, three American astronauts, Frank Borman, William Anders and James Lovell became the first humans to orbit the moon as they spent Christmas in space aboard Apollo 8, returning safely to Earth a few days later. From New Year's Day to year's end, or so it must have seemed, around the world people took to the streets in protest: against war, against capitalism, against communism, against liberalism, against authoritarianism and against authority in general. As the *Time* magazine essayist Lance Morrow put it 20 years later, there was 'blood in the streets of Chicago and Paris and Saigon'.[5] And there were riots and violence and bloodshed on the streets of many more towns and cities around the world, as politics took to the pavement.

The war in Vietnam

Opposition to the war in Vietnam predates 1968; it existed from the time the French and then the Americans became involved in the country. But this long-standing opposition became rather more widespread and intense from very early in 1968.[6] As Mark Kurlasnky notes, the *New York Times* greeted the New Year with the headline: 'World Bids Adieu to a Violent Year'.[7] This optimism was to be short-lived. The year had begun with a cease fire, but any hopes of an extended peace were dashed by the launching of the Tet Offensive by the Viet Cong and the North Vietnamese Army in the early hours of 30 January, the first day of the New Year by the lunar calendar.[8] By almost any military measure, the offensive was less than successful, but it did prove to be a significant propaganda victory for the North Vietnamese in that it served to undermine public support for the war in America. In doing so, it also undermined the credibility of and the general support for the administration of President Lyndon Johnson, who was trying to convince the American people that the war was going well and that they held the upper hand. Like many concerned observers, CBS News's Walter Cronkite demanded to know 'What the hell is going on? I thought we were winning this war'. He again reflected the growing mood of a nation when he editorialized, 'We have been too often disappointed by the optimism of the American leaders, both in Vietnam and Washington, to have faith any longer in the silver linings they find in the darkest clouds'. America was, he added, 'mired in a stalemate that could only be ended by negotiation, not victory'. It is reported that President Johnson reacted to this by responding: 'If I've lost Cronkite, I've lost Middle America'.[9]

As Mark Barringer notes, the Tet Offensive 'led many Americans to question the administration's veracity in reporting war progress and contributed to Johnson's decision to retire. After Tet American public opinion shifted dramatically, with fully half of the population opposed to escalation'. Both at home and abroad, 'dissent escalated to violence'.[10] On 17 March, in London, more than 10,000 anti-war protesters joined a Vietnam Solidarity march on the United States Embassy. Beginning peacefully, the march turned into a violent riot with around 90 people injured and more than 200 arrested. Between 23 and 30 April 1968, upon learning of a link between Columbia University in New York City and an organisation affiliated with the United States Department of Defence, Columbia students occupied administration buildings and effectively shut down the university. That is, until they were forcefully and violently removed by New York City police. Similar protests took place on campuses across the country, along with raids on draft boards and attacks on companies perceived as supporting or profiting from the war. The riots and violent clashes between anti-war protesters and police at the 1968 Democratic National Convention in Chicago in late August highlighted the depth of feeling and the schism running through American society and between the generations.[11]

It is also important not to overlook the depth of animosity toward the United States around the world over its presence in Vietnam, which seemed to be aired in numerous protests, irrespective of their domestic motives. These protests and riots ranged from the anti-US riots in Tokyo in April, in which 110 people were injured and 179 arrested, to the numerous student protests across West Germany, to the anti-war marches and demonstrations that took place in major Australian cities.[12] Protests and riots continued beyond 1968 until the United States and its allies completely withdrew from Vietnam and the subsequent fall of Saigon in 1975. Among the most notable of these protest actions was the incident at Kent State University in Ohio, where on 4 May 1970 the Ohio National Guard opened fire on anti-war student protesters, killing four students and wounding nine others. The following year, the *New York Times* published the leaked Pentagon Papers, revealing the depth of deception of the American people by successive administrations in respect to the war in Vietnam. What little support there was left for the American involvement in the war in Vietnam soon evaporated.

Paris, May 1968: Night of the Barricades

Setting aside the French Revolution of the late eighteenth century, the events in France of May 1968 were generally unprecedented and largely unexpected.[13] As Tariq Ali recalls, France literally 'exploded' into what was later described as the 'biggest strike and the largest mass movement in French history' as students and workers united to oppose, among other things, the management of universities, the excesses of capitalism, the war in Vietnam and the government of Charles de Gaulle more generally.[14] At the time, it was thought that France was in the grips of nothing less than a revolution.[15] In the end that was not the case, but there was no shortage of rioting across France throughout much of the year, and during May in particular.

Despite the preceding running battles between students and authorities, Friday, 3 May 1968 purportedly started out 'like any other Friday, with no sign of the storm ahead'.[16] On the day prior, the University of Paris at Nanterre had been shut down following ongoing student demonstrations. On the next day, activists from Nanterre came together with students from the Sorbonne to protest the closure and the laying of disciplinary charges against some of the students who had been involved. The Sorbonne was then closed with the students being forcefully removed by the police; as many as 100 were injured and about 600 were arrested. By 6 May, tens of thousands of students, teachers and supporters had taken to the streets where they were hastily confronted by thousands of police. Almost inevitably, violent clashes ensued, and a range of temporary barricades were soon established by the demonstrators. Up to 1,000 people were injured in the running battles, including more than 300 police, and hundreds more protesters were arrested. The following day, tens of thousands of demonstrators again took to the streets of Paris to demand that the police retreat from Nanterre and the Sorbonne, so that they could be reopened. The demonstrators also sought the release and the dropping of all charges against those who had been arrested. Over the next few days, demonstrations continued, and further riots broke out in Nantes, Rennes and Toulouse, while in Lyon, students were joined by protesting workers. After a week of protests, on 10 May, huge crowds gathered in Paris and erected dozens of barricades in anticipation of yet more violent confrontations. They were not to be disappointed, for at approximately 2 in the morning, baton-wielding police deployed tear gas and forcefully attacked the barricading protesters. During the night that was to become known as 'the night of the barricades', more than 1,000 people were injured, many of them seriously, and another 400 or more were arrested.

In response to the heavy-handed tactics of the government and the police, French labour unions called for a general strike, and on 13 May as many as 1 million demonstrators marched through the streets of Paris in support of the students. The Prime Minister Georges Pompidou intervened in proceedings to order the reopening of the Sorbonne and announced that convicted students would get another opportunity to have their cases heard. The reopened Sorbonne and Nanterre were soon to be occupied by students and reclaimed as autonomous people's universities. At the same time, factories were also occupied by workers, while by 18 May as many as 2 million workers were on strike, rising in the following week to as many as 10 million or roughly two-thirds of French workers. As a result of the widespread public disorder, the value of the French franc plummeted, and fuel and other necessities of life became increasingly harder to come by as, fearing the worst, people began to stockpile food. Amidst ongoing rioting and protests – now also including farmers – on 24 May a police officer was killed in Lyon along with a demonstrator in Paris, while hundreds more were injured, perhaps as many as 1,000. Another 800 or so were arrested in rioting that had spread across the country.

For all intents and purposes, for the best part of May and into June, much of France was near ungovernable as violent riots engulfed the capital and cities across the country. After a round of political jockeying by Prime Minister Pompidou, Francois Mitterand and Pierre Mendés France and an aborted referendum, with the government on the verge of collapse, it seemed as though de Gaulle was on the way out. However, through a series of politically astute manoeuvres, he managed to reassert control over the country and on 30 May de Gaulle dissolved the parliament and called elections for 23 and 30 June. At the same time, as many as 1 million backers of de Gaulle also marched through the streets of Paris in support of the president and his actions. While strikes and protests continued and occasionally flared into violence, almost as quickly as the would-be revolution started, it similarly faded away. Come the elections, with the leftist opposition divided, the Gaullists were somewhat surprisingly returned to office with an even tighter grip on power.

While the protests and riots of May 1968 might not have brought down the government, they did have a lasting impact in liberalising the social, cultural and intellectual landscape of France. As noted above, when it comes to hindsight, not everybody looks back over time and events and sees quite the same thing. In alluding to the enduring impact of May 1968 upon taking up the French presidency in May 2007, Nicolas Sarkozy suggested that his electoral victory 'was the final nail' in the coffin of May 1968.

Tlatelolco massacre in Mexico

Back across the Atlantic, there was also growing unrest among students and wider general dissatisfaction with the increasing authoritarianism of the government of President Gustavo Diáz Ordaz in Mexico. Morrow later noted: 'If there seemed an ultimate unseriousness about Paris in May, the events in Mexico City some months later were a trauma and tragedy'.[17] Those events, in the lead-up to the Mexico City Summer Olympics, culminated in the death of perhaps as many 300 anti-government student protesters when the police and military opened fire on a crowd of thousands gathered in Tlatelolco Square on the evening of 2 October 1968. At the time, the government claimed that only four people were killed and a further 20 wounded. Accounts of 20 years later reported that 20 were killed and 75 wounded.[18] To this day, the actual death toll remains unclear.

Protests against the authoritarian regime of Diáz Ordaz had begun some months earlier, including on 26 July to coincide with the anniversary of Fidel Castro's 26 July Movement and the Cuban Revolution. On this occasion, student protests were violently broken up by the police, leaving at least ten dead. A month later, on 27 August, as many as 300,000 students, parents, workers and peasants took to the streets to demonstrate against the government and its heavy-handed tactics. A considerably smaller protest took place in silence on 13 September. Five days later, government troops closed or occupied a number of universities, including the largest, the National Autonomous University, and took as man as 3,000 prisoners – not discriminating between students, academics and parents. On 22 September, supported by many of the local working poor, students came together again and barricaded themselves into Vocational School No.7 in the Tlatelolco region of the city, from where they fought running battles with the police for around two hours. On this occasion, the police retreated.

On 2 October, ten days before the start of the Summer Olympics, and with athletes and officials already arriving in the city, somewhere between 10,000 to 15,000 students and workers took the opportunity to grab international attention and marched through the city denouncing the government. Again making their way toward the Plaza de Las Tres Culturas in the Tlatelolco section of the city, by late afternoon around 5,000 of the protesters remained gathered in what was intended to be a peaceful protest. Soon thereafter, the police and military personnel began to surround the square in large numbers, deploying tanks and armoured vehicles as helicopters flew overhead. Come sunset, the government forces surrounding the protesters indiscriminately opened fire on the crowd. The offensive continued into the night as the police and military then went door-to-door through the neighbourhood searching for protesters. Despite the violent crackdown on protesters highlighting the nature of the governing regime, and despite calls for a boycott by prominent figures such as Bertrand Russell and Jean-Paul Sartre (also outspoken opponents of the war in Vietnam), ten days later the Mexico City Olympic Games opened on schedule without a hitch.

It has since come to light through the release of official documents in both Mexico and the United States that snipers from the Presidential Guard had taken up positions on buildings around Tlatelolco Square and had fired the first shots. This led the police and military to think that they were being fired on from the crowd of protesters and hence returned fire. In 2005, the Minister of the Interior who was in charge at the time of the massacre, Luís Echeverría Alvarez, was indicted on charges of genocide, but the case was subsequently dismissed. On the 25th anniversary of the student uprising and the subsequent massacre, the Mexican government granted permission for the erection of a memorial in Tlatelolco Square; only 20 names were actually listed on the monument.[19] Raul Álvarez Garín, a student leader and survivor of the massacre stated some years after the massacre: 'All of us were reborn on October 2. And on that day we also decided how we are all going to die; fighting for genuine justice and democracy'.[20] It took another three decades for the Institutional Revolutionary Party (PRI) to be forced from office via the ballot box in the elections of July 2000 after more than 70 years in power. Reflecting on the 40th anniversary of 1968, Enrique Krauze has suggested that 'the government's actions in 1968 were the real beginning of the end for the vaunted "Mexican political system"'. He further argues that the student movement and the wider mass protests of 1968 were the 'embryo of Mexican democracy' and 'a fundamental moment for the coming of democracy to my country', Mexico.[21]

Prague Spring

Just as the events of 1968 in Mexico marked the beginning of the end of authoritarianism in that country, so too the revolutionary movement of 1968 in Czechoslovakia, known as Prague Spring, is said to be the beginning of the end of communism and the Soviet Union. After two decades of Stalinist-like authoritarianism, the majority of them under the leadership of Antonín Novotný, Czechoslovakians began to seriously agitate for change and greater reforms at the Fourth Congress of Czechoslovak Writers in June 1967. The government's response was to take control of the Writers' Union journal *Literární Noviny* away from the authors and hand it to the Ministry of Culture. Inspired by the writers, following a small demonstration in early May, again in late October that year Czechoslovak students similarly became more vocal in agitating for reform, greater freedoms and improved services and conditions for students at Charles University Prague – Czechoslovakia's largest

As elsewhere, the protesters were confronted by police who violently broke up the gathering.

At around the same time, the Plenum meeting of the Central Committee of the Czechoslovakian Communist Party was taking place amidst something of a power struggle for control of the party between Novotný and a reform-minded Slovakian, Alexander Dubček. In the struggle for power, Novotný had sought support from Moscow, in particular Soviet leader Leonid Brezhnev, who travelled to Prague in December 1967 but did not expressly support the incumbent. At a subsequent meeting of the party on 5 January 1968, Dubček was elected by the Central Committee to succeed to Novotný as first secretary, ushering in an extensive reformist agenda. By the end of March, Novotný was also succeeded as president by Ludvík Svoboda, a former army general, who then helped facilitate much of the reform process.

The reform and liberalization process included the lifting of censorship, greater freedoms of speech, association and travel, less scrutiny of the media, greater democratization and electoral reform, including a new Central Committee, implementation of a federal system geared to greater Czech and Slovak autonomy, and steps toward decentralising in general, including governance of the economy. While remaining committed to communism, it was to be a system that Dubček described as 'socialism with a human face'. The reforms, known as the Action Plan, were to be undertaken in a systematic and controlled manner under the direction of the Communist Party. Despite certain radical elements and progressive forces urging more immediate and wide-ranging changes, Dubček sought to maintain a balance between the more conservative and liberal forces at work both within the party and beyond.

Alarmed at the speed and general direction of the reforms, under Soviet leadership, the Warsaw Pact countries sought reassurances from Prague that the Dubček government remained committed to the socialist cause and to the Pact. On 3 August, along with the German Democratic Republic, the Hungarian People's Republic, the Polish People's Republic and the Union of Soviet Socialist Republics, the Czechoslovak Socialist Republic signed the Bratislava Declaration affirming its 'unwavering loyalty to Marxism-Leninism' and reiterating its full commitment to the Warsaw Pact. Despite this pledge, in the ensuing months, the Soviets continually questioned the degree of Czechoslovakia's commitment to the cause. On the night of 20 August, under the guise of the Brezhnev doctrine, a joint duty to defend socialism and subordinate national interests to those of the Soviet bloc, troops from the armies of Bulgaria, Hungary, Poland and the Soviet Union invaded and occupied Czechoslovakia in order to preserve the pact. In the process and in the ensuing protests against the occupation, as many as 100 people were killed and hundreds more injured. Dubček, who was initially arrested and taken to Moscow, was later returned to power in Prague to oversee moderate and approved reforms. This, however, was short-lived as he was succeeded in early 1969 by Gustáv Husák, who quickly began to wind back reforms while purging the party of its reform-minded elements. Soon thereafter, Dubček found himself banished to western Slovakia working in forestry administration. The only significant reform that was to survive Prague Spring was the introduction of the federal system of government in 1969, which created the autonomous Czech Socialist Republic and Slovak Socialist Republic. [22]

Ralf Fuecks notes that while the protest movements of 1968 did not bring down governments or 'lead to a dramatic overturn of the political order like the French or Russian revolutions', Prague Spring, often overlooked 'when we speak of 1968...came closest to being the revolutionary overthrow of a regime'. As many have argued following the collapse of communism and the Soviet Union, 'communist hegemony in Eastern Europe was doomed from that moment. It was only a matter of time until a system incapable of reform collapsed'.[23] Fred Halliday makes a similar point in noting that the 'most dramatic events of 1968, and the ones with the greatest long-run consequences', took place in the communist world. It turned out to be a world where 'the repression of 1968 contained the seeds of the demise of the regimes that deployed it'.[24] It would appear that Dubček had a good idea of what was likely to come, for in the lead up to the Mexico City Olympics he wrote to the Czechoslovakian team urging them that if things did not go quite to plan in terms of success, 'don't hang your heads: What will not succeed today, may succeed tomorrow'.[25]

Conclusion

These are a few of the key riotous and rebellious events of 1968 from around the world; there are many others, large and small. There were student protests and demonstrations in numerous countries and at countless university campuses around the world, too many to mention. In Britain alone, there was serious unrest and disturbances at the London School of Economics, and at the Universities of Birmingham, Bristol, Essex, Hull and Leicester, among others.[26] In speaking of student uprisings 20 years on, Morrow suggested the whole world seemed to be 'going through its youth, its atomic youth'. Around the world the 'spasms of unrest seemed almost psychologically coordinated, as if a mysterious common impulse had swept through the nervous system of a global generation. The theme of the protests, and of the generation, was...what? To challenge authority. To change the world. To take possession of the world. To announce itself'.[27] In many cases, the passage of history has not made answers to these questions all that much clearer or any less contentious.

When civil rights leader Martin Luther King was assassinated in Memphis, Tennessee, on 4 April 1968, despite the emotional urging for calm and restraint by Robert F. Kennedy, violent riots broke out across the United States. The worst of the rioting was in Washington, DC, Baltimore, Chicago and Kansas City, but there were also riots in cities large and small across the country, more than 100 cities in all.[28] With some of the riots lasting weeks, tens of thousands of army troops and National Guardsmen were ordered onto the streets in an attempt to restore law and order. The eruption of violent race riots was in some ways difficult to disentangle from opposition to the war in Vietnam and the apparent unfair application of the draft system that was seen as disadvantaging and targeting the poor and minority groups. Race riots, widespread student unrest and growing opposition to the war were all part of what Morrow referred to as the 'nervous breakdown of 1968'.[29] It was a breakdown that would have ramifications for decades to come.

Robin Blackburn has suggested that the conglomeration of 'events of 1968 mark the birth of globalization.' While each was a global event of sorts, each event also 'intermingled with the other to make something new'.[30] Immanuel Wallerstein has made a similar point arguing that the 'revolution of 1968' was indeed a revolution. It was 'a single revolution' whose significance and impact cannot be analysed and measured by individual events and local contingencies. Rather, the revolution of 1968 must be considered and weighed up *in toto*. He notes that while 1968 has long since ended as an event, it remains 'one of the great, formative events in the history of our modern world system, the kind we call watershed events'.[31] As a watershed event or turning point in history, Fuecks argues that one of the 'fundamental changes' it ushered in 'was an *expansion of the political public*. The protest movements were precursors of a new global public. New media and new forms of action expanded the public sphere'. While each of the various protest movements or failed revolutions 'were all characterized by national contexts, they still constituted a cosmopolitan movement'.[32]

A related enduring theme or legacy of 1968 is that it was a time of discovery in terms of *'doing politics in the street'*. It was a time when people 'came to recognize their city streets as *public space'*, but those same streets and cities were also increasingly recognized as 'turning into very violent places'.[33] This form of political participation was referred to by the Trilateral Commission in one of its first publications as a 'crisis of democracy', that is, the unruly masses were seen to be getting too involved in politics.[34] It was a time when the personal became political and the political increasingly personal. As Morrow described it: 'the air of public life seemed to be on fire, and that public fire singed the private self'.[35] In essence, 'the sixties was the beginning of thirty years of politics in the street'. Vivian Gornick describes it in terms of agency being the 'name of the game. To not exercise agency was to be written out of history by those who *do* exercise it'.[36] And in this regard, it could be argued that not much has changed.

As Morrow explains, it was a time when the 'whole world [was] watching' a seemingly endless series of events and a year of enduring images – violent riots, assassinations of leaders, the war, would be revolutions, black power salutes and more – that were all linked together by new electronic media that beamed them into living rooms around the world. 'Never before had an *annus mirabilis* transpired before the television cameras in Marshall McLuhan's global village: the drama played to a capacity house, the audience of mankind'.[37] Waxing lyrical about 1968 two decades later, Morrow wrote: 'Nineteen sixty-eight was more than a densely compacted parade of events, more than the accidental alignment of planets. It was a tragedy of change, a struggle between generations, to some extent a war between the past and the future'.[38] And for some, it is a war that persists, one that many commentators and self-appointed guardians of history seem unable to let go of.

Writing another 20 years on to mark the 40th anniversary of 1968, Michael Walzer wrote that for those 'who were part of it, the left upsurge in the 1960s, the politics of civil rights and opposition to the Vietnam War, was wonderfully exciting. It brought large numbers of men and women, mostly young men and women, into a life of political engagement'. But he adds that ultimately 'it did not produce a sustainable politics; its institutional legacy is virtually nil. In fact, it contributed to forty years of rightward momentum that, only now, is there any prospect of stopping'.[39] This would seem to be at odds with Nicolas Sarkozy's recollection and account of the events and legacies of 1968. It also diminishes the importance of the 1960s in regard to the foundation and establishment of Green political parties as serious players in some European countries.

It is true that individual and collective protest movements of 1968 did not bring down 'the system'; on the contrary, conservative governments held on to power or were elected to it, such as de Gaulle in France and Richard Nixon in the United States. But as the saying goes, Rome was not built in a day; nor was it torn down overnight. Changes take time, and whether it is environmental movements, feminist movements or civil rights, in all of these arenas there have been considerable shifts in thinking and practice in the decades since 1968. And not insignificantly, advancements in these aspects of the human condition are, in some measure, legacies of 1968. As Mitchell Cohen notes: 'the racial ancient regime has crumbled in significant ways thanks in part to the 1960s'. In more general terms, 'it was a different world before 1960s feminists questioned "normal" authority patterns and how personal and political matters intersect'.[40]

While the emergence of Green politics and advances in the rights of women and racial minorities all owe something to the movements and sacrifices of the 1960s, as Fred Halliday notes, radical and terrorist organizations such the 'Rote Armee Fraktion (RAF) in Germany, the Brigate Rosse in Italy, the Black Panthers and Weather Underground in the United States were (as much as hippies, anarchists and proto-environmentalists, though with far more damaging effects) also the children of 1968'.[41] Bearing in mind the setbacks to the civil rights movement and the state of race relations in the United States in 1968, it is significant that 40 years after the dream died with the assassination of Martin Luther King, Barack Obama became the first Black American elected to the Presidency of the United States of America. In some respects, things have come a long way in 40 years indeed. Yet, it is also significant that the United States is still fighting wars in far off places against insurgents and terrorist organizations that are still fighting against what they perceive to be the forces of Western imperialism. This cycle of events is enough to remind one of the old saying that the more things change, the more they stay the same. Forty years is both a long time and a blink of the eye. For some, 1968 marks the beginning of an era of monumental change; for others, it changed nothing much at all.

Notes

1. See David Caute, *Sixty-Eight: The Year of the Barricades* (London, 1988); Mark Kurlansky, *1968: The Year That Rocked the World* (New York, 2005); Charles Kaiser, *1968 in America: Music, Politics, Chaos, Counterculture, and the Shaping of a Generation* (New York, 1997); Christopher Dickey, '1968: The Year That Changed Everything', *Newsweek*, 19 November 2007; *1968: The Year That Shaped a Generation* (Portland, 2008); and '1968: The Year That Changed the World?', *BBC Radio World Service*, 25 November–16 December, 2008.
2. Jules Witcover, *The Year the Dream Died: Revisiting 1968 in America* (New York, 1997).
3. Traiq Ali, 'The Year That Changed the World', *Sydney Morning Herald*, 5 January 2008. See also Traiq Ali, *1968 and After: Inside the Revolution* (London, 1978).
4. Gerard Henderson, 'I Remember 1968, and I Was There', *Sydney Morning Herald*, 8 January 2008.
5. Lance Morrow, '1968 Like a Knife Blade, the Year Severed Past from Future', *Time*, 11 January 1988. Retrieved from http://www.time.com/time/printout/0,8816,966422,00.html
6. See generally, Fred Halstead, *Out Now! A Participant's Account of the American Movement Against the Vietnam War* (New York, 1978); Kevin Williams, 'Vietnam: The First Living-Room War', in *The Fog of War: The Media on the Battlefield*, ed. Derrik Mercer, Geoff Mungham and Kevin Williams (London, 1987), pp. 213–60; Charles DeBenedetti, *An American Ordeal: The Antiwar Movement of the Vietnam Era* (Syracuse, 1990); and Adam Garfinkle, *Telltale Hearts: The Origins and Impact of the Vietnam Antiwar Movement* (New York, 1995).
7. Kurlansky, *1968*, p. 3.
8. See James H. Willbanks, *The Tet Offensive: A Concise History* (New York, 2009).
9. Morrow, '1968 Like a Knife Blade, the Year Severed Past from Future'; and Tom Wicker, 'Broadcast News', *New York Times*, 26 January 1997.
10. Mark Barringer, 'The Anti-War Movement in the United States', in *Encyclopedia of the Vietnam War: A Political, Social, and Military History*, ed. Spencer C. Tucker (Santa Barbara, 1998), pp. 33–35.

11. See David Farber, *Chicago '68* (Chicago, 1988); Frank Kusch, *Battleground Chicago: The Police and the 1968 Democratic National Convention* (Chicago, 2004); John Schultz, *No One Was Killed: The Democratic National Convention, August 1968* (Chicago, 2009); and John Schultz, *The Chicago Conspiracy Trial*, rev. ed. (Chicago, 2009).
12. As a US ally, Australia was also involved in the war in Vietnam.
13. Roger Absalom, *France: The May Events 1968* (London, 1971), p. xi. See also Alain Touraine, *The May Movement: Revolt and Reform: May 1968—the Student Rebellion and Workers' Strikes—the Birth of a Social Movement*, trans. Leonard F.X. Myhew (New York, 1971).
14. Ali, 'The Year That Changed the World'; and Kristin Ross, *May '68 and Its Afterlives* (Chicago, 2002).
15. Patrick Seale and Maureen McConville, *French Revolution 1968* (Harmondsworth, 1968); Charles Posner (ed.), *Reflections on the Revolution in France: 1968* (Harmondsworth, 1970); and Peter Steinfels, 'Paris, May 1968: The Revolution That Never Was', *New York Times*, 11 May 2008.
16. Caute, *Sixty-Eight*, p. 183.
17. Morrow, '1968 Like a Knife Blade, the Year Severed Past from Future'.
18. Caute, *Sixty-Eight*, p. 345.
19. Kurlansky, *1968*, p. 343.
20. For a detailed account of events, see Elena Poniatowska, *Massacre in Mexico*, trans. Helen R. Lane (Columbia, 1992); and Kurlansky, *1968*, pp. 321–44.
21. Enrique Krauze, 'Symposium: 1968: Lessons Learned', *Dissent*, Spring 2008, p. 18.
22. See Kieran Williams, *The Prague Spring and Its Aftermath: Czechoslovak Politics, 1968–1970* (Cambridge, 1997); Caute, *Sixty-Eight*, pp. 159–82; and Kurlansky, *1968*, pp. 287–305.
23. Ralf Fuecks, 'Symposium: 1968: Lessons Learned', *Dissent*, Spring 2008, p. 12.
24. Fred Halliday, '1968: The Global Legacy', *openDemocracy*, 13 June 2008. Retrieved from http://www.opendemocracy.net/article/1968-the-global-legacy
25. Quoted in Kurlansky, *1968*, p. 305.
26. See Caute, *Sixty-Eight*, pp. 302–29.
27. Morrow, '1968 Like a Knife Blade, the Year Severed Past from Future'.
28. The city of Boston was an exception to the rioting, remaining tense yet relatively peaceful thanks in large part to a James Brown concert at Boston Garden on 5 April that was initially cancelled but was then allowed to go ahead and was broadcast across Boston on both radio and television.
29. Morrow, '1968 Like a Knife Blade, the Year Severed Past from Future'.
30. Robin Blackburn, 'Symposium: 1968: Lessons Learned', *Dissent*, Spring 2008, p. 8.
31. Immanuel Wallerstein and Sharon Zukin, '1968, Revolution in the World-System: Theses and Queries', *Theory and Society*, 18 (1989), pp. 431.
32. Fuecks, 'Symposium: 1968: Lessons Learned', p. 12; emphasis in original.
33. Marshall Berman, 'Symposium: 1968: Lessons Learned', *Dissent*, Spring 2008, pp. 5–6; emphasis in original.
34. See Noam Chomsky, 'Noam Chomsky on 1968', *New Statesman*, May 2008. Retrieved from http://www.newstatesman.com/politics/2008/05/iraq-war-chomsky-1968-vietnam
35. Morrow, '1968 Like a Knife Blade, the Year Severed Past from Future'.
36. Vivian Gornick, 'Symposium: 1968: Lessons Learned', *Dissent*, Spring 2008, pp. 14–15; emphasis in original.

37. See Marshall McLuhan and Quentin Fiore with Jerome Agel, *The Medium Is the Massage: An Inventory of Effects* (1967; rpt. Berkeley, 2001); and Marshall McLuhan and Quentin Fiore with Jerome Agel, *War and Peace in the Global Village* (1968; rpt. Berkeley, 2001).
38. Morrow, '1968 Like a Knife Blade, the Year Severed Past from Future'.
39. Michael Walzer, 'Symposium: 1968: Lessons Learned', *Dissent*, Spring 2008, p. 25.
40. Mitchell Cohen, 'Symposium: 1968: Lessons Learned', *Dissent*, Spring 2008, p. 10.
41. Halliday, '1968: The Global Legacy.'

14
Making Other Worlds Possible? Riots, Movement and Counter-Globalisation

Tadzio Mueller and Sian Sullivan

A long day of carnival and peaceful protest...timed to coincide with the start of the G8 world leaders' conference in Cologne...turned into a riot yesterday afternoon as demonstrators trashed a McDonald's, wrecked part of the Futures Exchange, set fire to a bank, and destroyed cars and empty flats in the City of London. ...many people were injured as the police used water cannon and baton-charged up to 2,000 mostly peaceful demonstrators on horseback. By early evening, there were running battles in side streets with a hard core of protesters hurling stones and bottles, breaking into buildings, throwing out files, setting fire to papers and breaking ground floor windows.[1]

London, 1999

Riot police launched canisters of tear gas [on] Saturday at about 2,000 protesters trying to breach a safety perimeter a day after one man was killed during demonstrations outside the Group of Eight summit in Genoa, Italy. ... Ninety-three people were wounded Saturday, including eight police. Police arrested 36 demonstrators. ... As they marched, hundreds of extremists broke off from the larger group and set fires in plastic garbage cans, overturned cars, broke shop windows and hurled stones at police. Some called the police assassins.[2]

Genoa, 2001

Police have used rubber bullets, tear gas and water cannons against anti-globalization protesters in Swiss and French cities near Evian where the Group of Eight (G8) summit is being held. ...In the Swiss city of Geneva authorities spent more than nine hours battling with demonstrators as they rampaged through the city centre. ...Shop windows were smashed and stores looted, leaving the city streets awash with broken glass and choking fumes from tear gas canisters.

After protesters began to hurl rocks and petrol bombs, the German police were brought in for reinforcements, storming the front line to scatter the rioters and chasing ringleaders all over the city.... In Lausanne demonstrators wearing black face masks blocked roads with burning barricades and attacked the hotel area where some summit delegates were staying before being driven away by riot police with tear gas. Several demonstrators were injured, one seriously.[3]

Evian, 2003

There were fresh clashes between police and anti-G8 protestors early Wednesday ahead of the official opening of a gathering of world leaders from the Group of Eight (G8) nations at Gleneagles in Scotland.... Police had been attacked with bottles and other missiles, the BBC said. Late on Monday, riot police clashed with anti-G8 protestors in Edinburgh, the Scottish capital, leading to up to 100 arrests.... Police said [on] Tuesday that demonstrators bent on violence would meet a 'robust response' from the authorities.[4]

Gleneagles, 2005

Germany was shocked this weekend by images of violence in the Baltic port city of Rostock, where violent anti-G-8 protesters clashed with police just days before the start of the G-8 summit in Germany. Around 1,000 police and demonstrators were injured in violent clashes which followed an otherwise peaceful demonstration, with anarchists throwing stones at police and setting cars on fire.[5]

Heiligendamm, 2007

'I predict a riot!'[6] Globalization and its malcontents[7]

A Utopian dream is etched into the modern militant imaginary. A dream of revolution as rupture. An ecstatic storming of the Bastille, of the Winter Palace. Animated by a longing for something different, by fear in the face of repression, and by the (im)possibility of victory. 'Under the cobblestones, the beach' – the revolutionaries of 1968 wrote on the walls of Paris, articulating their realistic demand for the impossible. Their dream remains with us, returning as a global social movement once again picks up the cobblestones both to reveal and to make the worlds that might be possible in the absence of neoliberalism's enclosures and apparent certainties.

In this chapter, we trace the emergence of this complex and diverse global social movement: a movement that has become variously celebrated and vilified for its association with violence in the key public events of the street protests accompanying the meetings of world leaders promoting the neoliberal cause.

We attempt a summary of political, economic and cultural tendencies that in the last few decades have produced a dissenting, and sometimes rioting global movement with significant events and actors located in Western Europe. And we continue with some theoretical reflections regarding the nature and utility of 'the riot act' in this context. We do not see this as writing a history of riots, in the sense that a historian might be able to present a relatively detached history of the modern bread riots in England. We are writing the present, as people who were at and involved with producing the events we write about, and who share at least some of the dreams and affects of others who were there.[8]

Emergence 1: Seattle and the time when we were winning

In tracing the history and emergence of a social movement, an impossible question arises: when and where does it start? In the case of the 'counterglobalisation' movement – also constructed as the 'alterglobalisation movement', the 'antiglobalisation movement', the global justice movement and even the 'movement of movements'[9] – we are drawn to what would later become known as the movement's 'coming-out party':[10] the spectacular protests in Seattle against the November 1999 'Ministerial' of the World Trade Organization (WTO). This event drew together an unlikely coalition of comrades – anarchists and communists, environmentalists and trade unionists, catholic nuns and queer activists – who defied the cold, rain and scores of well-armed riot police to shut down the summit, preventing the opening ceremony from taking place and arguably contributing to the collapse of the trade negotiations conducted there. It was with Seattle and accompanying solidarity events elsewhere[11] that a diverse yet powerful global movement appeared, seemingly out of nowhere. From the depths of a history that was supposed to have ended with neoliberalism, a multiplicity of voices suddenly were loudly proclaiming that 'other worlds are possible!' That perhaps there might be alternatives to the liberalization of trade and capital markets, and to the privatization and enclosure of common lands and resources: to a world safe for capital but not necessarily for life.

Since then, an array of major protest events associated with the counterglobalisation movement have occurred in northern Europe, with many key moments taking place in both Britain and France. As the vignettes above indicate, the escape of these events from permissible civil society strategies of contestation into 'uncivil' provocative engagements, including both defensive confrontations with police and physical damage to the property and symbols of capital,[12] has been a key element of their impact. Two tendencies, in particular, have been noticed for their embrace of proactively confrontational tactics. These are the black bloc, stereotyped as the black-clad, masked and hooded youths who violently pierce capital's apparent peacefulness through the smashing of its symbols and windows whilst maintaining a confrontational stance towards police; and the Italian-inspired *tute bianche*, dressed in white overalls and everyday materials that serve as protective padding, in order to approach and break through police lines – a consciously bio-political practice[13] intended to draw out the tendency for violence towards protestors by police as always constitutive of the state's biopower.[14]

Naming the enemy: neoliberal globalisation and *The End of History*

Seattle was the moment when the global left regained a sense that it might be 'winning'. But in order to understand the emergence of the movement that 'came out' in Seattle, we need to dig deeper, to go further back into history, to understand *who* it was that protested, blockaded and rioted on the streets of Seattle and in other cities across the globe, and *why* they were doing so. To begin to make sense of the counterglobalisation movement, we need to understand the process of neoliberal globalization that had been restructuring the world since its emergence in the 1970s. And in turn, the neoliberal project can only be explained by considering the crisis of 'Fordism', the supposedly 'golden' period of relatively steady post-war capitalist growth that came to its end in the early 1970s.

From a class perspective, Fordism was based on a compromise between largely nationally organized productive capital and a (largely male and white) industrial working class organized in trade unions, the relationship between the two stabilised by a Keynesian welfare state. In terms of production and consumption, it relied on productivity growth and the development of internal markets for mass consumption. Comparatively well-paid factory workers were able, both in the global north and the so-called developmentalist states of the global south, to buy an ever-increasing number of products, thereby generating social peace. Towards the late 1960s, however, productivity increases began to slow down, and the model entered a crisis.[15] In 1971, the president of the United States, Richard Nixon, responded to the crisis of the international economic system by abandoning the gold-dollar-standard, thus ending the Bretton Woods system that was one of the pillars of the Keynesian mode of regulation. The crisis of the international currency regime was part of the fundamental crisis of Fordist capitalism in the 1960s and 1970s. During this time, an escalation of global struggles combined with international instabilities, as well as fiscal and legitimation crises experienced by many states,[16] to produce an extended period of global social upheaval.

But far from leading to emancipation, the outcome of this 'crisis of Fordism' was a further entrenching of capitalist structures through the emergence and subsequent victory of the neoliberal project. Dumenil and Levy[17] define neoliberalism as 'the expression of the desire of a class of capitalist owners and the institutions in which their power is concentrated, which we collectively call 'finance', to restore – in the context of a general decline in popular struggles – the class's revenues and power'. This reassertion of power occurred *vis-à-vis* labour (for example, in the battles that Ronald Reagan and Margaret Thatcher fought and won against the air traffic controllers and miners, respectively, in the 1980s), as well as other factions of capital, such as industrial/ productive capital.[18] One of the central characteristics of the regime of accumulation underpinning and emerging from this new class project are the 'new enclosures',[19] or 'accumulation by dispossession':[20] a frequently violent, *political* (qua state), 'liberation' of new resources for productive investment accompanied by the creation of a globally mobile and increasingly precarious proletariat (or what some are terming the 'precariat').[21]

In June 1989, as the Eastern Bloc was crumbling, political scientist Francis Fukuyama published an article declaring that *history* had come to an end:[22] '[t]oday...we have trouble imagining a world that is radically better than our own, or a future that is not essentially democratic and capitalist'.[23] The global neoliberal offensive seemed to have consigned every potential challenge to the scrap yard of history. The so-called post-1960s 'new social movements' still existed, but appeared incapable or unwilling to issue a direct challenge to the power of capital through what came to be derisively called their 'single-issue politics'.[24] With the collapse of the Berlin Wall, there appeared to be no force that could constitute an 'anticapitalist' project. And yet, to take up a somewhat tired metaphor, neoliberalism, at the same time as it was wiping out its remaining enemies, was busily creating its own gravediggers or, at least, its next challengers. Key strategies of the neoliberal offensive were 'accumulation by dispossession' through privatization and commodification; accompanied by a rearticulation of states into agents of upward redistribution of wealth, and of international economic institutions into agencies of structural adjustment. It was at these frontlines that new networks and forms of resistance began to grow and coalesce.

Emergence 2: The end of *The End of History*

In the first half of the 1990s, diverse social movements worldwide existed relatively independently of each other: by and large, they were not perceived, nor did they generally perceive themselves, as being linked in a 'glocal'[25] movement against neoliberalism. For that, the end of history had to end, and come to an end it did. If there is a date that heralded the birth of current global post-capitalist politics and consciousness – whereby the 'nodes' of these localities and concerns became 'networked' in a globalizing awareness of 'a common enemy' – it is New Year's Day, 1994. On this date, Mexico entered NAFTA[26] and the Zapatista National Liberation Army[27] emerged from its mountain refuges in the state of Chiapas, southeast Mexico, to seize the city of San Cristobal de las Casas and several other towns.[28] Under the declaration of 'Ya Basta!' – 'Enough!' – their campaign was against the president, the army, 500 years of oppression since the 'discovery' of the Americas and 40 years of 'development'; and for free elections, land rights, self-governance and the autonomy to live and die with dignity according to established cultural practices.[29] Tanks, Swiss aeroplanes, US helicopters and 15,000 troops were employed by the government to counter the rebellion, and a heavy military presence still remains in Chiapas. Three distinctive elements have constructed 'Zapatismo' as a cogent symbol of contemporary glocal self-determination politics, embodying the style and content, as well as the state's response, of counterglobalisation politics today. First is the powerful imaginary of the metaphorical David challenging the Goliath of neoliberal modernity and its protective and well-armed state forces. Second is the mystique conferred by the masking of participants. Pragmatically, this affords some protection of identity. Symbolically it also becomes a conscious statement of antipathy towards the cult of individualism associated with modernity, as well as representing the structural silence and invisibility of those rendered voiceless and faceless by colonialism and neoliberalism. And finally, there is the paradoxical intermingling of an affirmation of tradition with a looking to the future and the new – represented by skilful use of the emerging internet to popularize the Zapatista struggle and concerns,[30] as well as by a committed challenge by both women and men against the 'macho society' of their traditional past.[31]

In combination with the brilliant and poetic Zapatista uptake of globalisation technologies in their use of an emerging internet to publicize concerns and desires, the 1 January 1994 acted as a catalyst that pulled together seemingly disparate struggles in a consciousness of sharing a common enemy: namely, the alienations and dispossessions normalized by the conceptual and material enclosures demanded by neoliberalism. It is this contemporary history that made possible the heroic moment of Seattle 1999, as movements worldwide became entrained through the 1990s into the riotous and mutinous energy of a global counterglobalisation movement.

Reading the riot act: will the destruction be constructive?

But what is it about the riot act that fascinates so many of us, political radicals, commentators and spectators alike? While mainstream pundits usually focus on the seemingly mindless smashing of material property as well as confrontational attitudes towards police, arguably it is precisely the rupturing of 'normal' political space and time – the transgression of civility that occurs in riots – that is able to achieve something that everyday political practice cannot. As we write, activists throughout Europe and beyond are beginning to pour their energies into mobilizing for the international climate change summit in Copenhagen in December 2009. And once again, the question has erupted: what is the political point of this kind of confrontational politics? Given this live debate, we seek now to offer some reflections on the riotous summit protest as an enactment of the dream of revolution as rupture, asking: what are the possibilities and limits of such an event-focused political practice? We start with an example to set the scene:

The Annemasse blockade, G8 Evian 2003

> Without any warning, the police attacked our totally peaceful demonstration with massive volleys of teargas.... Even though for most of us this was the first time in such a situation, we never panicked.... Soon one felt how fear was overcome and washed away by courage.... While in the front some people held the police at bay by throwing stones and others extinguished the gas grenades right in front of the police lines, the Attac-campus groups supplied the barricade with wood for protection from gas. In the midst of all this, a large group of 'Pink & Silver' danced and sang carnival-rhythms.[32]

Nothing was *supposed* to happen at the blockade in Annemasse in 2003, making what did happen that much more significant. The attempt to blockade one of the highways leading to the conference centre hosting the 2003 G8-summit in Evian, France, had been organized largely by groups within the moderate counterglobalist ATTAC network,[33] not known for 'kicking off' against the police. We were both at the G8 protests in Evian/Annemasse in 2003, and one of us (Tadzio) joined this blockade, not expecting any confrontation with the police. At least, not the type of confrontation where the protesters fight back.

Tadzio recalls:

> On the march to the planned blockading point, I talked to several activists, most of whom had never been in potentially confrontational situations, and were anxious about the possibility of a police attack. After walking for some hours, we arrived at a line of police reinforced by water cannons – and were attacked with tear gas within thirty seconds. What seemed surprising in this situation was not the tactics of the police, but the way the crowd responded: after initially retreating about fifty to one hundred metres and recovering from the initial shock of the attack, a number of masked protestors began building a barricade and setting it alight, while others threw stones at the police. Very soon, almost the whole march participated. This 'stand-off' continued for several hours, after which the march returned to the camp. Intriguingly, although we had not achieved our goal to block the road we had

planned to, the general feeling was one of victory. At an evaluation meeting in Berlin some days after the action, several of the speakers invoked what had become known among the march's participants as 'the spirit of Evian'. In spite of criticism for breaking the ATTAC-network's line or discrediting the movement in the eyes of the 'wider public', many of those who participated in the blockade that became a riot felt that something had changed: for them, the riot transformed what they could think and do politically.

How are we to understand the transformative effect of this mini-riot in Annemasse? We recognize that it is impossible to generalize from one riotous event to the 'nature' of riots in the counterglobalisation movement. One riot is not like another: they vary both in their impacts and acceptability across time and space,[34] and a riot in a society where no one ever throws stones at the police is likely to have a very different meaning to one where this happens all the time. In what follows, we draw on some key theorists of the riotous event to elucidate the varied occurrence and manifestations of riots associated with the counterglobalisation movement in Europe, and to contribute to current debate regarding the meaning and effect(s) of these events and practices.

Effervescent crowds

We draw first on the work of Emile Durkheim to explicate a sense that – as with the riot in Annemasse described above – there indeed have been riots in this movement that have opened up political space; that have changed what can be thought and done and thereby displaced the limits of the socially and politically possible. Durkheim[35] suggests that '[i]n the midst of an assembly that becomes worked up, we become capable of feelings and conduct of which we are incapable when left to our individual resources'. Sometimes this means that mass gatherings merely reaffirm a social collective's underlying principles as transcending each single individual. But sometimes it can mean that the very principles of a collective are transformed: that new social and political spaces are opened, in a moment of what Durkheim called creative or 'collective effervescence'.

The starting point of Durkheim's analysis is the potentially ecstatic nature of mass events. The coming together of a normally dispersed group of people, a description that clearly applies to contemporary European counterglobalist protestors (though he was drawing on research regarding Australian indigenous people), disrupts the monotony of everyday life, producing events where 'a sort of electricity is generated, [which] quickly launches [the participants] to an extraordinary height of exaltation'. This effervescence – also associated with a carnivalesque reversal of social norms[36] and the transgressive noise of the potentially revolutionary Festival[37] – produces 'passions so heated and so free from control' that they can lead to generally 'outlandish behaviour'. Durkheim argues that it is in such riotous moments and epochs – producing an intense 'world of sacred things' – that societies (or movements) are born:[38]

> Under the influence of some great collective shock in certain historical periods, social interactions become much more frequent and active. ... The result is the general effervescence that is characteristic of revolutionary or creative epochs. ... People live differently and more intensely than in normal times. The changes are not simply of nuance and degree; man [*sic*] becomes something other than what he was.[39]

But how do riots actually produce the changes in established subjectivities that can open new political spaces? First, they encourage participants to stretch the boundaries of 'normal' social morality. As Farge and Revel note in their study of a set of riots in mid-eighteenth century Paris, the bourgeois involved in the street fighting temporarily broke the boundaries of their class and their morality.[40] Second, these changes in subjectivity induced by riots might last beyond the riotous event itself. Here, an elaboration of Durkheim's original concept of effervescence is useful. Durkheim, in fact, describes two different categories of effervescent events without properly distinguishing them. These are those that produce a certain intensity of feelings, which in turn reconstitutes and reiterates group cohesion, such that no lasting transformation of participants' sense of the possible occurs. Alternatively, there are those that constitute genuinely creative events, where, 'for some reason, these collective interactions become extraordinarily powerful and intense';[41] permitting some transformation of norms and values, and thereby shifting the individual and social identities that otherwise reconstitute and reproduce those norms and values. The positive feedback generated in such events induces lasting transformations in a way that everyday, 'run-of-the mill' riotous 'rituals' do not.

For such effervescent riots to be further effective, however, requires that their political energy diffuse and take hold beyond a circle of immediate participants. Aristide Zolberg's analysis of riots and other collective effervescent events as 'moments of madness' illustrates some ways in which this might occur. He argues that moments of madness are intensive learning processes, where new ideas spread to larger publics; that these ideas become institutionally located in the networks of social relations established during the moments; and that the aggregate experiences of individuals does indeed matter in producing possible transformation.[42]

Moments of madness: transgression produces transformation?

The practical question now becomes: do riots in counterglobalisation politics constructively open and reorganize political space in ways that survive the event and produce emancipatory social change? There are many ways in which we might engage with this question. Recall the account of the Annemasse protest given above. Contrary to behaviour expected from ATTAC activists, the participants of the march responded to the police's assault by drawing on a repertoire of protest – the burning of a barricade, the throwing of stones at the police – which by and large was new and alien to them. Although it was the non-ATTAC protesters at the front who started building the barricade and throwing stones at the police from the front lines, others quickly became caught up in the dynamic of the event and felt empowered to confront the police. This confrontation contributed to a transformation of protestor subjectivities by opening up new political spaces of contestation, and changing a sense of what is politically possible.[43] It was this changed sense of the limits of the possible that became the basis for post-summit evocations of 'the spirit of Evian'; and that allowed participants to break the long-established non-confrontational guidelines of ATTAC and to form linkages with other militant anti-capitalists in Berlin, thereby creating networks that subsequently were very active in the mobilization for the G8 summit in Heiligendamm in 2007. ATTAC activists from Leipzig felt similarly empowered by the event, and afterwards were more inclined to confront the police as well as engage in other forms of direct action.

If the Annemasse blockade described above was only a little mad, the riotous carnival planned in the city of London's square mile to coincide with the G8 summit in Köln, Germany, on 18 June 1999 could be construed as bordering on 'insanity'. In this event, 10,000 protestors wearing carnival masks and accompanied by driving samba rhythms, a punk band, and sound-systems, noisily and unexpectedly took over the disciplined space of the city. Its effects penetrated right to the heart of the city's sacred cow of speculative finance: the London International Financial Futures Exchange (LIFFE).[44] Over £10 million of damage was caused, the basement of the LIFFE building was flooded through 'release' of one of London's 75 buried rivers, and 16 people were arrested on the day with around 50 more arrested in connection with the event up to a year later. Among many counterglobalisation protesters, this event consolidated distrust of the state and its institutions. At the same time, within the United Kingdom, it generated a plethora of questions regarding the utility of all the time, energy and resources devoted to the staging of one-off spectacular events and the socio-political validity of a secretive vanguard of activist organizers orchestrating events requiring participation of broader publics.[45] Nevertheless, it could be argued that this 'carnival against capitalism' that became a riot was effective in wreaking havoc on a key stronghold of capital, and thereby creating a symbolic challenge that went beyond the state's monopoly of violence, attacking the sanctity of private (commercial) property, as well as capital's contemporary enclosure of public space.[46] It fed into and spawned an array of similar carnivalesque approaches to summit protests, contributing to a common strand in counterglobalisation tactics of identifying potent buildings and symbols of neoliberal capitalism as targets for attack.

But in what way does this 'symbolic' challenge really matter? Ernesto Laclau[47] suggests that the normalization of every social relation of domination requires an accompanying act of forgetting its origins in *political* operations of power and violence: effecting a silencing and closure of discursive, political and epistemological alternatives. One reading of the spectacular protest events mentioned is that they challenge this social forgetfulness, bringing to the fore the antagonisms and struggles that infuse normalized social relations. They demonstrate that the police's monopoly on violence and the sanctity of private property are not in the natural scheme of things, but are politically constituted and policed. In this reading, riots are events that can create a space of intensity where such social myths are more easily revealed and challenged than in relatively routine moments of everyday interaction.

Although perhaps, we should not over-valorize the smashing tactics of confrontational engagements with police and property in counterglobalisation politics? While the immediacy of an event might contribute to possibly transformative effects on the political subjectivities of those involved – feeding desire for other possible worlds[48] – at broader scales inciting the violence of the state might indeed do exactly that; so as to reinforce and justify violence at repressive intensities that become more of the same rather than generating something other. If 'transgression does not deny the taboo but transcends it and completes it',[49] then in this reading a transgressive politics that bubbles over into riotous violence might reinforce rather than smash the taboo of the state's monopoly on violence. This, then, invites greater thought and reflexivity so as to amplify subjectivities that refract, rather than reproduce, the violences underpinning capitalism's enclosures.

Running riot with Deleuze and Guattari

A further reading of the possibility for transformative excess in the production and experience of riotous counterglobalisation events might come from the poststructuralist philosophers Gilles Deleuze and Félix Guattari. The quasi-religious concept of revolution invoked at the beginning of this section (of revolution as total, immediate rupture), and which underpins Durkheim's notion of effervescence, has been problematized and, to some extent, replaced in today's counterglobalisation movement with the idea and necessity of building 'other worlds' through long, drawn-out processes of social change that nonetheless do not abandon an accompanying promise of the 'radical' and 'ruptural'. How, then, can we theoretically conceive of this type of social change? Here we use some of the tools provided by Deleuze and Guattari, who combine a subtle understanding of social change both as ruptural *and* as gradually constructed through time and space, with that rarest of academic qualities: revolutionary optimism.

The basis for their optimism lies in the world that Deleuze and Guattari encounter. It is in principle disorderly, a world of becoming, not of being, of nomadic movement through relatively undisciplined and bounded spaces. It is a world of multiplicity and difference, irreducible and indivisible. Here, unity and stability can only ever result from the operations of power, capture and *territorialization*,[50] such that order is not the almost unchangeable status quo, but rather a tenuous construct, which at all points has to be re-established by the state and other 'apparatuses of capture'.[51] The target of these constant attempts at capture is 'a pure and immeasurable multiplicity, the pack, and irruption of the ephemeral and the power of metamorphosis'. This is what they refer to (perhaps problematically) as the *war machine*, which 'brings a *furor* to bear against sovereignty, a celerity against gravity, secrecy against the public, a power (*puissance*) against sovereignty, a machine against the apparatus'.[52] The war machine – akin also to Hakim Bey's *Temporary Autonomous Zone*[53] – thus is not a tangible institution, but the irrepressible desire for nomadic transformation, for becoming. It is present only in its metamorphoses,[54] in moments of invention and creation:

> [a]nd each time there is an operation against the State – insubordination, rioting, guerrilla warfare, or revolution as act – it can be said that a war machine has revived, that a new nomadic potential has appeared, accompanied by the reconstitution of a smooth space or a manner of being in space as though it were smooth.[55]

Of course, not each and every riot generates creative flashes of the war machine; 'smooth' space is not generated every time a roving band of (mostly) guys in hooded sweaters lobs some rocks at the police. And presumably, Deleuze and Guattari would not think so either, for the destruction and 'violence' they advocate is not simply a 'nihilistic form ... of physical destruction', but rather a creative, generative (Nietzschean) form of constructive destruction.[56]

In this reading, then, an imputed act of political radicalism is transformative to the extent that it escapes as a *line of flight*, drawing into the world – manifesting – *other* subjectivities, spaces and possibilities. Imagine the striated space of the state, where all movement is relative to, and overcoded by, the centre – then an instance where the 'war machine' flashes up, where there is an escape from the regularized lines of stasis and movement of the state effecting 'a deterritorialization, through a movement which interrupts or suspends familiar, confining, formal possibilities ... a movement out of which the participating bodies are drawn along new vectors in experimental ways'.[57]

The riotous drawing of a line of flight creates new possibilities, opens up new political spaces and produces other worlds – both through, and in contexts beyond, the 'riot act'. It occurs in the moments where creative violence and excess is not subordinated to conventional political reason; where risk and chance have outcomes which cannot be predicted, and where connections are created between elements hitherto unconnected.

Open ends

We have come a long way. In the course of this political and reflective journey, we have ripped up the pavements of Annemasse and London, seen barricades burn and celebrated the creative excess of contemporary confrontations between the counterglobalisation movement and the institutions of global capital. Having arrived where we are now – what, finally, of that famous beach? The answer must remain open: it is as if we have ripped up the cobblestones to find sand – and then realized that we still do not know whether it really is the beach, or just another desert. It is ultimately only in the processes within which spectacular events are embedded that their political meaning is constituted.

The dream of revolution as a singular, one-off rupture has been discarded by most within the counterglobalist movement. But the desire for ruptural politics has not, and for good reason. We have suggested here that riots can be events that rupture 'normal' political time and space, that speed up history and open new political spaces for contesting otherwise normalized, 'sedimented' social relations of domination. They can generate an effervescence that might create new collective solidarities: in other words, they can create 'movements' where before there was only relatively isolated groups – this much we learn from Durkheim. They can create 'militants' where before there were protestors unable to challenge the power of the police. Speaking strategically, then: there is good reason to be critical of an exclusive focus on organizing protests, and every reason to attempt to build movement links beyond a one-off event. But there are no reasons to stop organizing altogether for moments of excess, of madness, of effervescence. Radical politics cannot live without the intensity created in such moments: it is those moments that make other worlds possible.

Notes

1. John Vidal and Libby Brooks, 'Day the City Turned Into a Battleground', *The Guardian*, 19 June 1999. Retrieved from http://www.guardian.co.uk/uk/1999/jun/19/johnvidal.libbybrooks.
2. Alessio Vinci and Kelly Wallace, 'G8 Leaders Condemn Violence as Protesters, Police Clash', *CNN.com/world*, 23 July 2001. Retrieved from http://edition.cnn.com/2001/WORLD/europe/07/21/genoa.violence/.

3. 'Protesters Rampage in Geneva'. Retrieved from http://news.bbc.co.uk/1/hi/world/europe/2954190.stm.

4. 'Fresh Violence Erupts Near Gleneagles G8 Site', 6 July 2005. Retrieved from http://www.monstersandcritics.com/news/uk/news/article_1031220.php/Fresh_violence_Erupts_near_Gleneagles_G8_site. This webpage is no longer active.

5. 'Politicians Call For Crackdown on Violent G-8 Protesters', 4 June 2007. Retrieved from http://www.spiegel.de/international/germany/0,1518,486573,00.html.

6. Kaiser Chiefs, *I Predict a Riot* (London, 2004).

7. Named after a much-circulated short article elaborating the militarizing of corporate interests apparent in the 2003 Iraq War and celebrating the massive and global anti-war movement that emerged in that year. Norman Solomon, '"Globalization" and Its Malcontents', *Media Beat*, 20 February 2003. Retrieved from http://www.alternet.org/story/15219/%22globalization%22_and_its_malcontents. This of course also revisits the title of the widely read critique of neoliberal economic policies written by the International Monetary Fund's own chief economist, Joseph Stiglitz, who published *Globalization and Its Discontents* (London, 2002). In the 'vignettes' presented here, we draw here on corporate media reports of protests against the G8, the Group of the world's eight most industrialized countries (the United States, Japan, Germany, United Kingdom, France, Italy, Canada and Russia). The G8 is only one international organisation whose summit meetings form a focus for intense policing effort and counterglobalisation protest. Others are the World Bank, the International Monetary Fund, the World Economic Forum and the European Union, all of which have attracted large-scale summit mobilizations involving a multiplicity of protest tactics. We use the G8 here as a convenient acknowledgement of the symbolic and material inequalities expressed as a current configuration of institutions comprised of a minority agree on economic, military and environmental policy that arguably sustains the global inequalities and ecological damage, determining the lives of a global majority.

8. Also see Tadzio Mueller, 'What's Really Under Those Cobblestones? Riots as Political Tools, and the Case of Gothenburg 2001', *Ephemera*, 4 (2004), pp. 135–51; Sian Sullivan, '"We Are Heartbroken and Furious!" Rethinking Violence and the (Anti-)Globalization Movements', in *Critical Theories, World Politics and 'The Anti-Globalization Movement'*, ed. B. Maiguashca and C. Eschle (London, 2005), pp. 175–94. Also published in 2004 as *CSGR Working Paper* no. 133/04. Retrieved from http://www2.warwick.ac.uk/fac/soc/csgr/research/workingpapers/2004/wp13304.pdf; and Sian Sullivan, '"Viva Nihilism!" On Militancy and Machismo in (Anti-)Globalization Protest', in *Globalization of Political Violence: Globalization's Shadow*, ed. R. Devetak and C. Hughes (London, 2008), pp. 203–43. Also published in 2005 as *CSGR Working Paper* no. 158/05. Retrieved from http://www2.warwick.ac.uk/fac/soc/csgr/research/workingpapers/2005/.

9. Tom Mertes (ed.), *A Movement of Movements: Is Another World Really Possible?* (London, 2004).

10. Naomi Klein, 'Reclaiming the Commons', in *A Movement of Movements*, ed. Mertes, p. 219.

11. UK London N30 1999. Retrieved from http://bak.spc.org/N30london/.

12. For a comprehensive review of protest tactics and consideration of their problematic categorizations as 'violence', see Amory Starr, '(Excepting Barricades Erected to Prevent Us from Peacefully Assembling)': So-Called "Violence" in the Global Alterglobalization Movement', *Social Movement Studies*, 5 (2006), pp. 61–81.

13. Michel Foucault, 'The Birth of Biopolitics', in *Ethics: Subjectivity and Truth*, ed. Paul Rabinow (New York, 1997), pp. 73–79.
14. Also see Sullivan, 'We Are Heartbroken and Furious'; and Starr,'(Excepting Barricades Erected to Prevent Us from Peacefully Assembling)'.
15. Michel Aglietta, *A Theory of Capitalist Regulation: The US Experience* (London and New York, 1987).
16. David Harvey, *The Condition of Postmodernity* (Oxford, 1989), pp. 141–42, 171.
17. Gerard Dumenil and Levy Dominique, *Capital Resurgent: Roots of the Neoliberal Revolution* (Cambridge, 2004), pp. 1–2.
18. Ibid.; cf. Stephen Gill, *American Hegemony and the Trilateral Commission* (Cambridge, MA, 1990).
19. 'The New Enclosures', *Midnight Notes* no. 10. (1990). A process that saw its first expression in Britain's 'enclosure movement' which opened in the early Middle Ages and saw major consolidation with the General Enclosure Acts of the early 1800s. For an excellent analysis of the radically transformative effect that this process has, particularly in terms of disembedding economy from the regulatory effects of both nature and other social institutions, see Karl Polanyi, *The Great Transformation: The Political and Economic Transformations of Our Time* (1944; rpt. Boston, 2001).
20. David Harvey, *The New Imperialism* (Oxford, 2003), pp. 137–79.
21. For example, 'Precarious, Precarization, Precariat? Impacts, Traps and Challenges of a Complex Term and Its Relationship to Migration', *This Tuesday: Logs on Migration, Labor, Transnational Organizing*. Retrieved from http://05.diskursfestival.de/pdf/symposium_4.en.pdf. Of course, capitalist production has always relied on migrant labour in variously precarious positions, as in the emerging colonies, and through the production of a landless underclass via the Enclosure Acts in west Europe.
22. Francis Fukuyama, 'The End of History', *The National Interest*, 16 (1989), pp. 3–18; republished as a book length monograph as *The End of History and the Last Man* (London, 1992).
23. Fukuyama, *The End of History and the Last Man*, p. 49.
24. George Katsiaficas, *The Subversion of Politics: European Autonomous Movements and the Subversion of Everyday Life* (New Jersey, 1997), p. 262.
25. The term 'glocal' is being used increasingly by social scientists and others to refer to the conceptual and material collapsing of global and local spheres of organization, made possible by new and rapidly globalising communications technologies, particularly the internet. For a consideration of this term and associated organisational phenomena, see Sian Sullivan, 'Conceptualising Glocal Organization: From Rhizome to E=mc^2 Becoming Post-Human', in *Metaphors of Globalization: Mirrors, Magicians and Mutinies*, eds Marcus Kornprobst, Vincent Pouliot, Nisha Shah and Ruben Zaiotti (Basingstoke, 2008), pp. 149–66.
26. The North American Free Trade Agreement between Mexico, United States and Canada.
27. That is, EZLN – Ejército Zapatista de Liberación Nacional. For further information go to one of the many websites that focus on the Zapatistas, for example, http://www.mexicosolidarity.org/programs/alternativeeconomy/zapatismo/en.
28. Guiomar Rovira, *Women of Maize: Indigenous Women and the Zapatista Rebellion* (London, 2000).
29. Gustavo Esteva, 'Basta! Mexican Indians Say "Enough"!', in *The Post-Development Reader*, ed. Majid Rahnema and Victoria Bawtree (London, 1997), p. 302.

30. See Harry Cleaver's archive 'Zapatistas in Cyberspace' at http://www.indigenous-people.net/zapatist.htm.
31. In the Spirit of Emma, *Zapatista* (London, 1999), p. 9.
32. Lukas Engelmann, Oliver Pye und Pedram Shahyar, *Auswertung der Evian-Kampagne* (Berlin, 2003). Retrieved from http://gipfelsoli.org/Home/Evian_2003/551.html.
33. Bernard Cassen, 'On the Attack', *New Left Review*, 19 (2003). Retrieved from http://www.newleftreview.net/NLR25303.shtml.
34. Anonymous (ed.), *On Fire; The Battle of Genoa and the Anti-Capitalist Movement* (London, 2001); The Free Association, *Moments of Excess* (Leeds, 2004). Retrieved from http://freelyassociating.org/moments-of-excess; John Drury, Steve Reicher and Clifford Stott, 'Transforming the Boundaries of Collective Identity: From the Local Anti-Road Campaign to Global Resistance?', *Social Movement Studies*, 2 (2003), pp. 191–212.
35. Emile Durkheim, *The Elementary Forms of Religious Life* (1912; rpt. New York, 1995), pp. 211–12.
36. Mikhail Bakhtin, *Rabelais and His World* (Bloomington, 1984).
37. Henri Lefebvre, *Everyday Life in the Modern World* (London, 1984); Sian Sullivan, 'On Dance and Difference: Bodies, Movement and Experience in Khoesān Trance-Dancing—Perceptions of a Raver', in *Talking About People: Readings in Contemporary Cultural Anthropology*, ed. W.A. Haviland, R. Gordon and L. Vivanco (New York, 2006), pp. 234–41.
38. Durkheim, *The Elementary Forms of Religious Life*, pp. 218–19; cf. The Free Association, *Moments of Excess*.
39. Durkheim, *The Elementary Forms of Religious Life*, pp. 212–13.
40. Arlette Farge and Jacques Revel *The Rules of Rebellion: Child Abductions in Paris in 1750* (Cambridge, 1991).
41. David Lockwood, *Solidarity and Schism: The 'Problem of Disorder' in Durkheimian and Marxian Sociology* (Oxford, 1992), p. 34.
42. Aristide Zolberg, 'Moments of Madness', *Politics and Society* 2 (1972), pp. 206–7; The Free Association, *Moments of Excess*.
43. Cf. Drury, Reicher and Stott, 'Transforming the Boundaries of Collective Identity'.
44. We draw here on the description of 'J18', in *We Are Everywhere: The Irresistible Rise of Global Anticapitalism* (London, 2003); and anonymous, 'May Day: Guerrilla? Gardening?', *Do or Die*, 9 (2000), pp. 69–81.
45. For example, anonymous, 'May Day: Guerrilla? Gardening?'; anonymous, 'Give Up Activism', *Do and Die*, 9 (2001), pp. 160–66.
46. Naomi Klein, *No Logo: No Space, No Choice, No Jobs* (New York, 2000).
47. Ernesto Laclau, *New Reflections on the Revolution of Our Time* (London and New York, 1990), pp. 32–34.
48. Cf. Sian Sullivan, 'An *Other* World Is Possible? On Representation, Rationalism and Romanticism in Social Forums', *Ephemera: Theory and Practice in Organization*, 5 (2005), pp. 370–92.
49. Georges Bataille, *Eroticism*, trans. Mary Dalwood (1957; rpt. London, 1987).
50. Gilles Deleuze and Felix Guattari, *A Thousand Plateaus: Capitalism and Schizophrenia* (London and New York, 2004), p. 9.
51. Also see Michel Foucault, *The Will to Knowledge: The History of Sexuality*, trans. Robert Hurley (1976; rpt. London, 1998).
52. Deleuze and Guattari, *A Thousand Plateaus*, p. 388.

53. Hakim Bey, *The Temporary Autonomous Zone*. Retrieved from http://www.hermetic.com/bey/taz3.html.

54. Deleuze and Guattari, *A Thousand Plateaus*, pp. 397–98.

55. Ibid., p. 426

56. Julian Reid, 'Deleuze's War Machine: Nomadism Against the State', *Millennium*, 32 (2003), p. 69.

57. John Hughes, *Lines of Flight: Reading Deleuze with Hardy, Gissing, Conrad, Woolf* (Sheffield, 1997), p. 46.

15
Riots in Thatcher's Britain

Peter Hayes

It cannot have been wholly coincidental that Margaret Thatcher's period as prime minister was one of recurrent rioting. She had entered 10 Downing Street in May 1979 praying, in the words of Saint Francis, that 'where there is discord may we bring harmony'. But she had gone on to say 'where there is error, may we bring truth', and as she later explained in her account of her years in office, this was a very important qualifying statement. Her political agenda was *the truth*; the agenda of her opponents was in *error*. For truth to triumph over error there was inevitably going to be a certain amount of discord.[1] This discord took the form of rioting in three notable arenas. First, there were the urban riots in the inner cities, beginning with a small riot the Saint Paul's area of Bristol on 2 April 1980; the riot in Brixton, South London from 10 to 13 April 1981 was far bigger and drew the most attention. Occurring over a long weekend, it was extensively documented by the media, and by Sunday there were a considerable number of spectators. The Brixton Riot was followed by a summer of rioting in various parts of England, including Moss Side in Manchester; in Wolverhampton, Smethwick and Birmingham in the West Midlands; in Leeds; Leicester; Nottingham and in various parts of London including Southall and again in Brixton. The most extensive of the summer riots was in Toxteth in Liverpool from 3 to 6 July 1981. There were riots for a third time in Brixton in November 1982, and in Handsworth, Birmingham in 1985. The second form of rioting was associated with the 1984–85 miners' strike. Throughout the strike, there were violent incidents as pickets confronted working miners and the police, with the most spectacular confrontation at Orgreave coke depot. The third riot was the poll tax riot that took place on 31 March 1990 in the centre of London. This followed a series of disorderly demonstrations in several cities. Popular opposition to the poll tax strengthened Thatcher's opponents within the Conservative Party, and contributed to the successful campaign to depose her in November 1990.[2]

The violence of the miners' strike and the poll tax riot are explicable as intense manifestations of the broader political conflict between left and right that was played out during Thatcher's years in office. This conflict included a long internal battle between the right and left wings of the Labour Party, and this split tended to muddy the party's response to the riots, something that Thatcher was adroit at exploiting. Aside from their disputed home in the Labour Party, those with left-wing views had power bases in two sets of institutions: the unions and local government, and Thatcher was determined to defeat them in both arenas.[3] The miners' strike was the principal battle between Thatcher and the unions, and the poll tax protests were the principal location of her battle with local government. By contrast, the urban riots were something of a surprise and cannot be neatly placed into a broad strategic conflict between the left and right. The far left was willing to take a share of the credit for them, but they did not initiate the riots and while there is evidence that, from Brixton onwards, left-wing activists arrived to exacerbate the trouble as best they could, this probably had only a marginal impact on the course of the rioting. The riots appear to have arisen with little prior organized political involvement and were directed primarily against the police, although the extent to which the police were the real target of the rioters as opposed to being the whipping boy for less accessible or tangible objects of grievance is open to dispute.

The urban riots

The model for the urban riots of the summer of 1981 was the Brixton riot. Even as the riot was minutely analysed in a public inquiry headed by Lord Scarman, it simultaneously provided the inspiration for rioters in other areas. On Friday, 10 April 1981, as Scarman described it, a young black man in Brixton was stabbed and chased; the police tried to help, their actions though were misconstrued by a gathering crowd, a riot started, and the police were stoned.[4] More radical commentators added that this misperception was understandable. Mike Cole, identifying the stab victim as Dave Shepherd, described how he met three friends. Parodying the style of the Scarman report, Cole explained:

[The friends] warned him that there were police youths about, spoiling for trouble. Ignoring their warnings he continued down the road quickly. Mr Shepherd was in considerable pain. When he came to the road junction he saw one of the police youths, who began running towards him. Reasoning that the youth might be about to harass him, he attempted to leave, but was grabbed and forced to the floor with the police youth on top of him.[5]

On Saturday, rioting started again. This time the spark was a stop and search for drugs under 'Operation Swamp'. In the afternoon, before the riot recommenced, Scarman cited witnesses who said that some white men appeared and taught the local young men, mainly black, who were waiting expectantly on the street, how to make petrol bombs.[6] The rioters threw these at the police and set cars aflame, the police threw stones, chanted war whoops and banged their shields.[7] The rioters, Scarman comments, 'were enjoying themselves'.[8] He does not comment on whether or not some of the police may have also gained enjoyment from the occasion. While police and rioters were confronting each other across burning barricades, the looters arrived. Some had travelled some distance to take advantage of the riot and the white looters, in particular, were described as deliberate and systematic.[9] The looters burned some of the buildings they entered, and when firemen arrived, they chased them away and stole their fire fighting equipment.[10] On Sunday, there was another riot and more looting but it was not as bad, and there was a small riot on Monday.[11]

There were two principal causal preconditions to the riots that were mooted in the extensive public discussions about what had taken place. The first was economic disadvantage, particularly high levels of unemployment; the second was racist policing. Thatcher accepted that the police might have been racist and sometimes brutal in their attitude towards members of the public in the inner cities. She and the government trod a delicate line between rhetorical support for the police while at the same time initiating reforms to reduce 'stop and search' procedures and change recruitment and training practices.[12] The link between rioting and unemployment, however, was highly problematic for the Conservatives, because a rise in unemployment was an inevitable by-product of their economic reforms. The Conservatives had fought the election campaign of 1979 with the help of an ubiquitous poster of a line of actors pretending to be in a queuing to sign on the dole. The accompanying slogan was 'Britain Isn't Working Under Labour'. The problem was that, at least in the short term, Conservative economic objectives of denationalization, efficiency savings and the ending of public subsidies, ensured that the dole queues would increase. Thatcherites believed that the end justified the means and that 'you can't make an omelette without breaking eggs', but it was almost impossible to articulate this case. Appeals to macro-economic logic and 'labour market flexibility', which after the Thatcher revolution have become truisms, were bitterly contested in the 1980s.

Given that the rise in unemployment was a consequence of Conservative strategy, it was also inaccurate and more pertinently politically impossible to put blame for the plight of the unemployed on the unemployed themselves. Norman Tebbit, Secretary of State for Employment between 1981 and 1983, had tried to do this in a speech in which he at once refuted the causal connection between unemployment and rioting and implied that if the unemployed had more determination, they might find other work. In a speech to the Conservative's annual conference on 15 October 1981, Tebbit said that when his father had lost his job in the 1930s 'he didn't riot. He got on his bike and looked for work. And he kept looking till he found it.'[13] This comment was skilfully exploited by political opponents to become one of the three revelatory statements of the Thatcherite creed (the others were 'there is no such thing as society' and 'greed is good'). The suggestion that the unemployed might find work if they tried harder was emphasized and 'on yer bike' was endlessly repeated as the summation of Conservative policy towards those who had lost their jobs (the relationship, or not, between unemployment and rioting in Tebbit's anecdote was ignored). The Conservatives were somewhat hamstrung by this line of attack, and this helps to explain why the infrastructure of social support for the unemployed remained largely intact under Thatcher's term in office. Indeed, it was not until the accession of New Labour in 1997 that a more Tebbit-like approach to the unemployed became standard policy.

In her statements on the urban riots, Thatcher appeared to reject any connection between them and unemployment. Her explanation placed the riots in the context of a series of broader processes of urban and moral decline in the postwar period. She identified the tension created by large-scale immigration; the creation of poorly designed public housing that had uprooted people and undermined their sense of community; the rise of the dependency culture in welfare payments that discouraged people from taking a sense of responsibility for their actions; and the decline of established sources of authority at home, school and church. She emphasized particularly the corrupting effect of television on working-class values, including the traditional values of immigrants. All of these things combined to allow high-spirited rioters 'to enjoy a fiesta of crime, looting and rioting in the guise of social protest'.[14] Given this analysis, Thatcher, implicitly realized that unemployment was a further contributing factor to the riots – which she eventually admitted in Parliament.[15] The unemployed are more likely to become welfare dependent and are not subject to the discipline of work. Indeed, given the significance that Thatcher gave to television, it can also be pointed out that the unemployed had more time to watch it. Their economic position makes them prone to exactly fit into the situation she identified in which community ethics are lost and traditional sources of authority are weakened.

Thatcher articulates her concept of discord, in two characteristic steps. First, the gap between truth and error is elided into a Manichean struggle between good and evil. Thatcher has a tendency to describe contending political forces without intervening shades of grey, without acknowledging that opponents may have reasonable arguments and without admitting to any failings on the side of truth and good, or any redeeming features of the side or error and evil. Second, the side of truth/good is identified with the majority and with democracy and the side of error/evil with the minority and with dictatorial or mob rule. In her public condemnation of the riots, Thatcher conformed fairly closely to this pattern. However, she had an underlying recognition that things were not so simple; she admitted the need for police reform, and offered a relatively sophisticated analysis of the causes of the riots that was not slotted in to the titanic battle between good and evil as neatly as it might have been. There was an element of open mindedness in Thatcher's analysis – she allowed herself room for thought and room for manoeuvre. As Thatcher continued in government, however, the subtleties of her thinking gave way to the simple dichotomies. Her triumphs in the Falklands and over the miners, her successive election victories in 1983 and 1987, and the victory of the west in the Cold War all seemed to encourage an ever more doctrinaire and inflexible view of the divide between truth and error until, in the poll tax debacle, she became trapped inside her own rigid categorizations.

The miners' strike

When the Conservatives came into government in 1979, it was obvious that a miners' strike was coming; it was not a matter of whether it would happen, but merely of when. The Conservative policy of privatization (mining was a nationalized industry), together with their assault on union power, were quite sufficient to signal the likelihood of conflict. On top of this, the National Union of Mineworkers (NUM) and the Conservative Party had a history of antagonism. A strike by the NUM had precipitated the general election of February 1974, with the Conservative leader Edward Heath campaigning under the question 'Who governs Britain?' – the government or the unions. The Conservatives lost their parliamentary majority in the election, and a minority Labour government had formed, which became a majority government after a further general election in October the same year. What finally made a strike inevitable was that the election of Thatcher in 1979 was followed by the election of Yorkshire NUM president, Arthur Scargill, to the national presidency in 1981. Assisted by the Marxist scholar, Vic Allen, and activist, Peggy Kahn, Scargill had developed highly accurate predictions of the Conservative's intentions for running down the mining industry. At the time, Scargill was accused of exaggerating but, with hindsight, if Scargill can be faulted, it is in understating the extent of government hostility. Scargill suggested that the Conservatives wanted to halve the size of the industry.[16] This is exactly what they did after the strike, and coal mining in Britain has now ceased altogether.

Armed with his foreknowledge of Conservative intentions, Scargill initiated three strike ballots: two in 1982 and a third in 1983. Here the unstoppable strike momentum was checked, as in each case a majority rejected the strike call. The Conservatives were providing considerable financial latitude to the

National Coal Board (NCB) management to make generous wage settlements, and there were no compulsory redundancies yet made as pits slowly started to close. All the while, the government was building up coal stocks and transferring them away from the pithead. This was done slowly and incrementally so that the miners, it was hoped, would not notice the growing piles of coal. In 1984, Scargill adopted a new tactic. Unable to secure a national strike through balloting the NUM membership, he turned to a second method: creating a national strike in a kind of domino effect, using a mobile group of activists, the 'flying pickets'. In the riots and other forms of violence that followed, the decision to mount the strike without a national ballot but rather through picketing was of crucial importance to the split between striking and working miners.

The spread of the strike through picketing began in March 1984 in Yorkshire. Pickets were then sent out throughout the coalfields. Several hundred pickets would converge on a single pit, turn the workers away, and then move on to another. Once the flying pickets had initiated a strike, an activist core at the pit would maintain it by promoting the idea that the strike was an expression of community and class solidarity and move quickly to attack any 'scab' that returned to work. This method quickly extended the stoppage until around 80 percent of the miners were on strike. There were, however, five coal mining areas where the majority of miners rejected joining a strike without a ballot. A banner at a rally attended by working miners put their argument succinctly:

No Ballot
No Strike
Scargill's Mob Rule
Out!![17]

The largest and most productive area where most miners continued to work was Nottinghamshire, and the others were South Derbyshire, Leicestershire, the Midlands and the North West.[18]

Only 39 percent of the miners who voted had backed a strike in the two most recent ballots in 1983. Why then did 80 percent go out on strike without any further balloting in 1984? In the literature on the strike, this question often focuses on the dissident minority, particularly in Nottinghamshire, who did not go on strike. The notion that this was because of the failure to hold a ballot is dismissed, and deeper economic historical and social explanations are sought; thus it is sometimes suggested that the working miners in Nottinghamshire and elsewhere somehow lacked the sense of community found amongst strikers.[19] On the contrary, it is suggested here that the explanation of working miners that they were democrats who wanted a ballot can be taken at its face value. The more difficult question then becomes why a strike that was supported by only a minority of the balloted miners succeeded in gaining so much support through picketing.

To answer this question, it is necessary to draw on two apparently conflicting explanations. First, for supporters of the strike, the presence of pickets and their presentation of their case raised the level of consciousness of the miners going in to work and persuaded them to join the strike. The activists who converged on a pit to engage in a mass picket succeeded through the power of argument, the appeal of class solidarity and by giving miners an enhanced sense of acting as part of a community. This form of action could be contrasted with balloting, where voters did not have the same immediate sense of solidarity with their fellow workers and where the propaganda of the NCB, government and mass media had more of a hold. Second, critics of mass picketing, including working miners, suggested that the tactic worked by creating a physical barrier that it was impossible to cross, and by having an underlying intimidatory threat of violence: it was, in a sense, 'bully boy tactics'.[20]

To bring these contrasting explanations together, it can be noted that support and fear of an organization are not exclusive propositions, and that fear can lead to support. Someone who yields to the threat of violence against their better judgement undermines the sense they have of their own dignity and courage. To retain a sense of dignity, it is possible to fall into line with the demands of the threatening organization by deciding that you support them. By acceding to the idea that striking was a principled act of solidarity, miners turned away by pickets were able to maintain their sense of dignity. It is insufficient, therefore, to suggest that the psychological processes involved amongst those who voted against the strike but ended up supporting it after being picketed can be characterized in terms of a raised consciousness, because the preservation of their dignity required the suppression of the consciousness of their fear. The initial fear was of the mass picket, but far more frightening was the prospect of reprisals by strike activists were they to return to work. The account of a member of 'the scab watch team' provides an insight into the level of fear. The author notes, with satisfaction, that working miners who were confronted on their doorsteps would soil themselves. Violence against 'scabs' was justified as a response to their returning to work, an act that was described as a 'violent' attack on the community from which they came.[21]

If we now return to the exceptional areas where the miners continued to work, it can be suggested that miners who were against a strike without a ballot had the organizational ability to continue to work as a group; they were not individualized by picketing and the threat posed by activists. Arguments that attempt to portray the working miners as having a poorly developed sense of community are misleading; rather they had a level of community organization that was sufficient to rival the organizations of strike activists. A characteristic form of violence during the strike, therefore, was where two organized groups, working miners and striking miners, were in confrontation with each other, particularly in Nottinghamshire where mass picketing was concentrated.

A further area of violence was where striking miners attempted to disrupt the supply of fuel for power stations and to heavy industry, and the most famous of these occasions was at Orgreave. Without a continuous supply of coke, the furnaces at the Scunthorpe steel works would be forced to shut down and were under some threat of cracking. Learning of this danger, striking miners determined to try and close the steel works by preventing the transfer by lorry of coke from the Orgreave depot. This lead to a series of confrontations, starting in May 1984 and peaking on 18 June. Exactly what happened at Orgreave, and the relative number of police and pickets each day is subject to differing interpretations, although according to one estimate, there were around 10,000 pickets and 4,000 police on 18 June.[22] However, even if the police were outnumbered, the confrontation at Orgreave was rather one sided.

After the urban riots, the police began the long-term effort to overcome racism in the ranks. This, however, was not the only reform that was taking place, there were also much more immediate and practical lessons that were being learned. In Bristol, in 1980, the police improvised shields from milk crates.[23] Four years later at Orgreave, the police were well equipped and tightly organized. They had long and short shields, they had their own cavalry and dog units, and they had boiler suited special forces with their police numbers obscured. Some of the images of the battle that ensued are reminiscent of Romans versus Celts. The police are seen helmeted and shielded in thick wedge-like lines. The pickets, many shirtless in the warm weather, range before them. While coming together to push and shove when the lorry convoys arrived, the pickets otherwise tended to break up into small autonomous groups from each pit. Some pickets would hurl missiles at the police, but there are conflicting accounts of their level of violence. It is generally admitted that stones were thrown and that there were also eggs filled with paint. However, quite how many missiles were thrown is unclear, and it has been suggested that they were fairly intermittent.[24] The police, it is implied, should have put up with a few stones and were wholly disproportionate in their response. Certainly, there are indications that the pickets were taken by surprise by the sudden ferocity of police attacks on 18 June. Arthur Scargill marched up and down the police lines pretending to inspect them, and was later hit on the head with a riot shield in retribution. The account of one picket, corroborated by photographs, is that a fair proportion of the miners allegedly hurling missiles, were actually picnicking.[25] In any event, the wall of shields parted, and the mounted police charged out. Pickets report being pursued by horsemen into the nearby terraces, with police riders jumping over garden fences and urging their horses down the interior passageways between the houses.[26] The mounted police wielded their truncheons, the police on foot used their shields as weapons, the dog handlers let slip their dogs. Pickets strung a wire across the street, although there are conflicting reports as to whether this was designed to catch policeman at the neck or whether it was placed at stomach height.[27]

Commenting on Orgreave and on parallel events in Scotland at the end of May 1984, Thatcher contrasted the mob with the people of Britain:

> [T]he overwhelming majority of people in this country are honourable, decent and law abiding and want the law to be upheld and will not be intimidated, and I pay tribute to the courage of those who have gone into work through these picket lines, to the courage of those at Ravenscraig and Scunthorpe for not going to be intimidated out of their jobs and out of their future. Ladies and Gentlemen we need the support of everyone in this battle which goes to the very heart of our society. The rule of law must prevail over the rule of the mob.[28]

After the events of 18 June, Thatcher's comments in the House of Commons followed a similar pattern: 'The lorries got through; the coal is getting through. I hope that that will continue, as I hope that the overwhelming majority of workers in this country will join all people of good will to see that mob violence does not prevail'.[29] In characterising the miners' strike in this way, Thatcher hardened her vision of a struggle between good/truth and evil/error. The good workers and people were the vast majority; the evil pickets were a small minority, linked to Marxism, to 'left-fascism' and to the hostile foreign powers of the Soviet Union and Libya. They blended imperceptibly into terrorists.[30]

The miners' strike never succeeded in disrupting power supplies. The Orgreave picket failed, and the Scunthorpe furnaces stayed open. In addition to the coal from Nottinghamshire and other working areas, the government arranged for coal imports to be landed at small harbours all around the country, avoiding the large unionised ports. The winter proved to be a mild one. Strike breaking accelerated as groups of miners at street, village or pit level, returned to work. After a year, the remaining strikers gave up.

The poll tax

The poll tax or community charge was first introduced in Scotland in 1989 and then rolled out across England and Wales to take effect from 1 April 1990. Everyone received a cheerful yellow leaflet informing them of the change, with a reassuring little cartoon of members of a community – expectant mothers, Sikhs, punks and so on – all smiling at the news. The leaflet explained that the rates were to be abolished, and a flat rate individual charge was to be levied to fund local government services. There would, however, be rebates, with 5 million people paying only 20 percent of the charge, and more than 4 million more qualifying for some reduction. The leaflet also warned gently that people who did not pay would be sent to prison.[31]

There was widespread public resentment towards the poll tax, which extended to a considerable number of Conservatives; on 18 April 1988, 38 of the Party's MPs voted against the government on the issue.[32] There was a campaign of non-payment, which had been initiated in Scotland under the slogan 'Can't Pay Won't Pay'.[33] The left seized upon the opposition to the poll tax and organised various demonstrations at local council meetings. Under the auspices of the All Britain Anti-Poll Tax Federation, a national demonstration was planned in London for 31 March 1990. This demonstration turned into the poll tax riot. The march attracted a huge crowd, with estimates varying from 50,000 to 100,000. The marchers had a petition, which they were prevented from delivering to 10 Downing Street. This sparked a peaceful sit-down protest amongst a small number of the demonstrators. Most moved on to listen to speeches in Trafalgar Square and then dispersed before the rioting began, but several thousand stayed. Back at the entrance to Downing Street, the police attempted to break up the sit-down protest, and some protestors began to throw missiles. Rioting escalated and spread to Trafalgar Square where scaffolding poles were pulled down and used as weapons. Groups of rioters went on into Covent Garden, Leicester Square, Soho and Tottenham Court Road, breaking the windows of shops and restaurants and looting. In Trafalgar Square, the police made horseback charges into the milling crowds. There was an official tally of 374 officers and 86 members of the public injured. Half of the 40 police horses were also injured.[34]

The good majority versus evil minority pattern that increasingly dominated Thatcher's utterances, appeared ideally suited to the poll tax protests. Before the 31 March riot had even began, the categories were in place, with the wicked minority extended to include the Labour Party under Neil Kinnock:

> In recent weeks, Marxist agitators and militants have organised mob violence. Policemen have been punched, councillors assaulted and shopkeepers have seen their shops looted. When hard-left campaigns of law-breaking are organised by Labour Party members, and publicly defended by Labour MPs, no weasel words from the Leader of the Opposition can alter the plain fact that they are inescapably Labour's responsibility.[35]

After the riot, Thatcher gave her analysis of the social and political background of the rioters:

> For the first time a government had declared that anyone who could reasonably afford to do so should at least pay something towards the upkeep

of the facilities and the provision of services from which they all benefited. A whole class of people – the 'underclass' if you will – had been dragged back into responsible society and asked to become not just dependents but citizens. The violent riots of 31 March in and around Trafalgar Square was their and the Left's response.[36]

Thatcher's concept of the underclass was drawn rather broadly to include all who were not paying directly into the rates, and this included all council house tenants. The popular policy of allowing tenants to buy their own council house had greatly increased private ownership and helped to provide the significant support that the Conservatives received from a section of the working class. For the rest, Thatcher appeared willing to lump them in with the Marxists. The 'Left' referred to by Thatcher were certainly at the demonstration, and some were involved in the rioting. Outside the left wing of the Labour Party, there were a number of small groups, of which the two most active and well-known were the Socialist Workers Party (SWP) and Class War. The SWP, with perhaps a few thousand members, was assiduous in attending demonstrations where they supplied banners with their logo always prominently displayed. They also published a newspaper, written in a dense style, that members were expected to sell but which few people read with much interest. Class War, by its own admission, had a membership that never rose above 150 and was often nearer 50. It had achieved notoriety, however, through its tabloid newspaper, which celebrated, in a semi-pornographic way, the enjoyment to be gained from inflicting violence on the class enemy. A regular feature was an exultant text accompanying a photograph of a police officer being attacked, perhaps on the ground being kicked.

As neither the hard left, nor the 'underclass' were the type of people that others wanted to associate with, and as they were unlikely to vote Conservative, there was a political logic to Thatcher's account of the poll tax riots. The contrast between the good majority and evil minority had worked well enough for the urban riots and for the miners' strike. Why then, when the same framework was used again, did it fail? The introduction of the poll tax was combined with a relatively generous financial package to local authorities, a settlement that was meant to have eased its impact and ensure that the tax would not adversely affect existing rate payers to any great extent. However, the opponents of Thatcher in local government had no interest in playing along. For them, the transition to the poll tax was to be as abrupt as possible, so they set the poll tax as high as possible. This strategy helps to explain why the average poll tax bill of £363 was 31 percent higher than the government's projected average bill £278.[37] These bills penalised a far wider group than merely those who had not previously been billed for rate payments, with an estimated 27 million households losing out and just under 8 million gaining.[38] Thatcher and other members of the government tried to suggest that the rises were the fault of the local councils, but the councils calculated, shrewdly and correctly, that it was the government who would shoulder most of the blame.

There were two strands of objection to the poll tax. The first was its unfairness, particularly of requiring the poorest in society to pay, even though there was the rebate. This was the principal stated objection of the protestors. Michael Heseltine, whose leadership challenge in November 1990 ended Thatcher's premiership, said that tax drew no distinction between 'the rich and the poor, the slum dweller and the landed aristocrat, the elderly pensioners living on their limited savings and the most successful of today's entrepreneurs'.[39] The second objection, somewhat less noble, was that after a decade of Thatcherism, public attitudes had changed sufficiently for many people to be aroused to indignation at the thought of paying more tax. This hard economic fact remained and could not be willed away by equating opposition to the poll tax with the error or evil of the minority. In contrast to the urban riots and to the miners' strike, where most of the public was on the sidelines, the poll tax had an immediate impact on everyone. The truth was that the majority were against it, and Thatcher had stumbled into error in thinking that the split could be viewed through her usual prism. In her determination to pursue the poll tax and to imagine opponents as a malign minority, she engineered her own downfall. But while her resignation caused considerable gloating by all who had opposed her, it was by no means the end of 'Thatcherism'.

Thatcher made one last appearance on the British political stage when she came to the aid of Chilean dictator, General Pinochet, who had covertly supported Britain in the Falklands War. Pinochet made the mistake of visiting the United Kingdom for a hospital operation in 1998. He was arrested and held under house arrest while the courts considered an extradition warrant issued in Spain for him to stand trial for some of the unspeakable atrocities that had been perpetrated under his regime. Thatcher, who had had the old dictator round for tea before his arrest, was vigorous in his defence. In a parody of her earlier self, she slotted Pinochet's case into the same good majority versus evil minority framework that she had used for the riots. The Marxist revolutionaries, she said, were once again behind things, while Pinochet stood for freedom and democracy. However contemptibly the Labour Government behaved, Thatcher assured Senator Pinochet that the British people remained loyal to him. Pinochet's house arrest, Thatcher added, could be compared with the actions of a 'police state'.[40] Considering all the torture and murder that followed Pinochet's coup, this last comment went beyond anything a satirist could invent. Pinochet was released in 2000 on the grounds of illness (possibly feigned). For Thatcher, the political analysis of truth and error that she had used so effectively in her early years in power had degenerated into its final pathetic form.

Notes

1. M. Thatcher, *The Downing Street Years* (London, 1993), p. 19.
2. Ibid., p. 849.
3. Ibid., p. 339.
4. Leslie George Scarman, *The Brixton Disorders 10–12 April 1981.* (London, 1981), pp. 3.4–3.12.
5. M. Cole, 'Teaching and Learning About Racism: A Critique of Multicultural Education in Britain', in *Multicultural Education: The Interminable Debate*, ed. S. Modgil and G.K. Verma et al. (London, 1986), p. 141.
6. Scarman, *The Brixton Disorders*, p. 3.104.
7. Ibid., pp. 3.60, 4.83, 4.85.
8. Ibid., p. 3.77.
9. Ibid., p. 3.61.
10. Ibid., p. 3.62.
11. Ibid., pp. 3.92–3.94.
12. Thatcher, *The Downing Street Years*, p. 144.
13. BBC Daily Politics and Sunday Politics, Top Ten Party Conference Speeches of All Time? 9 October 2014. Retrieved from https://www.facebook.com/video.php?v=982880971728761.
14. Thatcher, *The Downing Street Years*, p. 147.
15. House of Commons, Prime Minister's Questions, 14 July 1981, *Hansard* HC [8/973–78].
16. See P. Hayes, *The People and the Mob* (Westport, 1992).
17. R. Samuel, B. Bloomfield and G. Boanas, *The Enemy Within* (London, 1986), p. 81.
18. See Hayes, *The People and the Mob*.
19. P. Green, *The Enemy Without* (Buckingham, 1990), p. 191; J. Winterton and R. Winterton, *Coal Crisis and Conflict* (Manchester, 1989), p. 75.
20. D. Howell, *The Politics of the NUM* (Manchester, 1989), pp. 109, 102.
21. M. McGuire, 'The Scab Watch Team', in *A Year of Our Lives*, ed. D.J. Douglas (Doncaster, 1986), no page numbers; Hayes, *The People and the Mob*, pp. 125–26.
22. P. Gibbon and D. Steyne, *Thurcroft: A Village and the Miners' Strike* (Nottingham, 1986), p. 82.
23. J. Harris, T. Wallace, and H. Booth, *To Ride the Storm: The 1980 Bristol 'Riot' and the State* (London, 1983).
24. Gibbon and Steyne, *Thurcroft*; B. Jackson with T. Wardle, *The Battle for Orgreave* (Brighton, 1986).
25. Ibid.
26. Gibbon and Steyne, *Thurcroft*, p. 76.
27. Ibid.; Jackson, *The Battle for Orgreave*.
28. M. Thatcher, 'Remarks on Orgreave Picketing', 30 May 1984. Retrieved from http://www.margaretthatcher.org/speeches/displaydocument.asp?docid=105691.
29. House of Commons, Prime Minister's Questions, 19 June 1984. *Hansard* HC [62/137–40].
30. Thatcher, *The Downing Street Years*, pp. 351, 369, 378.
31. Department of the Environment, *The Community Charge (the So-Called 'Poll Tax'): How It Will Work For You* (London, 1989).
32. D. Butler, A. Adonis, and T. Travers, *Failure in British Government: The Politics of the Poll Tax* (Oxford, 1994), p. 120.

33. This slogan had previously been used in an abortive effort to maintain cheap public transport in London in the early 1980s.
34. Butler, Adonis and Travers, *Failure in British Government*, pp. 152–53.
35. M. Thatcher, 'Speech to the Conservative Central Council, Cheltenham, 31 March 1990', in M. Thatcher, *The Collected Speeches* (London, 1997), pp. 376–77.
36. Thatcher, *The Downing Street Years*, p. 661.
37. Butler, Adonis and Travers, *Failure in British Government*, p. 158.
38. Ibid., p. 157.
39. M. Heseltine, *Life in the Jungle* (London, 2000), p. 353.
40. M. Thatcher, 'Speech By Lady Thatcher to a Meeting in Blackpool Organised by the Chilean Reconciliation Movement on Wednesday, 6 October 1999'. Retrieved from http://www.margaretthatcher.org/speeches/displaydocument.asp?docid=108383.

16

France's Burning Issue: Understanding the Urban Riots of November 2005

Raphaël Canet, Laurent Pech and Maura Stewart

> The official discourse of equality of all before the law no longer manages to mask discriminations, notably racial, which are today recognized and on an unsuspected scale. The malaise resulting from these situations has never been so profound. It is translated into a widespread and dangerous loss of confidence in the values of the Republic.[1]

The facts

On the Thursday night of 27 October 2005, two adolescents from Clichy-sous-Bois, in the Parisian suburb of Seine-Saint-Denis, were electrocuted after entering an electrical power station in order to avoid a police check. On that same night, clashes erupted between local youths and the police, and 23 vehicles were torched. The next day, the then minister of the interior, Nicolas Sarkozy, exonerated the police services from all responsibility in what appeared then as an unfortunate accident. The young people from the neighbourhood did not accept this version of the facts, viewing instead this event as the tragic consequence of the highly confrontational relationship that reigned in the French suburbs between the young and the police. The social climate in these economically marginalized zones is such that adolescents usually prefer to flee when a police car approaches even if they have not committed any offence.

This balance of power between young people from the estates and police officers, between the street and the state, had been talked about for a few months by the minister of the interior himself who had publicly declared, when passing through several suburbs following some incidents, that he wanted 'to rid the town of hooligans', or 'to clean the *racaille* [scum] of the suburbs with *Kärcher* [a high pressure water washer brand]'.[2] In such a climate of mistrust, the deaths of 15-year-old Bouna Traoré, from a family of 11 children of Mauritanian descent whose father is a dustman in the city of Paris, and 17-year-old Zyed Benna, the youngest of a family of six children of Tunisian descent whose father is also a dustman in Paris, was going to be the element that triggered the spiral of violence that spread from the Parisian suburbs to the whole country. Nearly 300 cities were affected over a period of about three weeks.

Three periods can be singled out during these events of 2005.[3] First, the local riot, confined to the original town of the incident; second, a few days later, the extension of the acts of violence to the departments surrounding the Paris region. Finally, nearly ten days after the deaths of the two youths, violent action began to be registered in most areas of France. Here, however, is a noteworthy fact: Marseilles and its north districts, well-known for their tendency to erupt, likewise for Lyon's urban area that was behind the first riots of 1981 and 1990, were not to be affected by this phenomenon. The wave of violence reached its climax on the night of 7–8 November during which 1,408 cars were burned in 274 cities in the country, mostly outside of the Paris region. Then, the upsurge of violence subsided until 17 November, when a return to 'normal' took place, that is, 'only' a hundred or so vehicles were burned a day.

The 'riots' or 'urban violence'[4] of November 2005 ended in three deaths: the two young people electrocuted, as well as a retired worker in Stains (Seine-Saint-Denis) who was the victim of a despicable attack while he was monitoring the area surrounding his residence.[5] The material damage was estimated at 200 million euro. Nearly 10,000 private vehicles were burned, as well as 233 public buildings and 74 private buildings. Schools, gyms, buses, public buildings, and vehicles were all part of the collateral damage.[6] Fire was the rioters' favoured method of destruction, thus revealing a distinctive feature of this urban violence: the rarity of predatory acts. In short, there was an enormous amount of ransacking but very little looting.[7] Around 10,000 to 15,000 youths would have participated in the riots, mainly in small groups of ten to 15 people.[8] The average age of the rioters was 16.[9] On the police side, up to 11,500 officers were mobilized a day at the height of the crisis. Nearly 4,800 people, of which 1,000 were minors, were taken in for questioning during the riots but not more than 422 were subject to immediate criminal sanctions as they were caught red-handed.[10] Between 20 and 25 percent of all the people arrested were offenders known to the police.[11] One also finds an ethnic variety greater than what most commentaries, notably by journalists, had initially led to believe.[12] In Nord-Pas-de-Calais and Picardie, the most stricken regions of the Hexagon, the young rioters were more often the children and grandchildren of unemployed workers of French descent rather than young immigrants.[13] Furthermore, it is worth noting that the majority of these young immigrants ('second generation') were fully-fledged French citizens. Less than 10 percent of those arrested within the context of the riots appeared to be foreign citizens.[14] These facts, therefore, put into perspective the relevance of the analysis of those who only view the riots as the pure product of foreign criminals seeking to preserve their zones of influence. However, as we will see in more detail below, it is only one of several interpretations that have dominated the debate.

In our opinion, it must first be said that there is nothing surprising about the ongoing eruption of violence. Anyone familiar with the then controversial movie *La Haine* (released in 1995 and directed by Mathieu Kassovitz) would say that what is most surprising is the fact that widespread riots did not erupt before. In a way, on a smaller scale, they have been a typical occurrence in the *banlieues* since the 1980s. For instance, Strasbourg has now the dubious distinction of being well known for its New Year's Eve tradition of burning more cars than the year before to attract media attention for a few minutes. Irrespective of the exact reasons that caused the riots, it has been widely claimed – especially in the English-speaking media – that the riots represent the failure of the French republican model of integration.[15] We believe this diagnosis to be wrong. Our view is that, on the contrary, these riots should be interpreted as the manifest evidence that most of the frustrated young men feel entirely French and that they simply want to be accepted by the nation and, more prosaically, to be part of a modern consumerist society. Their frustration and anger is comprehensible when faced with the unfulfilled promise of socio-economic integration. In other words, the urban riots of November 2005, paradoxically, reveal on the one hand the success of the French republican model when it comes to teaching shared values and history, but on the other hand the failure of both the state, which has failed to translate into public policies the values it officially preaches, and the politico-administrative elites who are always keen to stress the benefits of 'republican' principles while delivering little when it comes to opening up access to key positions of power.

The clash of interpretations

'Why is France the only state in the European Union that is shaken ... by urban violence when the countries that surround us also have their underprivileged areas, their integration difficulties, their zones of exclusion and instability?', wondered the communist mayor of the town of Stains.[16] All types of arguments have been put forward: the ill-considered architecture and town planning layouts having led to a real human pileup; the unspoken convergence between social conflict and racial conflict (or ethnic, the terms varies according to the analysts); a police force that has become gradually out of touch with the population, or even the symbolic weight of the state and the republican idea that struggle, in fact, to fulfil their promises.[17] All in all, many wonder about the meaning of this explosion of violence. Why do youths from the suburbs engage in such acts of vandalism? What exactly do they want?

An illuminating study, carried out by a team of sociologists on the riots, which took place in the town of Aulnay-sous-Bois, confirms the plurality and diversity of the reasons for the November riots of 2005. It lists in descending order the following key reasons put forward by the young people involved in the riots:

- The desire to obtain recognition, in making their profound malaise known in the public space;
- The need to express their anger following the death of the two youths from Clichy-sous-Bois;
- The opposition to the Minister of the Interior and his declarations as well as police forces in general;
- School and professional relegation and employment discrimination;
- An opportunity to 'have fun';
- Peer-pressure;
- The pride felt in confronting the police;
- The breaking of the law and the increased prestige one could obtain from his or her peers;
- Competition between the estates with a view to obtaining a hypothetical first place in the media ranking of the most violent cities and a similar wish to have one's estate talked about on evening television.[18]

Beyond this great diversity of the reasons explaining a strong participation in the riots, reasons which can also greatly vary according to the town in question, it appears to us that the main problem resides in the fact that real political demands were unable to emerge from this rather disorganized wave of violence. But there is nothing surprising here insofar as the youths of deprived estates have become used to seeing violence as the only effective means of expressing themselves and, above all, of making themselves heard by the authorities. In any case, this violence fits only one catalyst: the anger about the Clichy-sous-Bois events. This anger was then clearly aggravated by Nicolas Sarkozy's statements.

An important matter is that of the singularity of the 2005 episode from a historical point of view. An analysis can be undertaken, for example, on the basis of the distinction between emotion and passion,[19] between *state violence* and *popular revolt*.[20] The 2005 riots were described by the entire media and political class as acts of urban violence, thus placing it in a more reduced historicity, dating back to the first urban outbursts in France, in Vénissieux or Vaulx en Velin at the end of the 1970s, then in les Minguettes (Lyon) in 1981. One must admit that these outbursts of violence have become almost a banal phenomenon in French society for nearly 30 years.[21] This phenomenon has, moreover, been inclined to gather pace since the revival of the riots in Vaulx en Velin in 1990. Since then, the list of towns affected has constantly grown longer: for instance, Mantes-La-Jolie and Sartrouville in 1991; the eighteenth district of Paris in 1993; Nanterre in 1995, Châteauroux in 1996; Dammaries-lès-Lys in 1997; le Mirail in Toulouse in 1998; Vauvert dans le Gard in 1999; Grigny, Corbeil-Essonnes and Lille in 2000; Metz and Vitry-sur-Seine in 2001; les Yvelines and Strasbourg in 2002, Nîmes in 2003.

However, it should be noted that the autumn riots of 2005, if they take place in the line of these recurring forms of urban flare-ups, differ on two points: their scale and duration. To that extent, the events of November 2005 constitute a relatively new social departure. The quest for meaning is not, however, neutral.[22] Defining a social situation, indeed, allows meaning to be given to the actions undertaken, whether the latter is directed towards protest or defence of the established order. It enables a certain form of intellectualization of the practice while obtaining a rational legitimacy for the collective and individual actions.[23] Thus, the events of 2005 have gone beyond the physical struggle in the public space to become the subject of symbolic struggles in the media space and more widely in the political space. Gérard Mauger judiciously described these symbolic struggles as 'the paper riot', thus rightly underlining that 'the conflicts of interpretation which were built up around the riots of November 2005 aimed to impose a legitimate definition (i.e. recognized if not by all, then at least by the great majority of people) of the riot and the rioter: the most gratifying as possible for some people, the most stigmatising for other people'.[24] Henceforth, it is this debate that we would hope to explore, through the analysis of four figures of rioters who confronted each other in the public space, in order to elucidate the events of November 2005.[25] It is important here to note that we find the first two figures to be remarkably simplistic and indeed inaccurate.

The Islamists

Certain media and commentators favoured the reference to 'Islamic groups'. In our view, this interpretation appears to partake in the political disqualification of the events of November 2005. To quote the philosopher Alain Finkielkrault: 'One would really like to reduce the suburban riots to their social dimension and see it as a youth revolt against discrimination and unemployment. The problem is that the majority of these youths are black or Arab and identify themselves with Islam. In France, there are other emigrants, Chinese, Vietnamese and Portuguese, who are having difficulties and they don't take part in the riots. Therefore, it is clear that we are faced with an ethnic-religious type revolt'.[26] Following such an analytical perspective, France would be plagued by a 'multiethnic Intifada'[27] as a result of the rise of communitarianism that is reinforced by multicultural discourse. The explosion of a tear-gas grenade close to the Bilal mosque, on 30 October, unfortunately made this argument more credible. In lumping Islamism and urban violence together, one resorts to a symbolic terminology with strong connotations in France, which was bound to strike the imagination in a context where the far right was on the rise.

Such a discourse was favoured by the English-speaking media for whom the rioters should be referred to as 'Muslims'.[28] Examples of this thoughtless and implicitly xenophobic tendency could easily be multiplied. But we will simply cite here the deplorable example of *Fox News*. Journalists on temporary assignments in France were especially criticized by the youths involved in the violence. In their view, the media broadcasted misleading, exaggerated images that gave the impression of being in the Bronx, in Baghdad or in Sarajevo. A report mentions the case of Moktar Farad who was requested to say in an interview conducted on *Fox*, by a journalist who had just returned from Iraq, that Muslims were to blame. The terrorist attacks in America in September 2001 and the 'war on terror' explain, but do not justify, the simplistic analytical perspective and ideological bias of some news outlets.[29] However, if one can state that there was a strong leaning towards simplistic analysis and bias in the English-speaking media's coverage of the riots, it is important to highlight a few examples of resistance against the widespread inclination to lump the rioters and Muslims together. As the editorial of *The Washington Post* asserted: 'France's upheaval is too important to be explained away by any single factor. And it is too important to be treated as a matter of satisfaction by Americans irritated by the French, on foreign policy or other grounds'.[30] The European editor of *The Observer* pointed out that 'analysts and commentators often seek to find evidence to support their well-established ideas in any given event'.[31] A columnist from *The Times* was more unequivocal: 'I do not try to believe things for which there is no evidence'.[32]

As regards to the key issue of 'evidence', it must be strongly emphasized that in no way did we know in November 2005 the religious beliefs or practices of the young persons involved in the unrest. If some of the rioters did possibly identify themselves as Muslims, it was more than likely 'a consequence of an ethnic solidarity maintained or preserved by the socio-economic conditions of segregation'.[33] In any case, we strongly believe, as emphasized by the authors of a report on equal opportunities, that 'referring to the North African (*Maghrébin*) by the term *"Muslim"* creates a new stigmatization when the overwhelming majority of North Africans in France do not practise Islam, even if the attachment to Muslim culture can find expression in the respect of certain rites and symbols such as eating Halal meat or respecting the period of Ramadan'.[34] Therefore, it seems unacceptable to us to designate each French citizen of North African descent as a Muslim as this practice denies them their freedom to not be defined by their religious practice.[35] In any case, it does not actually matter since it has been clearly demonstrated that the riots had absolutely nothing to do with religious freedom or about the place of Islam in the French society. In the same vein, to see the hands of Al-Quaeda in these tragic events simply revealed a very lively imagination.

Yet, the return of these themes of insecurity and Muslim fundamentalism were tempting from a political point of view. In claiming to be a defender of republican order, Minister Sarkozy could, indeed, build up some precious political capital, all the more so as the 2007 presidential election was looming. 'We will no longer tolerate no-go areas, where organized crime and mafia trafficking reign and where honest people are forced to keep quiet and lower their eyes...The police are the police of the Republic. They maintain republican order. If they didn't, what order would succeed it? That of the mafia or fundamentalists',[36] he asserted publicly. While no one objects to the rule of law and the maintenance of public order, it remains that radical Islamism did not play any role in the riots. On the contrary, these riots seem to show that Muslim religious institutions had very little control or influence on the youths involved in the riots.[37]

The 'natives' of the republic in conflict with neo-colonialism

Applying a neo-colonialist analytical framework to the unrest in the suburbs obviously contradicts the ethnic-religious (fundamentalists) reading of the events by putting the blame this time on the republic, which is accused of reproducing within its metropolitan territory a colonial conception of the social relations that it practiced long ago overseas, notably in Africa. These natives[38] of the republic would be nothing less than the contemporary figures of *the damned of the earth*,[39] victims of an 'interior colonization' that puts them under house arrest in their peripheral ghettos. This eminently political reading of the events of November 2005 results in the condemnation of a type of state racism[40] that can be detected by a generally stigmatising governmental discourse and is allegedly visible in the police's harassing behaviour when it comes to random checks of identification.[41] One should also mention that there was the strong symbolic power associated with the recourse to 3 April 1955 law in order to impose a state of emergency. The restoration of this law has been viewed as a reflection of the French government's 'colonial mentality'.[42] This colonial law was indeed historically adopted at the start of the Algerian War to quell the national liberation movement. It was used twice: in 1961 against the Algerian demonstrators and in 1984 against the local separatists in New Caledonia. The obvious irony has not been lost. The 1955 law was aimed 50 years ago at the grandparents of some of the current rioters.

In light of an allegedly unjustified police intervention, the accidental death of two French youths of African origin, the denial of the police authorities' responsibility as well as the introduction of repressive measures from the colonial legacy, some commentators rapidly stress the validity of this neo-colonial reading of the urban riots. Although it is not our intention to deny the importance of taking into account the appropriate historical background in order to understand better the riots of 2005, we do not believe in the relevance of analyses that emphasize the community drift in France,[43] a drift that would be based on historical or cultural factors. We are of the view that the most appropriate analytical framework is the one that takes fully into account the broader French socioeconomical context. But first, we should examine another popular figure in the media: that of the young offender.

The young offenders

Another popular interpretation, no doubt because the media love Manichean explanations, is based on the criminalization of the riots. According to this reading, the young perpetrators should merely be seen as regular offenders. This was, for instance, the position of the minister of the interior and his political entourage. In a speech before the French National Assembly, Nicolas Sarkozy argued that the central factor of these revolts resides in 'the willingness of those who have made crime their main activity to fight against the Republic's ambition of reinstating law and order in its territory'.[44] He further suggested that 75 to 80 percent of the rioters were known to the police for previous criminal acts.[45] The minister went as far as to make the themes of crime and insecurity the source of all the *quartiers difficiles'* problems: 'The main cause of unemployment, despair, and violence in the suburbs is neither discrimination nor the failure of schools. The main cause of despair in the neighbourhoods is drug trafficking, gang rule, the dictatorship of fear and the resignation of the Republic'.[46]

From this point of view, the events of November 2005 are deprived of all political significance. They are only large-scale echoes of acts of crime and spontaneous violence that punctuate periodically French current affairs. Such an analysis justifies strong measures to restore republican authority and order. That is how the then French president, Jacques Chirac, came to announce at the end of a special meeting of the Council of Interior Security, which brought together the ministers concerned by problems of law and order: 'the law must have the last word' and 'the Republic is naturally determined to be stronger than those who wish to spread violence and fear'.[47] The prime minister, Dominique de Villepin, intended, for his part, to fight against the no-go areas and reinforced the security operation by declaring a state of emergency on 7 November. The law on the state of emergency of 1955 authorizes the introduction of a curfew, which allows the closure of meeting places like cafés and theatres in 25 departments and empowers the police chiefs to expel foreigners taken in for questioning within the context of this urban violence. The following night was the most violent of all that period.

According to the available figures, this interpretation is not based on facts. In other words, the violent acts committed in November 2005 are not, in most cases, characteristic of young offenders.[48] This diagnosis is, moreover, shared by a governmental think-tank for which 'one cannot describe the people concerned as being deeply engaged in crime'.[49] If we are to subscribe to this diagnosis, it is worth mentioning that the lack of formal criminal records does not mean that we are dealing here with angels. It is not rare for a minor to escape formal sentencing by a court even though the police may have arrested him or her for a minor criminal infraction. Thus, one can be known to the police without having been formally subject to a criminal sentence. However, it remains that the criminal figure of 75 percent seems greatly exaggerated. As for the argument that criminals come from polygamous families, the numbers once again contradict the relevance of this view. For example, more than half of the people brought in for questioning by the police in Seine-Saint-Denis and brought to the Bobigny court come from traditional families, more than 30 percent from single-parent families, nearly 10 percent from reconstituted families and only 3 percent live in polygamous families.[50] What seems more important to us is the fact that these youths often come from large families (on average more than five children) and live in homes marked by insecurity as regards both to employment and housing. These findings also allow us to observe that the explanation that underlines France's colonial background cannot offer a fully satisfactory analytical framework.

The young unemployed rebels

According to this last interpretation, the socioeconomic profile of the young rioters is a key explanatory factor. It is especially important to stress that the proportion of youths over the age of 15 without any kind of school degree or diploma is 50 percent higher in the so-called Urban Sensitive Zones (*Zones Urbaines Sensibles or ZUS*) than in the average urban areas.[51] Unemployment is also 80 percent higher there, and it is obvious that these zones are being transformed into ghettos due to the combination of mass unemployment, residential immobility and discrimination towards '*visible*' minorities, factors that tend to force this population with little resources to reside there and to explain the departure of those who have the means to leave.[52] Furthermore, it is also important to note that children of North African immigrants as well as black people who have the same qualifications as the rest of the population incur a higher risk of unemployment: 'With degrees or the same qualifications, they are on average twice as likely to be unemployed. And one young graduate in two '*stemming from immigration*' finds that he/she is '*downgraded*' to a non-managerial position compared with the national average of one in five'.[53] One may also remark that the endogenous reproduction of French elites is easily shown by the fact that North Africans as well as black people – like children from underprivileged social classes for that matter – are 'almost invisible in the running of businesses, in institutions, intermediary branches, on the television and in the political sphere' and 'are also widely underrepresented in the civil service and in high profile (media) positions'.[54]

According to several sociologists, burning cars has become 'a banal type of expression in working-class areas'.[55] For a good number of young inhabitants from these impoverished suburbs, plagued by failure to obtain a degree and familial dereliction due to unemployment and poverty, the world of gangs and violent street culture may prove to be a tempting way to gain a sense of identity and a social status.[56] For some analysts, burning schools should be understood as the expression of a feeling of anger and frustration towards an educational system that failed them when it should have normally helped them get a good education and a job. As far as they are concerned, the 'system' has not really kept its promises. As other sociologists see it, the attack on cars incarnates a radical critique of consumer society,[57] and the attack on public transport represents a willingness to denounce the ghettoization and spatial compartmentalization of working-class people in peripheral urban areas.[58] All in all, in attacking state symbols – a phenomenon nearly banal in itself since the end of the 1980s – the rioters of 2005 would have shown that their violent acts are directed at the 'institutions'. Therefore, their gesture had, from this point of view, political connotations.[59] The violence can be interpreted as a readiness to show their presence in the public space in order to condemn how they were the victims of a denial of equality or even dignity.[60]

Beyond this demand to be heard and respected, the youths from the *'quartiers difficiles'* clearly suffer from the fact that they cannot easily find work or that they are subjected to discriminatory practices. Numerous studies and reports have documented, in particular, the reality of these practices. Thus, to cite only one example, *la Halde*[61] has received an average of ten complaints per day since the beginning of 2006. Two elements emerge very clearly from the list of complaints forwarded to it: discriminatory practices at the workplace are the principal subject of concern (about 45 percent) followed by discriminatory behaviours based on the 'origin' of the complainants (about 40 percent). But unemployment is only one facet of the problem that hits essentially the less qualified. One should also criticize the 'closed-in' nature of the French elites. Yazid Sabeg, doctor of economic science, company director and president of the 'Equal Opportunities' working group in the Montaigne Institute, notes, in an anecdotal but unfortunately revealing way, that a 'third generation of North Africans are old enough to work and I am still one of the very few North Africans to hold an important post in the French economic scene. Is it normal that my career should be constantly viewed as exceptional?'[62] It is also true that France, known for being slow as regards to women's access to electoral mandates, is worse still when it comes to minorities participating in the country's future. Although minorities account for about 12 percent of its population, only two of the 555 members of the lower house elected in metropolitan (non-overseas) France represent the country's blacks, Asians and North Africans. If one very much wishes to salute President Sarkozy's appointments to the French government of people such as Rachida Dati, minister of justice, Rama Yade, state secretary of foreign affairs and human rights, and Fadela Amara, state secretary in charge of urban policy, it is tempting to not see the phenomenon as a case of 'you can't see the wood for the trees'. If a clearly defined public policy of diversity is not implemented and mechanisms that allow for action on the severe causes of the phenomenon of low representation are not used, it is probable that we will constantly have to regret the lack of progress in this domain.

The practical shortcomings of the republican model

In this final part, the political dimension (or lack thereof) of the riots will be questioned. It will be argued, in line with the sociologist Gérard Mauger, that the riots should be understood as a 'proto-political' revolt, that is a collective revolt against state violence that lacked any form of collective organization and whose members were not politicized,[63] which has clearly revealed the striking gap between the noble ideology and the practical shortcomings of the so-called republican model and its emphasis on abstract equality.

According to police and intelligence reports, the vast majority of people brought in for questioning had no violent past, and Islamic groups had almost no involvement in the events:[64] 'It seems, in fact, that the rioters came first and foremost from working-class families, mostly immigrant, but also made vulnerable and impoverished by mass unemployment and insecurity. Those who were lacking in familial, school, career and thus, economic resources were also the favourite target of police harassment'.[65] However, for a number of experts, the audiovisual media, caught up in a logic of exhibitionism for the sake of an increased audience, played an important role in the national spreading of violence in two ways. First of all, in publicising and broadcasting a repertoire of action, they provided examples for future rioters lacking in inspiration. Then, in updating everyday a map of the cities that were engaged in the violence, they created a vicious circle with groups from different towns trying to outdo each other. Yet, one must also look beyond the influence of the traditional media to that of the new media such as the internet and mobile phones. The youths availed of these new 'tools and networks to coordinate with one another, exchange opinions and information, and to circulate calls to action'.[66] Blogs also challenged the control of information by journalists and politicians in allowing the audience to express their opinions in an unedited and uncensored manner. Several bloggers were actually arrested by the French police for inciting violence. Sarkozy recognized the power of this new media by taking out 'ads in Google to push his agenda'[67] and by agreeing to do a podcast interview.[68]

The political dimension of the events of November 2005, however, confronts us with a problem. For some, the riots should be understood as a real uprising rather than as ordinary riots,[69] on the basis of which the youths from the French suburbs would have brought politics into the arena, something that had been in practice denied to them, even though the themes of violence and insecurity, tied to the issues of immigration and the republican model, place them at the heart of French political discourse for more than 20 years. In other words, by resorting to mass violence, which was given a lot of media coverage and which seemed like the only course of action within their reach to draw attention to their social situation, 'they entered into politics, even those who supposedly don't vote and who lose interest in all things political'.[70] However, an important difference appears if one compares urban violence at the start of the 1980s to what has been taking place since the start of the 1990s. The former found expression in political demands that was not really the case after the 1990s. It should indeed be highlighted that the riots in *l'Est lyonnais* at the start of the 1980s were set in a climate in which the National Front was rising in power. In such a context, a quadruple murder with racist connotations in October 1982 followed by a police search was going to lead to clashes with the police in the *Minguettes* district in Lyon. The youths from the housing estates then developed a strategic course of action that led them to invest in the political arena. Police violence was met with a hunger strike, then, in October 1982, a group was created for the development of civil rights. This led to the so-called Walk for Equality the following year, which left Marseilles on 15 October 1983 and arrived in Paris on 3 December, greeted by more than 100,000 people. In the wake of this massive social turnout, a series of cultural and political associations (*SOS Racisme, France Plus, Convergence 1984*) were formed and gradually drew closer to the traditional political parties, particularly those on the left.[71]

Nothing like that happened in 2005. A few, of course, like the group *Devoirs de mémoires* which was sponsored by public personalities from the world of sport, music and cinema,[72] intervened to invite young people to play the electoral game by first registering and then voting in the presidential elections. Others, like the group *AC-Lefeu*, organized a French tour of the neighbourhoods to compile a list of grievances (*cahiers de doléances* – an obvious reference to the lists of grievances written by each major social group in the spring of 1789) which they then delivered to the National Assembly.[73] But these initiatives did not have any major and lasting impact. It may be that the political context has changed profoundly in the past two to three decades and that the focus on questions of national identity and public order leaves little room for debating the social ills of French citizens of foreign origin. Instead of discussing class struggle, the media and politicians favour discussing a possible clash of cultures. Similarly, the social question, which is centred on the problem of inequalities, is supplanted, in part, by the national question and the challenge of integration. This swing is particularly obvious when one observes the evolution of the French Communist Party (*Parti communiste français* or PCF). The PCF has continued to decline in the last quarter of the century and has been unable to 'politicize' youths from the troubled suburbs. This abandonment has also compounded the 'absence of formal representation within the French political structure' which has accompanied the 'gradual demise of the manufacturing industries'.[74] The PCF's electorate, traditionally established in the labouring classes, has been gradually moving from the far left to the far right of the French political scene,[75] to such an extent that the National Front became France's leading workers' party during the presidential election of 1995.[76] One should also obviously mention the 2002 presidential elections when, against all expectations, the far right candidate, Jean-Marie Le Pen, won nearly 17 percent of the vote, thus working his way to the second round of the election, behind Jacques Chirac (about 20 percent), the outgoing president of the republic, but in front of the socialist Lionel Jospin (about 16 percent), head of the government since 1997.

Since this infamous episode, the public debate seems to concentrate on the unruly suburbs and on the lack of integration caused by rigidities of an ethnic-religious nature. Furthermore, the mainstream political parties seem unable to attract or promote 'representative' youths. These factors would seem to explain why the acts of urban violence have yet to be translated into political actions and new public policies. In other words, what seems to be lacking today is not the political content and the political meaning of the events of November 2005, but rather the existence of a transfer mechanism that would allow a transformation of the public discourse on the suburbs' social and human problems. As Gérard Noiriel underlines: 'The second Italian generation identified with the working-class in the fifties and sixties, because the workers' movement at that time was strong enough to impose in the public space class criteria which the right and the employers had sought constantly to marginalize in favour of ethnic, religious or other kind of criteria. Today, working-class organizations are too weak to impose in the public space the social criteria with which the children and grandchildren of immigrants could identify themselves as well as in the past'.[77]

We are, therefore, dealing with a profound adjustment deficit in the frameworks of analysis,[78] not only with respect to the events of November 2005, but more generally as regards to the social situation of the French suburbs. On the one hand, this leads to a public debate dominated by questions of public order, and on the other, to a culturalisation of political and social conflicts, which is noticeable both in the discourse that condemns riots and in the rise of identity movements within anti-establishment social groups.[79] Whatever the style of action used, the violence or the condemnation of the colonial republic, French society is allegedly plagued by a logic of confrontation that could only lead to the fragmentation of the French political community of citizens[80] and the marginalization of the *République*'s egalitarian ideals. Left to themselves and held responsible for their own situation, deprived of organic intellectuals – as theorized by Gramsci – capable of giving meaning to their actions and merging them in a real social movement, the youths from the suburbs have violently expressed their rage.[81] With these destructive acts, this new 'flower of the proletariat' – to paraphrase Bakunin – has revealed the contradiction between the promises of the so-called republican model and the actions of the state and the ruling elites.

The republican model put to the test

Article 1 of the 1958 French Constitution perfectly sums up the essence of the French republican model of abstract equality: 'France shall be an indivisible, secular…Republic. It shall ensure the equality of all citizens before the law, without distinction of origin, race or religion'.[82] Accordingly, from a formal and legal perspective, there are no 'minorities' in France. Indeed, since 1789, the republic has always envisioned the unity of its citizens as 'without distinction of origin, race or religion'. Consequently, the legislator has always refused to recognize rights for groups that are formed on the basis of a community of common origin, belief, culture and language. In France, there is but one abstract community, that of its citizens. This conception has decisive practical consequences as it does forbid, legally speaking, any policy of affirmative action as long as it is based on a criterion prohibited by the constitution.[83] It similarly excludes any data collection stressing the origin, race or religion of the individuals concerned.[84] As a matter of principle, we see nothing wrong in the premises upon which the French integrationist model is based. Understandably, the rigid features of the French approach often astonish foreign observers. One should concede that in practice, it has important shortcomings. It does not perfectly allow French society to understand the specific problems faced by immigrants or the generation of people born in France of foreign parents. Yet, we would argue, that the fundamental problem is not the French model *per se* but rather the striking contrast that the French of Arab or African descent experience between the abstract principles officially proclaimed and what they endure in their daily lives.[85] For instance, the huge body of anti-discrimination law too often appears toothless or not rigidly enforced.[86] This is the crux of the matter, and this is not the first time France is faced with its own contradictions. Back in the times of the colonial empire, the public authorities used to teach the people submitted by force to French rule the merits of the Declaration of Human Rights of 1789 while denying their humanity.

Rather than seeking to blame the French integrationist model as most foreign media did in November 2005, our view is that, on the contrary, these riots should paradoxically be interpreted as evidence that the model has worked to a certain extent. Indeed, the following point must be stressed: it is because most French of Arab or African origin have believed in the idea of integration or assimilation that some are now tempted by nihilist attitudes. In other words, their frustration and anger is comprehensible when faced with the unfulfilled promises of social and economic integration.[87] Therefore, and contrary to what many 'multiculturalists' have argued, most rioters do not express their hate of France or demand 'cultural' rights for their 'communities'. Their frustration is huge because they feel that the efforts they have made have not been rewarded. Instead of promoting the vague notion of multiculturalism, the obvious long-term solutions would certainly be to create more jobs[88] and to face the failures of anti-discrimination policies. Even if one can legitimately cherish the republican model based on individual merit and abstract equality, more pragmatism and less ideology is today needed. As Azouz Begag, the then Minister for Equal Opportunities, put it in a radio interview at the time of the riots, 'the time for "blah blah blah" is past'.[89] More ambitious corrective measures should be taken in order to improve access to education and access to the civil service for those living in the *banlieues*. Another balance has also to be struck between prevention and repression. Police intervention has to be redefined, and the harassing of youth through checks of identification ought to be stopped. Yet, it is also decisive that police forces do not see their work annihilated by a deficient criminal system, freeing the same juvenile delinquents over and over. Political correctness and rigid republican ideology are still obstacles to a genuine debate on social justice, discrimination and criminality. Unfortunately, it is the far right that has always benefited from the unwillingness of our unprincipled leaders and embedded journalists to address poverty and racism in French society as well as from the overrepresentation of individuals of foreign origin in crime statistics.

As a final point, it appears important to place the riots in the larger context of a deeply frustrated and demoralized nation, frustrated by the inability of the elites to successfully manage the economy and fearful of its destiny in a globalized world.[90] In a famous study, *La société bloquée*, complemented with another powerful book, *La crise de l'intelligence*, Michel Crozier offered what may still be the best analysis of a country unable to reform itself.[91] At whose door should we lay the blame? For all intents and purposes, the responsibility of dysfunctional institutions and self-reproductive elites is tremendous. French society in its cultural and social diversity is simply not represented by Parliament. What is worse, the only chance to make it in this world (either at the higher civil service level or in the media) has more to do with genes rather than merits. The upper class has simply used the republican ideology as a protective shield to preserve its privileges through hidden networks of power and influence. As Ezra Suleiman points out: 'All end up closing ranks to defend an ideal, but also to defend their own positions'.[92] In proclaiming their despair to the whole republic, the youths from the euphemistically called '*quartiers difficiles*' have left the field wide open for possibilities, thus giving free rein to all sorts of reinterpretations and takeovers. Henceforth, it is up to political actors to do their share, to choose continuity with security withdrawal, communitarianism and racism, or to work towards reducing the gap between the haves and the have nots[93] and creating a more just and equal society. The unfortunate aspect of the last urban riots, however, is that rather than bringing together the people suffering from dramatic socioeconomic conditions, it has incited unscrupulous politicians to play a category of unemployed poor against another. What is ultimately needed is for the elites to get rid of a significant part of the privileges they have accumulated to the detriment of the public good and to favour action over spin.[94] We should rediscover the spirit of 1789. If not, some may eventually want to rediscover the letter of it with its bloody overtones.

Notes

1. Y. Sabeg and L. Méhaignerie, *Les oubliés de l'égalité des chances. Participation, pluralité, assimilation... ou repli?*, Rapport de l'Institut Montaigne, January 2004 (2005), p. 25. All translations are ours unless otherwise indicated.
2. While it is not our intention to justify the use of this word, it is important to note that Nicolas Sarkozy spoke in June 2005 following the death of an 11-year-old child, killed by two stray bullets during a shooting exchange between two rival groups, in the '*cité des 4000*' in the town of Courneuve. He subsequently described certain young people as '*racailles*' on 25 October 2005 during a visit to the infamous paving stone of Argenteuil, as a reply – therein lies its importance – to a tenant's question. It seems, therefore, necessary to exclude any premeditation. However, most well-intentioned commentators agreed to view this utterance as outrageous and enough of an excuse to incite more violence. Yet, this very word is used daily by people living in the poor neighbourhoods to describe the criminal youth. It does not imply that the utterance was a smart and dignified move but again, to accuse Sarkozy of racism was and still is singularly misplaced as he has constantly advocated the cause of (legal) immigrants, for instance, by defending, and against the dominant opinion, affirmative action and by arguing in favour of granting them the right to vote at the local level.
3. See Laurent Mucchielli, 'Les émeutes de novembre 2005 : les raisons de la colère', in *Quand les banlieues brûlent... Retour sur les émeutes de novembre 2005*, ed. Véronique Le Goaziou and Laurent Mucchielli (Paris, 2006), pp. 13–16.
4. Legally speaking, the penal code is not acquainted with an 'urban violence' or 'urban riot' offence. The riots or urban acts of violence are indeed protean. Thus, the majority of official reports on the violent acts committed from 29 October to 14 November 2005 have decided to include various offences (for instance, crimes or

offences committed against people who are agents of public authority, at a meeting or acts of destruction committed on property in certain specific areas).

5. Thus, in spite of the turmoil provoked by these events, which was echoed in the international press, these riots did not have much in common with the 54 deaths of the Los Angeles riots in 1992.
6. 'Le bilan chiffré de la crise des banlieues', *Le Monde*, 2 December 2005.
7. Fabien Jobart, 'Les émeutes urbaines : anatomie d'une crise', in *Universalia 2006*, Encyclopaedia Universalis, pp. 189–91.
8. Alèssi Dell'Umbria, *C'est de la racaille ? Eh bien, j'en suis ! À propos de la révolte de l'automne 2005* (Paris, 2006).
9. Hugues Lagrange, 'Nuit de novembre 2005. Géographie des violences', *Esprit*, no. 320, December 2005.
10. Jobart, 'Les émeutes urbaines', p. 191.
11. Hugues Lagrange, 'Autopsie d'une vague d'émeutes', in *Émeutes urbaines et protestations. Une singularité française*, ed. Hugues Lagrange and Marco Oberti (Paris, 2006).
12. For example, Cécilia Gabizon, 'Davantage de Noirs chez les émeutiers', *Le Figaro*, 11 November 2005, p. 9.
13. Alexandre Piettre, 'Les grandes émotions de novembre 2005. Perspectives pour un résistible nouvel échec politique à gauche', *Mouvements*, no. 43, January–February 2006.
14. Olivier Roy, 'Intifada des quartiers ou émeutes de jeunes déclassés?', *Esprit*, no. 320, December 2005. This rough estimate is confirmed by an official report, which examined the situation of people handed over (115 in total) to be tried immediately in the jurisdiction of the courts of Bobigny for diverse criminal acts committed from 29 October to 14 November 2005. The conclusion is that the great majority of 'rioters' are French (82 percent of those handed over to the courts) and were born on the national territory. Cf. Centre d'analyse stratégique, *Le traitement judiciaire des violences urbaines : leçons d'une étude de cas*, La note de veille no. 16, 19 June 2006, p. 2.
15. See, for example, 'Integration Has To Be Voluntary', *The Guardian*, 6 November 2005; 'While Paris Burns', *The New York Times*, 8 November 2005.
16. Thomas Ferenczi, 'Désintégration sociale', *Le Monde*, 11 November 2005, p. 2.
17. For a critical introduction to these arguments, see Véronique Le Goaziou and Charles Rojzman, *Les banlieues* (Paris, 2006).
18. Centre d'analyse stratégique, *Enquêtes sur les violences urbaines. Comprendre les émeutes de novembre 2005 – L'exemple d'Aulnay-sous-bois*, November 2006, p. 43. Retrieved from www.strategie.gouv.fr.
19. Alain Dewerpe, *Charonne, 8 février 1962. Anthropologie historique d'un massacre d'État* (Paris, 2006).
20. For the history of working-class revolts, see among others Charles Tilly, *La France conteste de 1600 à nos jours* (Paris, 1986); Eric Hobsbawm, *Les primitifs de la révolte dans l'Europe moderne* (Paris, 1966); Georges Lefebvre, *La grande peur de 1789*, and from the same author, *Les foules révolutionnaires* (Paris, 1988); Louis Chevallier, *Classes laborieuses et classes dangereuses à Paris pendant la première moitié du 19ème siècle* (Paris, 1978).
21. See generally M. Wieviorka (ed.), *Violence en France* (Paris, 1999).
22. We draw our inspiration here from studies conducted on the notion of symbolic violence developed by Pierre Bourdieu and Jean-Claude Passeron in their book *La Reproduction: éléments d'une théorie du système d'enseignement* (Paris, 1970), and on

the concept of *knowledge/power couple* explored by Michel Foucault, *Surveiller et punir* (Paris, 1975).

23. Frame analysis was developed in the sociological field of collective action and social movements by authors such as Charles Tilly, Sidney Tarrow, David Snow and Robert Benford. It allowed the development of a cognitive approach to explain social movements.
24. Gérard Mauger, *L'émeute de novembre 2005. Une révolte protopolitique* (Paris, 2006), pp. 82–83.
25. We are here indebted to the analysis developed by Mauger, *L'émeute de novembre 2005*.
26. Alain Finkielkrault, Interview in the newspaper *Haaretz*, 18 November 2005. For a brief and insightful alternative view on the presence of Islam in the French riots, see Olivier Roy, 'The Nature of the French Riots', 18 November 2005. Retrieved from http://riotsfrance.ssrc.org/Roy.
27. Bruno Frappat, 'La France des bas-côtés', *La Croix*, 7 November 2005, p. 1.
28. Although we mostly agree with the analyses developed in the International Crisis Group's report, *La France face à ses musulmans: Emeutes, Jihadisme et dépolitization*, Europe Report no. 172, 9 March 2006 (available online at: www.crisisgroup.org), we must regret the use of the term Muslim to describe populations who in no way identify themselves as such and who remain very little concerned with religious practice.
29. Centre d'analyse stratégique, *Enquêtes sur les violences urbaines*, pp. 35–36.
30. Jim Hoagland, 'French Lessons', *The Washington Post*, 9 November 2005, Editorial, p. A31.
31. Jason Burke, 'Comment: France and the Muslim Myth: The French Riots Have Been a Godsend for Those Who Oppose Integration and Progress', *The Observer*, 13 November 2005, p. 29.
32. David Aaronovitch, 'It's the latest disease: sensible people saying ridiculous things about Islam', *The Times*, 15 November 2005, p. 19.
33. Jocelyne Cesari, 'Ethnicity, Islam and Les Banlieues: Confusing the Issues', Web forum organized by the Social Science Research Council, 30 November 2005, p. 7. Retrieved from http://riotsfrance.ssrc.org/Cesari. According to the author, the conflation of issues such as poverty, ethnicity and Islam 'both in current political discourse and in political practice' can be attributed to the deteriorating social and economic conditions in the suburbs since the eighties and the 'top-down decisions regarding the assignment of populations within the housing projects [HLM, Habitation à Loyer Modéré, low-income housing]' (pp. 1, 3).
34. Sabeg and Méhaignerie, *Les oubliés de l'égalité des chances*, p. 46.
35. This fatuous practice is favoured by most English media. To cite the deplorable example of *The Economist*, a magazine that proclaims its intellectual rigour, but which did not hesitate to describe the two young people electrocuted on the night of 27 October 2005 as being 'two local Muslim youths' and to also evoke the existence of 'heavily Muslim *banlieues*'. See 'Two Years On', 25 November 2007. The same magazine also regularly describes Rachida Dati, the minister of justice, as 'the most prominent Muslim minister' of the current French government. See 'Trouble in the Court of Sarkozy', 6 December 2007. Yet, to the best of our knowledge, Dati has never claimed to be of Muslim faith and, what is more, she was for a time educated in a Catholic school.

36. Nicolas Sarkozy, 'Notre stratégie est la bonne', *Le Monde*, 6–7 November 2005, p. 15.
37. Bernard E. Brown, 'God and Man in the French Riots', *American Foreign Policy Interests*, 29 (2007), p. 183. The author recounts how Muslim clerics 'tried to calm down the young rioters by chanting' on 27 October 2005 in Clichy-sous-Bois. The rioters and the onlookers took up the chant. This scene was witnessed on live television and seemed to symbolize that the republic 'was being defied by militant Islam' (p. 183). However, the author affirms that the chanting ('glorifying Allah') did not effect a change in the rioters' behaviour. They 'continued their rampage that night and every night for three weeks'. Thus, this incident did not reflect 'Islamic fervor' but rather the 'exact reverse' (p. 185). Yet, Michel Wieviorka declares that if 'there is a problem, it is not Islamic violence, but the fact that the French Republic is resting on the capacity of religious leaders to organize the peace and social calm in popular areas', in 'Violence in France'. Retrieved from http://riotsfrance.ssrc.org/Wieviorka/.
38. This term was to be taken up by the director Rachid Bouchareb in his 2006 film *Indigènes* which recounted the story of the 130,000 young men from the colonies who joined the French army to free the *mother country* from the Nazi enemy during the Second World War.
39. Frantz Fanon, *Les damnés de la terre* (Paris, 1961).
40. Some go on to condemn French society on the whole for its so-called racist attitude. This ludicrous interpretation is invalidated by the rate of mixed marriages in France. As a noteworthy report on equal opportunities underlines, 'the French marry their daughters to North Africans who are said, however, to be the target of a certain collective hostility. Indeed, a French person, who is abstractly hostile to groups of different customs, does not view the individual who comes from this group as really being a carrier of his native culture, and accepts him or her individually into his or her family. *There is the big French paradox: combining a high vote for the far right with an ethnic mix just as high* (our emphasis)'. Cf. Sabeg and Méhaignerie, *Les oubliés de l'égalité des chances*, p. 66.
41. If we believe that this problem is very much real, it is important, however, to stress that the problem is of a structural nature. A long quote from a report devoted to the riots in Saint-Denis offers a convincing explanation of the latter: 'The essential tools that the police have at their disposal are identity checks, that is, tools which systematically increase the tension instead of reducing it. We now have in France young policemen of whom an overwhelming majority come from a rural background, are under-trained, and land abruptly in areas where they know nothing about the people who live there. They are afraid of them and they lack the competence that allows them to build up a peaceful solidarity with them. So they resort to what they have been given: identity checks which, on top of that, are based on physical attributes. The result: they get stoned! One is, therefore, very much in a logic of ever-increasing violence or in a cycle of reciprocal provocations'. Cf. Centre d'analyse stratégique, *Enquêtes sur les violences urbaines*, p. 46. Retrieved from www.strategie.gouv.fr.
42. Karima Laachir, 'France's "Ethnic" Minorities and the Question of Exclusion', *Mediterranean Politics*, 12 (2007), p. 100. See also Paul A. Silverstein, 'Postcolonial Urban Apartheid', 11 June 2006. Retrieved from http://riotsfrance.ssrc.org/Silverstien_Tetreault/. He contends (p. 10) that the riots were mainly due to 'the structural conditions set in place by the simultaneous cutting of public funding

to the *cités* and a protracted "war on terror" applied to an internal, postcolonial, marginalized, and racially-othered population'.

43. We refer to this title of L. Wacquant's book, *Parias urbains. Ghetto, Banlieues, Etat* (Paris, 2006). It maintains, in particular, that deprived French suburbs must not be compared with American-style ghettos.

44. Speech made by Nicolas Sarkozy, Minister of the Interior, at the French National Assembly, 15 November 2005.

45. See the complete report of the first session of Tuesday 15 November 2005 on the National Assembly website: www.assemblee-nationale.fr.

46. Quoted in Philippe Ridet's, 'M. Sarkozy durcit son discours sur les banlieues', *Le Monde*, 22 November 2005. However, it is worth highlighting the following argument. The French education system assigns teachers to schools 'based on a point system'. Teachers with the most points usually choose to teach 'in elite schools in posh neighbourhoods of Paris. Thus, it is young, inexperienced teachers who are systematically placed in suburban schools. Moreover, these teachers often complain that the pedagogical training that they receive in universities does little to prepare them for the realities of disciplinary problems and unsupportive families in the Parisian suburbs'. Yvonne Yazbeck Haddad and Michael J. Balz, 'The October Riots in France: A Failed Immigration Policy or the Empire Strikes Back?', *International Migration*, 44 (2006), p. 28.

47. Déclaration de M. Jacques CHIRAC, Président de la République, *Sur la sécurité, faite à l'issue de la réunion du Conseil de Sécurité intérieure*, Paris, 6 novembre 2005. Retrieved from http://presidence-de-la-republique.fr/elysee/elysee.fr/francais_archives/interventions/discours_Et_declarations/2005/novembre/reunion_du_conseil_de_securite_interieure_declaration_du_president_de_la_republique_sur_la_securite.31848.html

48. The minors who were previously brought before a court of law only 'represent, in fact, a third (34%) of the whole group who were handed over to [the criminal court of] Bobigny following the riots', A. Delon and L. Mucchielli, 'Les mineurs émeutiers jugés à Bobigny', *Claris. La Revue*, 93 (October 2006), p. 9.

49. Centre d'analyse stratégique, *Le traitement judiciaire des violences urbaines*, p. 2.

50. Ibid.

51. In 2002, more than 5 million people resided in 750 ZUS.

52. Sabeg and Méhaignerie, *Les oubliés de l'égalité des chances*, p. 130. See also Cesari, 'Ethnicity, Islam and Les Banlieues', p. 2, for a concise account of the development of ghettos in France.

53. Ibid., p. 26. See also Alain Frickey (ed.), *Jeunes diplômés issus de l'immigration: insertion professionnelle ou discriminations?* (Paris, 2005). For another perspective, see Bernard Salanié, 'The Riots in France: An Economist's View', 11 June 2006. Retrieved from http://riotsfrance.ssrc.org/Salanie/. The author argues (p. 2) that the combination of a costly minimum wage and a 'rigid' education system 'that has not found a good way to accommodate the needs of the children of immigrants' is the 'main culprit' when it comes to the youth unemployment rate.

54. Sabeg and Méhaignerie, *Les oubliés de l'égalité des chances*, p. 27.

55. Mucchielli, 'Les émeutes de novembre 2005', p. 19.

56. Gérard Mauger, *Les bandes, le milieu et la bohème populaire. Études de sociologie de la déviance des jeunes des classes populaires, 1975–2005* (Paris, 2006).

57. François Athané, 'Ne laissons pas punir les pauvres', in Dossier IPAM, *Le soulèvement populaire des banlieues françaises d'octobre-novembre 2005*, dossier, 15 December 2005.

58. Alain Bertho, 'Nous n'avons vu que des ombres', *Mouvements*, no. 44, March–April 2006, pp. 26–30.
59. Lucienne Bui Trong, *Violences urbaines. Des vérités qui dérangent* (Paris, 2000).
60. Piettre, 'Les grandes émotions de novembre 2005'. See also the authors of the report on the Aulnay-sous-Bois riots who have emphasized that in spite of the diverse motivation of those involved in the riots, the young inhabitants from the disadvantaged urban areas all express a strong demand for recognition and the possibility of making themselves heard by the local authorities as well as by the national authorities. Cf. Centre d'analyse stratégique, *Enquêtes sur les violences urbaines*, p. 43.
61. The High Authority for the Combat against Discriminations and for Equality (*La Halde: La Haute Autorité de Lutte contre les Discriminations et pour l'Égalité*) is an independent administrative authority created by law no. 2004–1486 of 30 December 2004.
62. Sabeg and Méhaignerie, *Les oubliés de l'égalité des chances*, p. 9. However, there have been some signs of '*ouverture*' in one of France's most elite schools, *Sciences Po*, which 'began recruiting students [in 2001] directly from low-performing suburban schools in *zones d'éducation prioritaires* (ZEPs), [...] who [...] have enjoyed a large degree of success at the elite school'. Haddad and Balz, 'The October Riots in France', p. 28. ZEPs or 'Zones of Priority Education' were launched in 1982 to improve educational achievement in socially disadvantaged areas. Yet, rather than an *ad hoc* policy of poaching the best ZEP students, it would be preferable to implement clearly defined policies to guarantee a fair and equal access to French elite schools. It would be a disaster if the students from the ZEPs are used as an excuse for not reforming the whole system, therefore guaranteeing the educational privileges of the well-off.
63. Mauger, *L'émeute de novembre 2005*, pp. 148–49.
64. 'Le rapport explosif des Renseignements généraux', *Le Parisien*, 7 December 2005. See also Hugues Lagrange, 'Autopsie d'une vague d'émeutes', in *Émeutes urbaines et protestations. Une singularité française*, ed. Hugues Lagrange and Marco Oberti (Paris, 2006).
65. Mauger, *L'émeute de novembre 2005*, p. 70.
66. Adrienne Russell, 'Digital Communication Networks and the Journalistic Field: The 2005 French Riots', *Critical Studies in Media Communication*, 24 (2007), p. 286.
67. Jeff Jarvis, 'Chaos Spreads From the Web to the Streets: The French Riots Have Exposed How Little We Can Control New Media, as Both Sides of the Conflict Use the Web for Their Own Ends', *The Guardian*, 14 November 2005, p. 3.
68. Russell, 'Digital Communication Networks and the Journalistic Field', p. 292. Sarkozy was interviewed by Loïc Le Meur, whose personal weblog has been one of the most widely read blogs in France.
69. Mehdi Belhaj Kacem, *La psychose française. Les banlieues: le ban de la République* (Paris, 2006).
70. Françoise Blum, 'Ils sont entrés en politique', *Le Monde*, 11 November 2005.
71. Adil Jazouli, *L'action collective des jeunes maghrébins en France* (Paris, 1986). Cf. also from the same author, *Les années banlieue* (Paris, 1992).
72. Among others the actors Jean-Pierre Bacri and Djamel Debbouze, the rapper Joey Starr and the footballer Liliam Thuram. Cf. 'Premier rendez-vous entre le collectif Devoirs de mémoires et des jeunes à Clichy-sous-Bois', *Le Monde*, 20 December 2005. For more information on the group *Devoirs de Mémoires*, see http://collectifddm.free.fr/collectif.htm.
73. The group covered 120 towns, collecting more than 20,000 statements and propositions. Among the major concerns one may note employment; the end of

discriminations and exclusion; accommodation; a fair judicial system and some control over police practices; education; and professional guidance. A summary of the Lists of Grievances is available online at http://aclefeu.blogspot.com.

74. David Waddington, 'The Madness of the Mob? Explaining the "Irrationality" and Destructiveness of Crowd Violence', *Sociology Compass*, 2 (2008), p. 684.

75. Pascal Perrineau, *Le symptôme Le Pen : radiographie des électeurs du Front national* (Paris, 1997).

76. Pierre Bréchon, *La France aux urnes. Cinquante ans d'histoire électorale* (Paris, 1998).

77. Gérard Noiriel, 'Itinéraire d'un engagement dans l'histoire', Propos recueillis par S. Laacher et P. Simon, *Mouvements*, no. 45–46, May-June-July-August 2006, pp. 209–19.

78. On these concepts, François Chazel, 'Les ajustement cognitifs dans les mobilizations collectives: questions ouvertes et hypothèses', in *Cognition et Sciences sociales*, ed. R. Boudon, A. Bouvier and F. Chazel (Paris, 1997), p. 193.

79. See, for example, the diagnosis adopted by the *Mouvement des indigènes de la République* (http://www.indigenes-republique.org).

80. Dominique Schnapper, *La démocratie providentielle, Essai sur l'égalité contemporaine* (Paris, 2002).

81. François Dubet, *La galère: jeunes en survie* (Paris, 1987).

82. French Constitution of 4 October 1958. English translation available at: http://www. conseil-constitutionnel.fr/conseil-constitutionnel/english/constitution/constitution.25740.html.

83. For further references, see the special issue of the review *Pouvoirs* on the concept of '*discrimination positive*', no. 111, 2004.

84. One should mention, however, a 2007 bill which, for the first time, initially allowed researchers to collect 'ethnic statistics' with a view of producing studies measuring the 'diversity of origins, discrimination and integration' in France. Remarkably, as it shows the prevalence of the traditional republican ideology, the main anti-racism association criticized this provision on the ground that it would reinforce racist stereotypes and an ethnicist vision of French society. See Laetitia Van Eeckhout, 'Faux débat sur les statistiques ethniques', *Le Monde*, 14 November 2007. Unfortunately, but not surprisingly, the *Conseil constitutionnel*, France's constitutional court, later found this legislative provision to be not compatible with Article 1 of the French Constitution previously quoted, and therefore struck it down. See Laetitia Van Eeckhout, 'Données ethniques : perplexité après la décision du Conseil constitutionnel', *Le Monde*, 24 November 2007. In our view, the French court did not pay sufficient attention to a competing constitutional right, the freedom of scientific research.

85. For an instructive account of the contradiction between the traditional republican discourse and institutional practice, see Nacira Guénif-Souilamas (ed.), *La République mise à nu par son immigration* (Paris, 2006). This book underlines (p. 33), and we can only subscribe to its analysis, that the youths of foreign descent from the suburbs merely 'demand the rights proclaimed by the republican aristocracy who obtain its legitimacy from them, yet hope that they will not be carried out'.

86. For an overall account, cf. Sabeg and Méhaignerie, *Les oubliés de l'égalité des chances*.

87. On the failures of the French welfare state to remedy inequalities, see recently Timothy Smith, *La France injuste : 1975–2006 : pourquoi le modèle social français ne fonctionne plus* (Paris, 2006). In English, Timothy Smith, *France in Crisis, Welfare, Inequality, and Globalization since 1980* (Cambridge, 2004). The author notes in

particular that the majority of 'social' spending serves to strengthen existing inequalities.

88. Andrew Moravcsik, 'Europe will get it right', *Newsweek*, 26 December 2005–2 January 2006. The article places the riots in a European economic context. It argues – rightly in our view – that the French riots were driven by socioeconomic reasons and implies that Europe needs to improve its economic performance 'in order to produce more jobs' by streamlining the 'traditional social democratic welfare state' and making it more 'sustainable'.

89. Alex G. Hargreaves, 'An Emperor with No Clothers?', Web forum organized by the Social Science Research Council, 29 November 2005, available at: http://riotsfrance. ssrc.org/Hargreaves.

90. See, for example, the impressive sales of the so-called *declinist* literature and in particular of Nicolas Baverez's emblematic book *La France qui tombe: Un constat clinique du déclin français* (Paris, 2003).

91. Michel Crozier, *La société bloquée* (Paris, 1999); *La crise de l'intelligence. Essai sur l'impuissance des élites à se réformer* (Paris, 1995).

92. Ezra Suleiman, 'France: One and Divisible', 18 November 2005, forum organized by the Social Science Research Council, available at: http://riotsfrance.ssrc.org/ Suleiman/printable.html.

93. This was ironically the major theme of the 1995 presidential campaign after Jacques Chirac mentioned the existence of a worrying *'fracture sociale'* in France.

94. Every new government has promised a Marshall Plan for the poor suburbs since 1988 and the appointment of the first minister in charge of urban policy. But it is a case of *'plus ça change'*. Thus, the 2008 plan for the suburbs is a ridiculous jumble of backward-looking ideas without, moreover, any serious financial guarantee. Cf. Speech made by the President of the Republic: 'Une nouvelle politique pour les banlieues', Élysée Palace, 8 February 2008 (http://www.elysee.fr/elyseetheque/). For a report advocating a complete reform of the administrative and legal framework as regards urban policy, see The Revenue Court Report, 'La gestion des crédits d'intervention de l'État au titre de la politique de la ville', annexed to the Senate Information Report no. 71, session 2007–2008 (http://www.senat.fr/rap/r07–071/ r07–0711.pdf). It is worth noting that there have been 19 successive ministers in charge of urban policy in 17 years, hardly a guarantee of continuity and a sign of the importance attached to the subject.

Select Bibliography

Archer, John E. *Social Unrest and Popular Protest in England 1780–1840* (Cambridge, 2000).

Beik, William. *Urban Protest in Seventeenth-Century France: The Culture of Retribution* (Cambridge, 1997).

Bercé, Yves-Marie. *History of Peasant Revolts: The Social Origins of Rebellion in Early Modern France*, trans. Amanda Whitmore (Ithaca, 1990).

Bohstedt, John. *The Politics of Provisions: Food Riots, Moral Economy, and Market Transition in England, c. 1550–1850* (Aldershot, 2010).

Bohstedt, John. *Riots and Community Politics in England and Wales 1790–1810* (Cambridge, MA, 1983).

Charlesworth, A. (ed.), *An Atlas of Rural Protest in Britain 1548–1900* (London, 1983).

Cobb, R. *The Police and the People: French Popular Protest 1789–1820* (Oxford, 1970).

Harris, T. *London Crowds in the Reign of Charles II: Propaganda and Politics from the Restoration until the Exclusion Crisis* (Cambridge, 1987).

Harrison, Mark. *Crowds and History: Mass Phenomena in English Towns, 1790–1835* (Cambridge, 1988).

Haywood, Ian, and Seed, David. (eds.), *The Gordon Riots: Politics, Culture and Insurrection in Late Eighteenth-Century Britain* (Cambridge, 2012).

Hilton, R. *Bond Men Made Free: Medieval Peasant Movements and the English Rising of 1381* (London, 1993).

Manning, R.B. *Village Revolts: Social Protest and Popular Disturbances in England, 1509–1640* (Oxford, 1988).

Outhwaite, R.B. *Dearth, Public Policy and Social Disturbance in England, 1550–1800* (Basingstoke, 1991).

Randall, A. *Riotous Assemblies: Popular Protest in Hanoverian England* (Oxford, 2006).

Randall, A., and Charlesworth, A. (eds.), *Moral Economy and Popular Protest: Crowds, Conflict and Authority* (Basingstoke, 2000).

Rogers, Nicholas. *Crowds, Culture and Politics in Georgian Britain* (Oxford, 1998).

Rudé, George. *The Crowd in History: A Study of Popular Disturbances in France and England, 1730–1848* (New York, 1964).

Rudé, George. *Ideology and Popular Protest* (Chapel Hill, 1995).

Rudé, George. *Paris and London in the Eighteenth Century: Studies in Popular Protest* (New York, 1970).

Rudé, George. *A Study of Popular Disturbances in France and England, 1730–1848* (London, 1967).

Scarman, Leslie George. *The Brixton Disorders 10–12 April 1981* (London, 1981).

Scott, J.C. *Weapons of the Weak: Everyday Forms of Peasant Resistance* (New Haven, 1985).

Sharp, B. *In Contempt of All Authority: Rural Artisans and Riot in the West of England 1585–1660* (Berkeley and London, 1980).

Shoemaker, Robert. *The London Mob: Violence and Disorder in Eighteenth-Century England* (London and New York, 2004).

Stevenson, John. *Popular Disturbances in England, 1700–1832*, 2nd ed. (London, 1992).

Stiglitz, Joseph. *Globalization and Its Discontents* (London, 2002).

Thomis, Malcolm I. *The Luddites: Machine-Breaking in Regency England* (Hamden, CT, 1970).

Thompson, E.P. 'The Moral Economy of the English Crowd in the Eighteenth Century', *Past & Present*, 50 (1971), pp. 76–136.

Tilly, Charles. *The Contentious French: Four Centuries of Popular Struggle* (Cambridge, MA, 1986).

Tilly, Charles. *Popular Contention in Great Britain 1758–1834* (Cambridge, MA, 1995).

Walter, John. *Crowds and Popular Politics in Early Modern England* (Manchester, 2006).

Wood, A. *The Politics of Social Conflict: The Peak Country 1520–1770* (Cambridge, 1999).

Index

Printed and bound in the United States of America